The Hidden History
of Coined Words

Also by Ralph Keyes

We, The Lonely People: Searching for Community
Is There Life after High School?
The Height of Your Life
Chancing It: Why We Take Risks
Timelock: How Life Got So Hectic and What You Can Do About It
Sons on Fathers: A Book of Men's Writing
"Nice Guys Finish Seventh": False Phrases, Spurious Sayings,
and Familiar Misquotations
The Courage to Write: How Writers Transcend Fear
The Wit & Wisdom of Harry Truman: A Treasury of Quotations,
Anecdotes, and Observations
The Wit & Wisdom of Oscar Wilde: A Treasury of Quotations,
Anecdotes, and Repartee
The Innovation Paradox: The Success of Failure, the Failure of Success
(with Richard Farson)
The Writer's Book of Hope: Getting from Frustration to Publication
The Post-Truth Era: Dishonesty and Deception in Contemporary Life
The Quote Verifier: Who Said What, Where, and When
I Love It When You Talk Retro: Hoochie Coochie, Double Whammy,
Drop a Dime, and the Forgotten Origins of American Speech
Euphemania: Our Love Affair with Euphemisms

The Hidden History of Coined Words

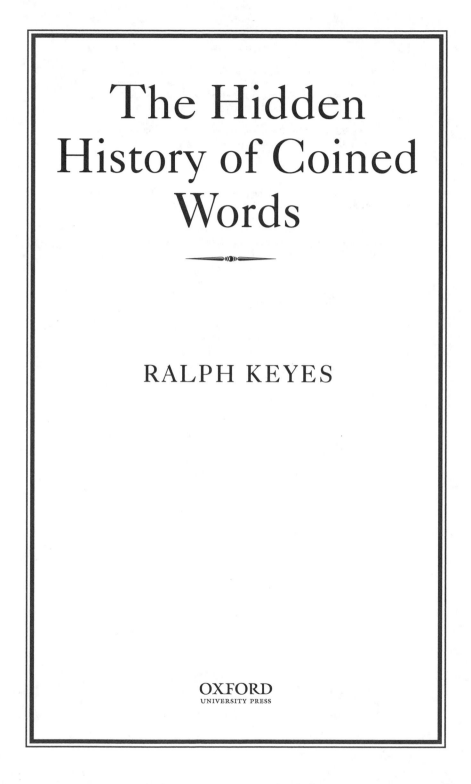

RALPH KEYES

OXFORD
UNIVERSITY PRESS

OXFORD
UNIVERSITY PRESS

Oxford University Press is a department of the University of Oxford. It furthers
the University's objective of excellence in research, scholarship, and education
by publishing worldwide. Oxford is a registered trade mark of Oxford University
Press in the UK and certain other countries.

Published in the United States of America by Oxford University Press
198 Madison Avenue, New York, NY 10016, United States of America.

Library of Congress Cataloging-in-Publication Data
Names: Keyes, Ralph, author.
Title: The hidden history of coined words / Ralph Keyes.
Description: New York, NY : Oxford University Press, [2021] |
Includes bibliographical references. |
Identifiers: LCCN 2020041480 (print) | LCCN 2020041481 (ebook) |
ISBN 9780190466763 (hardback) | ISBN 9780190466770 (pdf) |
ISBN 9780190466787 (epub)
Subjects: LCSH: English language—New words. | English language—Etymology.
Classification: LCC PE1574.K45 2021 (print) | LCC PE1574 (ebook) |
DDC 422—dc23
LC record available at https://lccn.loc.gov/2020041480
LC ebook record available at https://lccn.loc.gov/2020041481

1 3 5 7 9 8 6 4 2

Printed by Sheridan Books, Inc., United States of America

To my grandchildren—Leila, Elias, and Neko—
with all my love.

Contents

III. *Coinage Syndromes*

List of Illustrations

A Word with the Reader . . .

HOW DO WORDS get coined? That question has intrigued me for years. Some time ago I began collecting coined words for a possible book on the subject. This book would combine a collection of neologisms with information about their etymology. How little I knew. Its thousands of entries would have made that compilation a heavy lift, literally. Verifying its contents would be problematic, to put it mildly. (According to linguist Ben Zimmer, for the most part "etymologists haven't the foggiest idea who first hatched a given coinage.") Finally, a collection of coined words per se just didn't seem that intriguing. What *was* intriguing were the origin stories that I kept stumbling across while exploring how words have been created. In most cases these accounts were little known. They comprised a hidden history of coined words.

This history revealed how many terms in our language have been coined whimsically, to taunt, even to prank. More than a few weren't even coined intentionally; they resulted from happy accidents. Neologizers themselves come from diverse quarters. They include not just learned scholars and literary lions but cartoonists, columnists, children's authors, and children as well. *Neologize* itself was one of Thomas Jefferson's many invented words, ones for which he was sternly reprimanded by language guardians in the home country.

The history of word coinage is filled with fierce battles that have pitted word coiners against language purists who think we have more than enough perfectly good words already (and if we did need more, they should be provided by the proper authorities). Skirmishes between competing claims for coining a particular term are also common. An online search of "coined the term stakeholder," for example, turns up three different claimants in the first page alone. "Coined mobocracy" does too. "Supermodel" is another word with multiple people claiming authorship. (Why they'd want to is another question.)

Word coining sagas incorporate not just competition for credit but repeated examples of earnest futility by creators of words that quickly disappeared. By contrast, many coiners did not expect their new words to join the lexicon. They were just trying to have fun. Silliness, sarcasm, and slips of the tongue are just as likely to refresh our language as carefully crafted amalgams of clauses from Latin and Greek. Wisecracks. Throwaway lines. Invective. All have been capital sources of new words. Again and again, this book will show how often terms that weren't meant to be taken seriously went verbally viral, astonishing their coiners as much as anyone, then ended up in reputable dictionaries.

The key idea of *The Hidden History of Coined Words* is that successful neologisms are as likely to be created by chance as by intention. In some cases, those who have come up with a usable new word didn't even know they'd coined one, as when Isaac Asimov used *robotics* in a short story without realizing that this term was his own invention. In a case such as this, it's clear that a word coiner had no intention of giving us a new term. In other cases, evidence confirms how often a neologizer didn't anticipate how many of us would adopt a term they invented. These constitute some of the most fascinating stories in the history of neology.

No existing book has brought together these little-known accounts of how words have been coined. *The Hidden History of Coined Words* fills that void.* Its first section looks at the many unique ways in which words have been created: by accident, for laughs, as insults, or as hoaxes. The second section considers diverse sources of coined words: cartoons, newspaper columns, books for children, science fiction, works of literature, and ones of scholarship. A final section covers coinage syndromes: words coined deliberately, nonstarters, old terms revived, as well as disputation about coinage credit, battles fought over the merits of neologisms, and regret about coining a word or phrase. A concluding chapter offers tips on how to successfully coin a word for those who would like to try.

Success consists of inventing a term that others use. A successfully coined word is one that becomes part of our discourse. In his thoughtful book *Predicting New Words*, Allan Metcalf concludes that to be considered successful, a new word must remain in common use for at least two generations. (The linguist Sol Steinmetz thought it took even longer.) In some cases, newly coined words disappear—for generations even—then reappear when needed, to claim a place in the lexicon. As we'll see, this was the fate of one our most popular words: *serendipity*.

Although a freshly minted term is the purest form of coinage, related types of word creation recur throughout this book. In particular, *recoining* consists of giving a new meaning to an old word. It is *reborn*, as it were. *Cookie* is a classic recoin, converting a foodstuff into a technoterm. Words such as *gay, granular,* and *tweet* have been recoined in a similar fashion. Recoinages that are explored

---

* A few elements of this book have appeared in previous books of mine (which are listed in the bibliography), augmented here with recent findings and other revisions.

in this book include *summit, containment, disrupt,* and *hookup.* The backstories of such recoined words are at least as interesting as those involving terms coined from scratch. So are stories about the many terms that were escorted into our discourse by someone who recognized their value better than the originators did themselves. These terms include *jitterbug, tipping point,* and *Joe Six-Pack.*

Because the coinage process is so unpredictable, researching this topic can't rely on the usual methods and sources. One cannot simply search "coined" on the Internet, harvest the results, then cobble them together into a book that purports to be accurate. Consider the name of the search engine used most often to do such work: *Google.* While exploring the origins of that term, I found an assertion by a Pulitzer Prize–winning *Washington Post* columnist that Charles Dickens had written about King James I's "google eyes." Further exploration determined that Dickens actually wrote that the king had "goggle eyes." Other accounts of the birth of "google" rely on a popular but implausible story about this word popping from the mouth of a nine-year-old boy some eight decades ago. Its roots go back further than that, however, as I discovered by chance. When looking up *goon* in an old dictionary of "Americanisms," my eye happened on an earlier use of *google* than any I'd seen elsewhere, buried within a definition of another term.

Doing research for this book involved many such happy accidents. That's why writing it has been such a pleasure. While investigating Snoop Dogg's nickname (which derived from the comic strip character Snoopy), I discovered that the rapper had accidentally created a new word by mishearing an old one. When searching unsuccessfully for the magazine article where a scholar named Brander Matthews was said to have introduced the word *blurb*, I found an essay by Matthews himself in which he denied being the source of that word and correctly identified its actual coiner.

Experiences such as these made it clear that exploring the history of coined words called for sailing uncharted waters. Some of the most intriguing information about their birth comes not from works of etymology and lexicography but ones of history, biographies, press accounts, blog posts, and personal contact with those involved. And for good reason. Multiple etymological sources report that the word *tweed* resulted from a clerk's misspelling of "tweel" (the Scottish spelling of "twill"). In her 2017 book *Tweed*, however, art historian Fiona Anderson discredits that origin story, then suggests more plausible alternatives. And, although the prominent developer James Rouse is widely assumed to have coined *urban renewal*, according to his biographer Joshua Olsen this euphemism for slum clearance originated with a friend of Rouse's.

Like Rouse, many a presumed "coiner" of a term was actually its publicist. New words spoken by others but never recorded are their stock in trade. Quite a few of the neologisms I write about—including *yuppie, affluenza, fashionista,* and *gonzo*—were circulating on the street long before being committed to print by someone who got (and often took) credit for coining them.

This illustrates the challenge of trying to ascertain a new word's actual parent. There is no such thing as an etymological DNA test. Like Ben Zimmer, etymologists generally concede how difficult it is to say unequivocally where, when, and how most neologisms were born. In her delightful book *Word by Word: The Secret Life of Dictionaries*, lexicographer Kory Stamper concludes that "we will probably never know who coined a particular word, and when they used it."

As Stamper points out, at the outset, new words are more likely to be spoken than written. Typically they are introduced somewhere, sometime, by someone who utters them out loud, as slang, say, or wordplay, or within repartee (as was the case with *gerrymander*). Those that don't blow away in the wind may then show up in an email, a text message, or—back in the day—an actual letter (as *serendipity* did). Like *serendipity*, a fortunate few migrate to a printed page, where they give those who study word origins evidence of "earliest use." This is not the same thing as proof of coinage, but is often the best we can do when it comes walking neologisms back to their trailhead. In *The Stuff of Thought*, Steven Pinker reminds us that "etymologists can trace most words back for centuries or more, but the trail goes cold well before they reach the actual moment at which a primordial wordsmith first dubbed a concept with a sound of his or her choosing."

Hang on, you may be wondering, if this book can't tell me who actually coined a word, why should I bother reading it? Good question. For starters, in a surprising number of cases that I write about, we *can* ascertain where a word most likely originated, and how. Even when we can't, exploring their provenance leads to one fascinating backstory after another surrounding the birth of words. I liken it to a genealogical quest that may not lead to one's earliest ancestors but does turn up intriguing tales of those encountered along the way.

Technology is a mixed blessing in our quest to discover the birthplace of neologisms. On the one hand, computers give us powerful tools to search for their origins. They also create an invaluable pixel trail with which to trace words that originated online (which is one reason for Pinker's caveat that contemporary coinages lend themselves to being explored "in real time"). Finally, the Internet's forms themselves have become a source of neologisms. An entirely new type of coinage consists of Twitter hashtags such as *#MeToo*, *#BlackLivesMatter*, and *#MAGA* (the acronym for Make America Great Again that has become a word unto itself).

Balancing the Internet's virtues as a neology resource is the fact that it's so rife with misinformation, about word origins no less than other topics. Search engines are as dependable for etymological counsel as they are for medical advice: helpful, but not reliable (to put it mildly). Google's impressive Ngram feature, for example, promises to show—in an instant!—when words and phrases first appeared in their vast database of historic publications, then display graphically how often they appeared thereafter. Examining the data used to create such graphs unearths a host of problems, however. According to Ngram, "bad hair day" was being used early in the twentieth century. In fact, it's the phrase "had their day" that they cite (in a 1905 poem by Edwin Markham). "Booty call" did indeed show up in an ancient hymn in Sanskrit, as reported by Ngram, but in this form: "Men in the strife for booty call on Indra."

Such miscues are beyond even the estimable powers of autocorrect. Since it is so determined to "correct" new words, this tool is the mortal enemy of neology. *Cuttage*, an early-twentieth-century neologism, is routinely autocorrected to *cottage* by Microsoft Word. Dr. Seuss's *zummers* gets "corrected" to *summers*. My own term *palpiness* (for a heart's tendency to palpitate) becomes *pulpiness* with autocorrect's helpful guidance. And when I search *hangry*, Google wonders if I didn't mean *Hungary*.

You see what we're up against while trying to pin down the provenance of coined words. Those who do try invariably end up humbled. That's why—although I've endeavored to mind my etymological p's and q's—this book isn't meant to be a work of etymology per se. By telling the stories surrounding coined words I've tried to put them in their historical context, without always presuming to claim that an apparent coinage was indeed original.

This calls for being discriminating, of course. A reference to "email" in 1480 obviously had nothing to do with messages conveyed electronically. (Back then it referred to a form of embossing.) When Tad Dorgan referred to "think tanks" in 1901, the cartoonist-columnist meant this as slang for "brains." During Dorgan's time, "tipping point" referred to the moment when a car would roll over in a sharp turn. And when, more than four centuries ago, Shakespeare used *unfriend* in *Twelfth Night* ("unguided and unfriended"), he wasn't referring to trimming one's Facebook roster.

Speaking of Shakespeare, will this book have lots of words coined by him? It will not. For one thing, the Bard's coinages have already been picked over to a fare-thee-well (including in an entire book called *Coined by Shakespeare*). They are hardly part of a "hidden history." For another, trying to determine which words used by Shakespeare were his own invention is a formidable task. I've seen estimates that range from "nearly 10,000" to "something like 3000," "over 2000," "2000," "over 1700," "close to 1700," "some 1500," "more than 1000," "more than 500," "over 200," and "229." In his book *Authorisms*, Paul Dickson took pains to point out how many words thought to have been coined by Shakespeare did not actually originate with him, only to be chided by a reviewer for concluding that the playwright had created neologisms such as *eyesore* and *smilet* (a half-smile) that actually antedated him. "It's always impossible to know who first coined a word," observes Michael Macrone in *Brush Up Your Shakespeare*, "—and not much easier to know who first wrote it down." As if to make Macrone's case, modern plagiarism-detection software has found a plethora of words thought to be original to Shakespeare in an unpublished manuscript by his contemporary George North, a minor member of the royal court.

The same type of confusion surrounds neologisms attributed to the likes of Chaucer and the deity him/herself (in the King James Bible), who already have books of their own: *Coined by God*, or, in Chaucer's case, multiple Internet sites devoted to compiling his word creations. Although I note their contributions along the way, the stories of such neology rock stars are so thoroughly covered elsewhere that I felt no need to rehash them in this book. Instead I've focused on lesser-known coiners such as George Ade, Gelett Burgess, and Sir Thomas Browne, as well as little-realized neologisms created by better-remembered figures like Charles Dickens, Dr. Seuss, and Sir Winston Churchill.

I
_____

How Words Are Coined

Zen and the Art of Word Creation

WHILE HARD AT work, Winston Churchill hated to be distracted. Members of his staff kept their voices down. The keys of office typewriters were muffled. Because the bang of a stapler disturbed Churchill's concentration he had assistants connect sheets of paper with pieces of cord inserted through quietly punched holes. Churchill called the instrument that punched these holes a *klop* (after the sound it made). When he asked a new secretary to fetch him his klop, the bewildered woman brought him a multivolume work of history called *Der Fall de Hauses Stuart* by one Onno Klopp. "Christ almighty!" her boss responded.

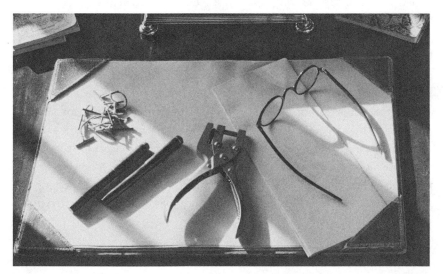

Winston Churchill's desk, "klop" in the middle, along with a pile of connecting cords and cord-connected documents.

Klop was just one of many words coined by Britain's two-time prime minister. If no existing term said well enough what he wanted to say, Churchill simply made one up. "Churchill's love of English was nowhere more agreeably expressed than in words and expressions he created," observes Richard Langworth in *Churchill by Himself*.

The avid amateur artist considered settings worth painting *paintatious*. He referred to his famous still life of bottles as a *bottlescape*. "Winstonian" is what their creator called such words. Some of Churchill's most inspired word creations were malicious, as when he said that far from being utopian, the Labor Party's socialistic program would lead to a *queuetopia* where citizens stood in line a lot. Other Churchillisms noted by Langworth include *fearthought* (useless worrying) and *afterlight* (retrospect).

Few of Churchill's verbal inventions have become part of the lexicon, however. They were used by no one but their inventor (and perhaps a small circle of friends). That's the typical fate of intentionally coined words. Most die with their coiner. This doesn't mean that Churchill made no lasting contributions to the English language. Sir Winston actually left quite a few terms and expressions behind, just not ones he necessarily considered dictionary-worthy.

In a 1908 letter Churchill referred to "the social security apparatus," which the *Oxford English Dictionary* cites as its earliest known use of *social security* in the modern sense. Other terms the dictionary found were first used by Churchill include *fly-in*, *seaplane*, and *under-employed*. In 1906 he coined *terminological inexactitude* for "inaccuracy," a phrase that became euphemistic for "lie" in the post-truth era. *Battle of the Bulge* is a phrase Churchill used in private conversation to describe a 1940 skirmish, one that took place four years before the more famous combat in the Ardennes woods. During a BBC broadcast early in World War II Churchill referred to the Local Defence Volunteers as the *Home Guard*, their most common appellation thereafter. Late in the war he wrote to his Minister of Works, "We must have a better word than 'prefabricated'. Why not 'ready made'?"*

Another Churchillism, *jaw, jaw*, comes from a misquotation of his 1954 observation that "meeting jaw to jaw is better than war." Press accounts had Churchill saying "jaw, jaw" (etc.), leading Prime Minister Harold Macmillan to misquote his predecessor in 1958 when asserting that "Jaw, jaw is better than war, war." As so often happens, this misquote improved on the real quote, leaving *jaw, jaw* behind as a presumed coinage by Churchill that we continue to find useful when discussing ways to avoid armed conflict.

---

* Three decades earlier Marcel Duchamp had called his found-object works of art "ready-mades," not likely to have been Churchill's inspiration.

Sir Winston's most enduring contribution to the lexicon was actually a recoinage. In the midst of a 1950 campaign speech, Churchill said that world leaders should have "a parley at the summit." After Churchill made this suggestion gatherings of world leaders became known as *summit conferences*. In time, get-togethers of many kinds came to be called *summit meetings*. Finally we dispensed with a second word altogether. Any meeting deemed important can now be called *a summit*. ("The prime minister will take part in a summit.") In recent times even the "important" requirement has been dispensed with. Churchill's recoinage can now refer to a meeting of any kind. Today we have a multitude of safety summits, opioid summits, biofuels summits, even a "cheeseburger summit" at the White House in which the Senate minority leader chatted over that repast with the president. Those who attend such gatherings engage in *summitry*. They *summit*, making a verb out of Churchill's noun.

I've little doubt that the word-proud Churchill did not consider "summit" to be one of his better contributions to the *Oxford English Dictionary* (hereafter the *OED*), let alone the most lasting. Yet if Winston Churchill hadn't talked of gathering at "the summit," would we?

Churchill's inadvertent word donation illustrates vividly the premise of this book: that the long, colorful history of word coinage is characterized as much by happenstance as by intention. The most successful verbal creations, even of happy word creators like Sir Winston, routinely have been ones they hadn't meant to be keepers. While it's true that many a usable new word has been coined deliberately, over the course of its history English terminology (and that of other languages as well) has been continually replenished with neologisms that appeared by chance.

Although I refer to words being *coined* throughout this book, this is something of a misnomer. That term implies earnest intentionality: words being minted much like medallions of currency. Why do we use the verb *coin* to characterize a helter-skelter process that in many ways is the antithesis of manufacturing money? Using this word to describe the creation of new words may reflect a forlorn wish that language could be replenished in as orderly a fashion as money is minted. This wish has a long history, one marked by constant controversy.

The Word Mint

In Horace's time, learned Romans generally favored traditional terms they thought had been "born" over "fabricated words" created by contemporaries. Such *ficta verba* were considered shoddy merchandise. That's why Horace felt he had to defend his right as a poet to "add a few words to the stock." As with Churchill, some of Horace's best verbal additions were meant to disparage. Horace mocked the type of poet who used flowery language as *promissor*. He called the use of pompous language *ampullatur*. Horace tapped the existing word *sesquipedalia*, meaning "a foot and a half long," as the basis of *sesquipedalian*, his way of referring sarcastically to using unnecessarily long words. (*Sesquipedalian* remains part of the English lexicon, referring to windy verbiage, and in 2011 was included in Merriam-Webster's list of "Top 10 Favorite Words.")

"Why should I be criticized," Horace said of his neologisms, "if I am able to acquire a few words, when the tongue of Cato and Ennius enriched our national language and brought forth new names for things? It has been permitted, and always shall be permitted, to mint a new word marked with the current stamp."

As Horace's apologia suggests, minting money and creating words have long been associated. In 1589 George Puttenham used *coin* as a verb when he wrote in *The Arte of English Poesie* that pretentious young scholars "will seeme to coigne fine words out of the Latin." **

Puttenham's lament illustrated a common ambivalence about creating new terms: using a neo-neologism of his own (*coigne*) to belittle ones created by others. As we'll see throughout this book, those who think words coined by others are debasing the currency don't necessarily think this applies to ones of their own creation. Puttenham himself was no mean coiner of words. In *The Arte of English Poesie* its author introduced neologisms such as *insect*, *predatory*, and *rotundity* in place of terms he didn't care for. Other coinages of his included *over-reacher* (hyperbole), *insertour* (parenthesis), and *cuckoo-spell* (repeating a word for rhetorical emphasis). Puttenham took pride in addressing the ear, the mind, or both with his coined words. He called them *auricular*, *sensable*, and *sententious*. Puttenhamisms that have enjoyed more success include *major-domo*, *grandiloquence*, and *indecency*. Their author realized that new words such as these can sound jarring to those accustomed to older ones, scholars especially, and was therefore concerned that reading his odd-sounding inventions "may move them to laughter." This didn't stop him from coining more.

Word coining was a common term of reference during Elizabethan times. In Shakespeare's 1607 play *Coriolanus*, Roman general Caius Marcius proclaims, "So shall my Lungs Coine words till their decay." Eight years later, a popular book on homemaking advised English housewives that although fancy chefs "may coine strange names" for their dishes, the readers themselves were perfectly well equipped to cook tempting meals by deft use of ordinary ingredients.

** Although the author of *The Arte of English Poesie* was unnamed, it is generally assumed that George Puttenham wrote it.

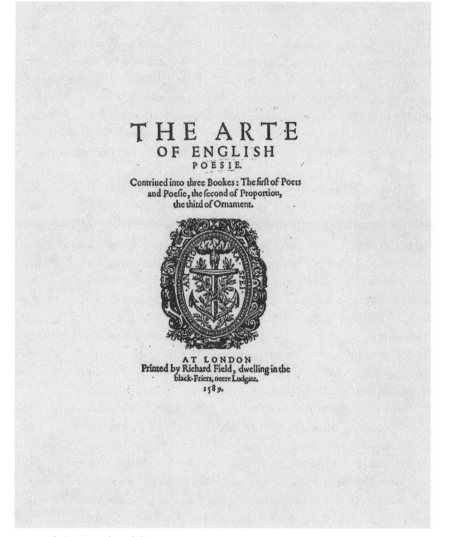

Cover of *The Arte of English Poesie.*

To Coin or Not to Coin

According to the *OED*, *neologism* refers to a word that is "newly coined" or "new to the language." It comes from *neologisme*, a French term based on the Greek *neo*, meaning "new," and *logos*, meaning "speech." In the not-too-distant past, calling words *neologisms* was disdainful. (Flaubert considered them "the ruination of the French language.") Verbal relatives such as *neology* and *neologist* were no more complimentary. After scouring the *OED* for early uses of these words, linguist

John Algeo determined that they "began life with a bad odor." *Neologism* and its offshoots often appeared in conjunction with terms such as *disfigured, corruption, barbarous, censured, reproach, avoid, presumption, crept, hostile, infirmity, caprice, armed, vicious,* and *debases.* Only one reference uncovered by Algeo was positive: the 1841 observation by British scholar Isaac D'Israeli (Benjamin Disraeli's father) that "neologisms have fertilized the barrenness of our Saxon." Balzac was another friend of neology, an inveterate word coiner whom his sister Laure called a *néologue.* "The French language has accepted the new words of my predecessors," Balzac proclaimed. "It will accept mine. Upstarts will become aristocrats in time."

This was a minority view, however. In Balzac and D'Israeli's time, as in that of Horace, coining words was considered a shady practice best left to pseudo-scholars, posturing poets, crowd-courting playwrights, and slang-addicted newspaper columnists. When an American writer named Leon Mead contacted hundreds of authors, academics, and prominent public figures (including Henry James, Mark Twain, Paul Laurence Dunbar, and Theodore Roosevelt) at the turn of the twentieth century to ask which words they'd coined, most vehemently denied doing anything of the kind. One author said that if he'd ever been guilty of creating a new word, it was not with conscious intent. Another told Mead that she considered most neologisms contrived. Yet a third wondered why he should invent a new word when there were so many old ones that he couldn't spell and whose meaning he didn't know.

Mead summarized such responses in his 1902 book *Word-Coinage.* In addition to reporting the disdain for neologisms expressed by so many correspondents, Mead's book included neologisms from a handful who admitted that they'd coined a word or two. Such confessions were made rather sheepishly, however. Typically this involved a disclaimer to the effect that the correspondent saw no need to create new words and considered the practice both suspect and unnecessary. Since Mead had asked, however, here were some terms they'd coined. A lengthy list of largely forgettable and forgotten neologisms would follow.

They included *feminology, irreluctant, broodle, fraternia, societology,* and *littleist* (to name just a few). An American composer told Mead that he'd coined *metropoliarchy* for a Fourth of July oration in which he said of the French, "Under this mask of a republic they form a metropoliarchy governed by the bourgeoisie . . ." A prominent horticulturist sent Mead a number of words he'd created for his professional work: *cuttage, graftage, layerage, seedage, inter-tillage, centrogenesis, dipleurogenesis, pseud-annual, communal intensity, cultural degeneracy,* and *pleur-annual,* among others. Mead was too polite to cast aspersions on such head-scratchers, but did say he was favorably impressed by a coinage the prominent Harvard naturalist Ernest Ingersoll sent him: *quotated* (referring to a paragraph bordered by quotation marks). Users themselves were less favorably impressed. That coinage quickly sank from sight.

Unlike Mead's confessed word coiners, Henry James and Mark Twain told him that they hadn't created any neologisms at all. (Twain did say he might have given currency to slang terms he'd picked up in Western mining camps such as *struck it rich*, *petered out*, and *grubstake*.) Theodore Roosevelt said that he could not recall being the source of a single new word. This from the man who enriched the English language with *pussyfoot*, *muckrake*, *loose cannon*, *lunatic fringe*, *hat in the ring*, *hyphenated-American*, *strenuous life*, *bully pulpit*, and *big-stick diplomacy* (as well as *weasel words*, a magazine writer's coinage that TR popularized).

The Golden Age of Word Coinage

Mead's coinage-deniers were born too soon. In the decades since his book was published, reticence about creating new words has given way to hubris. Horace may have had to defend his right to create new words, but today the creation of a neologism used by others is considered a feather in one's intellectual cap. When Terry Gross had Timothy Wu on her National Public Radio program *Fresh Air*, she introduced the Columbia University professor and former Federal Communications Commission chair by saying, "My guest is Tim Wu, best known for coining the term *network neutrality*."

As Gross's introduction suggests, inventing new words has gone from being a practice considered shameful to one that's bragworthy. In 2005 the pioneering gay activist Frank Kameny said, "I'd like to be remembered for coining the slogan 'Gay is Good' in 1968." Kameny had reason to feel that way. No matter what else they've accomplished in life, those thought to have created a neologism that entered the lexicon are lauded for that achievement. When an author of fifty-seven books died in 1999, the *New York Times* headlined his obituary, "Wayne E. Oates, 82, Is Dead; Coined the Term 'Workaholic.'" A few weeks later, the *Times*' obituary for a prominent psychologist was headed "Herbert Freudenberger, 73, Coiner of 'Burnout,' Is Dead." After a longtime Manhattan psychotherapist passed away in 2017, the *Times*' obituary said, "George Weinberg dies at 87; Coined 'Homophobia' After Seeing Fear of Gays." (Many more such coinage-celebrating obituaries will be noted in pages to come.)

One reason for neology's improved reputation is the speed with which social norms and structures are evolving. Our demand for new terms to discuss a constantly changing social landscape has led to open casting for neologisms. There is no shortage of aspirants. A website called "Word Spy" tracks the many neologisms that come and go in contemporary discourse. In 2004, its creator, Paul McFedries, published a compilation of such new words. Many were quite serviceable. When reading *Word Spy* more than a decade later, however, what's most striking is how few of the hundreds of neologisms collected by McFedries have stood the test of time. We haven't heard recently about *elderweds* (those who marry late in life), *flava* (one's personal style), or *machinima* (films created on personal computers).

When it comes to neologisms, supply far outstrips demand. Coined words are like swarms of salmon eggs: few hatch, fewer mature, and only a handful make it upstream. Even those that do survive seldom endure. That's why trying to predict which new words will last is so challenging. When *Grexit* was coined for Greece's possible exit from the European Union, I flagged it as a nonstarter and was right. When *Grexit* begat *Brexit*, I made the same prediction and could not have been more wrong.

Predicting coined-word survival rates is not for the faint of heart. In 2009 linguist Grant Barrett assessed the likelihood that entries on a list of new words might stick around. They included *frugalista*, *gay-marry*, and *fang-banging* (sex with a vampire). The linguist figured *Netflix divorce*, for couples driven apart by conflicting tastes in video streaming, showed promise, as did *spenduplus*, a word beloved by conservatives to describe governmental stimulus spending. A decade later the only term on Barrett's list that's endured is *reset button* in the political sense ("hit the reset button," now typically shortened to "hit reset" or simply "reset"). At the end of 2011 Barrett tried again, listing twenty-five words he thought might have staying power, such as *occupy* for the anti–Wall Street movement that disappeared quickly, and *Arab Spring*, which didn't survive the collapse of the uprisings that phrase described. Of them all, only *humblebrag* got widespread, lasting traction. (In the dodgy coinage-prediction business, one out of twenty-five isn't a bad batting average.)

Word-coining is a tough racket. Many audition; few are cast. Only a smattering win the linguistic Oscar of continued use. Attempting to anticipate which newly minted terms will strike our fancy, and why, is a daunting task. One thing we do know is that when it comes to coining terms others will use, intention matters about as much as intending to write a bestselling novel. This is something that word-coining columnists routinely discover, to their dismay. During his long tenure at the *New York Times,* columnist David Brooks has floated one coinage after another, usually to no avail. After his book *Bobos in Paradise* was published in 2000, Brooks's nickname for bourgeois bohemians did enjoy a brief vogue in the U.S. and a longer one in France, but ended up being used primarily by its coiner. The same thing is true of various names Brooks has given demographic cohorts. They include *the orchid generation* for emotionally fragile millennials, *organization kids* for hardworking twenty-somethings, and *manly upscale proles* for affluent white-collar men who get tattoos, listen to hip-hop music, and ride Harley-Davidson motorcycles. Brooks called millennials who can function easily in multiple settings *amphibians.* Periods of post-adolescent meandering are *the odyssey years.* Nary a one of these Brooksisms has caught on.

Given the odds against success, why do David Brooks and so many others try so hard to coin and promote new terms? "To name something is to own it," Brooks's colleague Thomas Friedman has explained of his own passion for word creation. Like most determined neologizers, this *Times* columnist has had far more misses than hits. Despite his efforts to expand our vocabulary with terms such as *petropolitics, Fayaadism, electronic herd, MIDS* (*Microchip Immune Deficiency*), and *The Great Inflection,* to name just a few, Friedman has succeeded only with *flat world.* This phrase was inspired by the observation of InfoSys head Nandan Nilekani that technology was leveling the world's playing fields. After Nilekani told Friedman this in 2004, the columnist contemplated his observation. "What Nandan is saying is that the playing field is being flattened," he thought. "Flattened? Flattened? My God, he's telling me the world is flat!" (In other recountings the columnist replaced "My God" with "Holy mackerel.") Soon afterward, Friedman says, he whispered in his wife's ear, "The world is flat." This became the title of his next book and a catchphrase that for a time enjoyed more cachet than most Friedmanisms.

Ironically, Thomas Friedman's most enduring contribution to the vernacular, *the Pottery Barn Rule* ("you break it, you own it"), was first challenged by the housewares company itself—Pottery Barn has no such rule—then routinely misattributed to Colin Powell.

The Futility of Intention

As prolific word coiners like Friedman and Brooks routinely discover, deliberately creating a new term in hopes that others will adopt it is generally an unfruitful way to refresh our language. This approach seldom has the desired outcome. It's too self-conscious. The scaffolding is too visible. Verbal creations tend to be overly clever, too intent on displaying wit and creativity. Far more important than a word inventor's wish to create a new term for the rest of us to use (and admire) is that consumers take to a neologism and find uses for it. This is why deliberate word inventions routinely disappear into lexical black holes while ones that do appeal to us are so often the product of happenstance. Regardless of their point of origin, neologisms that fill a verbal void or improve on an existing term may eventually show up in dictionaries. Who cares where they come from? By contrast, too many terms coined by determined neologizers, even distinguished ones, don't necessarily add anything to ones already in use. "We can make words up," says linguist Barbara Wallraff, "we can love the words we make up; we can feel, *well, that really nailed it*; but we can't make them enter the language. The language is very democratic, and until a lot of people decide that this is a word that belongs in mainstream English it just doesn't happen. Nobody can make it happen."

That's what Richard Dawkins, author of *The Selfish Gene*, discovered when he urged others to adopt a private word he and his wife liked: *dundridge*. This term is one they used for officious, by-the-book bureaucrats (after a character named Dundridge, in Tom Sharpe's 1975 novel, *Blott on the Landscape*). "'Dundridge' is a coining I am trying to introduce into English," tweeted Dawkins. "It means a petty, bossy, bureaucratic little rule-hound." When a jar of honey was confiscated from his luggage by an airport security inspector, Dawkins raged in tweets about "rule-bound dundridges." In a 2013 memoir he exhorted readers to "please use dundridge and give it currency." But this eponym had little resonance outside the Dawkins household and was ridiculed to death online.

The daunting odds against getting others to use their neologisms obviously hasn't kept determined neologizers like Richard Dawkins from trying anyway. As they typically discover, however, most of us enjoy being advised what new words we should use about as much as we like being told to floss our teeth. Instead of having such terms pushed upon us, we might prefer to come upon them ourselves. In the verbal marketplace, fancies of consumers count for far more than ambitions of producers. No matter how admirable, a coined word that few adopt has as much currency as a mural painted by Michelangelo on the wall of a food pantry. Users determine with their mouths, pens, and keyboards which neologisms will live (a few) and which die (most). When questioning the Oxford Dictionaries word of the year for 2017, *youthquake*, the *New Yorker*'s Louis Menand argued that this was a term more likely to be seen in a headline than heard in conversation. "People prefer to have their neologisms boil up unbidden from the global electronic soup," observed Menand.

Everyday assessors of new words seldom care a fig whether ones they find useful and ear-pleasing pass muster with linguists, lexicographers, and dictionary editors. This is particularly true of those who speak English. Unlike languages that have formal procedures for vetting neologisms, English is open-source. Anyone is free to propose new words or phrases. The only criterion for their success is that users adopt such terms. This has led to a word-creation process that's something of a free-for-all. And thank goodness. One reason English is such a lively, user-friendly language is that it's so receptive to new and needed terms regardless of their point of origin.

Where Do They All Come From?

When L. Frank Baum's fable *The Wonderful Wizard of Oz* was published in 1900, readers took right away to a word in its title: *Oz*. Baum's coinage remains a very useful way to refer to fantasy worlds. ("He's like from Oz.") How did the author come up with that appealing word? Speculation ranges from its resemblance to Job's Land of Uz to the thought that *Oz* might be a mashup of the

"Ooh's," and "Ah's" Baum hoped to excite among readers. Baum himself suggested the most likely if least logical explanation. During an interview three years after *The Wonderful Wizard of Oz* was published, the author said that while musing about where that Wizard might live, his eye landed on a nearby file cabinet. Its three drawers were labeled "A–G," "H–N," and "O–Z." This inspired Baum to use those two letters for the name of his wizard's homeland: *Oz*. Assuming Baum's origin story wasn't concocted post facto (as many are), by that unlikely process one of our most popular new words was created.

This is how it often goes in the wonderful world of word creation. In case after case, usable new terms have been coined with little intention or forethought. That's a confounding idea to those who are hard at work inventing words they hope the rest of us will use. Earnest neologizers who are intent on "naming and framing" our public discourse with carefully crafted new words are no more likely to succeed than a children's author whose roving eye settled on a filing drawer's label. Popular words like *Oz* routinely come from random sources, then are voted into common parlance by continued use. It isn't self-appointed guardians of "proper" speech on the one hand, or champions of new words on the other, who determine which neologisms will join the lexicon. It's those who decide which ones they like. This is a trickle-up process in which slang, sarcastic remarks, and throwaway lines sidle haphazardly into the vernacular more than a trickle down of staid words from learned sources marching into our lexicon in disciplined formation. Far from erudite neologizers (whoever they might be), it is everyday users who decide which new words meet their needs, and which ones don't, regardless of where they originated. In the free market of word coinage, Dr. Seuss and Snoop Dogg are every bit as likely as Thomas Jefferson and Thomas Friedman to add words to the lexicon.

The Inadvertent Coiner

In 1956 Elvismania was at its peak. Mobs of teenage girls who packed his sold-out concerts screamed in near-hysteria while the rocker sang, thrummed his guitar, and swiveled his hips. When a frenzied mob wouldn't leave a packed Toledo auditorium on Thanksgiving Day in 1956, promoter Oscar Davis took the microphone and assured the rocker's fans that "Elvis has left the building." Only then did they slowly drift out. A month later (by his own testimony), Horace "Hoss" Logan, creator of the radio program *Louisiana Hayride*, used the same tactic to induce spectators to leave a performance by Elvis in Shreveport, Louisiana. Over time, "Elvis has left the building" became a popular, lasting catchphrase meaning "Time to leave." When Hoss Logan died in 2002, the *New York Times* headlined his obituary "Horace Logan, 86; Coined Elvis Catchphrase."

A year after Elvis's Toledo and Shreveport concerts, the *Times* headlined a 1957 obituary "Robert H. Link, 60, Dead; Ex-Scoutmaster Coined Word 'Boondoggle' in 1925." This was the year that Link's namesake son was born in Rochester, New York. According to the *Times* and other sources, Robert Link Jr. needed a nickname to distinguish him from his father. So Robert Sr. came up with "Boondoggle." Link then borrowed his son's nickname to describe the lanyards that Boy Scouts braided from pieces of leather to gather their scarves, hold their whistles, or use as hatbands. When members of his troop used this term during the 1929 Boy Scouts World Jamboree in England, locals were charmed, especially after the Prince of Wales wrapped one around his Scout hat. " 'Boondoggle,' " *Punch* noted at the time. "It is a word to conjure with, to roll around the tongue; an expressive word to set the fancy moving in strange and comforting channels; and it rhymes with 'goggle,' 'boggle,' and 'woggle,' three of the most lighthearted words in the English language."

An ear-pleasing word like *boondoggle* can't be limited to lanyards, however. In its April 4, 1935, issue, the *New York Times* headlined an article "$3,187,000 Relief Is Spent to Teach Jobless to Play . . . Boon Doggles Made." This mid-Depression article reported on hearings being held by members of New York's Board of Aldermen that were investigating make-work projects for welfare recipients. A staff member of one such project told the *Times* that he was being paid to teach them how to make "boon doggles," or gewgaws created from strips of leather. It did not take long for this term to be applied to all manner of unproductive activity. Over time, *boondoggle* became a common way to describe fiascos such as badly built levees in New Orleans, and Boston's over-budget, long-past-deadline traffic tunnel known as the Big Dig. But its most bittersweet use occurred during the war in Vietnam when *boondoggle* proved to be an unusually apt way to describe America's misbegotten military incursion into Southeast Asia. When we found ourselves once again mired in unending conflict, in the Middle East during the early aughts, a new phrase was called for to describe our misadventures there. This term was discovered in an unlikely setting: a video arcade.

When Aaron Fechter invented the arcade game "Whac-A-Mole" in 1976, he probably did not foresee that its name would become a common allusion. This took time, however, awaiting a need. That need emerged during the 1990s. During a 1993 congressional hearing, Undersecretary of State Tim Wirth testified about elusive terrorist threats confronting the United States: "It's a little bit like Whac-a-Mole," said Wirth. "Have you ever been to an amusement park and seen that game Whac-a-Mole? You put in a quarter and you get so much time and you're whacking down as things pop up. You're whacking over here and they pop up over here. And we have to continue to play Whac-a-Mole."

After this first-known figurative use, *Whac-a-Mole* appeared only sporadically as an allusion. Then the United States invaded Afghanistan in 2001 and Iraq in 2003. As insurgents in both countries routinely vanished in one place only to reappear in another, Whac-a-Mole re-emerged as the go-to analogy for this frustrating type of warfare. "What I worry about is we're playing a game of Whac-a-Mole here," said Senator John McCain in 2006, as our military presence in the Middle East devolved into a maddening attempt to engage with an elusive enemy. When explaining his reluctance to send more American troops to Iraq and Afghanistan, President Barack Obama continually pointed out that we were playing Whac-a-Mole in those countries. During the Covid-19 pandemic, epidemiologists reprised the name of Aaron Fechter's arcade game when they said that suppressing this coronavirus in one place only to have it pop up in another was like playing Whac-a-Mole.

Coinage Chaos Theory

As *Whac-a-Mole* and *boondoggle* illustrate, sources of new words can be fluky and unpredictable. The process by which they are created and adopted is anarchic. Coining usable terms resembles scribbling free verse far more than composing haiku. There is no equivalent of a Neology Board whose sage members scrutinize new words before approving those they think pass muster. Far from being minted in an orderly manner with vigilant quality control, the creation of new words is more like the chaotic process by which the solar system was born. One might even postulate a Chaos Theory of Word Creation in which usable neologisms pop up almost at random, after some word or phrase emerges by chance, strikes a chord, and then takes its place in the verbosphere. Rather than currency mints, one might better look to casinos with their games of chance for a suitable analogy to the word-coining process.

2

Coined by Chance

FROM THE STANDPOINT of English lexicography, Super Bowl XXXVIII should be no more memorable than Super Bowl XXXVII, say, or Super Bowl XXXVIV. Yet it is. For the sake of our vernacular, that 2004 football game— its halftime, in particular—was a seminal event. During this nationally televised interlude, while singing "I bet I'll have you naked by the end of this song," Justin Timberlake yanked off Janet Jackson's bustier. Before cameras cut away, nearly ninety million TV viewers could see Jackson's naked breast for 9/16th of a second.

Was this nipple-exposure intended or accidental? Only the performers knew for sure. According to Jackson, viewers were only supposed to see her red bra once Timberlake did his thing. Jackson's spokesperson Stephen Huvane said the fuller view was due to "a malfunction of the wardrobe." Timberlake concurred, explaining that Jackson's bra ended up in his left hand because of a "wardrobe malfunction." Although it's unlikely that Justin Timberlake thought he'd be contributing a most useful phrase to our national conversation, that's exactly what he did. *Wardrobe malfunction* caught on quickly as a sly, winking euphemism for the exposure of skin. In the years since Super Bowl XXXVIII took place, flesh-flashing, and this droll way to describe it, has become more common than ever—among figure skaters in skimpy outfits, sunbathers in meager bikinis, and teenagers wearing dangerously droopy drawers.

Like *wardrobe malfunction*, many a successful new term has been added to our language by chance. In *Word-Coinage*, Leon Mead estimated that no more than 20 percent of usable neologisms are deliberate creations. The rest, as he put it, simply "crept into the language."

Consider the word *schooner*. According to nautical lore in coastal New England, this word for a sleek new type of ship was coined spontaneously in the early eighteenth century when a prototype was launched into the waters off Gloucester. By this account the ship's builder, Capt. Andrew Robinson, overheard a bystander exclaim, "Oh, how she scoons!"

"A scooner let her be!" Robinson is said to have responded. While generally wary of that type of origin story, the *OED* calls this one "not at all improbable" (for them a ringing endorsement).

According to the *OED* countless words in the English language were coined not just by chance but by accident. They called terms that resulted from typos, misspellings, and other miscues "ghost words." Founding editor James Murray identified nearly a hundred of them in other dictionaries. He dreaded the thought that some might show up in theirs. Before being caught in the knick of time, an illustrative quotation they'd planned to use included the "word" *cairbow*, a misspelling of *caribou*.

Although the *OED*'s founders may have abhorred this type of lexical miscue, in his book *Clichés and Coinage*, literary scholar Walter Redfern called the coining of words by mistake "blunderful." Rather than an orderly process, Redfern suggested, language expansion takes place "largely in bits and pieces, by collective participation, and with some intervention from accident." The author didn't consider this something to be concerned about. Quite the contrary. Redfern endorsed "chance, slips and all the other ways language bursts out of the corsets forced on it by the very ones who should be grateful for its diversity." As Marcel Proust observed about his own language, "The French words that we are so happy to pronounce correctly are themselves nothing but blunders made by Gaulish mouths, mispronouncing Latin and Saxon words."

Improvisational Word Coinage

Among the multitude of ways in which words are born, many are spontaneous. Think of your own family. Families typically have a private language that parallels the one they use in public. Its vocabulary is a hodgepodge of made-up words, mispronounced ones, inside jokes, and shared allusions (such as the Dawkinses' *dundridge*).

When William Gladstone was asked how he felt about being appointed vice president of Britain's Board of Trade in 1841, he responded, "Bathing feel." *Bathing feel* turned out to be an expression used by members of his wife's family to describe an antsy sense of anticipation when undertaking a formidable task, much like a baby about to be plunged into bath water. The family of Gladstone's wife, Catherine Glynne, used so many idiosyncratic words and expressions that in 1851 Catherine's brother-in-law published a glossary of "Glynnese." This compilation included terms such as *grubuous* for looking indisposed, *twarly* for peevishness, and *niobe* for being in a tearful state.

The Glynnes weren't the only English family of their time who had an extensive private vocabulary. So did the family of author Maurice Baring (1874–1945),

whose private words were known as *Baringese*. They included *dewdrop* for a compliment, and *Molly Corkering* for a hasty, superficial housecleaning (because a
housekeeper of theirs named Molly Corker tended to straighten up by shoving
things beneath the sofa).

Such terms seldom show up in any dictionary, of course. How could they?
Most are based on shared history and celebrate that history. Members of our family say giveaway items left by the street are available at *curbmart*. *Encroachment*
refers to hogging more than one's share of a double bed. *Gumyak* is what we call
the solid contents of soup, because that's what my mother called them. I have no
idea why. Perhaps she coined it as a child.

Children are natural-born neologizers. When they don't know a word for
what they want to say, they just make one up. A ten-year-old neighbor of ours
once told us that the reason she took so many wild shots when playing basketball
was because she was *chanceful*. We've always liked that coinage and sometimes
use it ourselves. *Chanceful* is a good way to describe the process of family word
creation as a whole, and, by extension, language growth in general. As the linguist
Allen Walker Read once observed, families constitute "the matrix in which we see
the bubbling up of linguistic experimentation."

In at least one case, a family's private word became the accepted term for a
commercial product. That family was the Mullanys of Fairfield, Connecticut. In
1953, twelve-year-old David Mullany kept saying he could "whiff," or strike out his
playmates, when they played stickball with a plastic golf ball. This led his parents
to begin referring to their son's "whiffle" ball. When David Mullany Sr. developed
a baseball-sized version of his son's plastic ball, he dropped the *h* and capitalized
the *w* to create its brand name: *Wiffle*.*

Smurf is another term of great commercial value and widespread utility
that has an offbeat origin story. According to Belgian cartoonist Pierre "Peyo"
Culliford, while dining with fellow cartoonist André Franquin at a café, he
wanted to ask for the salt but had a brain cramp and couldn't think of that word.
So he made one up: *schtroumpf*. "Pass the schtroumpf," said Culliford. The two
cartoonists got such a kick out Peyo's spontaneous coinage that they used it as the
basis for a nonsense language all their own. This language was subsequently put
in the mouths of some miniature blue-skinned comic characters that Culliford
created in 1958 and called "Les Schtroumpfs." The name of these cute mini-figures
was subsequently translated into other languages, including *Smurfen* in Dutch,
and its English iteration: *Smurfs*. That version of Peyo's accidental neologism hit

---

* Long before there was a whiffle/wiffle ball, and before he turned to spinach, Popeye got his
oomph by rubbing the head of a *Whiffle Hen* named Bernice.

the verbal jackpot, becoming not just the name of a popular cartoon series but a generic way to describe smaller people. *Smurf* can also refer to a type of break-dance, an experienced gamer posing as a newbie, or simply to the state of "feeling Smurfy."

Linguists are keenly aware of the role happenstance can play in word creation. In their book *Aspects of Language*, Dwight Bolinger and Donald Sears note how often simple mistakes fertilize our lexicon. "Raw material," they call such words born in error. All mistakes are not created equal, however. "Most of them come to nothing," write the linguists, "—mispronunciations, mistakes in grammar, artificial coinages, attempts at verbal humor, poetic distortions—the majority pass unnoticed, or are noticed and disregarded, or are briefly taken up but soon dropped. It is only by being noticed, appreciated, and adopted that a few make their way in to stay."

Quark is one. This now-ubiquitous word was born during an early-1960s brainstorming session in which physicist Murray Gell-Mann and his colleague Richard Feynman noodled with names for the subatomic particles that Gell-Mann considered the building blocks of matter. Gell-Mann tossed out "squeak" for these quirks of nature, then the nonsense word "squark." He pronounced that word "kwork," however. The two physicists both liked Gell-Mann's garbled version and began to use it with colleagues.

But how to spell the term they liked so much? A few weeks after his brainstorming session with Feynman, Gell-Mann thumbed through James Joyce's *Finnegan's Wake*, a novel he loved for its extravagant wordplay. One passage leaped out at him: "Three quarks for Muster Mark!" Like so many of Joyce's neologisms, the meaning of this one wasn't clear. Whatever Joyce's intent, other than creating a word to rhyme with "Mark," *quark* was just the spelling Gell-Mann was looking for. "The allusion to three quarks seemed perfect," he later explained (since the subatomic particles Gell-Mann called quarks bonded in threes). Others also thought this quirky term was appealing and found diverse uses for it: as the name of a French concept car, a Star Trek character, and a dog in the 1989 movie *Honey, I Shrunk the Kids*. Quarks all. For his research on subatomic particles, Gell-Mann received the Nobel Prize in Physics. Be that as it may, at the top of Gell-Mann's "Known For" list on his Wikipedia page is "coining the term 'quark.'"

Some figures, such as George W. Bush, have contributed more than their share of blunderful terms to the lexicon. America's forty-third president apparently had no idea he was expanding our vocabulary when in April 2006 he told his fellow Americans, "I'm the decider, and I decide what's best."** Bush's

---

** Centuries earlier "decider" was an esoteric term for those who adjudicate theological and legal issues, not something likely to have been Bush's source.

contribution to our political vocabulary was quickly adopted by journalists in a semi-ironic way, as when *Time* called a cover story on Supreme Court Justice Anthony Kennedy "The Decider," and *Newsweek* headlined a cover story about Hillary Clinton "What Kind of Decider Would She Be?" *Decider* eventually shed its mocking skin and become a verbal commonplace (as the name of a media website called *decider.com*, among other things). That's because there's no better way to describe someone who makes decisions. *Leader* comes close, and *manager*, or *executive*, but none are quite as descriptive or evocative. Nor is *decision-maker*, which author Leo Rosten claimed to have coined (although that phrase has been in use since the early twentieth century, referring to baseball umpires). *Decider* is the best of them all.

Other slips of Bush's tongue that enjoyed satiric reuse include *subliminable* and *misunderestimate.* (*Strategery* was a *Saturday Night Live* invention used by Bush impersonator Will Ferrell.) At the 2016 Democratic National Convention, *Saturday Night Live* alum Al Franken, then a senator from Minnesota, warned members of his party not to misunderestimate Donald Trump. Although Franken meant this as a joke, humor is a common way station for words minted accidentally to migrate into the language as a whole.

It says something that the verbally challenged George Bush contributed *decider* and *misunderestimate* to the lexicon while his more articulate successor Barack Obama added nary a word during eight years in the White House. The closest thing to a verbal contribution by our forty-fourth president was his 2009 reference to antsy Washingtonians being *wee-weed up*, a piece of street slang that enjoyed a brief vogue, among children especially, after the president gave it purchase. A year before Obama said this, his patronizing observation that Hillary Clinton was "likeable enough" became a catchphrase referring sarcastically to less-than-endearing figures such as Texas senator Ted Cruz. (During the 2016 primaries, a *Time* cover story on Cruz was headlined "Likeable Enough?") After Hillary herself referred to the *basket of deplorables* she thought contained many of Donald Trump's supporters, yard signs quickly sprouted proclaiming "DEPLORABLE—AND PROUD OF IT." T-shirts reading ADORABLE DEPLORABLE sold briskly. In the years that followed, *deplorable* continued to be heard in a defensively proud way by those who thought they might be in Hillary Clinton's basket. They considered themselves citizens of a *Deplorable Nation.*

During a debate with Hillary, Donald Trump promised, "I'm going to cut taxes big league and you're going to raise taxes big league." *Big league* was a phrase the developer had used for years, but he uttered it in such a way that many listeners thought he'd said "bigly." They rather liked this inadvertent coinage (a revival, actually: though seldom heard in modern times, the adverb "bigly," or "bygly," has been around since the Middle Ages), and it soon showed up in everyday conversation. During his confirmation hearing before the Senate Judiciary Committee, Supreme Court nominee Neil Gorsuch observed that John Hancock's name had become eponymous for signatures in general because he'd written his so distinctly on the Declaration of Independence. "No one remembers who John Hancock was," said Gorsuch, "but they know that that's his signature because he wrote his name so bigly—big and boldly."

Eggcorns

As with *big league* spawning *bigly*, it's not uncommon for new terms to result from old ones that are misheard. There's even a name for them: *eggcorns.* That's because, after reading an account by fellow linguist Mark Liberman about a woman who'd misheard the word *acorn* as *eggcorn* (a common mistake), Geoffrey Pullum proposed that we use this delightful mishap for the broader phenomenon of new words being created from misheard old ones. Although still not a household word, *eggcorn* has caught on enough to be added to the *OED* in 2010, and five years later to the *Merriam-Webster Dictionary.* There it joined *mondegreeen*, a word for misheard terms (in song lyrics especially), so named by essayist Sylvia Wright in 1954 because "Lady Mondegreen" was the way she'd heard the phrase "laid him on the green" when her mother recited an old Scottish ballad about the death of the Earl of Murray.

Examples of mondegreens and eggcorns abound, including one propagated by the rapper Snoop Dogg. While sharing a toke with Seth Rogen, Dogg was told by the actor-director about a hydroponic marijuana-growing operation he'd visited. The rapper misheard this as "hydrochronic." Clipping its first clause, Dogg began referring to marijuana as *chronic.* So did his fans.

Such inventions may not suggest verbal clumsiness or Freudian slips so much as creative brains at work. A coal miner's daughter, for example, once told me that as a girl she'd thought the mine elevator called a "man trip" was a "man trap." The woman thought her version was more appropriate.

Neurologist Oliver Sacks was something of a connoisseur of eggcorns, including his own. As his hearing declined with age, Sacks carried a notebook in which he recorded actual words in green and the way he'd misheard them in red. Sacks's notebook was filled with entries such as *choir practice* (for chiropractor), *pontillitis* (for tonsillitis), *Porsche* (for porch), and "*Kiss my feet!*" (for Christmas Eve). The neurologist was so taken with his cook's name for gefilte fish—*filter fish*—that he used this term as the title of an essay.

Many an everyday word began as an eggcorn. *Buttonhole*, in the sense of accosting someone, results from a mishearing of *button-hold*, or detaining someone by holding on to the buttons of their clothing. Bill Bryson's tally of eggcorns and their origin words includes *penthouse* ("pentice"), *shamefaced* ("shamefast"), and *sweetheart* ("sweetard"). *Duct tape* is so routinely misheard as *duck tape* that this is now a brand name.

Many Americanisms were essentially eggcorns that grew from attempts by early settlers to record Indian words phonetically. Capt. John Smith was a prime transcriber of such terms. Soon after he helped settle Jamestown in Virginia during the early seventeenth century, Smith did his best to record words he'd heard local Indians use. One of them was what Smith recorded variously as "rabougcums," "rahaughcuns," and "raugroughcuns," his best guesses for the spelling in English of what they called an animal who "scratches with his hands." Over time this phonetically spelled word morphed into *raccoon*.

Coined by Mistake

Random spellings like Smith's, and misspellings as well, are a rich source of new words. One such word appeared in a report put out by the Colorado Public Utilities Commission in the early 1980s. While perusing this report, clean energy advocate Amory Lovins and a colleague noted an odd word: *negawatt*. It was a typographical error. The report writer meant to say *megawatt*. But the more Lovins thought about it, the more sense that typo made. Why not call units of electricity that are saved rather than consumed *negawatts*? Lovins floated the neologism in a 1984 *Business Week* interview, then included it in a 1988 report called *Negawatts for Arkansas*, and in a 1989 speech titled "The Negawatt Revolution—Solving the CO_2 Problem." *Negawatt* caught on quickly and has been part of the alternative energy vocabulary ever since. In France an environmental think tank calls itself the *Association négaWatt*.

Mistakes are an integral part of language expansion. This process is analogous to the role errors play in evolution. A species' success depends on random mutations that evolve into valuable traits over time. In a similar sense, many usable new words have resulted from simple miscues such as typos, tongue slips, and mistranslations. "Verbal blundering is integral to language," Michael Erard writes in his book *Um . . .*, "not something that intrudes upon it. Because human language has ways to deal with accidents and interruptions, they must have evolved alongside language itself."

Negawatt is far from the only term to result from a typographical or transcription error. Another originated with Chaucer's reference, in his 1374 epic *Troilus and Criseyde*, to Troilus as a bold *dorrying don* (someone who dares). In 1430 poet John Lydgate adapted Chaucer's phrase to use as a verb in his *History of Troy* so that Troilus was now someone *dorrying do* (daring to do). When Lydgate's tome was reissued over a century later, *dorrying do* was misprinted as *derrynge do*. Elizabethan poet Edmund Spenser was so taken with this misprinted phrase that beginning in 1579 he employed it repeatedly in his poems, spelling it *derring-doe*. With the final *e* deleted, Sir Walter Scott and other romantics made sure that *derring-do* in the Spenserian sense (referring to manly chivalry) became part of the English lexicon. Shorn of its chivalry aspect, now referring simply to boldness, derring-do went on to characterize adventurous characters like Buck Rogers, the Hardy Boys, and Nancy Drew.

Words created by mistake aren't always this usable and this durable. Nor do they necessarily get used at all. To have even a shot at becoming part of the language, such terms must first see the light of day. Sometimes they are unearthed unexpectedly, as my wife, Muriel, and I discovered while tilling ground for a vegetable garden behind our San Diego home in the mid-1970s. Muriel's pitchfork hit a hard object that didn't feel like a rock. That object turned out to be Mason jar filled with crumbling love letters. In these letters the onetime lover of a married man who'd owned our property four decades earlier complained bitterly about the sexual demands of her new husband. "Tillie" (as I'll call her) was particularly incensed by how much *intercurse* her husband expected. I never knew if this was intentional, a typo, a Freudian slip, or perhaps one that wasn't so Freudian. If Tillie had made her complaint in public, as a tweet, say, this piece of mistakery might have joined our vocabulary. Or perhaps I could have used *intercurse* in a piece of writing, thereby escorting Tillie's word into the vernacular. It happens.

Escorts

After Franklin Roosevelt proposed that seven new justices be added the Supreme Court to supplement the nine who were blocking New Deal legislation, his cousin and companion Margaret "Daisy" Suckley asked the president whether he wasn't trying to "pack" the court. Roosevelt roared with delight at Suckley's characterization and began calling his erstwhile plan to enlarge the Supreme Court *court-packing*. That expression has endured as a way to refer to increasing a court's size in hopes of changing its opinions.

When inadvertent coiners like Daisy Suckley make little or no effort to promote their new terms, help is called for, someone who picks up on another person's coinage and ushers it into the lexicon. This requires paying attention to unusual words used in passing that others may take for granted. That's exactly what happened in 1970 after *Electronic News* columnist Don Hoefler was invited to lunch with some members of the budding high-tech community in California's Santa Clara Valley. His colleague Jim Vincler tagged along. During their lunch, one of the locals used the phrase "Silicon Valley." As Vincler later recalled, "I saw Don's eyes subtly light up like a poker player who had just filled a straight as he asked, 'Silicon Valley? Where'd that come from?'"

It turned out that this was slang used by Santa Clara high-techers who liked to say they worked in "Silicon Gulch," or "Silicon Valley" (after the silicon-based chips that were integral to the electronic gear being developed there). When heading west to check out that techno-industry, East Coast tech types in the know liked to say they'd be visiting the Silicon Valley. Outside the ranks of those who worked in that valley and others who swam in their wake, this term was seldom heard. That changed in early 1971 when Don Hoefler wrote a series of articles for *Electronic News* titled "Silicon Valley USA." This widely read series put that slangy phrase on the map. Though Hoefler is often credited with coining "Silicon Valley" (and sometimes took credit himself), at best he was its publicist. "How was I to know that the term would quickly be adopted industry-wide, and finally became generic worldwide?" Hoefler observed a decade after he escorted *Silicon Valley* into the vernacular. Not surprisingly, when Don Hoefler died in

Trombonist Harry White and bandleader Cab Calloway, coiner and popularizer of the word *jitterbug*.

1986, the *Spokane Chronicle* headlined his obituary, "Man Who Coined 'Silicon Valley' Dies."

Escorts of new terms are routinely thought to be their coiners. This is especially true when the escort is better known than the coiner. Because he recorded a song called "The Jitterbug" in 1934, bandleader Cab Calloway is typically given credit for inventing that beguiling new term. Apparently it was a trombonist named Harry Alexander White who came up with this word, however, one overheard by Calloway's trumpeter Edwin Swayzee. Swayzee then wrote "The Jitterbug," and Calloway made that song and the dance it inspired a national craze. But Swayzee and Calloway alike were the beneficiaries of a term coined by Harry White, not the creator of that term.

Evangelist Jerry Falwell was another such beneficiary. Because he was so identified with the Moral Majority movement, Falwell presumably invented its name. Its actual originator, however, was conservative activist Paul Weyrich. As Weyrich later recalled, during a conversation with Falwell in the late 1970s, "I turned to him and said, 'Well, you might say, out there, there is a vast moral majority, and if we could all get together—because we've been separated politically and denominationally and otherwise—we could probably be very powerful.' And he stopped me and he said, 'Wait a minute, wait a minute—what did you say? You said, out there, there was something'—and I didn't even remember what I had said. And finally, I said, 'out there, there is a vast moral majority.' And he turned to his people, and he said, 'that's the name of the organization.'"

Coining in Public

Some useful terms just slip out of mouths. Their value is recognized only by someone other than the one from whose mouth they slipped (which makes you wonder how many potentially useful new words blew away in the wind because no one recognized their value). They may not mint the words in question, but escorts do put them into circulation.

Around the time that *Silicon Valley* was becoming part of the national conversation, reporter Martin Nolan wrote an August 28, 1970, article in the *Boston Globe* titled "After the Soul of Joe Six-Pack." Although he's often credited with coining this now-ubiquitous synonym for *Average Joes*, Nolan told readers he'd heard *Joe Six-Pack* used several years earlier by a man who threatened to sue him if his coinership was revealed.

Another term often heard among those who take an interest in Six-Pack voters is *Astroturfing.* That's how pols describe the practice of artificially generating huge volumes of mail to send to public officials. It dates back to 1985 when Texas senator Lloyd Bentsen contrasted mass-mail campaigns with actual correspondence from concerned citizens. "A fellow from Texas can tell the difference between grass roots and Astroturf," Bentsen commented. In the wake of this remark, political operatives began calling assembly-line communication "Astroturf" (the original brand name for the artificial grass first used on the Houston Astros' baseball field). As a verb, *Astroturf* refers to generating such messages. Those who do so create ersatz groundswells of opinion. According to an article in *The Hill* about anti-Republican protesters, "Conservative talkers like Sean Hannity and former Speaker Newt Gingrich have fanned the notion on the right that the protests are 'Astroturf,' rather than grassroots." Although he apparently had no intention of adding a new term to the lexicon, Lloyd Bentsen was the source of this recoinage. It took political operatives and reporters to convert Bentsen's droll Texasism into a usable term that has become integral to America's political palaver.

With so many of their words on the record, public figures are vulnerable to having ones they didn't consider coinages become part of their verbal heritage. (Think of Churchill and *summit*.) Even the venerable lexicographer James Murray, fell prey to this syndrome. In an 1880 speech to London's Philological Society, the *OED's* founding editor discussed how often his pioneering work took him into areas that lacked a vocabulary. The common phenomenon of trimming letters from existing words to create new ones (e.g., abide/bide, alone/lone, espy/spy), for example, had no name. Therefore Murray gave it one. He called the letter-clipping process *aphesis*, a neologism the editor used for years afterward. Words shorn of an initial letter or letters were *aphetized*. They became *aphetic*. Despite occasional use by colleagues, this term didn't catch on. Another Murrayism, one that did become part of the lexicon, wasn't one he thought of as a neologism. During the same speech in which he introduced *aphesis*, Murray noted the lack of "a good English word for the French *mot d'occasion*, indicating a word invented for the nonce." This inspired *nonce word*, referring to terms created for a single occasion. Murray's incidental coinage remains in common use among those who take a serious interest in language. In time he himself began to talk of "nonce words."

James Murray is just one of many figures on both sides of the Atlantic whose casual use of a word or expression became a major part of their lexical legacy. Teddy Roosevelt is another. Roosevelt was prone to say *bully* the way children a century later would say *awesome*. Whatever he liked was "bully." This intensive was common during Roosevelt's time, particularly in his native New York. (It had originated in England centuries earlier but died out there before being revived in antebellum America.) When TR called the presidency a "bully pulpit," he meant that it was a first-rate platform for promoting his positions. To him, pulpit was a noun, bully an adjective. Today "bully pulpit" is more likely to be used as a catch-phrase. Because the "bully" part of that phrase is typically thought to reference coercion, *bully pulpit* has developed overtones of arm-twisting never intended by its creator. Nonetheless, more than a century after Teddy Roosevelt introduced it, *bully pulpit* remains among our most popular political phrases.

Another phrase that the twenty-sixth president used in passing, while talking with his young aide-de-camp Douglas MacArthur in 1906, later got a second wind. When MacArthur asked Roosevelt what he considered the key reason for his popularity among the masses, the president replied, "To put into words what is in their hearts and minds but not their mouths." Nearly six decades later, Lyndon Johnson said about our military venture in Vietnam, "The ultimate victory will depend on the hearts and minds of the people actually live out there." Like so many enduring TRisms, this is one for which he did not take credit, and probably didn't even consider uniquely his.*** *Hearts and minds* was simply a casual expression used by the voluble president that found a lasting home in the American conversation.

This is not an uncommon form of language expansion. Many a coined or recoined word has become part of popular discourse after being used in passing by someone who did not seem intent on contributing a word to the lexicon, let alone anticipate that this might happen.

In 1996, a Boston web developer named Bob Donahue asked members of an Internet chat group if anyone had tapes of the *The X-Files* that he could borrow. Donahue promised that after "some MASSIVE binge-watching" he'd return them promptly. In time, *binge watch* became a routine part of everyday discourse, especially after Netflix and others began releasing series episodes all at once. When British writer Steven Poole asked Donahue if he realized that he was the first known user of the now-ubiquitous phrase, and may have coined it, Donahue said he didn't. "What a cool revelation!" Donahue told Poole two decades after asking for *X-File* tapes. "To be honest, I have zero recollection as to whether I made up the phrase off-the-cuff, or I was using something I had heard before." Whether or not the phrase originated with him, Donahue said he himself still calls his tendency to consume certain shows during marathon viewing sessions *binge-watching*. In 2015 the *Collins English Dictionary* named *binge watch* its word of the year.

The next year Collins chose *Brexit* as its word of the year for 2016. Its provenance could be traced to a 2012 blog post in which the head of a British think tank named Peter Wilding converted *Grexit*, the newly coined term for Greece's proposed withdrawal from the European Union, into *Brexit* for Britain's possible

---

*** A decade earlier, French general Louis Hubert Gonzalve Lyautey had emphasized the importance of winning the hearts and minds of natives along the Indochina–China border to suppress the Black Flags rebellion there.

exit. In the years that followed, Wilding was astonished to find that this had become the go-to term for Britain's exit from the European Union, an entry in the *OED*, and Collins's word of the year. As Wilding told Steven Poole, by 2019 he'd resigned himself to the idea that *Brexit* would probably "go down in history," with him as a footnote.

Wilding's experience has counterparts among other surprised contributors to the lexicon whose contribution was more casual than intentional. Four cases in particular that we'll explore in the next chapter show how certain terms have gone viral due more to enthusiasm on the part of consumers than determination on the part of their producers.

3

Casual Coinage

THE DAY AFTER Virginia seceded from the Union in 1861, three slaves—Frank
Baker, James Townsend, and Shepard Mallory—commandeered a boat and rowed
across the James River from Hampton to Fortress Monroe, where federal troops
were stationed. There they asked for asylum from Federal troops manning the fort.*

What seemed like a straightforward request was anything but. Should these
refugees be treated as freedmen who'd emancipated themselves? Or did the
Constitution and the Fugitive Slave Act of 1850, which remained the law of the

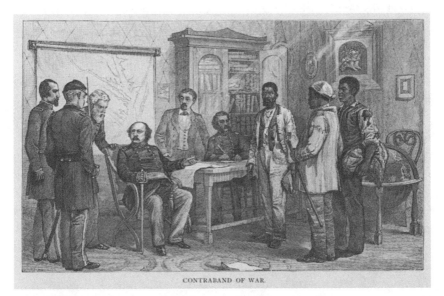

CONTRABAND OF WAR.

General Ben Butler receives escaped slaves.

---

* Although today's understandable tendency is to talk of the "enslaved" and their "enslavers,"
this section incorporates the vernacular of the period it depicts, including "slaves," "slaveown-
ers," "runaways," and "freedmen."

land, require that they be returned to their so-called owners? Complicating matters was the fact that slave owners in loyal border states such as Maryland and
Kentucky had been assured that the right to keep their human "property" was
secure. President Lincoln hoped that the same pledge would keep Virginia from
seceding as well. Giving asylum to the three runaways would belie this guarantee.

That was the dilemma confronting Fort Monroe's commander, Major General
Benjamin F. Butler. A Massachusetts lawyer and Democrat who'd supported
Jefferson Davis as his party's nominee for president a year earlier, this squat, pop-
eyed Union officer was no abolitionist. Yet Butler realized that he could hardly
order his troops—many of whom were antislavery New Englanders—to detain,
shackle, and return escaped slaves to secessionists who were aiming guns at them
from batteries across the river. If returned, the runaways would almost certainly
be put to work building these batteries.

As Fort Monroe's commander cogitated on these issues, a tall, erect soldier
wearing the blue-green uniform of the 115th Virginia Militia and a plumed officer's hat approached the fort's entrance on horseback, beneath a white flag of
truce. When General Butler rode out to meet him, this officer introduced himself as Major John Baytop Cary. Cary, in civilian life a school principal, had met
Butler at the previous year's Democratic convention. After reminiscing about
their contact there, Cary told Butler that the three escaped slaves belonged to
Colonel Charles Mallory, who was in charge of the artillery company of the 115th.

"I am Col. Mallory's agent and have charge of his property," Cary said. "What
do you mean to do with these negroes?"

"I intend to hold them," Butler responded.

"Do you mean, then to set aside your constitutional obligation to return
them?"

"I mean to take Virginia at her word, as declared in the constitutional obliga-
tions to a foreign country, which Virginia now claims to be."

"But you say we cannot secede, and so you cannot consistently detain the
negroes."

"But you say you have seceded, so you cannot consistently claim them," he told
Cary. "I shall hold these negroes as contraband of war, since they are engaged in the
construction of your battery and are claimed as your property. The question is simply whether they shall be used for or against the government of the United States.
Yet, though I greatly need the labor which has providentially come to my hands,
if Colonel Mallory will come into the fort and take the oath of allegiance to the
United States, he shall have his negroes, and I will endeavor to hire them from him."

Since both men knew perfectly well that was out of the question, their meeting ended on this note. But the rationale Butler had given for retaining Col.
Mallory's slaves didn't end there. After Butler's exchange with Cary was reported

in the press, it became a popular topic of conversation among northerners, and eastern Virginia's slaves too. "Within a few days," noted Lincoln biographers John Nicolay and John Hay (at the time his secretaries), "a new phrase was on every one's lips, and the newspapers were full of editorials chuckling over the happy conception of treating fugitive slaves of rebel masters as contraband of war."

Commentators marveled at how quickly the key word of Butler's phrase— *contraband*—became a way of characterizing runaway slaves. "Never was a word so speedily adopted by so many people in so short a time," wrote a Union officer named Charles Cooper Nott several months after Butler used it. *Contraband*, Nott reported "leaped instantaneously to its new place, jostling aside the circumlocution 'colored people,' the extrajudicial 'persons of African descent,' the scientific 'negro,' the slang 'nigger,' and the debasing 'slave.'" Nott, a lawyer in civilian life, concluded that "those who love to ponder over the changes of language and watch its new uses and unconscious growth, must find in it a rare phenomenon of philological vegetation."

This wasn't just a matter of philology, however. As word raced around the nation about Butler's so-called Fort Monroe Doctrine, it quickly became clear that this doctrine provided a perfect rationale for not returning escaped slaves without relitigating arguments about slavery that had convulsed Americans for decades. While having the desired result of providing sanctuary to runaways, calling them *contraband* sidestepped the larger issues involved. Butler's recoinage, concluded historian James McPherson, "turned out to be the thin edge of a wedge driven into the heart of slavery."

Before the general's new take on this term, "contraband" had been an obscure term relating primarily to maritime law. Butler did not intend to recast that word the way he did, let alone suggest a concept that would influence the course of the Civil War. His reference to "contraband of war" was almost facetious; he did not even consider it worth mentioning in his official report about meeting with Major Cary. Nor did Cary, in his own report. Long after members of the press had adopted Butler's casual coinage, in official dispatches the Union general himself continued to refer to "slaves," not "contrabands."

Although abolitionists such as William Lloyd Garrison and Frederick Douglass considered this term demeaning (Douglass thought it was more suited to a pistol than a person), among northerners *contrabands* was used synonymously with "escaped slaves" throughout the Civil War. "Several contrabands came into the camp of the First Connecticut Regiment today," reported a Northern newspaper soon after Butler declared his doctrine. The thousands of slaves who followed were housed in "contraband camps."

Why was Ben Butler's recoinage so popular? Because characterizing runaways as confiscated enemy property was far more palatable politically than treating them as free men and women. North of the Mason-Dixon line, support for preserving the union far outweighed any passion for emancipating slaves. Treating them as enemy property to be confiscated was for many an acceptable alternative. "The venerable gentleman who wears gold spectacles and reads a conservative daily, prefers confiscation to emancipation," noted abolitionist-journalist Edward L. Pierce early in the war. "He is reluctant to have slaves declared freemen, but has no objection to their being declared contraband."

Regarding runaways as *contraband* therefore proved to be an invaluable way to consign them to a verbal purgatory: neither slave nor free. But the term didn't just convey a useful ambiguity. *Contraband* was also cheeky, a bit of a wink. (Escaped slaves themselves might rather have been called *freemen*, but *contraband* was certainly better than *slave*.) Throughout the war, songs were composed about "contrabands," poems written, paintings painted. Louisa May Alcott wrote a story titled "My Contraband." Winslow Homer published drawings of life in contraband camps (and following the war painted a watercolor titled "Contraband" that portrayed a Union soldier sitting beside a young black boy). Many other artists incorporated this word into their work, including one who drew a determined-looking runaway astride a white horse who is galloping away from a camp flying a Confederate flag and toward one displaying the stars and stripes. It is titled "Contraband: Changing Quarters."

Contraband art: *Contraband: Changing Quarters* (artist unknown).

In a thorough analysis of the rapid diffusion of this word, historian Kate Masur concluded that it was a "placeholder," a way to characterize runaway slaves pending their actual emancipation. By overemphasizing the role Butler's "contraband of war" concept played in highlighting the ambivalence northerners felt about escaped slaves, however, Masur thought her fellow historians had underestimated their enthusiasm for the term *contraband* itself. In the stories they told about contrabands, songs they sang, and pictures they drew, "Northerners sought to fill with meaning a term that was, by definition, transitional and unstable."

Following the Confederate surrender, some questioned whether Butler had actually uttered the phrase "contraband of war" in his exchange with Maj. Cary, or just took retroactive credit for doing so. Three decades after they'd met, Cary confirmed that Butler had used those very words during their meeting on horseback. It was the first time he'd heard the term "contraband" used this way, Cary added (in a letter to Butler).

In his 1892 memoir, Butler acknowledged the rationale that this phrase had provided for giving asylum to runaways, but said its public reception astonished him. Despite the admiration these words brought to this man of considerable ego, Butler took no pride of authorship for recoining *contraband of war*. "It was a poor phrase," Butler wrote. "The truth is, as a lawyer I was never very proud of it, but as an executive officer I was very much comforted with it as a means of doing my duty." Like it or not, *contraband* belonged to him. Long after the war ended, Butler conceded that words like the one he'd conjured "will stick to the man they belong to. This one will stick to me in spite of all efforts to the contrary."

Decades later an American diplomat had the same experience, inadvertently recoining an existing word in a way that proved to have even greater lasting impact and an indelible association with its recoiner.

Containers

During three tours of duty in Moscow's U.S. embassy, George Kennan had a front-row seat to observe both the Soviet Union's wartime devastation and its postwar attempts to create satellite states in Eastern Europe and foment Communist-led insurrections in Western Europe. Before leaving Russia in 1946, the forty-three-year-old diplomat sent the State Department a long telegram spelling out his concerns about the Kremlin's attempts to bring more countries into its orbit. Because Soviet expansionism posed a threat to world order, Kennan argued, the United States needed to curtail its territorial ambitions. In a subsequent *Foreign Policy* article based on this telegram, Kennan wrote, "It is clear that the main element of any United States policy toward the Soviet Union must be that of a long-term, patient but firm and vigilant containment of Russian expansive tendencies."

Containment was just one of eight thousand words in Kennan's article. He hadn't meant that word to be its focus. Years later, the diplomat recalled choosing this term "light-heartedly." His casually chosen word ended up having an inordinate influence on world affairs, however. In the assessment of historian Gregg Herken, Kennan "inadvertently coined the term that would henceforth be used to describe the country's new approach to the Soviet Union." This new approach grew out of the need to *contain* Soviet expansionism. The Soviet Union had to be *contained* within its existing borders. Our policy toward that country should be one of *containment*.

Obviously Kennan didn't coin the word "containment" any more than Ben Butler coined "contraband," but he breathed new life into that old term, making it a diplomatic concept that would dominate American thinking throughout the Cold War. Long after Kennan added *containment* to the diplomatic lexicon, this concept continues to describe a policy for limiting the ambitions of expansionist powers. How that should be accomplished was left up to the container (as it were).

Because he put so little weight on this word, Kennan hadn't bothered to spell out exactly what he meant by containment. Over time, others did that for him, generally in ways he hadn't intended. As its author hoped, the concept of *containment* at first occupied a middle ground between inaction and military action. Kennan meant it to refer simply to isolating the Soviet Union and its allies. Armed intervention wasn't necessarily called for. Since the Red Army had been so devastated by the war and the Soviet people were so exhausted, Kennan didn't think the USSR posed an immediate military threat to Western democracies. Others felt otherwise. Cold warriors such as John Foster Dulles, secretary of state under President Dwight Eisenhower, gave *containment* a bellicose spin, considering it synonymous with a "rollback" of postwar Communist gains. In time, this became the accepted notion. Some five decades after George Kennan wrote his long telegram, *Safire's Political Dictionary* defined containment as a "policy of limiting the aggressive expansion of Communism by military means."

To Kennan's lifelong dismay, the military aspect of *containment* subsumed the diplomatic and economic pressure he'd meant to emphasize. As he came to realize, the ambiguity of that term made misinterpretation nearly inevitable. It was a word too easily adapted to whatever purposes the user wished (which is what made it so useful). This card-carrying member of America's foreign policy establishment was both alarmed and chagrined by how much weight was put on a single term he'd used in the *Foreign Policy* article based on his initial telegram and the many ways in which it was misinterpreted. "My thoughts about containment," Kennan told an interviewer in 1996, "were of course distorted by the people who understood it and pursued it exclusively as a military concept; and

I think that that, as much as any other cause, led to 40 years of unnecessary, fearfully expensive and disoriented process of the Cold War."

Years after he first called attention to the need to contain Soviet expansionism, Kennan wrote that his creation of this concept made him feel "like one who has inadvertently loosened a large boulder from the top of a cliff and now helplessly witnesses its path of destruction in the valley below, shuddering and wincing at each successive glimpse of disaster."

As subsequent events would show, George Kennan wasn't the only parent of a term who came to feel this way about his wayward offspring.

Shifting Paradigms

In a classic *New Yorker* cartoon, a comely young woman wearing bell bottoms tells a balding, paunchy man in urban safari gear "Dynamite, Mr. Gerston! You're the first person I ever heard use 'paradigm' in real life." That cartoon appeared in 1974. During the decades since, *paradigm* has become a regular entry on lists of overused words. So has its close cousin *paradigm shift*. In addition to being ubiquitous in semi-learned discourse, this phrase is now the title of several books, one record album, and a YouTube channel.

How did *paradigm* become such a used, and overused term? To answer that question, we must go back to 1947, and to the Harvard dormitory room where a graduate student named Thomas Kuhn stared out the window at vine-covered walls of a nearby building and contemplated why Aristotle's ideas about physics were so wrongheaded. In what he later called an "epiphany," Kuhn realized that Aristotle wasn't wrong; he simply was working in a context very different from our own. Trying to interpret Aristotle's ideas with modern concepts allowed us to overlook his profound insights. They were neither better nor worse than subsequent versions, Kuhn concluded, just different. Aristotle was working in an entirely distinct *paradigm*.

That was the word Kuhn chose to describe his unfolding ideas about how scientific progress occurs. Although it was already in play (adapted from the word "paradeigma" that Aristotle and other ancient Greeks used to mean "exemplar"), Kuhn gave "paradigm" a bigger, broader, more robust meaning.

This meaning evolved in his head as he taught an introductory science course at Harvard. While explaining the fits and starts of scientific progress to undergraduates, Kuhn concluded that the history of science had less to do with a forward march toward generally accepted truths than with continual shifts in which one frame of reference replaced another. Fifteen years after that conclusion began to dawn on him, Kuhn published a book in 1962 called *The Structure of Scientific Revolutions*. His title tipped the author's intentions, referring as it did to multiple "scientific revolutions," rather than a single "scientific revolution." This notion, commonplace today, but radical at the time, exploded like an intellectual bomb in the world of science. By the time its author died in 1996, *The Structure of Scientific Revolutions* was considered one of the most influential books of the twentieth century. It still is.

In his book Kuhn not only talked repeatedly about the paradigm of accepted concepts in which scientists work (analogous to *conventional wisdom*, a term that had recently been introduced in John Kenneth Galbraith's 1958 book *The Affluent Society*), but posited that when an existing paradigm withers away because of questions that can't be dealt with within its assumptions, a new version crops up that allows us to reassess old information in a new light. Kuhn called this process a "paradigm shift." Examples include the Darwinian revolution that forced naturalists to think in terms of evolution instead of creation, Einstein's theory of relativity that replaced one of stasis, and Crick-Watson's upending of our conceptions of molecular biology with their discovery of the double-helix structure of DNA.

Kuhn's notion of shifting scientific paradigms attracted the attention not only of colleagues but nonscientists as well. *Paradigm shifts* began to be identified not just in the physical sciences but in social sciences too. Keynesian theories were seen as constituting a paradigm shift in economic thinking, followed by post-Keynesian ones that led to yet another shift. The paradigm of Freudian psychology that questioned accepted notions of human behavior was subsequently challenged by Jungian and Skinnerian paradigms. Shifts came to be seen all over the intellectual milieu as one venue after another embraced this concept: management, marketing, the arts, theology, politics, and even sports (as when an innovative Major League Baseball team was lauded for its "paradigm-shifting" approach to the game). In the ultimate sign of widespread diffusion, Kuhn's notions cropped up in the thickets of popular culture, reaching some sort of crescendo when a rock band named Korn called their 2013 album *The Paradigm Shift*.

How did its creator feel about the popularity of his coinage? Not too good. Although Thomas Kuhn clearly hoped his peers would adopt his neo-neologism, which appears throughout *The Structure of Scientific Revolutions*, he hadn't thought it would be used so promiscuously and was appalled when it was. By the time Kuhn was interviewed by John Horgan for a 1991 *Scientific American* profile, he lamented how "hopelessly overused" and "out of control" the use of *paradigm* had become.

From a linguistic perspective it was *too* successful. *Paradigm* and *paradigm shift* have been described as a sort of verbal virus, spreading from one discipline to another and finally to an entirely undisciplined use of the phrase. One could just as easily say *example*, or *matrix*, or *pattern*, or *context* instead of *paradigm*, but where would the oomph be? The prestige? The gravitas? And should you choose to put your own spin on Kuhn's terminology, so be it. After all, the author himself had used *paradigm* in a wide variety of ways (if not twenty-one, as one critic concluded). Kuhn realized that the success of his book—which has sold well over a million copies—was due in large measure to the useful ambiguity of its key concept. This in turn led to the multitude of ways in which it's been used. One commentator suggested that the meaning of *paradigm shift* has drifted so far from Kuhn's original version that it should no longer be attributed to him.

The fault was partly his, Kuhn conceded, for making the "dreadful mistake" of not defining *paradigm* more clearly in his book. In a second edition of *The Structure of Scientific Revolutions* the author pleaded with readers to replace *paradigm* with *exemplar*. Few heeded his plea. In time, Kuhn resigned himself to being saddled with *paradigm* and accepted his fate. "If you've got a bear by the tail," he told Horgan, "there comes a point at which you've got to let it go and stand back."

Disruptive Behavior

A fellow Harvard PhD knew just how Kuhn felt. In 1995 this junior faculty member at the Harvard Business School coauthored a *Harvard Business Review* article based on research he'd done for his PhD thesis that showed how new technologies had turned the computer disk-drive industry on its head. It was titled "Disruptive Technologies: Catching the Wave." Rather than stick to technologies that satisfied customers' current needs, this article argued, innovators needed to adopt ones on the cutting edge that would best serve customers of the future, even if doing so disrupted the lives of those they served in the present.

Two years after this article was published, coauthor Clayton Christensen wrote a book called *The Innovator's Dilemma*. His title referred to the challenge faced by business leaders who had to choose between continuing to operate a successful business on existing terms or embracing innovations that might threaten the success their enterprise was enjoying. But failing to do so ensured long-term failure at the price of short-term success. Because they didn't want to tamper with a winning business model, companies such as Sears, Radio Shack, and Railway Express had to step aside to make way for rambunctious mold-breakers such as Amazon, Apple, and Federal Express. "The list of leading companies that failed when confronted with disruptive changes in technology and market structure is a long one," Christensen wrote.

The Innovator's Dilemma became a big-league bestseller. In the process it gave fresh meaning to the terms *disrupt, disruptive, disruption,* and *disruptor.* Before Clayton Christensen gave it a positive spin, "disrupt" referred to causing a commotion. Messing things up. Being a nuisance. The 1974 edition of *Webster's New*

Collegiate Dictionary defined *disrupt* as "to break apart," "to throw into disorder," "to cause to break down." Parents who were summoned for a chat with the principal about their child's *disruptive* behavior did not look forward to this meeting. *Disruptors* of any age were considered antisocial nuisances. Street-corner haranguers. Unruly soccer fans. Rowdy dissidents at stockholder meetings. *Disruption* was what happened when such mischief-makers held sway. At least before Clayton Christensen began to preach his gospel. Today it's the cornerstone of a faith system. Historian Jill Lepore even suggests that "disruption" has become a form of secular theology, filling a gap left by the decline of traditional religion.

The trappings are certainly there: revival-type meetings with speakers shouting, "Let me hear it: *DISSS-RUPPTTT!*" Or a "Festival of Disruption" sponsored by the website TechCrunch. Is there any way Clayton Christensen could have anticipated that Taco Bell would hire a Resident Disruptor? Or that a "Disruptive Toothbrush" would one day be sold online?

Like *paradigm* and *paradigm shift*, *disrupt* and its many variations have become buzzwords bordering on clichés. They lie at the heart of what's considered the most influential management concept of modern times. Far from referring to misbehaving in class or acting up at a stockholder's meeting, *disrupt* now depicts a difficult but necessary transition to genuine innovation. *Disruptors* are no longer troublemakers; they're buccaneers, prophets, and visionaries who can breathe new life into hidebound organizations by enduring short-term failure for the sake of long-term success. To prepare for the future, such organizations need to hire the type of difficult disruptor that personnel directors usually usher out of their office as quickly as possible. In an interesting twist on the concept of coinage, the website of his Christensen Institute says, "The theory of disruptive innovation was first coined by Harvard Professor Clayton M. Christensen." This is the first time I've heard of a theory being "coined."

Did Christensen anticipate how much impact his new take on this old term would have? Yes and no. Although he hammered home the need for *disruption* in years of articles and books that followed his original reconception of this term, I doubt that Christensen had any inkling that it would make its way into the neological hall of fame. *Disrupt* appeared in the titles of only two of his many books. Nearly all of them, on the other hand, included the term "innovation."

Due in part to the efforts of Clayton Christensen, *innovation*—like *disruption*—has become a positive concept in recent decades (to put it mildly). This wasn't always so. During the Middle Ages, those who tried to *innovate* risked their necks to do so. In 1548 the king of England issued a *Proclamation Against Those That Doth Innovate*. Religious dissenters were punished severely for being *innovators*. (When an English Puritan named Henry Burton was accused of propagating theological innovation in 1636, his ears were cut off and he was sent to prison.) Not just theological but political dissidents were denounced as advocates of *innovation*. Edmund Burke reviled the French Revolution as "a revolt of innovation." American Federalists called themselves "enemies to innovation." Noah Webster's definition of this term in his 1828 dictionary advised readers that "innovation is often used in an ill sense, for a change that disturbs settled opinions and practices without an equivalent advantage." Only in the mid-twentieth century did the reputation of this concept become redeemed after economist Joseph Schumpeter began to talk of innovation in positive terms as a process by which new products were introduced, then famously proposed that capitalism itself was based on a "perennial gale of creative destruction." As Lepore points out, Schumpeter's seminal idea was the intellectual godfather of "disruptive innovation."

When Clayton Christensen made his contrarian case for *disruption*, this notion dovetailed nicely with the modern reverence for *innovation*. What he hadn't anticipated was how ubiquitous the concept of disruption would become, not just in the lexicon of management but in popular discourse as well. In its modern iteration, *disrupt*—and its many verbal offshoots—has become one of the most used, overused, and misused words in the English language. Nobody realized this better than Clayton Christensen himself. Two decades after he recoined it, Christensen expressed concern about the "almost random use of the word 'disruption.'" The management professor was sure that few of the many people who propagated that term had made any serious effort to understand its implications. "Too frequently, they use the term loosely to invoke the concept of innovation in support of whatever it is they wish to do," he lamented. Two decades after *The Innovator's Dilemma* was published, Christensen echoed the second thoughts of George Kennan and Thomas Kuhn when he told an interviewer, "What we didn't anticipate, and what in many ways was a fault of mine, was that the term disruption has so many different connotations in the English language, that it allows people to justify whatever they want to do as, 'Oh, this is disruptive,' . . ."

In retrospect, Christensen wished that instead of *disrupt* and *disruption* he'd used terms such as "type 1 innovation," and "type 2 innovation." Those who wanted to invoke those concepts would then have to study what he meant by them. But that's precisely why they would have gone nowhere. Who wants to read a book in order to use a term? The ones we prefer can stand on their own, like *disrupt*. If new words have a bit of zest, like that one does, more's the better. Better yet is that they evoke a smile.

4

Just Kidding

DURING THE POST–WORLD War II era, Alfred Kinsey's books didn't just provide exciting information about the sex lives of human beings, they gave us a vocabulary to discuss this information. On the pages of Kinsey's *Sexual Behavior in the Human Male*, one phrase in particular caught our attention: *missionary position*. In his 1948 book, the Indiana University biologist reported that anthropologist Bronislaw Malinowski said this was how Trobriand Islanders referred to the man-astride version of sexual intercourse that Western missionaries advised them to practice. According to Kinsey, Malinowski had reported in a 1929 book that "caricatures of the English-American position are performed around . . . campfires, to the great amusement of the natives who refer to the position as the 'missionary position.'"

However, in his 1929 book *The Sexual Life of Savages in North-Western Melanesia*, Malinowski wrote no such thing. Kinsey's claim was part of an oceanic myth. (Malinowski did mention an old-timer who dismissed public displays of affection among young couples in the Trobriand Islands as *mmnan si bubunela*, or "missionary fashion.")

So where did "missionary position" originate? Based on extensive research, anthropologist Robert J. Priest has concluded that the first appearance of *missionary position* was in . . . *Sexual Behavior in the Human Male*. This would point the finger at Alfred Kinsey himself as its probable source. Whether Kinsey simply misspoke when attributing that term to Malinowski or whether he wanted to protect himself by crediting a lighthearted coinage of his own to the distinguished anthropologist has never been determined.

Another possibility is that this phrase originated as an inside joke among anthropologists familiar with prudish Western missionaries who considered the proper position for lovemaking to be man above, woman below. *Missionary position.* Get it? Chuckle, wink, nudge to the ribs. In response to Priest's report of his findings, American folklorist Alan Dundes shared an old joke: a French sexologist gives a lecture on seventy positions for making love. Afterward an audience member calls out, "What about the missionary position where the man lies on top of the woman?" The sexologist responds, "Oo la la! Ziss I never heard!"

A second responder, Australian anthropologist Kenelm Burridge, reported that upon returning from naval duty in World War II he'd heard veterans discuss their time in India with a heavy emphasis on the Kama Sutra, sexually explicit temple carvings, and other forms of South Asian erotica. The comparison of such candid, unabashed, and imaginative representations of sexual behavior contrasted vividly with more reserved Western treatments of the same subject. During bawdy conversations among these veterans, Burridge said he'd heard the phrase "missionary position" in a way that suggested it was part of British Army lingo long before Alfred Kinsey put the expression in print.

Robert Priest doesn't buy it. He thinks that anyone who referred to the "missionary position" after World War II most likely got it from *Sexual Behavior in the Human Male*. Although it would take several years after publication of that book for "missionary position" to become a common expression, its imagery and humor ensured that this phrase would join the erotic vocabulary. By now, it's not just a humorous but a straightforward way to refer to man-on-top lovemaking. "Missionary position" has also become part of Spanish terminology as *postura del misionero*, Dutch as *missionarishouding*, German as *Missionarsstellung*, and French as *position du missionnaire*. Among English speakers, "missionary position" is now so commonplace that we sometimes dispense with its second word. In Craig Lesley's novel *River Song*, a woman tells a man that she's lost weight by playing softball. "What position?" he asks. "Mostly missionary," she responds.

The Joy of Coining Words

Whimsy is integral to the word-creation process and always has been. Many of our most durable words and phrases were created for fun. "Jubilance is an explanation for a lot of the things that happen in language," Allen Walker Read once observed. This distinguished linguist considered "the play spirit" an integral part of word coinage. That spirit, the Columbia University professor suggested, "may even have been the prime mover in the development of language itself."

Closely related to being playful is being facetious. When an English linguist dismissed slangy neologisms as little more than "the ghosts of old facetiousness," H. L. Mencken responded that facetiousness was "the most powerful of all the stimulants that keep the language alive and growing." This is more true than ever in a world where language is being continually fertilized by whimsical bloggers, wisecracking comedians, and sundry quipsters who are less intent on expanding our vocabulary than on enjoying themselves. Any number of neologisms began as little more than quips, punchlines, and flippant remarks whose widespread adoption surprised their coiners as much as anyone. When Andy Warhol observed a half-century ago that there would be a time "when everyone will be famous for fifteen minutes," I doubt that he thought his fey prediction would inspire one of our most useful expressions. Following an early appearance in a 1967 issue of *Time*, Warhol's throwaway line became commonplace in conjunction with the rise of celebrity culture. "Fifteen minutes of fame" describes perfectly the status of today's many transiently famous demi-celebrities. Anyone who enjoys a brief period of recognition is apt to describe it as "my fifteen minutes of fame." By now the key words of Warhol's whimsical remark are so familiar that "fifteen minutes" alone can suffice when referring to a fleeting period in the public eye. ("She's had her fifteen minutes.")

Another ubiquitous expression began its life in a similar spirit. This one was born in a hotel room where Muhammad Ali met with publicist John Condon and boxing photographer George Kalinsky in 1974. Ali was anxious about his upcoming fight with the taller, heavier, and stronger George Foreman. As the three discussed Ali's anxiety, Kalinsky recalled a photograph he'd once taken of the boxer sparring. In that photo Ali lounged against the ropes to create distance from his sparring partner. "Why don't you try something like that?" said Kalinsky. "Sort of a dope on the ropes. Letting Foreman swing away but, like in the picture, hit nothing but air." John Condon picked up on this idea, compressing Kalinsky's suggestion into the crisper "rope-a-dope."

That described Ali's strategy for fighting Foreman in Zaire: lounging against the ropes as his increasingly frustrated opponent exhausted himself trying to lay a glove on him. Near the end of the eighth round Ali dispatched Foreman with a left hook and a right cross. Foreman fell to the canvas and didn't get up. Afterward Ali called this strategy "rope-a-dope." The rest is history, pugilistic and philological. Nearly half a century after the Rumble in the Jungle, we still rely on *rope-a-dope* to describe strategies that involve frustrating an opponent with feints and dodges. The Taliban's evasive tactics in Afghanistan have been called "military rope-a-dope" by a CNN correspondent. According to a financial commentator, in early 2018 the American dollar had gotten off the canvas, "first to do a little rope-a-dope, and then come out of that defensive position, swinging and landing some heavy blows on the currencies and metals."

Amusing candidates have an edge when it comes to neologizing. Like Allen Walker Read, many linguists consider fun-seeking an ill-appreciated motivation for creating new words. This motivation is on vivid display in the American version of English. Examples of playful terms that were born in the exuberant atmosphere of the American frontier, according to Read, include *discombobulate, hornswoggle*, and *lollapalooza*. He could have added *mugwump*. Referring to a feisty political independent, this term was heard often after the Civil War in part because it was so much fun to say. Apparently *mugwump* was based on *mugquomp*, Algonquian for an important tribal leader. Before focusing on political outliers, it referenced leaders of many kinds. When a group of Republicans bolted from their party during the 1884 presidential election to support Democrat Grover Cleveland, the *New York Sun* taunted them as "Little Mugwumps." Shorn of "Little," *mugwumps* went viral, referring both to political renegades and self-important leaders. This popular appellation soon begat *mugwumped, mugwumpery, mugwumpism*, and *mugwumpian* for leaders who are more officious than official.

H. L. Mencken was a fan of *mugwump*, whose provenance he discussed in his monumental book *The American Language*. In this book Mencken argued that the vitality of America's version of English lay in its exuberance. He defended his country's often-derided "Americanisms" by pointing out that such neologisms don't just fill gaps in the English vocabulary but do so with gusto. According to the journalist-linguist, "There survives in the American something that seems to have faded out of the Englishman: an innocent joy in word-making for its own sake, a voluptuous delight in the vigor and elasticity of the language." The Americanism *hoosegow* may not have improved on *jail*, or *prison*, he pointed out, but was a lot more fun to say. *Flimflam* felt better in the mouth than *swindle*, and *rubberneck* was a more agreeable verb than *crane*.

Mencken had a keen ear for Americanisms new and old, along with their origin stories. That's why a collection of his articles titled *On Politics* was subtitled *A Carnival of Buncombe*. Therein lies a story.

Talking Buncombe

During the Sixteenth Congress (1819–21), Representative Felix Walker of Buncombe County, North Carolina, liked to interject during speeches that he was "only talking for Buncombe." Walker's earnest assertion amused his colleagues, who began to use it themselves. "Talking for Buncombe" soon became a popular catchphrase, then simply "talking Buncombe." Respelled as *Bunkum*, the key word in that expression showed up in *The Attaché*, an 1856 novel by humorist Thomas Chandler Haliburton. In Haliburton's yarn, a Yankee visiting England tells a local, "Almost all that's said in *Congress* . . ., and all over America, is *Bunkum*. Well, they talk *Bunkum* here too as well as there. . . . Slavery speeches are all *Bunkum*; so are reform speeches too."

Over time, *Bunkum* was shortened to *bunk*. As a synonym for "nonsense," *bunk* proved to be just the sort of satisfying, blunt word users crave. It gained

notoriety in 1916 when Henry Ford dismissed history as "more or less bunk."
Seven years after that an American author named William Woodward published
a farcical takedown of American business practices called *Bunk*. Woodward's
characters raged continually about the power of *bunk* in modern life. Bunk, one
said sarcastically, was "the most colossal, constructive power in the world. What
would the great war [World War I] have been without bunk? Why, it would have
fizzled out in almost no time, and history would have been cheated out of her
most glorious pages. . . . mankind needs its bunk and thrives on it."

To challenge bunk's power, the protagonist of Woodward's novel becomes a
professional *de-bunker*. His job is to "take the bunk out of things." He *de-bunks*.
This newly created verb appears throughout *Bunk*. "Recently we de-bunked the
head of a large financial institution," this man reports. However, he adds, "To
keep the United States thoroughly debunked would require the continual ser-
vices of not less than half a million persons."

By now *debunk* is heard more often than *bunk* alone, and has become a term
unto itself. Apparently there's something about the *de-* prefix that adds power
to a word. Nowadays we're less likely to get *briefed* than *debriefed*. In academic
circles *deconstruct* is a more knowing term than *construct*. *Debug* is another case in

Page from logbook of Admiral Grace Hopper's Mark II team with bug attached,
September 9, 1947.

point. For that very useful neologism we have a U.S. Navy admiral named Grace Hopper to thank. During World War II Admiral Hopper was renowned for her technological skills. Soon after the war ended, she was detached to work on Mark II, an early computer being developed at Harvard. In 1947 a member of Hopper's team removed a moth that had taken residence between two relay contacts of a malfunctioning Mark II. An entry in their logbook for September 9, 1947, reads "1545 Relay #70 Panel F (moth) in relay. First actual use of bug being found." The offending moth was taped to this page of their logbook (which was later put on display at the Smithsonian). For years thereafter, in her writing and speeches, Hopper pointed out that even though others had already referred to "bugs" in glitchy devices, as far as she knew this was the first time such a device had been literally *de-bugged*. Decades later we still say malfunctioning computer hardware and software needs *debugging*.

Cyberspeak

If ever a subject cried out for neologisms, it's digital technology. Since this type of technology was so brand-spanking new in the postwar era, there was, and is, a desperate need for terms to talk about it. That's particularly true among the self-described propeller heads who toil in its vineyards. This crowd's geek-speak brims with whimsically invented terms, many of which have migrated to the broader national conversation.

Wiki, for example, grew out of the rumination of programmer Ward Cunningham, about what to name an online collaboration program he'd created in the mid-1990s. "Quick web" was a possibility. This described what Cunningham was trying to accomplish, but wasn't much fun to say. What would suggest the playful spirit he wanted to convey? As he deliberated, Cunningham recalled his visit to Hawaii several years earlier. After landing at Honolulu's airport, he'd boarded a *Wiki-Wiki* shuttle bus. Its name, Cunningham had been told, was Hawaiian for "quick." Might he be able to borrow this delightful word for his program? He could, and did. When introducing this program in 1995, Cunningham called it *WikiWikiWeb*. Ever since, all manner of collaborative online ventures have been called "wikis."

Nowhere is jubilance on better display than among high-tech entrepreneurs like Ward Cunningham. In the land of bean bag chairs and hallway Ping Pong games, a playful workplace has produced a continual stream of whimsical new words to fill gaps in our language. Like *wiki*, fanciful terms such as *Google*, *Twitter*, and *Uber* are integral to the culture of that sector, especially when verbized to *google*, *tweet*, and *uber* ("I ubered over here"). *Bluetooth* was a jokey placeholder name for a wireless system being developed in 1997 (adopting the moniker of a tenth-century Scandinavian king with a tooth so decayed it looked blue) that no one took seriously except users. Now millions do.

Software is another term that may have begun as an inside joke among early computer programmers before jumping the fence to become part of common parlance. In an online memoir, pioneer programmer Paul Niquette says he coined this term during the early 1950s "more or less as a prank." According to Niquette, his neo-antonym for "hardware" at first evoked shrugs and smirks among fellow programmers. Niquette says he and his colleagues used this coinage for years, but only among themselves. He never even recorded it. Why not? Because, the programmer explains, he'd always thought such a word was better suited to idle banter than serious discourse. Princeton statistician John Tukey—who'd earlier coined *bit* as a contraction of "binary digit"—had no such compunction. In a 1958 paper Tukey referred to "software." Because that is the first known appearance of this term, he's generally assumed to have coined it. Paul Niquette begs to differ. Assuming Niquette's origin story is accurate (as with so many oral coinages, there's no rock-solid way to confirm or debunk it), "software" is just one among many geeky jests-among-friends to achieve widespread usage.

Blog is another. This term originated in 1997 when one Jorn Barger began calling his regular online jottings a *web log*. Others compressed those two words into *weblog*. In early 1999 Barger's fellow netizen Peter Merholz commented on his website, "I've decided to pronounce the word 'weblog' as wee'-blog. Or 'blog' for short." Since weblogs constituted a kind of "information upchucking," Merholz recalled telling a friend at the time, why not give them a name that was "roughly onomatopoeic of vomiting."

Merholz was being facetious, of course, not seeking a ticket of admission into the *OED*. It ended up there nonetheless. Virtually overnight *blog* became the preferred term for weblogs. Those composing them soon came to be known as *bloggers*. One blogger named Brad Graham mused online about other words that this coinage might spawn. "Is blog- (or -blog) poised to become the prefix/suffix of the next century?" asked Graham on his own weblog. "Will we soon suffer from (and tire of) blogorrhea? Despite its whimsical provenance, it's an awkward, homely little word. Goodbye, cyberspace! Hello, blogverse! Blogosphere? Blogmos?" Fellow bloggers liked the sound of *blogosphere* and, to an amazed Brad Graham, adopted that word to describe their venue.

Jeff Howe is another amazed (and amused) neologizer. To mock the penchant for portmanteaus such as *shareware*, *vaporware*, and *clickbait* in the Silicon Valley, the onetime *Wired* writer began calling online consultation among large groups of people *crowdsourcing*. As Howe later confirmed in an email, "Crowdsourcing, as a neologism, is at least in part a joke. 'Spoofy' is about right. We truly did need a new word to describe a heretofore largely uncharacterized phenomenon, but we were also poking fun at a portmanteau-crazed Silicon Valley." Though meant to be sardonic, in all seriousness this term became one of the most successful coinages of modern times. In 2009 Howe himself published a book called *Crowdsourcing.*

The Power of Whimsy

As Jeff Howe and many other whimsical neologizers have discovered, terms meant to be fanciful can change flavor as they wend their way into the national conversation. That's because spoofiness is conveyed better in person than in print. Well before Andy Warhol's famous catchphrase made its hard copy debut in *Time*, the artist had talked drolly about enjoying "fifteen minutes of fame." In person, the ironic flavor of his remark would have been clear. While actually conversing, a cock of one's eyebrow, a bit of a smirk, or nudge to the ribs conveys the message "Just kidding." No such tipoffs are available in emoji-free text.

Published coinages, no matter their intent, are taken more seriously than verbal ones. That's what Erica Jong discovered after her 1973 novel *Fear of Flying* became a bestseller. The most attention-getting passage in Jong's book depicted a spontaneous, passionate, drawer-dropping, guilt-free coupling that the author called a *zipless fuck.* "Zipless," she wrote, "because when you came together zippers fell away like rose petals, underwear blew off in one breath like dandelion fluff. Tongues intertwined and turned liquid. Your whole soul flowed out through your tongue and into the mouth of your love." Apparently enough readers had enjoyed this kind of sex, or wished they had, that *zipless* quickly joined the erotic vernacular and stayed there. More than three decades after *Fear of Flying* was published, *New York Times* columnist Ross Douthat wrote that Bill Clinton's sexual escapades were tolerated because they represented "a Europe-envying vision of perfect zipless adult bliss." In his book *Zipper*, social historian Robert Friedel notes how the scope of "ziplessness" has broadened to become an allusion to "dispensing with the barriers that and complications that men and women set up between themselves." In time, *zipless* came to refer to all manner of spontaneous activity. Jong's coinage proved to be one of those diverse terms that has utility far beyond its original use, as when a *New Yorker* writer referred to an abortive "zipless coup" in Iraq.

Writers take heed: conjured terms you'd meant to be facetious are apt to be taken seriously, then become a lasting part of your literary legacy that can embarrass you for the rest of your life. This has been the experience of Philadelphia author Stephen Fried. In his 1993 book *Thing of Beauty: The Tragedy of Supermodel Gia*, Fried referred to many of those he wrote about as *fashionistas.* The author said he'd coined this term to depict the motley players, wannabes, and hangers-on who populated the world of haute couture that his book portrayed. (As we'll see, Fried's claim of authorship is contested.) At a time when the nightly news often featured Nicaraguan *Sandinistas*, and Starbuck's *baristas* were coming into their own, the suffix *-ista* was the source of much humor among friends who attached it incongruously to nouns. Thus: *fashionista*.

Although Fried's wife thought this term was contrived, the author used *fashionista* four times in *Thing of Beauty*. He didn't think that neologism would attract much attention, and at first it didn't. During the year after his book's publication, *fashionista* appeared only once: in a *New York Times* review of *Thing of Beauty* that took its author to task for making up "corny labels." Others didn't concur, though it took time for this to become clear. A database search that *Times* reporter Penelope Green conducted found *fashionista* being used by journalists three times in 1994, 26 times the year after that, 54 times in 1996, 74 in 1997, 243 in 1998, and 225 by mid-1999. Writer Michael Musto told Green that he used this term all the time, considering it "one of those wonderful words like 'tofu' that could mean anything you want depending on the inflection."

To explain why the *OED* was thinking about adding *fashionista* to its pages, an editor there told Green, "The word fills a linguistic gap created by the rise of haute couture as a highly visible industry over the past couple of decades." Pointing out that the Spanish-derived suffix *-ista*, like its English counterpart *-ist*, referred to a type of believer, the editor said terms including this suffix suggested devotees of many kinds (e.g., *Fidelista, feminist*). When the *OED* did add *fashionista* to its lexicon in 2002, Stephen Fried said he was "flabbergasted." Fifteen years later, according to a Google search, *fashionista* had appeared in print on- and offline more than eighty-five million times.

The experience of Fried and Jong is not uncommon. Nor is it modern, or limited to pop culture expressions. Far from it. Over the centuries, any number of mainstream terms began life as witticisms.

Scientists

During an 1833 meeting of the newly formed British Association for the Advancement of Science, a lively discussion took place about the need for a name that would encompass those who toiled in different branches of their profession. *Natural philosopher* was too broad and too lofty, the discussants agreed. *Savans* was rather assuming, and, in any event, French. The German term *natur-forschur* ("nature-pokers") was rejected as too susceptible to ridicule. In keeping with the lighthearted spirit of the evening, a Cambridge University professor named William Whewell suggested *scientist*. To make sure his colleagues realized this suggestion was jocular, Whewell noted its similarity not only to *artist* but to *atheist*, and *sciolist* (an ill-informed person who pretends to be knowledgeable). "The suggestion was obviously frivolous," notes science historian Sydney Ross, "and could not have been considered seriously for a moment."

Six years after he made this "frivolous" suggestion, Whewell repeated it, this time more seriously, in an 1840 book (where he still couldn't help himself, noting the resemblance of *scientist* to *artist*, *journalist*, and *tobacconist*). When geologist Adam Sedgwick reached this section of Whewell's book, he scribbled in the margin, "Better die of this want [for a professional title] than bestialize our language by such a barbarism." Five decades later, Royal Society president Thomas Huxley was still proclaiming that "to any one who respects the English language, I think 'Scientist' must be about as pleasing a word as 'Electrocution.'" Despite such outrage, *scientist* was so well suited to its purpose that it eventually became part of common parlance, first among the laity, and, eventually, grudgingly, among scientists themselves.

One reason whimsical word creations can catch on in all seriousness is because so many are just the type of term users covet. We love terse, earthy, vivid words, propriety be damned. Earnestly coined terms, by contrast, can be too self-conscious, too intent on making the coiner look clever or erudite. End users just want to enjoy themselves. This underlies the unlikely creation of one of history's most popular words.

OK!

During the early spring of 1839, Charles Gordon Greene, the editor of the *Boston Morning Post*, decided to have some fun. In a satirical piece on grammar, Greene referred to "o.k.," saying it meant "all correct."

Shouldn't "all correct" be abbreviated as "a.c."? Indeed it should. But in antebellum America, screwball spelling was all the rage. "No go," for example, became "know go." Andrew Jackson's cabinet was called his "Kitchen Kabinet." Members of the press were particularly fond of this type of spoofery. Newsrooms have always been hotbeds of eccentric spelling. Among journalists, "lede" is the beginning of a piece of writing, and "graf" is short for "paragraph." To amp up the humor involved, many a phrase has first been misspelled by journalists, then abbreviated. Thus *ow* stood for "oll wright," *K.G.* meant "know go," and *tk* signified "to come." This placeholder for a textual gap remains common among writers and editors.

K was and is a particularly popular letter to use in deliberate misspelling. Which gets us back to *OK*. Along with other goofy abbreviations, after making its debut in 1839, *OK* continued to appear now and again in the pages of the *Morning Post* and other newspapers. If that had been its only press appearance, *ok* undoubtedly would have suffered the fate of its close cousin *ow* and been little more than a long-forgotten verbal curiosity. During the presidential election of 1840, however, President Martin Van Buren—who was nicknamed Old

Kinderhook (after his hometown in upstate New York)—made "OK" part of a campaign slogan: "Vote for OK." Its repeated appearance during the 1840 campaign kept *ok* alive in the American vernacular.

OK might not have outlived that campaign, however, were it not for a fortuitous prank involving Andrew Jackson. Like Dan Quayle and George W. Bush, Van Buren's predecessor was the butt of many a jest based on his supposed mangling of the English language. During the Battle of New Orleans, Jackson was said to have commanded his troops to "elevate them guns a little lower." When given an honorary degree by Harvard, the president known as Old Hickory allegedly tried to impress his learned audience by reciting the only Latin he knew: "*E pluribus unum,* my friends, *sine qua non.*" Much of the canon of apocryphal Jacksoniana was based on his presumed inability to spell. Even though this allegation combined one part truth with many parts hogwash, it was accepted enough that in 1840 the editor of an anti-Jackson newspaper in New York could plausibly suggest an etymology for *ok* that involved the president's spelling problems. According to this yarn, Jackson had an aide label some official papers "OK" for "all correct." In an early example of actual fake news, that etymological hoax was reprinted throughout the country as if it were authentic. This account gave the public a plausible, amusing origin story for *OK*. In the process, *OK* was riveted into the American lexicon, and, eventually, that of many other languages as well.

Speculation about the origin of *OK* did not cease with the apocryphal Jackson fable, however. For decades, trying to determine the provenance of this term kept the nation's etymologists busy. Some thought it might have originated as an abbreviation of the telegraph term "Open Key." Others searched for its origin in European languages, or Indian ones, or as a Civil War term for biscuits favored by Union soldiers that were stamped "O.K." by a Chicago baker named Orrin Kendall.

Amid all this speculation, it took the etymological prowess of Allen Walker Read—the linguist who considered jubilance a major impetus for word creation—to chase down *OK's* actual source. After long hours spent leafing through dusty old newspapers in the pre-Google era, Read happened on the probable first appearance of *OK* within Charles Gordon Greene's satirical piece in the March 23, 1839, edition of the *Morning Post.* He then tracked its subsequent evolution into one of the most ubiquitous terms in our discourse.

Building on Read's work, his fellow linguist Allan Metcalf in 2012 devoted an entire book to recounting the genesis of *OK* and exploring the many ways it's been used over time. In Metcalf's opinion, this two-letter word became such a popular part of our discourse not only because of its crispness, but because *ok* conveys an invaluable sense of ambiguity. *OK* indicates affirmation but not necessarily approval. Saying something is *OK* (or okay) needn't imply concurrence. Simply that it is all right. It's *OK*.

A particularly intriguing aspect of the origin story of this term is the fact that after being born as a whimsical prank among journalists, *OK* was kept alive by means of a hoax involving Andrew Jackson. It is far from the only neologism born in this fashion. Pranking turns out to be an effective way to insert new words into the English language.

5

Prankery

THE OCTOBER 26, 1809, edition of New York's *Evening Post* included a notice titled "DISTRESSING." That attention-getting headline was followed by this announcement:

> Left his lodgings some time since and has not been heard of, a small elderly gentleman, dressed in an old black coat and cocked hat, by the name of *Knickerbocker*. As there are some reasons for believing he is not entirely in his right mind, and as great anxiety is entertained about him, any information concerning him left either at the Columbian Hotel, Mulberry Street, or at the office of this paper will be *thankfully* received.
>
> P.S. Printers of newspapers would be aiding the cause of humanity in giving an insertion to the above.

This notice was reprinted in several other New York newspapers. At first no one reported seeing a little old man wearing old-fashioned clothes. Then, on November 6, a correspondent who called himself "A TRAVELLER" said passengers on the Albany stagecoach had spotted a man answering to this description resting beside the road. "He had in his hand a small bundle tied to a red bandana handkerchief," the letter-writer reported, "he appeared to be traveling northward and was very much fatigued and exhausted."

Ten days later, the *Evening Post* published a notice from Seth Handaside, who identified himself as the landlord of the Independent Columbian Hotel on Mulberry Street. According to Handaside, his missing guest was still missing. Possessions he'd left behind included the manuscript of "a very curious kind of written book." Assuming Mr. Knickerbocker was still alive, said the hotelier, if he didn't return soon to settle his bill, "I shall have to dispose of his book to satisfy me for the same."

These notices caused quite a stir. The missing author, the circumstances of his disappearance, and the possible content of his book aroused fevered speculation among New Yorkers. One New York official wondered whether the city should offer a reward for information about the whereabouts of Mr. Knickerbocker.

It didn't, he did not resurface, and on December 6, 1809, yet another notice appeared in the *Evening Post*. This one announced the publication of a two-volume history of New York: "Containing an account of its discovery and settlement, with its internal policy, manners, customs, wars, &c., &c., under the Dutch government, furnishing many curious and interesting particulars never before published, and which are gathered from various manuscript and other authenticated sources, the whole being interspersed with philosophical speculations and moral precepts." With so much prepublication buzz, *A History of New York from the Beginning of the World to the End of the Dutch Dynasty, by Diedrich Knickerbocker* became an instant bestseller.

Far from being a serious work of scholarship, however, *A History of New York* turned out to be a prior-day mockumentary. Its dedication to the New-York Historical Society was a tipoff (this group having had little cachet at the time). So was the fact that there was no Independent Columbian Hotel on Mulberry or any other street in New York.

Diedrich Knickerbocker's history was filled with fanciful etymology, including the origin of his own surname, from the Dutch *knicker* (to nod) and *boeken* (books), suggesting one who dozed off while reading books. According to Knickerbocker, the name "Manhattan" may have been inspired by the fact that early Dutch settlers encountered women on that island who wore men's wool hats. Hence Mann-hatta, or Man-hat-on. Knickerbocker added that early colonists civilized Manhattan's natives by supplying them with "rum, gin, brandy and the other comforts of life."

In Knickerbocker's history, an early governor of New Amsterdam named Wilhelm Kieft, aka "William the Testy," was given to flowery proclamations "written in thundering long sentences, not one word of which was under five syllables." During a time of tension with settlers from other countries, the diminutive Kieft dispatched forces that were "armed to the very teeth with one of the little governor's most powerful speeches, written in vigorous low Dutch." A subsequent skirmish with nearby Swedes was portrayed in Homerian terms: "Bang! went the guns—whack! went the broad swords—thump! went the cudgels—crash! went the musket stocks—blows—kicks—cuffs—scratches—black eyes and bloody noses, swelling the horrors of the scene!" (In fact, in 1655 a small village of Swedish settlers outside New Amsterdam had surrendered meekly to Dutch forces.)

Not long after this lively book appeared in Manhattan bookstores, its actual author was revealed. Washington Irving, editor of the satirical journal *Salamagundi*, had written the fanciful "history" of New York. There was no

Diedrich Knickerbocker; his book was a hoax, and the "disappearance" of its author a prank.

Which isn't to say that the faux historian's book had no impact on our history. It did, but more in the realm of language than scholarship. Since the rambunctious tone affected by "Diedrich Knickerbocker" so successfully captured the voice of a certain type of New Yorker, these lively citizens came to be known as *Knickerbockers*. That neo-eponym was applied primarily to New Yorkers of Dutch descent whose happy-go-lucky manner contrasted with that of more staid settlers from New England. Unlike these Puritanical Yankees, Knickerbockers liked to read fiction, go to the theater, hang around taverns, and generally enjoy themselves. In 1856, Henry Wadsworth Longfellow derided "the dreadful Knickerbocker custom of calling on everybody." Over time, their nickname was used not only for Dutch-descended New Yorkers but residents of that city in general.

Although it may not have been his intention, Irving was pleased to see the surname he'd given his mock-historian become a household word. *Knickerbocker* became the name of an influential literary magazine, an insurance company, a beer, and an early baseball club (the New York Knickerbockers). An 1830 edition of Knickerbocker's *History of New York*, illustrated with sketches of Dutchmen

"Diedrich Knickerbocker," portrayed in an 1849 edition of Washington Irving's *A History of New York*.

wearing loose knee-breeches drawn by Charles Dickens's illustrator George Cruikshank, led to that type of garb becoming known as *knickerbockers*. This garment's appellation in turn inspired the name of a type of women's underwear, eventually shortened to *knickers*. ("Don't get your knickers in a twist.") In contemporary Ireland, disposable plastic bags flapping in trees are known as "witches' knickers." By perpetrating a successful hoax, Washington Irving gave us a most useful neo-eponym.

Beyond Amalgamation

Verbal vacuums cry out for new words. Ones created to prank can fill them as well as any, and in some cases even better. The history of word-coining is rich with cases of neologisms created as part of a hoax that went on to fill gaps in our vocabulary.

One such gap involved intermarriage. Many nineteenth-century Americans were alarmed by the prospect of blacks marrying whites and producing mixed-race offspring. Before, during, and after the Civil War, a fear of "mongrelization" was widespread, on both sides of the Mason-Dixon line. That word wasn't suited to polite conversation, however. Nor was "race-mixing." "Amalgamation" was more respectable, but rather stuffy. How could Americans discuss the specter of intermarriage without using such problematic terms? Late in the Civil War an answer presented itself.

During the presidential campaign of 1864, a seventy-two-page booklet appeared on the streets of Manhattan. This publication was titled *Miscegenation: The Theory of the Blending of the Races, Applied to the American White Man and Negro*. It cost 25 cents. According to the booklet's anonymous author, "miscegenation" was a word he'd created by combining the Latin root words *miscere* (to mix) and *genus* (race). This, the pamphleteer explained, was a more scientific term than *amalgamation*, which he considered a "poor word" to describe white-black relationships.

The author then expounded at length about the virtues of miscegenation that would inevitably follow a Union victory in the Civil War. "The miscegenetic or mixed races are much superior mentally, physically, and morally to those pure or unmixed," he wrote. For this reason, "it is desirable that the white man should marry the black woman and the white woman the black man . . ." When Asians and Indians were added to the mix, he continued, the result would be an improved race of "miscegens."

This position may not sound preposterous in today's multicultural world, but in the racially charged atmosphere of Civil War-era America, it was incendiary. The idea that intermarriage would be not only an inevitable but a desirable

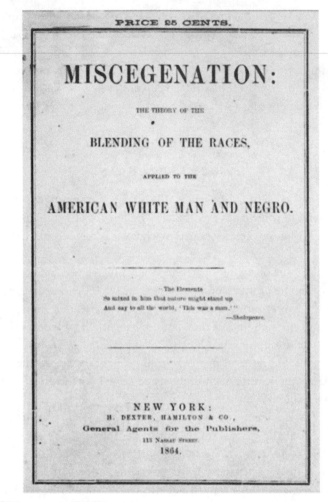

PRICE 25 CENTS.

MISCEGENATION:

THE THEORY OF THE

BLENDING OF THE RACES,

APPLIED TO THE

AMERICAN WHITE MAN AND NEGRO.

The Elements
So mixed in him that nature might stand up
And say to all the world, 'This was a man.'"
—Shakspeare.

NEW YORK:
H. DEXTER, HAMILTON & CO.,
General Agents for the Publishers,
113 Nassau Street.
1864.

Cover of *Miscegenation* booklet, 1864.

consequence of emancipation was a radical and—to northerners and southerners alike—appalling prospect. Yet this was exactly what *Miscegenation* proposed.

To increase the impact of his booklet, its author sent copies to a number of prominent Americans. The one that went to Abraham Lincoln was accompanied by a note extolling "human brotherhood." This message expressed hope that the president would stand four-square for equality between "the white and colored laborer," an inflammatory suggestion in working-class neighborhoods of racially and ethnically polarized cities such as New York. Although Lincoln did not endorse *Miscegenation*, some abolitionists who received copies did. A few anti-slavery publications, including the *Anglo-African Review* and the *National Anti-Slavery Standard*, reviewed it favorably.

The contents of *Miscegenation* quickly became a focal point of campaign oratory. As the 1864 election approached, talk of "miscegenation" dominated America's political discourse. In Washington, D.C., a Polish expat wrote in his diary, "The question of the crossing of races, or as the newly-invented sacramental word says, of *miscegenation*, agitates the press and some would be *savants* in Congress." Slavery-tolerant Democrats used this neologism to bludgeon antislavery Republicans who, they said, were hell-bent on mongrelizing the white race. Democratic publications warned that race-mixing would be the logical consequence of Abraham Lincoln's "Miscegenation Proclamation." The *Cincinnati Enquirer* advised its readers to beware of "zealous miscegenators." A Democratic newspaper in New Hampshire ran a widely reprinted article headlined "Sixty-Four Miscegenation," which claimed, falsely, that sixty-four abolitionist schoolteachers in New England had given birth to mixed-race babies. On the other side of the debate, humorist David Ross Locke, a staunch Republican and a favorite of President Lincoln, incorporated the new word into his portrayal of a clueless, semiliterate Confederate named Petroleum Vesuvius Nasby. "Lern to spell and pronownce Missenegenegenashun," Nasby/Locke advised. "It's a good word."

But not one that was genuine. *Miscegenation* turned out to be the creation of two New York journalists who weren't advocates of race-mixing at all. Their booklet was a hoax: a political dirty trick meant to sabotage Republican prospects in the election of 1864. Years after *Miscegenation* was published, its authors were unmasked as David Goodman Croly and George Wakeman of New York's Democratic newspaper *The World*. By coining this word and using it as the title of their provocative booklet, Wakeman and Croly hoped they could undermine Republican candidates by making the controversial issue of intermarriage a focal point of political discourse.

Without naming its perpetrators, a *World* article headlined the "Miscegenation Hoax" that appeared two weeks after Lincoln's 1865 inauguration, expressed horror at the way avid abolitionists had overlooked "the barbaric character of the compound word 'miscegenation.'" This article predicted that "the name will doubtless die out by virtue of its inherent malformation. We have bastard and hump-backed words enough already in our verbal army corps." In fact, the *World* concluded, as a usable word, *miscegenation* had already "passed into history."

As we've seen, predicting the fate of coined words is a dicey endeavor. Although the uproar surrounding "miscegenation" did die down after Lincoln's reelection, the word itself did not. By now it's a well-established part of our vocabulary. In a sort of professional hat tip, the renowned hoaxer (and Republican stalwart) P. T. Barnum devoted an entire chapter of his 1866 book *The Humbugs of the*

World to detailing the shrewd composition and brilliant rollout of *Miscegenation*. The successful propagation of this mock neologism was due to "one of the most impudent as well as ingenious literary hoaxes of the present day," wrote Barnum. Even though it wasn't meant to be taken seriously, or outlive its devious intent, *miscegenation* caught on and stuck around because, following the Emancipation Proclamation, a scientific-sounding term was needed to help us navigate the controversial topic of intermarriage. In the absence of anything better, *miscegenation* fit that bill. To this very day, that word is used so commonly for racially mixed relationships that it doesn't even elicit synonyms in an online thesaurus. It has even spawned a verb. As Walter Redfern writes, "The urge to miscegenate counteracts racism."

David Croly had mixed feelings about his role in coauthoring a word that became so ubiquitous. Long after he died, Croly's widow recalled the way *miscegenation* was conceived as her husband and a colleague (George Wakeman) composed their tract by that title. "I remember the episode perfectly, and the half joking, half earnest spirit in which the pamphlet was written," she said. Be that as it may, Mrs. Croly concluded, her husband's coinage "added a new, distinctive, and needed word to the vocabulary."

One American who didn't agree was David Croly himself. Croly considered *amalgamation* a perfectly good term, one he used until his death in 1889.

Vim and Vigor

Following the Civil War, an ex-Union officer and homeopathic physician named Augustin Thompson decided to go into the patent medicine business. After experimenting with various formulas, in 1876 Thompson produced a beverage that he eventually called Moxie Nerve Food. This tonic promised its users that they would enjoy renewed vim and vigor. According to its advertising, Moxie Nerve Food could treat "brain and nervous exhaustion; loss of manhood, imbecility and helplessness."

"It has recovered paralysis, softening of the brain, locomotor ataxia, and insanity when caused by nervous exhaustion. It gives a durable solid strength, makes you eat voraciously, takes away the tired, sleepy, listless feeling like magic, removes fatigue from mental and physical overwork at once."

With carbonation added and its last two words dropped, "Moxie" became a popular beverage. Even after the Pure Food and Drug Act of 1909 put an end to Moxie's medicinal claims, a reformulated version sold briskly as a soft drink. The jingle *Just Make It Moxie for Mine* rang in many American ears for some time. "The Moxie Trot" enjoyed a vogue among vigorous dancers. Bottles of Moxie were a fixture at fairs, resorts, dance halls, and other settings associated with vim and vigor. "Moxie Mobiles" toured the country promoting this beverage.

Along the way, the name of this soft drink became synonymous with audacious gumption ("That kid's got moxie!"). Where did its name come from? According to Augustin Thompson, his beverage was named after a West Point classmate named Moxie who as a young Army officer discovered the drink's secret ingredient—a sugar cane–like plant with powerful restorative properties—while trekking in the Andes. Various versions of Lieutenant Moxie's saga included one where he was stricken with a fever during his trek and restored to health by an Andean healer's herbal concoction. Moxie then shipped a bale of this herb to his fellow West Pointer. The rest is history, or fake history. Augustin Thompson had not attended the United States Military Academy. Nor had anyone named Moxie. Lieutenant Moxie existed only in Dr. Thompson's fertile imagination. According to one version of the Moxie saga that Thompson propagated over the years, his friend's name was originally spelled "Macksey," but he'd respelled it as "Moxie." In the process, Thompson added, "I believe I coined a word." In his 1885 trademark application, however, Thompson conceded that far from being someone's name, Moxie was an "arbitrary word."

But was it? While researching *The Moxie Encyclopedia*, author Q. David Bowers found many settings on old maps of Maine that incorporated the word "Moxie." As far back as 1815, there was a Moxy Pond and Moxy Mountain in Maine. Other historic settings Bowers located in that state included Moxie Cove, Moxie Falls, Moxie Trail, Moxie Woods, and Moxie Camp on Moxie Lake (incorporating a word that may have originated as the phonetic spelling of one used by local Indians). All had been named long before Augustin Thompson filed his trademark application and undoubtedly were familiar to this Maine native. The name of Dr. Thompson's health drink was no more the surname of a young army officer than it was a word of his own creation. What it actually was, was an inspired piece of marketing moxie.

Pranking the Enemy

During Moxie's heyday, what came to be known as the Great War erupted across the Atlantic. During its first year, German artillery, machine guns, and poison gas inflicted appalling losses on French and British troops. Allied attempts to attack German trenches protected by barbed wire only increased casualties among its soldiers.

Toward the end of 1915, Britain's First Lord of the Admiralty, Winston Churchill, convened a group of military and government officials to oversee development of an armored military vehicle that could smash through barbed wire and maneuver over trenches. Since the vehicle they envisioned was called a "landship," this group was titled the Landships Committee. Those working on prototypes of that vehicle gave it names of their own, including "Centipede," "Mother," "Wilson," "Big Willy," and "Little Willy." No such slangy monikers would do as an official name, however. ("Willy" is British slang for penis.)

What the committee needed was a name that camouflaged this weapon's actual purpose. At first its members called the armored vehicle they were developing a "water carrier" (e.g., "Water Carrier for Mesopotamia"). Then it occurred to them that, in an initials-rich environment, this would undoubtedly be condensed to wc, the British abbreviation for "water closet" (lavatory). A subcommittee was therefore created to come up with a term that improved on "water carrier" but had a similar flavor. After considering and discarding "container," "reservoir," and "cistern," they finally settled on the generic term *tank*.

This mechanical behemoth made its debut at the Battle of the Somme in France in July 1916. Those operating fifty of these vehicles were dubbed members of the *Tank Corps*. Then, as now, *tank* proved to be a perfectly usable word. Like the weapon it named, that term was tough, straightforward, and rugged. Despite being conjured as a ruse, the term *tank* proved to be as durable as the vehicle itself, becoming commonplace on both sides during the first world war and many wars to come.

Early tank in action, France, 1916.

Gobbling Turkeys?

Late in World War II, a Texan named Maury Maverick was appointed head of the federal government's Smaller War Plants Corporation.* This onetime U.S. congressman and former mayor of San Antonio was a political powerhouse in his native state. Short, barrel-chested, and cantankerous, Maverick had a longstanding aversion to bureaucratic jargon and what would later be called politically correct speech. He once chastised an ex-professor for using the word "nodule" to refer to political groupings. In addition to being annoying, said Maverick, this word sounded "like a sex perversion."

Maverick found new fuel for his fire in the inflated vocabulary of federal bureaucrats, including ones who reported to him. In a 1944 memo, he advised staff members to "stay off the gobbledygook language." Circulating far beyond its intended audience, Maverick's memo caused a sensation. At the request of the *New York Times*, its author wrote an essay about his neologism for the Sunday magazine. In that essay Maverick said he'd coined *gobbledygook* because all the inflated rhetoric he encountered in Washington reminded him of "the old bearded turkey gobbler back in Texas who was always gobbledy-gobblin' and struttin' with ludicrous pomposity. At the end of this gobble there was a sort of . . . 'gook.'"

Maverick's charming account of how he coined *gobbledygook* is celebrated in the annals of neology. It is probably apocryphal, however, and something of a prank to boot. In Maury Maverick's time *gobblegoo* or *gobbledegoo* was slang for performing fellatio (growing out of an earlier expression, *gobble the goo*). Maverick, who was well known for his salty tongue, undoubtedly knew this. "His private speech was extremely earthy and nearly always generously interlarded with profanity," writes biographer Richard Henderson. According to Henderson, many of the amusing anecdotes and comments in his subject's letters and conversation were unprintable. Maverick was quite a prankster too, notorious for clowning around and playing practical jokes. (He once said that in order to be more sensitive to racial sensitivities he would henceforth refer to "chiggers" as "chigros.") Maverick very likely concocted the turkey-gobbling story as a cover for stealthily inserting a bit of profanity into respectable discourse. Asking us to accept that Maury Maverick's coinage of *gobbledygook* was merely coincidental with the existing word *gobbledegoo* strains credibility. Since he died in 1954, however, we can't ask him.

---

* Years earlier, the surname of Maverick's paternal grandfather, Samuel Maverick, had become an eponym for those straying off the range because he refused to brand his cattle, leading neighbors in south Texas to call any unbranded cows on the loose "Mavericks."

Whether based on turkey talk or oral sex, *gobbledygook* became an instant and lasting part of the lexicon. There is a constant demand for words to mock inflated verbiage. When *gobbledygook* made its debut some seven decades ago, there were already several synonymous terms in the English vernacular: *poppycock, balderdash, doubletalk, gibberish,* and *claptrap,* among others. *Bureaucratese* appeared just before Maverick's coinage, and *bafflegab* just afterward. But *gobbledygook* remains our most popular word for stilted, jargony language.

Bigfeet

On October 5, 1958, a column titled "Giant Footprints Puzzle Residents Along Trinity River" appeared in California's *Humboldt Times.* According to columnist Andrew Genzoli,

> There is a mystery in the mountains of Humboldt County, waiting for a solution . . . Who is making the huge 16-inch tracks in the vicinity of Bluff Creek? Are the tracks a human hoax? Or, are they actual tracks of a huge but harmless wild-man, traveling through the wilderness? Can this be some legendary sized animal? [Jerry] Crew said the men refer to the creature as "Big Foot."

Jerry Crew was a part of a road crew that had stumbled upon some huge footprints—sixteen inches long—within Six Rivers National Forest. Genzoli's report of their discovery provoked a frenzy of speculation about the possibility that a gigantic, elusive creature might be found deep within one of our national forests. In follow-up accounts, the columnist shortened "Big Foot" to "Bigfoot." Extensive media coverage throughout the country followed suit. As a result, this mysterious humanoid is still referred to by the term Genzoli introduced to our vocabulary and our imaginations some six decades ago. Countless articles were written about the search for that beast, media reports broadcast, and books written (typically titled *Bigfoot*). Research conducted on this subject is called *bigfootology* by some; those who conduct it are *bigfootologists.* They want to know: Was the creature whose footprints were discovered in Six Rivers a gorilla-like being? A type of bear? A nearly extinct tribe of Native Americans?

Jerry Crew himself thought the footprints were a sign from above that the case for evolution needed rethinking. Others suggested more terrestrial explanations. In 2002, however, after a member of Crew's outfit named Ray Wallace died at eighty-four, his family revealed a different possibility altogether: prankery. According to them, Wallace—a consummate prankster—had crafted huge wooden feet that he used to create the footprints his road crew had found. Not that this revelation dampened interest in Bigfoot. If anything, fascination in this subject has grown during the years since Wallace died, even inspiring a podcast called *Wild Thing* that's devoted to all things Bigfoot. True or false, with help from Jerry Crew and Andrew Genzoli, Ray Wallace's prank gave us a useful, evocative word to discuss our theories about this creature: *Bigfoot.* High-powered figures in many endeavors are commonly called *bigfoots.* That term has also become a verb meaning to throw one's weight around: *to bigfoot.*

Some think the synonymous term *sasquatch* gives the reclusive beast a tonier name. That word was introduced in a 1929 magazine article, "B.C.'s Hairy Giants: A Collection of Strange Tales About British Columbia's Wild Men as Told by Those Who Say They Have Seen Them." According to this article, an Irish-Canadian schoolteacher and Indian agent named J. W. Burns came up with the term *sasquatch* to refer to large, hairy creatures that were thought to inhabit woods near the Chehalis Indian reservation where he taught, just over the border from Washington state. Burns said that this was what members of the Chehalis tribe (now called the "Sts'ailes First Nation") called that creature. Since this article appeared in the April 1, 1929, edition of *Maclean's*, some speculated that it had less to do etymology than with April foolery. However, Burns seems to have been sincere in his claim that *sasquatch* was a phonetic adaptation of a Halkomelem word for the huge, hirsute beings that Chehalis Indians thought lived in nearby forests.

Not all pranky words enjoy as much success as *bigfoot, Moxie,* and *gobbledygook.* In fact, few do. Yet some of the many terms that were concocted as part of a hoax but didn't join the lexicon enjoyed success of a different kind.

Coined to Con

A late-nineteenth-century inventor named John Keely deserves some sort of Creative Neology award for the many fanciful words he coined. In his time, this self-educated carpenter, mechanic, and sometime carnival barker became famous, then infamous, for inventing a contraption he called a "hydro pneumatic pushing vacuo machine." Better known as the Keely Motor, its inventor claimed that this engine could run on small amounts of water. Through a process he called "aqueos disintegration," water converted into "etheric vapor" would power his engine. A train fueled by aqueos disintegration could travel from Philadelphia to San Francisco on a quart of water, Keely said. One gallon would get a steamship from New York to Liverpool. A full bucket of water would "produce a power sufficient to move the world out of its course."

Keely's astonishing claims motivated a businessman as shrewd as John Jacob Astor to invest in this inventor's startup. But John Keely was to Thomas Edison as Bernie Madoff is to Warren Buffett. None of his many promised engines was ever completed, let alone shown to be viable. Nothing other than hot air ever emerged from Keely's workshop—that and an impressive glossary of neologisms that left his listeners both dazzled and confused. Keely discussed his "inventions" in language so arcane that listeners were hard-pressed to know whether he was engaged in doubletalk or they were too dense to grasp the profundity of his discourse. When the entrepreneur reported that one engine he was working on "requires introductory mediums of differential gravities, air and water, to induce disturbances of equilibrium on the liberation of vapor, which only reached the inter-atomic position and was held there by the submersion of the molecular and atomic leads in Generator I then used," Americans didn't know whether to be impressed or dumbfounded.

John Keely proved to be far better at inventing words (some 1500 of them by one estimate) than machinery. Despite repeated assurances that he would produce a glossary of technological neologisms such as *vaporic, triune, etheric, dynaspheric, vibratory, sympoathietic,* and *interatomic,* Keely never did. He died in 1898, at the age of sixty-one, without defining his terms, let alone demonstrating any functional engine. When a friend asked how he'd like to be remembered, the prankster-inventor responded, "Keely, the greatest humbug of the nineteenth century."

John Keely and his "Keely Motor."

Prank-Words, Mountweazels, and Nihilartikels

Nearly a century after John Keely's death, the *New York Times* published an article about "Grunge" culture in Seattle. That November 15, 1992, account appended a glossary of slang terms used by scruffy northwestern rockers. Titled "Lexicon of Grunge: Breaking the Code," this list included words such as *lamestain* (uncool person), *Tom-Tom club* (uncool outsiders), *cob nobbler* (loser), *wack slacks* (old ripped jeans), *fuzz* (heavy wool sweaters), *plats* (platform shoes), *harsh realm* (bummer), and *swingin' on the flippity flop* (hanging out).

Three months after the *Times* article appeared, a twenty-five-year-old receptionist at Seattle's Sub Pop Records named Megan Jasper admitted that she was the creator of these words. When asked by *Times* reporter Rick Marin if grungers had their own slang terms, Jasper simply made some up. Even though none of these neologisms made it into the vernacular, members of a band called Mudhoney did help perpetuate Jasper's ruse by using fanciful terms during interviews.

Spoofy terminology is created not just to bamboozle and con but for practical reasons as well. One is to sniff out copyright infringers. This tactic dates back more than a century, when the last entry in Rupert Hughes's 1903 *Music Lovers' Encyclopedia* was *zzxjoanw*. That supposed name of a Maori drum was clearly spurious, there being no *z*, *x*, or *j* in the Maori language. Nonetheless, it wasn't exposed as a hoax until 1976. Its purpose had been to spot those who purloined content from the encyclopedia (as many did).

Such pseudoneologisms are known as *mountweazels* in the U.S. and *nihilartikel* abroad, a word combining the Latin *nihil* (nothing) with the German term *Artikel* (article). *Mountweazel* was inspired by a putative photographer named Lillian Virginia Mountweazel, who first appeared in the 1975 edition of the *New Columbia Encyclopedia*. This mythical native of Bangs, Ohio, was said to have been renowned for her photographs of rural mailboxes that were published in a book titled *Flags Up!* Mountweazel reportedly died at thirty-one, while photographing an explosion for *Cumbustibles* magazine.

The first known use of *Mountweazel* as an eponym occurred in a 2005 *New Yorker* article by Henry Alford that discussed words created to catch copyright infringers. In this article, Alford noted that a new edition of *The New Oxford American Dictionary* included *esquivalience*, meaning "the willful avoidance of one's official responsibilities." The creator of that fake word turned out to be an editor at Oxford named Christine Lindberg.

Five years later, Google began including bogus words such as *tarsorrhaphy* and *hiybbprqag* to trap its rival search engine, Microsoft's Bing. Bing dutifully added several of Google's phony coinages to its search terms (confirming how little human attention is paid to vetting such terms). Those who searched *hiybbprqag* on Bing were sent to a fake website about seating at an imaginary Los Angeles theater, one that was imagined by Google as part of its sting.

Less sting operation than research strategy was a menu created by the U.S. Army in the mid-1970s as a tool for surveying food preferences among soldiers. Along with actual dishes on this menu, the Army's poll asked GI's how they felt about ones such as *funistrada*, *buttered ermal*, and *braised trake*. All were contrived names of nonexistent dishes, intended to test the authenticity of responses. Many of those who took part in this survey said they preferred the fake dishes to real ones such as cooked lima beans, grilled bologna, and apricot pie. *Funistrada* took on a life of its own, however, as the name of a race horse, and a restaurant in Burdickville, Michigan, called *Trattoria Funistrada*.

Irving Again

Two years before he'd conferred the sobriquet "Knickerbockers" on New Yorkers, Washington Irving gave residents of that city another nickname, one he hadn't meant to be taken seriously. In several essays Irving wrote for *Salamagundi* during the early 1800s, the author called residents of Manhattan *Gothamites*. This referenced the residents of a medieval English village called Gotham who were celebrated as "wise fools" for feigning lunacy in order to fend off royal tax collectors. In time, a popular form of humor was based on the "fools of Gotham." Eventually, the fools of Gotham were recast ironically as the "wise men of Gotham." A dictionary of slang published in 1699 defined a Wise Man of Gotham as "a Fool." In his 1755 *Dictionary of the English Language*, Samuel Johnson called a *gothamist* "one who is not wise," citing an ironic old saying, "As wise as a man of *Gotham*." In 1802—five years before Irving used the term in his essays—Charles Lamb referred to "dizzards, fools, gothamites."

Obviously Irving hadn't meant to flatter New Yorkers when he called them *Gothamites* any more than calling the city itself *Gotham* was affectionate. Over time, however, Irving's taunt lost its sting and became yet another nickname for New York, one on a par with Big Apple, the Empire City, and the City That Never Sleeps. *Gotham* took on added cachet after the creators of Batman used that name for the city he and Robin patrolled in the mid-twentieth century. This became such a common way to refer to New York that a 1998 history of the city was titled *Gotham*. By then, being called a *Gothamite* was no more derogatory than being called a Manhattanite. In a 2015 obituary, the *New York Times* referred to a recently deceased centenarian as a "gleeful Gothamite." This wasn't the first time that a term meant to taunt was embraced by the taunted, and certainly won't be the last.

6

Taunt Terms: Euro

FOLLOWING WORLD WAR II, the British Broadcasting Corporation hired astrophysicist Fred Hoyle to do commentary on cosmology. With little time per comment and no visual aids, Hoyle knew he had to create vivid word pictures. This was why, when discussing the increasingly popular notion that our universe was born in a cataclysmic explosion, the caustic Cambridge University professor told listeners, "These theories were based on the hypothesis that all the matter in the universe was created in one big bang at a particular time in the remote past."

"Big bang cosmology is an illusion," Hoyle assured those listening, in a league with religious fundamentalism.

Hoyle never imagined that *big bang* would be taken seriously as a coinage, let alone one that would become a part of the lexicon, both scientific and lay. Nor was he seeking lexical renown with that phrase. All Hoyle wanted to do was use withering sarcasm to discredit the idea that our universe began with a huge explosion. During the years that followed *big bang*'s debut, Hoyle kept up the beat, continuing to disparage what he called the "big bang idea," "big bang assumption," and "supposed big bang." Only when it was too late did Hoyle realize how big a verbal black hole he'd dug for himself. Far from blowing the theory of cataclysmic universe creation out of the water, *big bang* put it on the verbal map. By giving imagery and resonance to what had been an abstract theory, these two vivid words quickly became the way that theory was most often described. They also became a central part of Fred Hoyle's legacy. When he died in 2001, his obituary in the *Los Angeles Times* was headlined "Sir Fred Hoyle; Coined 'Big Bang.'"

In hopes of improving on Hoyle's coinage, *Sky & Telescope* magazine sponsored a contest to replace it. This 1993 competition attracted more than 13,000 entries. They included *the Big Boot, Buddha's Burp, Hubble Bubble, Let There Be Stuff, Blast from the Past, Matter Morphosis, Immaculate Inception, Jurassic Quark, Bertha D. Universe, the Whole Enchilada, the Expanding Godhead, the Primal Billowing, Primal Pop, Jiffy Pop,* and *Doink.* (In Bill Watterson's comic

strip *Calvin and Hobbes*, Calvin proposed "The Horrendous Space Kablooie.")
None were better than the original, however, so *big bang* it remains. No entry
"even approaches the phrase 'big bang' in felicity," explained contest judge Carl
Sagan at the time.

Coinage by Contempt

Derision is a first-rate source of good new words. A will to disparage can inspire
neologisms that are vigorous and clear without being self-conscious. In this chapter let's look at coinage-by-contempt abroad, then explore its rich American tradition in the chapter that follows.

One unusually successful term meant to taunt was launched in a Derby court-
room in 1650 where George Fox was on trial for blasphemy. Fox was the founder
of the Religious Society of Friends, a Protestant denomination that detractors
thought comprised little more than deranged cultists. During his trial, Fox told
the magistrate that he should "tremble at the word of the Lord." This magistrate,
Gervase Bennet, did not appreciate Fox's advice. Bennet mockingly referred to
Fox and his followers as little more than "quakers." That name stuck, even among
Friends. Although other religious zealots had already been called quakers, Fox
himself, as well as historians of the Religious Society of Friends, attribute their
terser, better-known name to Magistrate Bennet.

Marshaling words to taunt others has a long history. As we've seen, Horace's
neologisms were rich with ones meant to disparage rival poets. Subsequent literary figures followed suit. In the early eighteenth century a British poet named
Ambrose Phillips was ridiculed by colleagues who disliked his Whiggish politics,
hated his saccharine verse, and were jealous of his renown. One of them, Henry
Carey, used the first syllable of Phillips's given name as the basis for a mocking
moniker that appeared in the title of a satiric verse Carey wrote in 1725: *Namby
Pamby*. Among its lines were

> *Little Subject, Little Wit.*
> *Namby-Pamby is your Guide;*
> *Albion's Joy, Hibernia's Pride.*
> *Namby-Pamby, Pilly-piss,*
> *Rhimy-pim'd on Missy Miss.*

In a 1733 edition of his classic mock epic *The Dunciad*, Alexander Pope used
"Namby Pamby" to denigrate other writers. Four decades later, the *Westmoreland
Magazine* referred to "A namby-pamby Duke." Over time, this phrase became an
established way to dismiss anyone considered weak, insipid, or wishy-washy. They
are *namby pamby*.

Taunt at Your Peril

Coining terms to taunt is a risky business. Those who create a derisive word to give someone's knuckles a smart rap commonly find that word being taken seriously. In the process it loses its derogatory flavor. To the dismay of those who create them, moreover, verbal brickbats can become boomerangs that return and haunt the taunter.

This was the fate of a French art critic named Louis Leroy. In 1874 Leroy attended an exhibit in Paris that featured work by fifty-five artists that had been rejected by the official Salon. The artists included Paul Cézanne, Edgar Degas, Pierre-Auguste Renoir, and Claude Monet, whose painting was sketchy in detail but rich in bold colors and light. Instead of literal representation these painters tried to capture a *sense* of what they were portraying with daubs, dabs, and minimal brushstrokes.

In a scathing review of this exhibit, Leroy—himself a painter—wrote that unfinished wallpaper was more complete than the works on display. Far from being works of art, these paintings were merely *impressions.* (In fact, one of Monet's works was titled *Impression: Sunrise / Impression: soleil levant.*) Leroy's epithet caught on quickly, but not in the way he'd intended. Within months the avant-garde artists he'd hoped to denounce came to be called, and to call themselves, *impressionists.* Their school became known as *impressionism.* What was meant to be a fatal stab from the nib of Louis Leroy's pen became not only an accepted term but an admiring one. Leroy himself, when remembered at all, is recalled primarily as the man who gave *impressionism* its name.

The French have exported many a term that began life as a Gallic taunt. This tradition antedated the Salon exhibit, going back as far as pre-revolutionary France when Jacques-Claude-Marie Vincent de Gournay became France's intendant (administrator) of commerce in 1751. Gournay had been instrumental in propagating the concept of market-based economics with his motto: *laissez-faire, laissez-passer* ("let it be, let it pass"). English speakers liked the flavor of *laissez-faire* at least as well as "free market," if not better. But this verbal export was transcended by one even more original to Gournay. After taking charge of France's commercial interests, Gournay was appalled by the number of government regulations he thought were stifling his country's economy. These regulations were administered by officials sitting at *bureaux* (French for "desks"). Gournay sarcastically called this *bureaucratie,* or "government by desks." The intendant used that mocking term in conversation, but never recorded it. Following his death, a colleague recalled in a letter that Gournay liked to say, " 'We have an illness in France which bids fair to play havoc with us; this illness is called 'bureaumania.' Sometimes he used to invent a fourth or fifth form of government under the heading of 'bureaucracy.' " A century after Vincent de Gournay coined this sarcastic term, Thomas Carlyle wrote of "the Continental nuisance called 'Bureaucracy.'" With its sharp edge dulled, this withering term became the more dispassionate *bureaucrat* and *bureaucracy*.

A year after the coiner of *bureaucracy* left government service in 1758, Étienne de Silhouette was appointed France's controller-general. Faced with rebuilding France's economy following the Seven Years' War, Silhouette enacted strict fiscal controls. In response, he was ridiculed on Paris streets. His surname inspired a contemptuous phrase. *À la silhouette* referred to anything reduced to its most frugal form: plain wooden snuff boxes, garments with no folds, pants without pockets. French aristocrats moaned that because of the controller-general's austere policies, inexpensive all-black profiles *à la silhouette* were the only type of portrait they could afford. Stripped of its pejorative flavor, that eponym lives on as the name of this type of picture.

Following France's revolution, the secretary of its newly formed Assembly proposed a ban on capital punishment. Not only was this practice cruel, he argued, it was inequitable. Commoners convicted of capital crimes were hanged in public. Those who could afford to pay for the privilege were beheaded discreetly, behind closed doors.

After failing in his attempt to get executions banned altogether, the Assembly secretary suggested that an efficient beheading machine for all might be more humane than snapping the necks of indigent prisoners or chopping the heads off of wealthier ones. Such a machine was subsequently designed by a French surgeon named Antoine Louis and built by German harpsichord maker Tobias Schmidt. The man who'd spearheaded the invention of this contraption, Joseph-Ignace Guillotin, made passionate speeches on its behalf. During one such speech, which he gave in late 1789, Dr. Guillotin made what he thought was a facetious observation: "With my machine, I cut off your head in the twinkling of an eye, and you never feel it!" Guillotin's flippant remark was met with derisive laughter by his colleagues. It struck the fancy of Parisians, however—its "twinkling of an eye" reference especially. A mocking song based on Dr. Guillotin's remark then appeared in a satirical publication:

> *And then off-hand*
> *His genius planned*
> *That machine*
> *That "simply" kills—that's all—*
> *Which after him we call*
> *"Guillotine"*

In years to come, the name of the man who made a comment he'd considered humorous was tied indelibly to the subject of his jest. Guillotin's mortification about

Joseph-Ignace Guillotin demonstrates model of a proposed execution machine to laughing members of the French Assembly.

this development was amplified by the fact that during the Reign of Terror, thousands of French citizens were beheaded by the machine named after him (though not Guillotin himself, as a popular myth alleges). Following Guillotin's death in 1814, Victor Hugo noted the irony that while Columbus could not get his name attached to the continent he'd discovered, Guillotin couldn't get his own detached from the beheading machine he'd proposed. When Dr. Guillotin's descendants failed in their efforts to have the government rename this beheading device, perhaps to *Louis-Schmidt*, after its actual creators, they changed their own surname to Mercier.

Ideologues

After Napoleon Bonaparte became France's emperor, his linguistic flair was noted at home and abroad. John Adams liked one neologism in particular that he attributed to France's leader. "Napoleon has lately invented a word which perfectly expressed my opinion," Adams observed in 1810, a decade after he left the White House. That word was *ideology*.

Adams's observation was problematic on several counts. In the first place, even though Napoleon had used the term *idéologie*, he'd done so to disparage impractical theorizing. Furthermore, he did not invent that word. It was coined in post-revolutionary France by a philosopher named Destutt de Tracy, to describe the science of ideas. Tracy considered *idéologie* a subset of *zoologie*. Recast as a political concept, its English translation went on to enjoy a long and robust life, as when Wonder Woman was said by a film critic to have a "feminist ideology."

Early in the twentieth century, that ideology was on vivid display as English feminists campaigned for women's suffrage. Although most were well-mannered, some didn't mind their manners at all. One group of suffragists led by Emmeline Pankhurst and her daughter Christabel chained themselves to the gates of Buckingham Palace to publicize women's right to vote.

At the same time that suffragists were agitating for women's right to vote, Londoners were being introduced to a new type of compact newspaper called *tabloids* (after a compressed pill whose brand name was Tabloid). One prominent version was the *Daily Mail.* While covering the Spanish-American War in 1898, a star reporter for this tabloid, Charles Hands, had been aghast when a "lady war correspondent" joined him and his male colleagues in Cuba. A few years later, he mockingly called a woman running for Parliament "the chieftainess." In a 1906 article, Hands dismissed the Pankhursts and their followers as unworthy of the name *suffragist.* They were mere "suffragettes."

Far from cringing beneath Hands's verbal lash, its targets grabbed the whip from his hand. The suffix *-ette,* they quickly realized, was more forceful than *-ist.* "There was a spirit in it," said Christabel Pankhurst about why they renamed their movement's newspaper the *Suffragette.* Christabel's sister Sylvia later wrote a book titled *The Suffragette Movement.* In 2015 a movie based on that movement was called simply "Suffragette."

Lumps, Bumps, and Meritocrats

The fact that practicing medicine offers fewer opportunities for invective than writing for tabloids doesn't keep doctors from coming up with ways to taunt each other. Following World War I, a capital opportunity to do so presented itself in the field of oncology. During the 1920s, a British surgeon named Geoffrey Keynes (the younger brother of economist John Maynard Keynes) began to simply excise tumors in breast cancer patients and radiate any remaining cancerous cells. Keynes concluded that this *modified mastectomy* had outcomes at least as good as those resulting from *radical mastectomy*—removing one or both breasts altogether, along with surrounding tissue, which was the preferred way to treat breast cancer. Few of his fellow oncologists agreed with Keynes, including surgical colleagues at St. Bartholomew's Hospital in London. "A built-in dogma of thirty years stand-ing dies hard," Keynes later wrote, "and I was regarded with grave disapproval and shaking of heads by the older surgeons of my own hospital."

This is classic British understatement. Surgeons who'd spent their careers cutting off entire cancerous breasts called the less drastic treatment pioneered by Keynes and a few others "lumpectomy." In his book *The Emperor of All Maladies*, physician-author Siddhartha Mukherjee compares this appellation to a "low-minded joke, a cartoon surgery in which a white-coated doctor pulls out a body part and calls it 'a lump.'" (Among themselves, surgeons refer to nonspecific growths as "lumps and bumps.")

It would be several decades before modified mastectomy began to replace radical mastectomy as the treatment of choice for breast cancer patients. In the process, *lumpectomy* became the standard, nonpejorative way to describe this alternative to breast removal. Journalist Jane Brody, who perhaps didn't realize the word's negative connotations among surgeons, made a casual reference to "lumpectomy" in the *New York Times* in early 1971. In Brody's article and other press coverage that followed, this term was usually set off by quotation marks, suggesting it would be unfamiliar to readers. Within a decade, however, the quotation marks began to disappear—and soon vanished altogether. *Lumpectomy* was here to stay. Unlike surgeons, who recognized the mockery inherent in this term, members of the general public did not. By the turn of the twenty-first century, *lumpectomy* was respectable enough to become the title of several books. In that case, a rehabilitated taunt term titled a book. In other cases, titles themselves introduced neologisms that were meant to disparage.

Soon after the end of World War II, a futuristic novel called *The Rise of the Meritocracy* was published in Great Britain. This dystopian saga, written by sociologist Michael Young, satirized the assessment of merit by credentials rather than performance. In such an environment, Young's 1948 book suggested, anyone with initials following their name would outrank even those of great achievement who lacked them. By the norms of meritocracy, any unpublished writer with a B.A. in English would be taken more seriously than the high school graduate who wrote *For Whom the Bell Tolls*, and the novels of Leo Tolstoy would be downgraded because their author had never been awarded a Nobel Prize.

The Rise of Meritocracy informed readers that "the origin of this unpleasant term . . . is still obscure. It seems to have been first generally used in the sixties of the last [twentieth] century in small-circulation journals attached to the Labour Party, and gained wide circulation later on." Thirty-six years later, in the introduction to a 1994 edition of his novel, Young confessed that he himself had coined "meritocracy," by merging the Latin *mereō* with the Greek suffix *-cracy*.* Why

---

* Although Young may have believed his own origin story, two years before his novel was published, sociologist Alan Fox had referred to "meritocracy" in a 1946 article in an obscure British journal called *Socialist Commentary*.

hadn't the author said so sooner? Because, Young explained, when he was coming up with his book's title, a classicist had warned him that creating a word from Greek and Latin roots would break the rules of proper usage and subject him to ridicule. As it turned out, even though the message Young hoped to convey in *The Rise of the Meritocracy* was controversial, the key word of his novel's title was not. ("Rather the opposite," Young noted drily.) This was why he now felt free to step forward and take credit for coining *meritocracy*. "The twentieth century had room for the word," Young wrote, even one he'd meant to be pejorative.

The Iron Lady

One beneficiary of an increasingly meritocratic society was a doughty grocer's daughter from Lincolnshire named Margaret Thatcher. After entering politics in the early 1970s, Thatcher rose steadily through the ranks of Britain's Conservative Party. Her combative style caught the eyes not just of fellow Brits but of Britain-watchers in the Soviet Union who considered this archconservative Tory inflexible, pig-headed, and too hawkish by half. Thatcher didn't improve her standing in their eyes by giving a speech on January 19, 1976, a few months after being elected head of the Conservatives, in which she warned that "the Russians are bent on world dominance, and they are rapidly acquiring the means to become the most powerful imperial nation the world has seen."

Five days after she uttered these words, the Red Army publication *Red Star* published an article titled "The 'Iron Lady' Sounds the Alarm." Its author, Captain Yuri Gavrilov, reported that this was what Margaret Thatcher's colleagues called her: the Iron Lady. Years later Gavrilov admitted that he'd invented this sobriquet himself. Including "Iron Lady" in the article's headline had been his idea too. How did he come up with this nickname? Three decades after he'd done so, Gavrilov told a *Daily Mail* reporter that Thatcher's call to arms made him think of Otto von Bismarck, Germany's "Iron Chancellor." Perhaps he could come up with a similar name for her. "Iron Conservative Party Leader" was a bit clunky, but "Iron Lady" was not. The fact that this brought *iron maiden* to mind, a coffin-like container whose spiked lid was apparently closed slowly on medieval torture victims, didn't hurt.

Thatcher's many detractors in the Soviet Union thought Gavrilov's disparaging nickname captured perfectly her brittle, obdurate leadership style. If readers of his article had been limited to Russian speakers, Gavrilov's coinage would undoubtedly have disappeared in Soviet archives. To gain reach a wider audience, *iron lady* needed an escort. Soon after Gavrilov's article was published, one appeared in the form of journalist Robert Evans, the head of Reuters's Moscow bureau. On a slow news day in late January 1976, the Russian-speaking correspondent killed time by leafing through publications at a Moscow newsstand. An article in *Red Star* caught his eye: "The Iron Lady Wields Threats" (his own translation) by one Yuri Gavrilov. Evans bought a copy, then used Gavrilov's article as the basis for one of his own. This dispatch, which was reprinted widely in Great Britain, informed readers that "British Tory leader Margaret Thatcher was today dubbed 'the Iron Lady' by the Soviet Defense Ministry newspaper *Red Star.*"

The target of that taunt quickly recognized its political value. Days after Robert Evans introduced her Soviet nickname to British readers, Thatcher donned a bright red evening gown to address a gathering of Tories. "I stand before you," she told them, "in my *Red Star* evening gown, my face softly made up and my fair hair gently waved, the Iron Lady of the Western world. Yes I am an Iron Lady. After all, it wasn't a bad thing to be an Iron Duke [the Duke of Wellington]."

Becoming known as the Iron Lady fast-tracked Margaret Thatcher's career. Her new nickname soon replaced an old one: "Thatcher the Milk Snatcher" (bestowed when she was an education secretary notorious for eliminating free milk from school menus). As a campaign slogan, it was instrumental in her rise from backbencher to opposition leader, then prime minister of the United Kingdom. *The Iron Lady* subsequently became the title of several books about Thatcher and a biopic starring Meryl Streep. After a 2006 statue of her was cast in bronze, Lady Thatcher commented, "I might have preferred iron, but bronze will do."

7

Taunt Terms: U.S.

AS MASSACHUSETTS'S GOVERNOR, Elbridge Gerry presided over the 1812 redrawing of its congressional districts. Members of Gerry's political party, the Democratic-Republicans, designed these districts to favor themselves. Their results were, to say the least, artistic. Benjamin Russell, editor of the Federalist *Columbian Centinel*, displayed a map of the Democratic-Republicans' artistically drawn congressional districts on the wall of his office. A visitor to Russell's office observed that one of these districts resembled a salamander. The visitor's companion, James Ogilvie, responded, "Why, let it be named a Gerrymander!"

After Ogilvie's appellation made the rounds, the *Boston Gazette* published an unsigned drawing—apparently sketched by an artist named Elkanah Tisdale—that portrayed this district as resembling a monstrous dragon-salamander. Tisdale's engraving, captioned "THE GERRY-MANDER. A new species of Monster," was reprinted in many other newspapers. Not just its eye-catching graphic but the whimsical caption went viral. A fledgling nation needed words to discuss new phenomena like creative redistricting; "Gerry-mander" fit that bill. In time, this term was converted to a verb, lowercased, and shorn of its hyphen. Two centuries after Elkanah Tisdale drew his dragon, *gerrymander* remains the verb most often used for the tortured design of electoral districts.*

Hoosiers

Four years after congressional districts were redrawn in Massachusetts, Indiana joined the union. Migrants to this new state were commonly called *hoosiers*. No one is quite sure why. Some said it was because the many North Carolinians who settled there were prone to say "Who's eyere?" when visitors knocked on their

---

* Since Elbridge Gerry pronounced his surname with a hard *g*, by rights *gerrymander* should begin with a hard *g* as well.

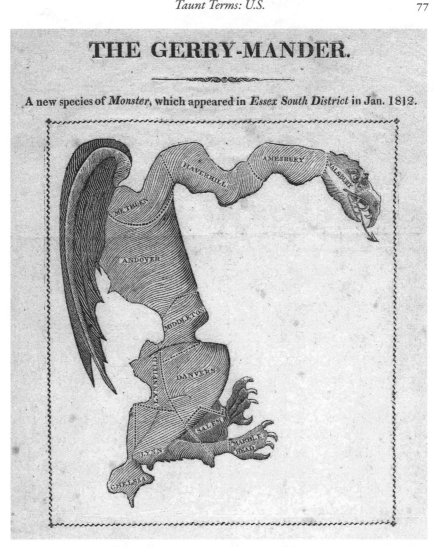

THE GERRY-MANDER.

A new species of *Monster*, which appeared in *Essex South District* in Jan. 1812.

Maiden appearance of "The Gerry-mander," in the *Boston Gazette*, March 26, 1812.

door. Others thought it might refer to the "hoosier men" who worked for an Indiana contractor named Sam Hoosier. Or to *hoozer*, a slang term for those hill dwellers who were later called hillbillies. Other plausible root words compiled by Indiana University librarian Jeffrey Graf include "Husher," a man bulky enough to stifle other men, "Hussar," from European mounted troops, 'Huzzah!' proclaimed after a victory of some sort, "Hoosa," an Indian term for corn, "Hoose," a bovine disease that gave cows a demented appearance, and "Whose ear?" asked about one torn off during a brawl.

As such etymologies suggest, "hoosier" wasn't meant to be complimentary. It suggested someone who was hopelessly backwoods. Based on his research, Graf concluded that *hoosier* originally denoted "a rustic, a bumpkin, a countryman, a roughneck, a hick or an awkward, uncouth or unskilled fellow." Over time, however, the derided embraced the derision and adopted it with enthusiasm. In his 1963 novel *Cat's Cradle*, Indiana native Kurt Vonnegut portrayed members of a futuristic cult who use *hoosier* as a normal name for Indianans. Today, being known as a hoosier is no more demeaning than being called a Hawkeye, a Buckeye, a Sooner, or a Tar Heel. At the behest of Indiana's senators, in 2016 the U.S. Government Publishing Office replaced "Indianan" with "Hoosier" as its official designation for residents of Indiana.

In 1821, members of Indiana's legislature met in the southern city of Corydon to determine where their state's capital should be located and what that location should be called. The first task was no problem: land in central Indiana was purchased from local Indians and platted for a city. Naming that city was more problematic. In keeping with Indiana's etymology as "land of the Indians," General Marion Clark—of Lewis and Clark fame—proposed *Tecumseh*, after the renowned Shawnee chief who'd lived nearby. That one didn't fly. Nor did other Indian names Clark proposed. The longer their deliberations lasted, the giddier legislators grew. Suggestions became more and more far-fetched. One member of the legislature proposed *Suwwarow*, explaining that this was the name of a plant in Mexico (he apparently was thinking of the saguaro cactus, not the recently discovered atoll of Suwarrow in the Cook Islands). Suwwarow went nowhere either. Finally Judge Jeremiah Sullivan of Jefferson County grafted *polis*, Greek for "city," onto Indiana and came up with *Indianapolis*. "The name created quite a laugh," Sullivan later recalled of his Indian-Greek hybrid. Indiana's governor liked it, however, and signed off on *Indianapolis*.

At the outset, derision far exceeded praise for Judge Sullivan's coinage. In Vincennes, the *Indiana Centinel* published an inspired denunciation:

> Such a name, kind readers, you would never find from Dan to Beersheba; nor in all the libraries, museums and patent offices in the world. It is like nothing in heaven, nor on earth, nor in the waters under the earth. It is not a name for man, woman, or child; for empire, city, mountain, or morass; for bird, beast, fish nor creeping thing; and mothering mortal or immortal could have thought of it, except the wise men of the East who were congregated at Corydon. It is composed of the following letters:
>   I-N-D-I-A-N-A-P-O-L-I-S
> Pronounce it as you please, gentle readers—you can do it as you wish— there is no danger of violating any system or rule, either in accent, cadence

or emphasis—suit your own convenience and be thankful you are enabled to do it, by this rare effect of the scholastic genius of the age. For this title your future capital will be greatly indebted, either to some learned *Hebraist*, some venerable *Grecian*, some sage and sentimental *Brahmin* or some profound and academic *Pauttowattomie*.

For years thereafter, the name of Indiana's capital excited more mirth than approval. In time, however, as Indianans and others grew accustomed to its multisyllabic cadence, "Indianapolis" developed a certain cachet. "I am coming to Indianapolis, the city with the musical name," one out-of-stater wrote a friend there in 1923. Due to its newfound popularity, communities in four other states (Texas, Colorado, Iowa, and Oklahoma) adopted the name of Indiana's capital, according to one commentator, "without the slightest regard for its meaning—City of Indiana—but solely for its melody and dignity."

Bloomers

In 1854, Mary Birdsall of Richmond, Indiana, purchased a publication called *The Lily*. Although Birdsall's name has been lost in the mists of history, the surname of the woman from whom she bought the monthly—Amelia Bloomer—has not.

Bloomer founded *The Lily* in 1849 to promote temperance and abolitionism. Over time issues involving women's rights were added to its agenda. Dress reform was one such issue. *The Lily*'s September 1851 edition featured pictures of Mrs. Bloomer and her feminist colleague Elizabeth Cady Stanton wearing a radically new type of garb consisting of a skirt that fell just below the knees, above baggy "Turkish trousers" (similar to what today we call harem pants). Patterns for the outfit were offered as a premium to new subscribers.

Women who donned this attire considered it both a political statement and a practical alternative to the heavy corsets, petticoats, and long, cumbersome skirts that collected dust, mud, and debris when those wearing them walked outside. Thinking she should practice what she preached, Amelia Bloomer began wearing this outfit herself while strolling the streets of Seneca Falls, New York, ignoring the hoots, whistles, and mocking jeers of men she passed. "There is a class of men who seem to think it their special business to superintend the wardrobes of both men and women," she later observed, "and if any dare to depart from their ideas of propriety they forthwith launch out all sorts of witticisms and hard names, and proclaim their opinions, their likes and dislikes, with all the importance of authorized dictators."

Although the garment that inspired such ridicule was designed by Bloomer's fellow feminist Elizabeth Smith Miller, it was not named after her. That honor

"The Bloomer Costume," by Nathan Currier, 1851.

was reserved for *The Lily*'s editor. Amelia Bloomer may have had nothing to do with the costume's creation, was not the first to wear it, and wasn't even the garb's most prominent advocate, but she did have one invaluable asset: her surname.

In an early indication of where things were headed, the *Boston Transcript* began referring to "the Bloomer suit," then "the Bloomer costume," and finally just "the Bloomer." Other publications followed suit, vying to come up with creative ways to mock this form of dress. Headlines of their sneering articles featured words such as "Bloomerism," "Bloomerite," and "Bloomers." Press artists caricatured cigar-smoking women wearing Bloomer Costumes—they cracked whips, walked bulldogs, and propped a foot on bar railings. P. T. Barnum organized a "Bloomer Parade" of young women dressed in that garb. Bloomer-clad minstrels performed on the New York stage. In London the Adelphi Theatre mounted a farcical revue called "Bloomerism, or the Follies of the Day." Members of the audience would be served a Grand Vegetarian Banquet, their announcement promised, and then be treated to "A Lecture on Bloomerism! Resulting in the BLOOMER POLKA! With twelve pretty bloomers all in a row." When a group of young blades in London organized a Bloomer Ball to which only women wearing

Caricature of cigar-smoking women wearing Bloomer-style outfits, 1851 lithograph, artist unknown.

a Bloomer Costume were invited, *Punch* magazine devoted a piece of doggerel to this event that included the lines "Oh, oh my Bloomers, chicken-hearted! Oh, my Bloomers, what a fall!" This humor magazine also ran a spurious exhortation from Amelia Bloomer herself urging all British brides to be married in a Bloomer Costume.

The imperturbable Mrs. Bloomer never rose to such bait, simply wearing the outfit named after her, appreciating the circulation boost it gave her newspaper, and ignoring those who taunted its wearers.

If Amelia Jenks hadn't married a lawyer named Dexter Bloomer, one can only imagine what the outfit named after her would have been called. Certainly not

Jenkses, let alone *Stantons*, *Anthonys*, or *Millers* after other feminists with whom it was associated. Mrs. Bloomer's married name was just so gosh-darned fun to say and write about. "Bloomer is a word that is difficult to pronounce without a smile," observes biographer Margaret Farrand Thorp. Late in life Amelia Bloomer noted how indelibly her name was associated with the outfit designed by Elizabeth Miller, "in spite of my repeatedly disclaiming all right to it and giving Mrs. Miller's name as that of the originator or the first to wear such dress in public." However, as Thorp notes, "Bloomer was a funnier word than Miller and the public declined to change."

Although the Bloomer Costume had largely disappeared on both sides of the Atlantic within a few years of its introduction, late in the nineteenth century a modified version resurfaced in England as part of a "rational dress" movement spearheaded by Lady Florence Harberton. In 1898, the formidable Lady Harberton was denied entrance to a hotel in Surrey because of her unusual garb. By then—like other apparel eponyms such as *cardigan*, *leotard*, and *raglan*—*bloomer* had become a common rather than a proper noun. However, that word still referred to what many considered questionable attire. As the *Cheltenham Chronicle* reported in early 1899, when Lady Harberton began her rational dress crusade, it took "a great deal of both physical and moral courage even to mention the word bloomers." Within decades that was no longer true. A century after Amelia Bloomer began strolling about Seneca Falls in the gear that would be named after her, *bloomer* found a lasting verbal home as a generic name for underwear.

Shifting Semantics

Taking the sting out of terms meant to mock is part of what linguists call "semantic shift," a significant alteration of a word's meaning. "Nice," for example, once suggested being rather dim. "Dude" has gone from referring to a dandy to characterizing any man at all. "Guy" serves the same purpose, even though its life began as a way to refer contemptuously to malefactors like the rebellious Guy Fawkes, after he was executed in 1605 for attempting to blow up Britain's House of Lords. Such miscreants were *guys*. (Fawkes himself preferred to be called "Guido.") In the colonies, however, "guy" became synonymous simply with "chap," "bloke," or "fellow." Among Americans, a *regular guy* was an admirable person. When the British writer G. K. Chesterton was called a regular guy while visiting the U.S., it took him a while to figure out that this was meant as a compliment.

Semantic shifts are all about. After Teddy Roosevelt accused certain investigative reporters of "raking the muck," that type of journalist became known derisively as a *muckraker* (already a slang term for those who stir up trouble). Meant to undercut them, the targets of this insult adopted it with pride. To the present day "muckrakers" is considered more complimentary than insulting among those trying to expose malfeasance.

"Spread" is another word whose meaning changed over time. Initially, *spread* referred to a meager meal that was distributed artfully on a table to make it look more bountiful. Now it simply means bountiful. The zoologist Stephen Jay Gould once observed that when John Scopes was charged with teaching evolution to high school students in Dayton, Tennessee, residents of this town welcomed lawyers for the prosecution and defense with "a spread of equal size."

The so-called Scopes trial in 1924 provided fertile ground for mockery by out-of-town journalists. H. L. Mencken called this proceeding *the monkey trial*, an enduring appellation. On the eve of his departure for Tennessee to cover that trial, Mencken wrote, "The old game, I suspect, is beginning to play out, even in the Bible Belt." This adaptation of existing phrases such as *corn belt, cotton belt,* and *snow belt* is the first known use of *Bible Belt* to refer to regions that are heavy with fundamentalist Christians. Mencken took inordinate pride in this expression, putting it at the top of a list of terms he'd coined (ahead of *booboisie* and *smuthound*).

The Sage of Baltimore referred to the *Bible Belt* repeatedly while covering the Scopes trial. As he told readers, "One need not live a long, incandescent week in the Bible Belt to know that jurisprudence becomes a new science as one crosses the border." Mencken dismissed residents of southeastern Tennessee as "morons," "hillbillies," "yokels," and "peasants" who didn't just live in the Bible Belt but in "the buckle of the Bible Belt." Long after leaving that region he called it "the Bible and Lynching Belt." Although Dayton residents (including John Scopes himself) were understandably miffed by Mencken's verbal brickbats, in time they embraced this disparaging name for their region. Fundamentalist southerners and residents of the lower Midwest became proud to say that they lived in the Bible Belt.

Whistlestoppers, Pollsters, and the Best and Brightest

As Harry Truman toured the Bible Belt and other sparsely populated regions of the United States while running for president in 1948, Republican senator Robert Taft of Ohio grew testy. Truman's campaign consisted of multiple speechmaking events, not only in cities of many sizes but communities so small that trains would stop there only when a passenger or conductor pulled a chord that signaled the engineer, who acknowledged this alert by blasting his whistle. During these brief stops, Truman would appear at the rear platform to castigate the "do-nothing Congress" controlled by Republicans such as Robert Taft, the Senate's majority leader. According to Taft, the president was "blackguarding Congress at every whistle station in the West." Taft's reference to "whistle stations" betrayed his ignorance of everyday speech. For decades, *whistle stops* had been slang for tiny towns whose names were little known outside their region and the offices of cartographers. It also was the title of *Whistlestop*, a popular 1941 novel that was made into a movie five years later.

Soon after Taft hurled his "whistle stations" gibe at Truman, the plain-spoken president himself got it right. During a campaign appearance in Los Angeles, Truman mocked the Republican senator by saying that Los Angeles was the biggest "whistle stop" he'd ever visited. When this elicited a roar of approval among his listeners, the president knew he was on to something. Far from having the desired effect, Taft's taunt didn't just insult residents of America's small towns but outraged mayors of cities such as Chicago, Seattle, and Los Angeles, where Truman had campaigned. The president cheerfully referred to Taft's sneer throughout what came to be known as his *whistle-stop campaign*. Presidential aide Clark Clifford called the senator's gaffe "a priceless gift." This proved true not just for our politics but our language. When Truman campaigned for Adlai Stevenson by train in 1952, the Associated Press called him a "whistle-stopper." During the decades that followed, multi-venue events of many kinds, not just political, would be called "whistle stop campaigns," or simply "whistle-stopping."

During the 1948 election, every major opinion poll predicted a victory by Republican presidential candidate Thomas Dewey. Elmo Roper was so sure of this outcome that his Roper Poll stopped surveying voters six weeks before they voted. Other voter polls followed suit. In response, one year later political scientist Lindsay Rogers published a scathing critique of those who surveyed public opinion. He called his 1949 book *The Pollsters*. This title referenced *The Hucksters*, a 1945 bestseller that skewered the advertising industry, and a 1947 movie based on that novel. As memories of the 1948 election faded and polling techniques improved, Rogers's coinage lost its derisive flavor. Today there is no shame in being called a pollster. Nonetheless, when Jill Lepore was interviewed about a *New Yorker* article she wrote in 2015 that noted the negative connotations of this coinage early on, the historian called those who survey public opinion *pollers* (as do others).

Lindsay Rogers wasn't the only American author of a book whose pejorative title underwent a semantic shift. David Halberstam had a similar experience following the publication of his 1972 book *The Best and the Brightest*. The title of this caustic portrayal of highly educated government officials who were so tragically mistaken about the war in Vietnam was meant to be bitterly ironic. Shorn of that flavor, however, "best and brightest" became one of the most repeated catchphrases of modern times. Today this phrase typically refers simply to a group of unusually smart, capable individuals. Several decades after Halberstam's takedown was published, a *Smithsonian* magazine cover story lauded "America's Best and Brightest."

"Cartoons"

Having discussed one art exhibit early in our consideration of taunt terms, let's conclude with another. This one was mounted at London's Palace of Westminster in 1843. It featured drawings of prominent British aristocrats that were meant to resemble the preliminary sketches that artists assembled into templates for murals, frescoes, or tapestries. Their name in English was *cartoons*, from the French *carton*, the Italian *cartone*, and the Dutch *karton*.

To satirize the patronizing pomposity of this display, *Punch* magazine artist John Leech drew an elaborate panel of shabbily dressed Londoners scrutinizing portraits of well-dressed members of the upper classes. Leech's panel, which ran in the July 1843 issue of *Punch*, was given the ironic caption of *Cartoon No. 1*. During the years that followed, *cartoon* became simply a way to describe the type of comic drawings produced by Leech and others. In addition to giving cartoons their name, Leech was the first caricaturist to be called a *cartoonist*. In the years that followed, those who adopted this appellation became a bountiful source of both amusing artwork and many a useful new word.

II

Sources of Coined Words

8

Coins in Bubbles

FOUR DECADES AFTER John Leech drew *Cartoon No. 1*, his successor at *Punch*, George du Maurier (the grandfather of novelist Daphne du Maurier), composed one that portrayed two women discussing a physician who is walking by:

Oh, that's your doctor, is it? What sort of doctor is he?
Oh, well, I don't know much about his ability; but he's got a very good bedside manner!

Although "bedside manner" had appeared in an 1849 British press account and "bed-side manners" in an American novel two decades later, du Maurier's 1881 *Punch* cartoon added *bedside manner* to the conversational mix in the way we use it today.

A subsequent *Punch* cartoon by du Maurier, captioned "True Humility," featured a stern-looking older bishop having breakfast with an earnest young curate who is struggling to eat a rotten egg. "I assure you, parts of it are excellent," this novice clergyman tells the bishop. Soon after that panel appeared in 1895, "like the curate's egg," or simply "a curate's egg" began to refer to something considered a mixed bag, and has ever since (among the English, anyway). In his mixed review of *The Crown*, a 2016 Netflix series based on the Windsors, a British historian called it "something of a curate's egg."

Despite being primarily a visual medium, cartoons and comic strips have contributed an inordinate number of new terms to the English lexicon. A picture may be worth a thousand words, but countless neologisms have been introduced in their captions and speech bubbles. According to comics scholar Thomas Inge, comic strips and cartoons "enriched" the English language by introducing "popular phrases, word coinages, and the revival of archaic usages." Bill Bryson concurs. "It is striking how many words have come into American English through comic strips," writes Bryson in his book on language *Made in America*.

Such strips were avidly consumed by young and old, the well-educated and self-educated, and white and blue collar readers alike. Like sports and the weather, they could be discussed by all. As a result, comics and cartoons have been a better source of terminology than words and phrases from movies or television shows, which tend to have a short shelf life. ("Kiss my grits." "No soup for you!" "Sock it to me!" "Dy-no-mite!" "Stifle it!") By contrast, a long list of enduring catchphrases from the funny pages include "good grief," "time's a wastin'," "for cryin' out loud," "blow me down!" and "We have met the enemy and it is us." Many commonly used catchphrases originated or were popularized as titles of comic strips: *Keeping Up with the Joneses*, *Mutt and Jeff*, and *Famous Last Words*. Their contributions to the vernacular are due in part to the fact that so many strips have had longer runs (more than four decades for *Li'l Abner* alone) than their counterparts in electronic media. In addition, space constraints keep cartoonists from using big words. Active, vivid language is their stock in trade.

"Comic strips are literally strewn with PLOPS, BLAMS, ZOTS, OOPS, SWOOSHES, and ZOOMS," noted *Beetle Bailey*'s creator Mort Walker. Coming up with such terms draws on the neologic powers of the cartoonist. As Walker pointed out, it's cheating to have a cartoon character dig a hole to the tune of "DIG, DIG, DIG, DIG." Instead, cartoonists need to vocalize an activity, "a bat hitting a ball, FWT! . . . foot kicking a garbage pail, K-CHUNKKK!" before finding terminology that sounds just right.

That terseness, simplicity, and zaniness has been at the heart of what's captivated cartoon fans of all ages. During the past century especially, words in comic strips, cartoons, and comic books were among the first ones children read in adult media, and at an impressionable age. This made the responsibility of cartoonists great, Winston Churchill once observed, because "many are the youthful eyes that have rested upon their designs, and many the lifelong impressions formed thereby." Since impressions gained from cartoons preceded the actual reading of history, he added, "They have a great power indeed, these cartoonists."

Fun for all

As a boy, Churchill pored over old collections of *Punch* cartoons in his school's library. Those devoted to events of the day provided his first lessons in history and politics. These cartoons also initiated Churchill's lifelong fascination with the American Civil War. One published early in that war showed Yankee soldiers running away from "a place called Bull Run." Later, a *Punch* cartoon depicted the North and South as two bedraggled knife-wielding men grappling on the edge of a dark abyss labeled "BANKRUPTCY." Following the assassination of Abraham

Lincoln, another *Punch* cartoon portrayed a grief-stricken Britannia laying a wreath at Lincoln's grave.

The president himself had been impressed by the work of editorial cartoonist Thomas Nast. Both Lincoln and Ulysses S. Grant acknowledged the impact of Nast's many pro-Union engravings, which they thought contributed to the Union victory. Lincoln called the cartoonist his best recruiting sergeant. Following the Emancipation Proclamation in 1863, a two-sided panel by Nast entitled "Emancipation" contrasted slaves being whipped, branded, and sold on one side, with drawings of freed slaves being paid for their work, educated, and raising families on the other. In between them was a bust of Lincoln.

If there is such a thing as graphic coinage, Nast was its exemplar. Uncle Sam as we know him—a tall, dignified, goateed man in tails and top coat—was Nast's improvement of a bumpkin-like version that appeared in *Punch*. The elephant and the donkey as icons of America's two major political parties were another Nast contribution to our political iconography.

Following the war, Nast crusaded against Tammany Hall's leader, William Marcy "Boss" Tweed. The cartoonist repeatedly sketched Tweed responding to charges of corruption, vote-rigging, and overall malfeasance by asking, "What are you going to do about it?" Over time, Nast's words were assumed to be Tweed's own (even by *Bartlett's*). His work was so acerbic that some mistakenly think *nasty* is an eponym based on his surname.

One beneficiary of Thomas Nast's legacy was Theodore Roosevelt. This benefit came into stark relief following a hunting expedition in Mississippi that Roosevelt took in 1902. During that trip Roosevelt refused to shoot a bear that his guides had tied to a tree. When word of TR's merciful act got out, *Washington Post* cartoonist Clifford Berryman portrayed the president sparing the life of an adorable cub.

This famous 1902 cartoon helped buff up Teddy Roosevelt's reputation as a humanitarian. According to a popular account promulgated by the Theodore Roosevelt Association and others, soon after Berryman's panel went viral, the owner of a Brooklyn candy store named Morris Michtom sought to capitalize on that reputation by displaying in his store's window a stuffed bear his wife, Rose, had sewed. They called it "Teddy's Bear." When multiple customers asked if they could buy this toy, the Michtoms sent it to the president for his children, asking permission to use his name in future versions. Roosevelt consented. Almost simultaneously, a German dollmaker began selling a stuffed bear with the same name. Both versions were a big commercial success. By 1906 a news article reported that "no novelty of recent years has been so popular as the Teddy Bears." A subsequent article speculated that this success was "due to their name—'Teddy-bears.'" The

Clifford Berryman's cartoon of Teddy Roosevelt sparing the life of a bear cub, *Washington Post*, November 16, 1902.

popularity of this stuffed animal and many to follow inspired the generic term *teddy bear*.

Nearly half a century after Clifford Berryman's cartoon helped inspire this new term, his successor at the *Post*, Herbert Block, himself helped add a new term to the political lexicon. As "Herblock," the editorial cartoonist became a fierce opponent of Wisconsin senator Joseph McCarthy. McCarthy was notorious for charging that those he opposed were either Communists or Communist sympathizers. Because so many of his fellow Republican senators condoned that practice, Herblock's March 29, 1950, cartoon portrayed four of them, including Robert Taft, pushing a reluctant GOP elephant toward an unsteady stack of leaking tar barrels. ("You mean I'm supposed to stand on that?" read its caption.) "For want of a better term to summarize the issue," Herblock later wrote, "I labeled the top barrel *McCarthyism*." The cartoonist denied any intention of adding this word to the political lexicon, but he did. *McCarthyism* has endured for decades as a way to refer to smear by innuendo.

Although Herblock is generally acknowledged as the coiner of *McCarthyism*, and undoubtedly launched that epithet into general discourse, on the day before his cartoon featured the term it had appeared in a *Christian Science Monitor* editorial. Since fewer people read editorials than consume cartoons, however, we can safely credit Herblock for being the primary purveyor of *McCarthyism*, if not its sole originator.

Editorial cartoonists may have loftier agendas than mere entertainment, but that's not true of their colleagues on the funny pages. They just want to have fun. "Anything for a laugh," said comic strip artist Billy DeBeck (voicing a common cartoonists' credo). According to DeBeck's colleague Jules Feiffer, working in a medium that many consider frivolous has certain benefits. "Irresponsibility is one," Feiffer explained. "Not being taken seriously is another. Junk, like the drunk at the wedding, can get away with doing or saying anything because, by its very appearance, it is already in disgrace. It has no one's respect to lose; no image to endanger."

No wonder cartoonists have been such fertile language refreshers. Their lack of "seriousness" gives those whose work relies on caricature and speech balloons lots of latitude to engage in wordplay. With no expectation that their language be respectable, cartoonists have always felt free to use whatever terms they pleased, including ones of their own invention. Some of these terms have joined the lexicon.

Tad

Early last century, Thomas Aloysius "Tad" Dorgan published a cartoon in the *San Francisco Bulletin* that portrayed a man in police court who is trying to juggle a bottle, pitcher, plate, and salt shaker. It was captioned "Duck soup." Well over a century after Dorgan's 1902 cartoon appeared, *duck soup* is still synonymous with "piece of cake."

Dorgan grew up in a San Francisco neighborhood that was filled with laborers, sailors, crooks, gamblers, and sundry lowlifes. From their talk and that of street hustlers, sport bettors, show business types, and underworld figures in his adopted home of New York City, Dorgan picked up a rich argot that he tapped throughout his career as one of the nation's most popular cartoonists.

At the age of eight, three and a half of Dorgan's fingers had been mangled by a house-moving cable. As with his colleague Al Capp, who'd lost a leg beneath a streetcar when he was nine, Dorgan's disability may have contributed to his jaundiced outlook. His cartoon characters liked to say about the *dumb bells* and *dim bulbs* whom they considered unusually stupid, "nobody home." As a result, for some time during and after World War I, *nobody home* was a popular American expression. *Boneheads* was another, an existing piece of slang Dorgan featured in a 1908 panel that referred to a "bunch of boneheads!" and then as the nickname of his baseball-playing character "Bonehead Barry."

Before World War I, one of Dorgan's characters said, "She and I were sitting there making love see—and I'm just goin' to make her for the coin when suddenly she goes plumb nutty, wallops my noodle and gives me the bum's rush." Other expressions coined or popularized by Dorgan included *bum steer, dog it, drug store cowboy, fall guy, hard-boiled, low down, plugged nickel, you said it, once-over, for crying out loud, get the gate, get the hook, got his goat, spill the beans*, and *send to the cleaners*. Many terms attributed to Dorgan turned out to be existing slang that he introduced to a broader vernacular. Cartoonists like him were magpies who put street argot in the mouths of characters. In the process, their work became a revolving fund of what contemporaries called *slanguage*. These propagators of slang would overhear new terms, use them in cartoons, then broadcast the results to a large audience who began using those words themselves.

When asked which of the many colorful terms he employed were ones he'd created and which were ones he'd heard on the street, Dorgan demurred. In an extensive survey of Dorgan's vocabulary, etymologist Leonard Zwilling flagged many that were falsely credited to him. They included *bunk, lounge lizard*, and *cat's meow*. Zwilling couldn't find *bum ticker, Chinese homer*, and *23 skidoo*— sometimes said to be Dorganisms—anywhere in his work. Although Tad is often credited with introducing the term *yes-men* in a 1913 cartoon, that coinage had already been used as the title of a story in *Century Magazine* the year before and (as determined by etymologist Barry Popik) in a newspaper article one year earlier. He did add *gate-crasher* to American parlance.

Dorgan was particularly partial to words meaning "nonsense" such as *malarkey* and *applesauce*. The first known use of *horsefeathers* in print, referring to nonsense, was in a 1927 panel by Tad whose caption included the words "Bah—Horsefeathers." This piece of slang, which inspired the title of the Marx Brothers film *Horse Feathers* (that appeared one year before their 1933 movie *Duck Soup*), was also attributed to Dorgan's colleague Billy DeBeck, who used it a year after Tad did.

Heebie-Jeebies and Goo-Goo Eyes

Billy DeBeck was a Chicago native who'd set out to be a painter but ended up as one of America's most popular cartoonists. The main source of DeBeck's popularity was a pint-sized, pop-eyed character whom he introduced in a 1919 strip titled *Take Barney Google, F'rinstance* (in time shortened to *Barney Google* alone). The surname of its hero, an amiable racetrack tout married to a formidable wife whom he called "sweet woman," played no small part in the success of this strip. At the time Barney appeared, *goo-goo eyes* was slang for simpering looks. In 1923 songwriter Billy Rose put them together in his hit tune "Barney Google, with the Goo-Goo-Googly Eyes."

When DeBeck's publisher, William Randolph Hearst, suggested that the cartoonist add an attractive woman to *Barney Google*, DeBeck complied. Naming her was a challenge, though. After scrolling through various possibilities (Jane, Annie, Muriel), DeBeck decided to simply call his vampy creation "Sweet Mama." When several newspapers refused to print the strips that featured this bombshell, DeBeck was told to drop his new character. But by then her name was on the nation's lips. Sweet Mama was a hit, due not just to her seductive allure but to her name, which swept the country as a catchphrase. Soon after being dropped, Sweet Mama reappeared. Her name became part of the lasting vernacular (along with spinoffs such as Red Hot Mama, Big Fat Mama, Motorcycle Mama, etc., etc.)

This verbal triumph prompted DeBeck to begin embellishing the language in *Barney Google*. In one 1923 strip, Barney kicked his swaybacked race horse Sparkplug, saying "You dumb ox—why don't you get that stupid look offa your pan—you gimme the heeby jeebys!" Respelled as *heebie-jeebies*, this DeBeckism was another hit, not just joining the vernacular to mean "the jitters," but inspiring a song and a popular dance by this name. A subsequent DeBeck coinage, *hotsy totsy*, his 1926 term for pretentiousness, quickly became the nation's term.

When Barney Google inherited land in the Appalachian Mountains, DeBeck's language took a new turn. To prepare for Barney's adventures there, the cartoonist didn't just tour the Appalachians, jotting down examples of local dialect, but scoured books about mountain culture for verbal inspiration. Folklorist Vance Rudolph later wrote DeBeck to say that since he'd borrowed so many idioms from his work, he could at least send him a signed copy of one of his panels. (The cartoonist complied.)

DeBeck's research provided the argot for a new cast of characters who lived in mountainous "Hootin' Holler." They included Snuffy Smith, a grizzled ne'er-do-well whose favorite activity was lounging against a tree, with a jug of moonshine in his hand; Snuffy's head-scarfed wife, Loweezy; their son, Jughaid, who wore a coonskin cap; and fellow residents of Hootin' Holler who used actual mountain idioms such as *plime blank* ("exactly"), *a lavish of* ("a lot of"), *bodacious* ("awesome"), and *discombooberated* (an alternative version of "discombobulated"). These authentic expressions were augmented by ones DeBeck invented: *time's a-wastin'*, *bus' mah britches*, *tetched in the haid*, *shif'less skonk*, and *balls-o-fire!* Unlike the circumspect Tad Dorgan, DeBeck told interviewers that adding his own words and catchphrases to the English vocabulary gave him great pleasure.

The Talk of Dogpatch

In the same year that Billy DeBeck began borrowing and coining mountain dialect, a rival creator of backwods terminology joined him, an irascible, chain-smoking, one-legged cartoonist named Al Capp. Capp proved to be an unusually fecund creator of zany terminology in the *Li'l Abner* strip that he introduced in 1934. The cartoonist blended "yokel" and "hokum" for the surname of his protagonist, Abner Yokum. Abner and other residents of "Dogpatch" used a colorful neo-hillbilly patois created by Capp. *Li'l Abner* lasted for forty-three years. At its peak, sixty million readers in nine hundred newspapers consumed Capp's neology. John Steinbeck thought the cartoonist's verbal prowess deserved a Nobel Prize for Literature, like the one awarded him. Capp, Steinbeck explained, "not only invented a language but has planted it in us so deeply that we can talk it ourselves."

Capp himself liked to call puzzling situations *amoozin' and confoozin'*, one of his favorite Dogpatch expressions. Others were *oh, happy day!*, *as any fool can plainly see*, and *if I had my druthers* (an expression based on the existing term *druthers*). Other Cappisms included *wimminfolk*, *corn-dishun*, *contrariwise*, and *natcherly*, the probable source of *natch*. Dogpatch's *skonk works*, where *Kickapoo Joy Juice* was brewed from dead skunks, old shoes, and miscellaneous detritus inspired members of the R & D operation at Lockheed Aircraft Corporation to call themselves the "skunk works" during World War II. So many other companies followed suit that, despite Lockheed's attempt to trademark the phrase, *skunk works* became generic for all manner of creative enterprises.

Then there were *shmoos*, cheerful self-reproducing hermaphrodites shaped like bowling pins whose only goal in life was to please humans, even when this meant allowing themselves to be eaten. Buttons could be made from their eyes, toothpicks from their whiskers. Cut thin, their hide made fine leather—cut thick, sturdy boards.

Shmoos were such a hit that *Time* magazine put them on its cover. During the 1948 election Thomas Dewey accused Harry Truman of promising voters "everything including the shmoo." One year later, Truman invited Al Capp to stand by his side as he introduced a savings bond illustrated with a shmoo. Americans in general and scientists in particular found diverse applications for Capp's creation. A survey instrument used in particle physics is still called a *shmoo*. So is a test pattern that electrical engineers employ. Creating those patterns is known as *shmooing*. *Shmooing* is also the name microbiologists have given the asexual reproduction of a type of yeast.

When asked why he called his creation a *shmoo*, the cartoonist explained, "That's what it was. You wouldn't call a moose anything but a moose would you?"

Notwithstanding Capp's nonchalance about his many neologisms, the cartoonist worked hard at creating them. He always kept a notebook at hand to jot down ideas and was known to revise his strip's dialogue half a dozen times and more. Capp sometimes spent hours trying to come up with just the right name for even minor characters. Like his Dogpatch expressions, some of these names joined the national conversation. Abner's pipe-smoking mother *Mammy Yokum* alluded to all manner of feisty old women. *Daisy Mae Scragg*—his voluptuous, scantily clad wife—became synonymous with innocently seductive women. Homely *Sadie Hawkins*, on the other hand, was so unlikely to attract a husband that her father created an annual event named after her in which unmarried women chased eligible bachelors. This inspired generations of *Sadie Hawkins Day* dances in high schools and colleges around the country.

One of Capp's most memorable characters was *Joe Btfsplk*, a forlorn little man in rags who wandered about with a cloud raining over his head, spreading gloom and doom. When asked how to pronounce his last name he'd reply testily, "B-t-f-s-p-l-k." Capp thought of Btfsplk's surname as onomatopoeic for a sputtering Bronx cheer. During *Li'l Abner*'s long run and for decades afterward, his name was synonymous with those thought to suffer chronic misfortune. As late as 2016, a commentator called then-congresswoman Loretta Sanchez "the Joe Btfsplk of California politics." In the same year, humorist Garrison Keillor continually referred to Donald Trump as "Mr. Bftsplk."

Another Capp creation, Evil-Eye Fleegle, was a zoot-suited hoodlum from Brooklyn who vanquished his foes with "THE UNLIMITLESS POWER OF THE HUMAN EYEBALL!" Fleegle unleashed this power by focusing one eye on his targets while pointing directly at them. That was a *whammy*. When Fleegle's televised mass whammy demanded that watchers turn green (to match his own complexion), Mammy Yokum was one of the few who refused to comply. "Druther not!!" she tells the New Yorker after he travels to Dogpatch to importune her. "I gotta give you th' whammy, Mammy!!" he responds.

Fleegle begins with a half-whammy. This sends Mammy reeling backward. When she still refuses to turn green he threatens her with a full whammy. "A FULL whammy got sufficient power to melt a locomotive," he boasts, "uproot 100 acres of giant redwood, an' toin the country radioactive for T'REE generations!!" When Mammy Yokum still refuses to do his bidding, Fleegle hits her with a double whammy, now focusing both eyes in her direction. Mammy stands her ground once again, however, the goodness of her heart successfully neutralizing the malevolent energy emanating from Fleegle's evil eye.

Although *whammy* and *double whammy* were sports slang at the time Capp introduced them to a national audience in the 1940s, both broadened their purview under his auspices. *Double whammy* is the most enduring of many Cappisms left behind by their creator, even more ubiquitous today than a single *whammy*. In an era of supersized meals, jumbo jetliners, and bloated SUVs, double whammies are the norm.

The Sailor Man

When they couldn't decide what to call a redesigned four-wheel-drive vehicle early in World War II, American soldiers thought about a cartoon character named Eugene the Jeep. This character, who first appeared in the comic strip *Thimble Theatre* in 1936, was a good-natured, preternaturally strong creature with a bulbous nose who could only say "Jeep, jeep, jeep." Jeep's surname fit the GI's rugged vehicle perfectly, making his creator, Elzie Segar, the source of a durable brand name.

Thimble Theatre made its debut in 1919. Ten years after that, Segar introduced a cantankerous sailor with big biceps who smoked a corncob pipe and had a sharp tongue. As *Popeye*, this character proved so popular that *Thimble Theatre* was renamed after him. Popeye's distinctive dialect included a credo that remains a favorite of many Americans: "I yam what I yam an' tha's all I yam." Segar's many readers incorporated terms such as these into their speech. *Goon* was one, inspired by the Goons, a repulsive family that lived on Goon Island. Alice the Goon—a big-nosed, hairy, eight-foot-tall character—was particularly ominous. After this family showed up on the funny pages in 1933, parents began to warn their children that if they didn't behave, "the Goon will get you." Gangs of toughs hired by employers to attack striking workers during the Depression were called *goon squads*.

Although this neologism had already appeared in a 1921 *Harper's Magazine* essay by Frederick Lewis Allen that contrasted heavy-handed types of people he called "goons" with lighter-touched "jiggers," it was Popeye who added *goon* to our vernacular. On college campuses *goon* became Depression-era slang for a stupid individual. When that iteration went into decline, a replacement word was inspired by another Popeye character: Dufus Jones. Soon after Elzie Segar's successor Forrest Sagendorf added this dimwitted character to *Popeye* in 1958, the respelled term *doofus* became slang for lamebrained individuals. Dufus Jones thus joined a large roster of lovable losers who have contributed their names to the American canon of eponyms.

Everybody Loves a Loser

When cartoonist H. T. Webster introduced *The Timid Soul* in 1924, he inadvertently created an eponym that would outlive him by six decades and counting. The slight, retiring hero of this cartoon series was a morbidly meek and pathologically unassertive man with white hair and a neat moustache who wore both belt and suspenders. His name suited him perfectly: *Caspar Milquetoast*. (*Milk toast*, toasted bread soaked in milk, echoed a nickname hung on meek and mild

Caspar Milquetoast.

men—*milksops*—ever since Chaucer used it that way in *The Monk's Tale*, at the end of the fourteenth century.) Although *The Timid Soul* lasted only for a few years, its protagonist's surname remains a synonym for pushovers, as when a *New Yorker* writer referred to Jimmy Carter as "a hand-wringing Milquetoast." Another writer for that magazine subsequently called a modest wealth tax proposal "milquetoastery."

During World War II, one more lovable loser made his debut, in the premiere issue of *Yank: The Army Weekly*. This one was featured in a regular strip introduced by cartoonist George Baker in June 1942. Its featured character was a hapless infantryman with a cucumber nose who couldn't adapt to military life. Baker called him the *Sad Sack*. In one strip, this sorry soldier made his bed, mopped the floor, shined his shoes, and donned a spiffy uniform only to be given kitchen duty peeling potatoes because a single pocket of his uniform wasn't neatly pressed. In another, the Sad Sack writhed and squirmed during a sex hygiene class, then pulled on a rubber glove to shake hands with a young woman after class.

Baker was cagey about the etymology of his protagonist's name, admitting only that it came from a "longer phrase, of a derogatory nature." This not-to-be-named-phrase was *a sad sack of shit*, prewar slang for sorry individuals. During the war itself, GIs applied that phrase to inept soldiers. After World War II ended, the Sad Sack was featured in a comic book series that lasted for four decades. To this day his name is synonymous with any pathetic person, so widely used that it's sometimes compressed into a single lowercased word (as when a film critic referred to a movie's protagonist as a "sadsack").

A more amiable, less beleaguered type of loser made its debut on the campus of Antioch College in Yellow Springs, Ohio. Antioch was where a young New Yorker named Herb Gardner enrolled following World War II. While there, Gardner took a course in American history taught by a short, squat professor with a bemused smile who often lectured with his hands folded before him. According to a classmate who sat next to Gardner, as he observed this man's quirky mien, the aspiring cartoonist sketched caricatures of him. These sketches provided the basis for cartoon characters he called "nebbishes" (from *nebbich* or *nebekh*, Yiddish for "poor soul"). An early version appeared in Antioch's college newspaper, titled "A Complete Guide to Falling Asleep During Classes (Especially Prepared for *NEBBISH* Students"). Drawings of distinctly nebbish-type characters illustrated Gardner's guide.

Like their professorial inspiration, a nebbish is short and plump, with a big nose, beetle brows, and quizzical expression. These figures appeared in a cartoon syndicated to several dozen newspapers from 1954 until 1960. For a time they also enjoyed a vogue as dolls, greeting card illustrations, and cocktail napkins featuring nebbishes saying things like "Next week we've got to get organized," and "I am so smart I make myself sick." One classic of minimalist humor portrays a squat nebbish with arched eyebrows, palms raised, and shoulders shrugged. Its caption reads, "So?" Compared to high-achieving nerds, nebbishes are ineffectual but lovable. Unlike a slob, their creator explained, "a nebbish is the victim of a slob. A slob spills things, and the things get spilled on the nebbish." Though long gone from the commercial scene, the name of Gardner's popular creation has endured, not just as a noun but as the root of an adjective. According to *The Daily Beast*, actor Don Knotts was "famous for playing hapless, nebbishy characters."

In the comic strip *Peanuts*, Herb Gardner's contemporary Charles Schulz introduced a nebbishy character named Charlie Brown in 1950. Well after Schulz's death in 2000, his recurring trope of having playmate Lucy Van Pelt assure Charlie Brown that she'll hold down a football for him to kick (sixty-one times according to one tally), only to pull it up as he swings his leg and lands on his back, remains a common way to refer to being repeatedly deceived. As political commentator Jeff Greenfield has written, "There is a history of North Korea playing Lucy with the football while the U.S., as Charlie Brown, whiffs badly."

An even more enduring trope involved Lucy's baby brother, Linus, clutching a blue "security" blanket to his temple while sucking his thumb. Schulz later called Linus's *security blanket* "the best idea I ever had." Infants' afghans are now routinely sold as "security blankets." To this day, we use that term for all manner of comfort sources. *Security blanket* can refer to anything from a dependable friend to NATO's presence in Eastern Europe.

The Far Side

Although few contemporary cartoonists have been as prolific as an Al Capp or a Billy DeBeck when it comes to neologizing, one did continue that tradition: Gary Larson.

In his late, lamented *Far Side* cartoons, Larson made screwball neology part of the action. One panel in which a man stumbled as two wolves chased him around a table is captioned "Luposlipaphobia: The fear of being pursued by timber wolves around a kitchen table while wearing socks on a newly waxed floor." Another *Far Side* cartoon that featured an anxious-looking man at a desk was captioned "Analidaephobia: The fear that somewhere, somehow, a duck is watching you." Larson later wondered if he hadn't overthought this one. His original versions were "quackaphobia" or "duckalookaphobia." But after determining that the scientific family name of ducks is Anatidae, he went with Analidaephobia. "And so," Larson conceded, "I ended up coining a word that twelve ornithologists understood and everyone else probably went, 'Say what?'"

Thagomizer enjoyed a similar fate. In the *Far Side* cartoon that introduced this term, a caveman points to three spikes in a picture of a dinosaur's tail and tells several prehistoric listeners, "Now this end is called the thagomizer . . . after the late Thag Simmons." Though hardly a household word, that Larsonism has enjoyed some currency among paleontologists. An indication of Larson's standing in the scientific community can be seen in the fact that three insects—the owl louse *Strigiphilus garylarsoni*, the Ecuadorian butterfly *Serratoterga larsoni*, and a beetle called *Garylarsonus*—have been named after him. Collectively, a type of madcap humor that is both funny and ominous is called *Larsonesque*.

9

Ink-Stained Word Coiners

WHILE TOURING THE United States at the end of the nineteenth century, a London drama critic named William Archer was struck by how much colloquial language he encountered. The slang in an 1896 book called *Artie* was particularly striking. This bestselling collection of newspaper yarns featured an office boy named Artie Blanchard, whose speech was filled with idioms such as "rubberneckin,'" "wise guy," and "cuts no ice."

Artie Blanchard was the creation of an Indiana journalist named George Ade. Ade based that character on an actual office boy he'd met while writing human interest stories for the *Chicago Record* in the 1890s. Though largely forgotten today, in his time the tall, skinny journalist was wildly popular not only among his fellow heartland residents but Americans across the country. Hundreds of thousands of everyday newspaper readers joined writers such as Mark Twain, Carl Sandburg, Theodore Dreiser, and Edmund Wilson in applauding George Ade. "I would rather have written *Fables in Slang* than be President," the editor and novelist William Allen White commented after a compilation of Ade's work by that title was published in 1900.

George Ade portrayed his fellow Midwesterners amiably, humorously, and with a sure command of their vernacular. Readers particularly liked his ear for colorful street argot such as *samoleons*, *bellhop*, *keen*, and *piffle*. This called for allowing his subjects—shopgirls, office boys, clerks, stenographers, elevator operators, and teamsters—to speak for themselves in a colorful patois that was sometimes embellished by Ade, then adopted by readers around the country.

Artie Blanchard's lingo was a particular favorite. In one account Artie said that upon joining a group of men, "they all give me the glad hand." In another, he said that a woman "puts out the glad hand." After being verbed as *gladhand*, this piece of slang became a lasting part of American speech.

In an 1896 story, Artie confronted a young woman he thought had been spending too much time with another suitor. Referring to the date books that Gilded Age women used to keep track of who they were seeing when, Artie told her, "I s'pose the other boy's fillin' all my dates?" In 1902, another character in an Ade fable referred to being "all dated up." This helped reposition the word *date* to refer to a ritual of courtship.

Ade later referred to a penny-pinching character as "undoubtedly the Tightest Wad in the Township," inspiring our current term *tightwad*. (The author was given to random capitalization.) Of another character, Ade wrote just before the turn of the century, "he had 'sized' the hustler for a 'panhandler' from the very start," an early use of *panhandler*. (Ade's use of quote marks suggests that this term didn't originate with him, and, sure enough, the *OED* records an earlier use of the term, in 1893.) One Ade character who mused in 1900 that "the Bunk was about to be Handed to him," introduced this contraction of *bunkum* to many of Ade's readers around the country. Ade also was a key disseminator of *OK*, a term he used repeatedly in his work.

Once it became clear that his characters' slangy speech was what particularly attracted readers, Ade retitled his syndicated column, "Fables in Slang" (and used that title for his 1902 anthology of those columns). The writer thought this gave him permission to use as many street terms as he pleased while alerting readers and colleagues that he knew what he was up to, that he wasn't some illiterate *mutt*, a vulgar *dub* who used—in his words—"barbarisms, Americanisms, colloquialisms, provincialisms, or any [other] 'ism' that stood on the doubtful list."

Ade once scrawled several pages of colloquial words and phrases that he might use in his column and stories. Although most were forgettable and quickly forgotten, this list included terms such as *excess baggage* and *damp firecracker*. By one accounting, Ade used nearly 1600 pieces of such argot during a half-century career that lasted until the advent of World War II. In A to C alone, an alphabetical compilation of slang he employed included *battle-axe* for a formidable woman, *beef* for complaint, *chair-warmer* for a place holder, and *cheap* for stingy. Other terms we still use that can be found in Ade's writing include *curtain raiser*, *Dew-dads*, *ding*, *foxy*, *piffle*, *slow-poke*, *snob*, *stuck up*, and *fly the coop*. His reliance on words and phrases like these could pose problems for those who'd never heard them, however. When a play Ade wrote opened in London in 1908, the theater's manager provided audience members with a glossary of Americanisms used by its playwright. On this list were *jerk-water railroad*, *campus*, *corker*, *quitters*, *rattled*, and *easy money*.

Ade's oeuvre has proved to be an etymological bonanza. His writing is filled with early and first use of words and phrases that we now use routinely. Ade didn't just record street talk, however. Because demand often exceeded supply, the writer sometimes had to create slang of his own. In one story Ade converted the athletic and military term *sidestep* into a verb when he wrote figuratively about a boy whose parents hoped he could "side-step the Pitfalls" of life. Ade subsequently referred to a "newly-arrived Delegate from the Asphalt Jungles," the first known appearance in print of a phrase that later became the title of a bestselling novel, and a movie based on that novel.

Ade's verbal inventiveness was what so impressed his colleagues. H. L. Mencken lauded his "extraordinary talent for devising novel, vivid and unforgettable phrases." Lexicographer W. J. Funk—who included George Ade in a 1933 list of America's top ten purveyors of slang—considered his verbal creations "funnier than real slang."

Like a Shakespearean actor consigned to roles in light comedies, the Purdue graduate was taken aback by discovering how many considered him little more than a "professional slangster" who was expected to engage in "verbal buck-dancing" on command. Although he made a point of using the King's English when being interviewed, Ade found that journalists routinely tried to lure him into answering their questions in lingo as colorful as that used by his characters. When he didn't comply, they'd often put some in his mouth anyway, then run the results under headlines like "SLICK SLANG-SLINGER HERE." But slang-slinging was what paid Ade's bills and then some, allowing him to live most of his adult life on a large Indiana estate, entertain lavishly, and winter in Florida, where he died in 1944.

Runyonese

George Ade once wrote a fan letter to another Florida snowbird telling him, "You not only get a story but you spice it with the correct vernacular." The recipient of that letter was Ade's fellow columnist, story writer, and slang-slinger Damon Runyon. A slight, poorly educated newsman, Runyon left his native Colorado in 1910 for New York City, where he became known as the Bard of Broadway (the street, not its theaters).*

Runyon's writing revolved around New York street life, some of which was compiled in a collection whose title and contents inspired the musical *Guys and Dolls*. Although the streets Damon Runyon covered in midtown Manhattan were quite different from the Midwestern sidewalks that George Ade considered his

---

* In a variation on the accidental coining of words, when a Colorado typesetter misspelled Damon Runyon's actual surname of "Runyan" as "Runyon," the journalist decided he liked that version better and adopted it.

beat, Runyon's coverage of its habitués relied just as heavily on the patter used by subjects whom he gave names such as Dave the Dude, Harry the Horse, Spanish John, Sam the Gonoph, Izzy Cheesecake, Meyer Marmalade, and Hot Horse Herbie. These characters carried *rods*. When arrested by the police, they were *collared* by the *fuzz*, *took the fall*, *packed it in*. Corrupt officials were *on the take*—bribed with *scratch*, *do-re-mi*, or *moolah* (a term Runyon attributed to a street hustler named Chuck Green). Runyon's mostly male characters called women's legs *gams*. Women themselves were *dolls*, *dames*, *molls*, *cupcakes*, *chickens*, *broads*, and *beautifuls*. As one of his characters noted, "Personally I always take a gander at a doll's feet and ankles before I start handicapping her."

Many elements of Runyon's vocabulary remain in play. In his writing *freeloaders* feasted on free lunches at saloons. Charitable meals served to hoboes were *handouts*. Runyon applied a term for failed plays—*turkeys*—to all manner of nonstarters. The racetracks he haunted provided him with *long shot* (as when writing about a triaging doctor who "cannot afford to waste time on long shots") and *photo finish*. A less-than-pretty woman to Runyon was "no worse than a photo finish for the most beautiful."

In his time Runyon's streetwise palaver came to be known as "Runyonese," a gumbo of underworld slang, Big Apple colloquialisms, vaudeville gags, and, in some cases, words gussied up by Damon Runyon if not coined outright.

Although Runyon denied that he invented words, saying he merely reported language used by his subjects, the actual story is more complicated. Like George Ade, Damon Runyon did sometimes augment terms he'd overheard with ones of his own creation. *Hoorah Henry*, a phrase that Runyon introduced in a 1936 short story, later became common in Great Britain, where it referred to upper-class bon vivants. *The Roaring Twenties* owed a debt to Runyon's term for midtown Manhattan: *The Roaring Forties*.

Original Runyonisms like these were in short supply, however. Following his death in 1946, close scrutiny determined that only a handful of the many terms associated with Runyon were original. After assessing hundreds of them, a French professor of American studies named Jean Wagner concluded that no more than ten could be attributed to Runyon. When it comes to neologizing, however, coining ten usable words is no mean accomplishment. In addition, as Wagner points out in his book on *Runyonese*, by importing what he called "quick coinages" from the street into his writing, Runyon extended the life of these spontaneously uttered terms. Without his patronage they would have suffered the brief life of most oral neologisms. And even if few of the many novel words used by Runyon were pure coinages, Wagner adds, many could be considered "quasi-coinings." Some, such as *bankroll*, simply converted existing nouns into verbs. Others added suffixes such as *-aroo*, *-ola*, *-er*, and *-us* to existing words, as when

Runyon created *mobster* from *mob* (as others had before him). Less successful were *stinkaroo* and *phonus bolonus*. Other nonstarters in Runyon's verbal oeuvre included *gongs* (medals), *alley apple* (rock), *meat house* (morgue), *smeller* (bad play), *phedinkus* (nonsense), *rooty-toot-toot* (machine gun), and *pizzolover* (melding pistol with revolver). Had the writer coined that word a few decades later, it undoubtedly would have been misconstrued as referring to a lover of pizza, and autocorrected to *pizzalover*.

In one case Runyon did have a go at outright word invention. When writing the screenplay of a 1942 movie based on his story "Butch Minds the Baby," Runyon coined *mooley* for a not-too-bright person, and *komoppo* for a wealth-flaunting woman. Those neologisms attracted the attention of movie industry censors who, in their never-ending search for hidden meanings, threatened to bowdlerize Runyon's script because they thought these unfamiliar words might be double entendres. Where did they originate? he was asked. "I made them up myself," Runyon admitted.

Slang-Slinging Columnists

Damon Runyon was just one of a long line of newspaper columnists whose colorful coinages and overheard slang became part of the American vernacular. They included a popular expression associated with another New York columnist, Walter Winchell: *make whoopee*. Winchell was very possessive of this phrase, claiming not only that he'd coined this sly reference to sex, but implying that *whoopee* itself was his own invention. When etymologists pointed out that *whoopee* could be found in any number of vintage songs and publications, including Mark Twain's *A Tramp Abroad*, and that the word *whoope* was a common part of Middle English, Winchell threw in the towel, at least part-way. "They contend *whoopee* is older than Shakespeare," Winchell conceded. "Well, all right. I never claimed it, anyhow. But let 'em take *makin' whoopee* from me and look out!"

The surname of this onetime song-and-dance man was originally spelled "Winchel." According to the columnist, after an extra L was appended to his last name on a theater marquee, like his friend Damon Runyon, Winchell decided he preferred the misspelled version. (In a biography of Winchell, Neal Gabler offers alternative explanations for the respelling of his surname.) Throughout his half-century career, the diminutive, chain-smoking Broadway boulevardier was a two-fisted slang-slinger. In his first fist was a gossip column that Winchell wrote from 1924 until 1967, one that fellow columnist Herb Caen called *three-dot journalism* (i.e., brief, tweet-like prose pellets separated by ellipses, a style Winchell was said to have adopted when the hyphen key on his typewriter was stuck). In Winchell's second fist was a Sunday evening radio broadcast that opened with

"Mr. and Mrs. North and South America and all ships at sea. Let's go to press!" At this broadcast's peak, in the late 1940s, some fifty million listeners hung on the frenetic words that followed, including many they'd never heard before.

According to Neal Gabler, Winchell "worked painstakingly as a lexicographer, collecting new phrases and coining his own." The mixed results were what came to be known as "Winchellisms" or "Winchellese." He was an early user of *whammy* as a non-sports term, writing in 1939 about a group of women who'd "put the whammy" on soap operas they found insulting. Movies to Winchell were *flickers* (*flicks* for short), an existing term that became part of the national lingo after he added it to his on-air vocabulary.

Winchell's own coinage, *moom-pitcher*, was less successful. So was *keptive* (mistress), *choongum* (chewing gum), *hush house* (speakeasy), and *certinney* (certainly). Other fizzlers included *get storked* for getting pregnant, *infanticipating* for being pregnant, *Reno-vated* for being divorced in Reno (Nevada), *giggle water* for liquor, and *Wildemen* for homosexuals, as well as *swastinkas* and *ratzis* for Nazis. Journalists he didn't care for were *presstitutes*. Close friendships were *chumships*. Winchell was especially fond of using *phffft* for anything that sputtered out like a wet firecracker, but few of his followers followed suit. *Pash*, Winchell's abbreviation for passion, didn't catch on. Nor did *maple massagers*, his name for night club dancers, or the term he coined for manicure shops: *paw empawriums*.

Other Winchellisms were more popular. The columnist's name for legs, *shafts*, enjoyed a brief vogue, as did *veddy*, Winchell's hoity-toity version of "very." *Ex* for a former spouse is commonplace today, as is *C* for a hundred dollars and *G* for a thousand. *Blessed event*, Winchell's name for childbirth, was a phrase his readers and listeners took to, one that can still be heard.

Winchell's use of *yada yada* in 1945 anticipated by half a century the appearance of that phrase on *Seinfeld* (with an extra *yada* added). Although it would take several decades to catch on, Winchell used the term *frienemies* in a 1953 column to suggest a way we could coexist with the Russians. "Howz about calling the Russians our Frienemies?" asked Winchell, the first known use in print of this modern-sounding term.

Winchell's archconservative colleague Westbrook Pegler would never have made such a suggestion. This Rush Limbaugh precursor devoted his first syndicated column in early 1938 to attacking congressional "bleeding hearts" who he thought were wasting too much time trying to outlaw lynching. Pegler later pinned that label (referencing the bleeding heart of Jesus) on socially conscious liberals such as Eleanor Roosevelt and fellow columnist Heywood Hale Broun, whom he called "Old Bleeding Heart." Pegler dismissed intellectuals in politics as *double-domes* (charging that FDR's New Dealers were "big-name bleeding hearts and double domes"), a pejorative that became common in his time, if not in ours.

Like Donald Trump a few decades later, Pegler's specialty was coming up with scathing nicknames to hurl at opponents. He mocked Supreme Court justice Felix Frankfurter as "Old Weenie" (which may have inspired the use of *weenie* to suggest cowardice). Vice President Henry Wallace was "Bubblehead," President Franklin Roosevelt "Moosejaw the First." When not referring to Eleanor Roosevelt as a bleeding heart, Pegler called the chatty, toothy First Lady "the Gab," "la Boca Grande," or "la Grande Bouche" (Spanish and French for "the big mouth"), an appellation that reappeared as "Madame de la Grande Bouche" in the Disney version of *Beauty and the Beast*.

During his heyday this columnist's take-no-prisoners journalism often hit its mark. A corrupt union boss who was about to go to prison after being dogged relentlessly in Pegler's column came up with his own neologism for that process. He'd been "Pegler-ized."

A less reactionary heir of Walter Winchell, Herb Caen of the *San Francisco Chronicle*, not only named the staccato *three-dot journalism* introduced by Winchell but practiced it himself. During the six decades he spent as a man-about–San Francisco, Caen was a mint of catchy coinages. Most reflected the dubious eye he cast on comings and goings in the Bay Area. Berkeley, in Caen's lexicon, was *Berserkeley*. Or *Baghdad-by-the-Bay*. Los Angeles was *Lozngeles*.

Herb Caen's most successful contribution to the lexicon came when—in a 1958 *Chronicle* column—he gave some scruffy North Beach poetry reciters their lasting name. For a picture spread in progress, Caen wrote, *Look* magazine had "hosted a party in a No. Beach house for 50 Beatniks." This coinage referenced author Jack Kerouac's own description of those like him. They belonged to a *beat generation*, the novelist had said, a phrase that begat *beats* for short. Caen's suffix *-nik* was adapted from a word recently in headlines: *Sputnik,* Russian for "one who travels around the earth," the name of the Soviet satellite that was launched in 1957. Caen later said this hybrid of *beat* and the last three letters of *Sputnik* had simply popped into his head the day before he introduced it in his April 2 column. The next day that coinage appeared in a *San Francisco Examiner* headline. To Caen's surprise, "beatnik" quickly became part of common parlance. "I didn't even know it was going to catch on," he observed years later. "I just fell into the word writing a column one day." Kerouac himself didn't like Caen's coinage, saying that he may have been a *beat* but was no *beatnik*. After this term became ubiquitous, Kerouac confronted the columnist at a San Francisco bar. "You're putting us down and making us sound like jerks," he told Caen. "I hate it. Stop using it."

Kerouac was not alone in taking umbrage. Caen's verbal invention made him a target of ire in hip gathering spots such as the North Beach bagel shop whose proprietor posted a sign announcing, "We feature separate toilet facilities for HERB CAEN." Kerouac's fellow beat, poet Allen Ginsberg, wrote a letter to the *New York*

Times Book Review objecting to a reviewer's repeated use of "the foul word beat-nik." Caen took it all in stride. He said he was particularly amused by a footnote in Norman Mailer's 1959 book *Advertisements for Myself* that told readers *beatnik* was "a word coined by an idiot columnist in San Francisco." There is no such foot-note that I can find. In *Advertisements for Myself* Mailer credited Caen for coining "beatnik," then noted that because *-nik* was a demeaning diminutive in Yiddish, *beatnik* had a condescending quality that pleased members of the press. Its coiner was not among them. Three years after he added *beatnik* to the vernacular, Caen confessed in 1961, "I've never been particularly proud of the word."

The Brothers Alsop

Not long after Herb Caen made this confession, the term *southern strategy* began to be bruited about. Most associated with Richard Nixon, that phrase was introduced in a 1963 *Saturday Evening Post* article by Stewart Alsop to char-acterize Barry Goldwater's approach to running for president, attributing it to Goldwater's nemesis Nelson Rockefeller. In a 1971 letter to *Business Week*, how-ever, Goldwater himself said the first person he'd heard use the words "southern strategy" was Joseph Alsop (Stewart's brother), while visiting the senator's office in the 1950s. By 1968 this strategy had come to characterize the racially divisive way Richard Nixon courted voters south of the Mason-Dixon line.

Joe Alsop also originated and named the concept of a *missile gap*—a presumed dearth of this weapon in America's arsenal relative to the Soviet Union's—that became a key campaign issue for John Kennedy in 1960. As a senator, Kennedy had read into the *Congressional Record* Alsop's August 1, 1958, column on the so-called *missile gap*, the first known appearance of this phrase.

The Alsop brothers were quintessential neologizing journalists, auditioning one coinage after another, some of which became part of the national conver-sation, most of which didn't. *Daddyknowsbestism*, for example, did not outlive Stewart Alsop's suggestion that this was a political problem. In one *Newsweek* column Stewart discussed what he called *Waltermittyization*, in another *the Clothespin Vote*. A 1974 column he wrote proposed that we adopt France's notion of *degringolade*, a hard-to-translate (let alone pronounce) word for the sudden collapse of society, which Alsop saw afoot in his own country. The *Irish mafia*, on the other hand, apparently was introduced by Stewart Alsop, with reference to John Kennedy's political entourage, and picked up by other correspondents (to the dismay of Kennedy himself).

Stewart Alsop's most successful contribution to the lexicon came when he and a colleague named Charles Bartlett abridged the existing terms *war hawks* and *doves of peace* in a December 8, 1962, article in the *Saturday Evening Post* that discussed the struggle between *hawks* and *doves* in the Kennedy White House during the Cuba missile crisis. (This article also quoted Secretary of State Dean Rusk as saying the US and USSR were *eyeball to eyeball* during that crisis, borrowing a piece of military slang that went back at least to the Korean War.) So-called *hawks and doves* subsequently engaged in fierce debates about the war in Vietnam.

Like so many poly-coiners, the Alsop brothers were given credit for neologisms they didn't create. It's been mistakenly reported that Stewart and Joe were responsible for *domino theory* and *light at the end of the tunnel*. Joe himself claimed original use of the *domino theory* to justify our military intervention in Vietnam (the idea that if they went Communist, so would surrounding countries, like a row of falling dominoes). Long before he used this analogy, however, Dwight Eisenhower had referred to "the 'falling domino' principle." When Joseph Alsop later wrote of seeing *light at the end of the tunnel* in Vietnam, he used an expression dating back at least to the post–World War I era. Joe also liked to talk of "the WASP ascendancy," and even co-wrote an essay by that title. (As we'll see, WASP was in play long before Joe Alsop picked it up.)

Egghead is another term attributed to an Alsop, including by himself. According to Stewart Alsop's own account, during the 1952 election he'd cast about for a way to characterize well-educated voters who were smitten with the demi-intellectual Adlai Stevenson, finally settling on *eggheads*. Both spiritually and physically, this term suited the baldheaded Democratic presidential nominee perfectly. Stewart said he'd first heard it used while following the campaign. As he wrote, "This reporter remarked to a rising young Connecticut Republican that a good many intelligent people, who would be considered normally Republican, obviously admired Stevenson. 'Sure,' was the reply, 'all the eggheads love Stevenson. But how many eggheads do you think there are?' " Alsop later admitted that the "rising" star he'd quoted was his brother John. John subsequently added "a large, oval head, smooth, faceless, unemotional but a little haughty and condescending" to the term depicting intellectuals that he thought originated with him. But John Alsop doubted that *egghead* itself was his own coinage. It wasn't. During the early twentieth century, *egg heads* was common newsroom parlance. In 1918, when he was a reporter for *Chicago Daily News*, Carl Sandburg wrote to a colleague that " 'Egg heads' is the slang here for editorial writers." Fifteen years later, the 1933 movie *Hallelujah, I'm a Bum* featured a leftish character named Egghead.

Regardless of their origin, terms such as *eggheads* and *double domes* are in constant demand to denigrate those we called *brains* or *bookworms* as children. You know, *nerds*. As so often happens with derisive neologisms, we've embraced this once-pejorative name for smart, socially inept individuals. What is its provenance?

10

Kiddie Lit

FOR YEARS LIBRARIANS, linguists, and etymologists struggled to determine the etymology of *nerd*. Some thought it might have derived from *turd*. Or perhaps it was *drunk* spelled backward (*knurd*). Or could it come from *nerts* (a slangy version of "nuts")? Maybe it began as an acronym for the Naval Enlisted Requiring Discipline sailors who languished in brigs during in World War II. Or was it a clip of the surname of ventriloquist Edgar Bergen's doll Mortimer Snerd?

After rigorous investigation, etymologists finally found nerd's probable point of origin: the 1950 book *If I Ran the Zoo*. In that book Theodor Geisel (aka Dr. Seuss) wrote, "And then, just to show them, I'll sail to Ka-Troo/And Bring Back an It-Kutch a Preep and a Proo a Nerkle a Nerd and a Seersucker too!"

When he composed this line, I doubt that Geisel foresaw that he'd be providing us with one of our most useful and durable words. Kids know a good word when they hear one, however, and *nerd* certainly qualifies. Boom babies of the 1950s who became teenagers of the 1960s and adults after that (chronologically speaking) took *nerd* along with them on their generational odyssey.

At first it was derogatory, of course. One did not want to be called a *nerd* any more than a geek, a dweeb, a dork, a twit, or a twerp. According to a 1951 *Newsweek* article, "In Detroit, someone who once would be called a drip or a square is now, regrettably, a nerd." After nerdy Bill Gates became the world's richest man, however, this word took on a new cachet. The richer Gates got, the better "nerd" sounded. By now it not only stands alone but has spawned *nerdy*, *nerdish*, and the verb *nerd up* (along with several dozen other variations on *nerd* that can be found in *Urban Dictionary*).

One secret for the success of a Seussism like *nerd* was the fact that their creator wasn't intent on thrusting new words into the lexicon. This onetime cartoonist was more interested in entertaining himself and his young readers. With his flair for zany word creation, Geisel was less the heir of Beatrix Potter than of Lewis

Carroll. "Seuss's willingness to experiment with words," writes biographer Philip Nel, "—even if that means breaking the rules—is one reason that his books are so fun to read."

In books by Dr. Seuss what "happens" is basically beside the point. It's all about wordplay. The words he played with were heavy on *b*'s, *x*'s, and *z*'s. *On Beyond Zebra!* features a "Floob-Boober-Bab-Boober-Bus." In the *Butter Battle Book* a nuclear device is called a "Bitsy Big-Boy Boomeroo." A song in *The Cat in the Hat Songbook* claims, "Somebody Stole My Hoo-to Foo-to Boo-to Bah!" The author's imaginary figures have names like *Zax*, *Zooks*, and *Zumble-Zays* as well as the inimitable *Yuzz-a-ma-Tuzz* and the *Zummzian Zuks*.

Unlike so many neologizers, Geisel didn't just adapt existing terms, cobble clauses together, or borrow roots from other languages. He cut new words from whole cloth. In doing so, Dr. Seuss paid careful attention to the sound of these words, realizing how important this was to members of his young audience and the adults who read to them. In the process he contributed more than his share of neologisms to our language. *Nerd* is the most successful one. *Grinch* isn't far behind, as well as *Lorax*, the prototypical quixotic environmentalist. Others— *zax*, *yuzz*, *vroo*, and *thneed* (for things we want but don't really need)—didn't make the cut but could have.

Such terms were not easy to coin. Geisel's writing methods relied heavily on work sheets, charts, lists, and word counts. This approach was based on *meticulosity*, he once told Maurice Sendak, adding, "Is that a word?" (It is, meaning focused on details.)

One Seussism was due to a happy accident. When Geisel's secretary typed his scrawled reference to a "uug under the rug" as "vug under the rug," the author decided he liked her version better. *Vug* clearly improved on *uug*, and that's how this word appears in the Dr. Seuss book *There's a Wocket in My Pocket!* Another fanciful word in that book is *Zillow*. This is the name Dr. Seuss gave to a furry creature who is a young boy's sleeping companion. "But the ZILLOW on my PILLOW always helps me fall asleep," reads the text above a picture of these two in bed.

Although the online real estate aggregator Zillow denies any Seussian inspiration for their name, many a Net commenter suspects otherwise. More recently, an app offering help to online resellers has named itself Yerdle. (Think: *Yertle the Turtle*.)

The name of Barnes & Noble's e-book reader may also have originated in a book by Dr. Seuss. Even though the bookstore chain has a more prosaic origin story for their *Nook* reader's name (based on the cozy "nook" in homes where books are often read), it's hard to imagine that somewhere deep in the memory bank of those who created that product, these words from *One Fish Two Fish Red Fish Blue Fish* hadn't been deposited:

> *We took a look.*
> *We saw a Nook.*
> *On his head he had a hook.*
> *On his hook he had a book . . .*

Since they're only "writing for children," and feel little need to observe the norms of proper speech, authors such as Theodor Geisel have license to create wacky words that their young readers like and continue to use once they grow up. *Voom*—which appeared in *The Cat in the Hat Comes Back* in 1958 ("Then the Voom . . . it went VOOM! And, oh boy! What a *VOOM*!")—makes an occasional reappearance in the mouths of adults. In 2007, half a century after *The Cat in the Hat Comes Back* was published, an energy consultant asserted that "many practitioners in the electricity industry have begun to yearn for a policy 'Voom' . . ." (Because he used *voom* this way, Geisel has sometimes been credited with coining *va va voom*, but that phrase was the title of a 1954 song written by actor Art Carney, and then appeared in Mickey Spillane's 1955 novel *Kiss Me Deadly*, two years before *The Cat in the Hat Comes Back* was published.)

Citing Dr. Seuss has become a common practice among jurists, such as Supreme Court justice Elena Kagan and a federal judge named Stephanie Thacker (who in 2018 quoted from *The Lorax* when admonishing the U.S. Forest Service to "speak for the trees, for the trees have no tongues"). A year earlier *New York Times* columnist Ross Douthat wrote of " 'Butter Battle Book'-style escalations in the judicial wars." Four years before that, during a 2013 speech denouncing Obamacare, Texas senator Ted Cruz said, "When Americans tried it, they discovered they did not like green eggs and ham and they did not like Obamacare either. They did not like Obamacare in a box, with a fox, in a house or with a mouse. It is not working."

I doubt that Theodor Geisel had the needs of jurists, journalists, and officeholders in mind when creating his neologisms. Contributions to adult discourse made by writers like him are seldom willful. A scholarly analysis of Dr. Seuss's imaginative vocabulary concluded that the appeal of its made-up words lay not in their usefulness but in their laugh-out-loud disorderliness. Unlike determined neologizers such as newspaper columnists but in tandem with cartoonists, authors of books for children don't necessarily expect their coinages to show up in dictionaries. Geisel's verbal creations were based more on rhyming, alliteration, and onomatopoeia than actual utility. When he needed a rhyme and an existing word couldn't get that job done, Geisel just coined one, as in "I can't blab such blibber blubber! / My tongue isn't made of rubber" (*Fox in Socks*).

In addition to coining such terms, Geisel escorted existing but obscure terms into general usage. So it was with *grinch*. At the time *How the Grinch Stole Christmas* was published in1957, *Scrooge* was the go-to name for grouchy Christmas skeptics. Since then, Ebenezer Scrooge has had to share that mantle with *the grinch*, who didn't just sneer at Christmas but tried to eradicate it altogether (at least in its modern, commercialized form). Over time, *grinch* extended its reach to grouches of all kinds. ("He is such a grinch!" "So grinchy!") Geisel actually identified with this cranky curmudgeon, whom he called a "nasty anti-Christmas character that was really myself." (His car's license plate read GRINCH.) A version of this word predated *How the Grinch Stole Christmas*, however: the French noun *grincheux*, referring to an ill-tempered person. Was that the source of Dr. Seuss's version?

Geisel wasn't saying. Like so many creative people, Theodor Geisel was cagy about the sources of his creativity. When asked where he got his ideas, the author would reply gravely that they came from a village in the Austrian Alps called Uber Gletch, where he went every year to have his cuckoo clock serviced.

Another children's author whose work was rich with nonsense words had no such reluctance to discuss their genesis. That would be Lewis Carroll. Like Theodor Geisel, this author was a dedicated coiner of fanciful words. Unlike Geisel, he liked to ruminate on the source of those terms, and share his rumination with others.

Lewis Carroll

While visiting his sister in 1874, Reverend Charles Dodgson took a walk in the countryside near her home outside London. As he walked, the clergyman—who would later become better known as "Lewis Carroll"—thought of this line: "For the Snark was a Boojum, you see." Dodgson later said that he had no idea what those words referred to. But he liked their meter, *snark* in particular (which he later decided was probably just a combination of "snail" and "shark"). This fanciful animal was subsequently featured in his 1876 poem *The Hunting of the Snark*.

Like *grinch*, *snark* may have owed something to another language: *snarken* in German, or *snarka* in Norwegian and Swedish. Or it could have been onomatopoetic, for the sound of snoring, say, or perhaps for a snort, if not a snarl. In a book on the evolution of this term, author David Denby suggests that snark's unpleasant flavor—"the ugly blunt sound of it, the single harsh syllable that expels a puff of insolent air in its wake"—may underlie its use as the root of an expletive. From the early twentieth century on, "snarking" was synonymous with nagging. By the 1960s, "snarky" referred to being biting, and still does.

Cover of *The Hunting of the Snark* (1876).

Charles Dodgson had been fascinated since childhood with word creation. Whether or not the words actually meant anything was immaterial. His verbal handiwork was on vivid display in *Jabberwocky*, the epic nonsense poem whose lines brimmed with freshly minted terms:

> 'Twas brillig, and the slithy toves
> Did gyre and gimble in the wabe:
> All mimsy were the borogoves,
> And the mome raths outgrabe.
> He took his vorpal sword in hand;
> And, as in uffish thought he stood,
> The Jabberwock, with eyes of flame,
> Came whiffling through the tulgey wood,
> And burbled as it came!

Jabberwocky appeared in *Through the Looking-Glass* (1871). When Alice wonders what its many puzzling words refer to, Humpty Dumpty tries to help her. "Slithy," he explains, combines "lithe" and "slimy."

"You see it's like a portmanteau—there are two meanings packed up into one word." (*Portmanteau* was a French word for a suitcase with twin compartments.) Dumpty thinks "mome" may have something to do with "home." "Outgrabe," he says, describes "something between bellowing and whistling, with a kind of sneeze in the middle." "Mimsy" is a portmanteau combining "miserable" and "flimsy."

One of Carroll's most enduring neologisms was *portmanteau* itself, a more popular name for what linguists call "blends." *Dumbfound* is such a word, combining "dumb" and "confound." *Twirl* blends "twist" and "swirl." In the U.S., *motel* and *electrocution* join *guesstimate*, *infomercial*, and *Spanglish* on the list of successful American portmanteaus, along with *bromance*, *mansplain*, and *humblebrag*. Due in part to Lewis Carroll's influence, creating one new word from two old ones is among our most common forms of coinage.

Carroll didn't just name this type of neologism, he created quite a few himself. *Chortle*, the author's blend of chuckle and snort, made its way into the *Oxford English Dictionary*, and contemporary speech in general. *Galumph*, combining "gallop and triumph" (which the *OED* defines as "to march on exultantly with irregular bounding movements") can still be heard on occasion.

Carroll's other specialty was creating whimsical words such as *boojum* (for an unusually treacherous type of snark). This nonsense neologism went on to become the name of a tree in Baja California after British ecologist Godfrey Sykes exclaimed, "It must be a boojum!" when he happened on that strange-looking plant in 1922. Boojum also provided the name of a geometric pattern and a cruise missile.

Carroll had no idea what many of his coined words referred to. He just liked the way they sounded and was confident others would put them to good use. As Martin Gardner notes in *The Annotated Alice*, Carroll inverted the admonition of his Duchess to take care of the sense of words and let the sounds take care of themselves. Carroll, wrote Gardner, "takes care of the sounds and allows the sense to take care of itself." As with boojum, this could take time. Decades after *vorpal swords* appeared in *Jabberwocky*, players of Dungeons and Dragons added those words to their game's vocabulary. A fantasy basketball game online pitted Team Jabberwock against Team Vorpal Swords. When asked by a young correspondent where *vorpal swords* came from, Carroll had responded that he didn't know, any more than he could explain the origin of *tulgey* wood. Of *Jabberwocky* itself, Carroll said, "The Anglo-Saxon word 'wocer' or 'wocor' signifies 'offspring' or 'fruit.' Taking 'jabber' in its ordinary acceptation of 'excited and voluble discussion.'" Over time *jabberwocky* came to mean nonsense speech of many kinds.

One *Jabberwocky* line included the phrase "as in uffish thought he stood." In *The Hunting of the Snark* Carroll later wrote, "The bellman looked uffish ..." When a young correspondent asked him what "uffish" meant, the author responded that this word made him think of "a state of mind when the voice is gruffish, the manner roughish, and the temper huffish."

Although few Carrollisms achieved broad circulation, a group of boarding school students in Rudyard Kipling's 1899 novel *Stalky & Co.* used them in their puerile conversations, particularly Jabberwockian terms such as *burble, beamish,* and *frabjous*. And here is how British astronomer Arthur Stanley Eddington compared oxygen to nitrogen in his classic 1927 book *The Nature of the Physical World*: "Eight slithy toves gyre and gimble in the oxygen wabe; seven in nitrogen. . . . We can now venture on a prediction: if one of its toves escapes, oxygen will be masquerading in a garb properly belonging to nitrogen." When some of Carroll's nonsense words joined those of poet Edward Lear in the *OED*, lexicographer Eric Partridge observed that the two "must, in their philological heaven, be chortling at the thought that they have frabjously galumphed into the English vocabulary."

Goops and Wimps

To make the point that space limitations can promote brisk prose, I sometimes read aloud from the directions on a small bottle of insect repellent cream to writing students. "Don't goop on," these directions advise. "Three drops for hands and face is plenty." We worry over the word "goop." Is it too colloquial? Too self-conscious? There's no better word for what the writer was trying to say, however. The only viable alternative is *slather*, which is even more self-conscious than *goop*. So goop it is. Besides, that word is terse, forceful, and fun to say. Where did it come from?

San Francisco, it turns out. That is where *goop* was coined by a humorist named Gelett Burgess. Though today remembered primarily for writing "The Purple Cow" ("I never saw a Purple Cow, / I never hope to see one, / But I can tell you, anyhow, / I'd rather see than be one!"), in his time, more than a century ago, Burgess was better known for a series of books he wrote about a group of unruly children called *The Goops*.

That series kicked off in 1900 with *Goops and How to Be Them: A Manual of Manners for Polite Infants, Inculcating Many Juvenile Virtues, Both by Precept and Example*. Devoted fans of these books included a young Theodor Geisel. Geisel's mother read books by Burgess to her young son during the early twentieth century. As she read, Mrs. Geisel carefully enunciated the many fanciful words their author used. "The Goops are gluttounus and rude," Burgess wrote of his balloon-headed protagonists. "They gug and gumble with their food."

> *The Goops they lick their fingers,*
> *And the Goops, they lick their knives;*
> *They spill their broth on the tablecloth—*
> *Oh, they lead disgusting lives!*
> *The Goops they talk while eating,*
> *And loud and fast they chew;*
> *And that is why I'm glad that I*
> *Am not a Goop—are you?*

Goop was too good a word to be limited to children, however. In time, it became a common way to describe slimy liquids (*goop, goopy, gooped*). Long after being coined by Gelett Burgess, *Goop* was adopted by the actress Gwyneth Paltrow for a line of lifestyle accoutrements whose customers call themselves "Goopies."

Burgess had a counterpart in England named Evelyn Sharp. In addition to writing books for children, Sharp was a militant feminist-pacifist who served time in prison for opposing Britain's participation in World War I. Several years earlier, in a collection of fairy tales, she'd introduced a group of children who were forever pranking others but burst into tears when anyone pranked them. Sharp called her can-dish-it-out-but-can't-take-it characters "The Wymps."

Before long, this term, respelled *wimp*, was applied to all manner of feckless individual. In a 1912 story George Ade referred to "a Wimp wearing Tortoise-Shell Spectacles." Ade's use of this term without explanation suggests that it was familiar to his readers. (Sinclair Lewis later wrote of "wimpish little men with spectacles," in his 1925 novel *Arrowsmith*.)

Following the war, Ade alluded to another children's book when he wrote an essay about the joys of single life in which he referred to a bachelor who "googles his way among the girls for six nights a week." Although it's tempting to attribute the popularity of "google" to Ade, or to Barney Google's creator Billy DeBeck, this word has a longer, richer history, one that's little known and often misconstrued.

Googling Around

The most popular origin story for *google* involves a stroll that mathematician Edward Kasner took with his nine-year-old nephew during the mid-1930s. As they walked and talked, Kasner wondered aloud what one might call ten to the hundredth power (the number 10 followed by 100 zeros). "A googol!" suggested

Covers of *Goops* (1900) and *Wymps* (1897).

Kasner's nephew. That's the word his uncle bestowed upon ten to the hundredth power, one we still use, along with its cousin *googolplex* (an unimaginably large number). When Larry Page and Sergey Brin introduced their search engine in 1998, the two said they respelled *googol* as "Google" for its name, after a colleague named Sean Anderson accidentally misspelled "googol" that way when searching domain availability. *Google.com* was available; *googol.com* wasn't.

There's more to the *googol/google* story, however, far more. For starters, since Edward Kasner's young nephew would not have spelled out his suggested word for ten to the hundredth power as Kasner did later ("googol"), that spelling almost certainly was the mathematician's doing, not his nephew's. More likely this boy had "Google" in mind, the surname of Barney Google, who was popular at the time. But "Google" has an even longer provenance than Billy DeBeck's choice of Barney's surname. From the late 1830s on, it had appeared in many different venues. During that century a type of duck found in the upper Midwest was called a "google-nose." In border states the Adam's apple of a hog was known as "the google."

Such examples illustrate how versatile "google" is, a fun word with lots of possible uses. In many early appearances this word was used primarily for its onomatopoetic quality. Before the Civil War, a journalist in Nashville wrote of his horror at the "guttural google-google-google" sound emitted by an opera singer. In 1912, the *Krazy Kat* cartoonist George Herriman portrayed Krazy's mouse nemesis Ignatz drinking water from a bottle to the tune of "Google, google." Louis Armstrong later restored a third google when recalling that "google, google, google" was the sound a man he knew in New Orleans made when guzzling beer.

At the time this man drank his beer, Barney Google would have been prominent in the nation's funny papers. But Barney's creator Billy DeBeck wasn't responsible for adding his character's surname to our vernacular. The search for who did takes us to England, where a series of children's books by Vincent Cartwright Vickers made its debut in 1913. The title of this series' first entry, *The Google Book*, adapted a cricketer's term for balls that follow unpredictable paths: *googly* (as when a British magazine in 1907 made reference to "googlies that do not google"). *The Google Book* featured a monstrous slug-like creature called "the Google" who inhabited a pond in Googleland. At night the Google slithered out of his watery lair to hunt birds with names such as the "Lesser Nockit," the "Shiver Doodle," and the "Blue-Billed Ork."

Were Larry Page and Sergey Brin aware of this antecedent when they named their company? If they weren't at the time, they certainly were later. When these visionary cyberpreneurs began digitizing the world's library of books, the first volume they scanned was *The Google Book*.

Tom Swift Sr. and Jr.

Brin and Page weren't the only branders to find inspiration in a series of books meant for children. John Cover was another. In 1974 this onetime NASA researcher patented the technology for an electronic stun gun. What to call it? Cover's search for a name took him back to his childhood hero: Tom Swift. Swift was a geek's geek, long before that slangy term had been reassigned to techies like him. (*Geeks* originally referred to freakish carnival performers who did things like bite the heads off live chickens.)

The series of books featuring Swift kicked off in 1910 with *Tom Swift and His Motor Cycle.* During subsequent decades this inventive young man, who was adventurous as well as precocious, provided wish fulfillment for many a techie lad. Unlike more dashing heroes such as Frank Merriwell or Jack Armstrong, Tom Swift's appeal had as much to do with his ingenuity as his derring-do. Tom's many inventions included electric cars, airships, submarines, radios, and futuristic weaponry.

One book in particular made a big impression on the young John Cover: *Tom Swift and His Electric Rifle, or Daring Adventures in Elephant Land.* This 1911 novel depicted a trip to Africa by Tom Swift and a group of pals who are keen to use a weapon he'd invented that shoots charges of electricity instead of bullets. Inspired by Tom's invention, six decades later Cover called his own electric weapon "TSER" for *Tom Swift's Electric Rifle.* After members of the company he created to produce this invention got tired of having to spell out its name when answering the phone, an extraneous "A" was added to make Cover's abbreviation an acronym: TASER. (The fact that TASER rhymed with *laser,* which had been named in 1960, didn't hurt.) *TASER* went on to become not just the name of a product but a verb which, in abbreviated form, highlighted a familiar quotation from an undergraduate about to be arrested by police at the University of Florida in 2007: "Don't tase me, bro!" The *New Oxford American Dictionary* subsequently called *tase/taze* a notable word of that year.

TASER's debt to Tom Swift is well known in the world of product naming. What's less well known is the nature of the book that inspired this brand. Its young inventor has a "colored" servant named Eradicate Sampson who calls him Massa Tom. ("Heah I is, Massa Tom! Heah I is!") After reading about a big hunt of elephants in Africa, Tom decides that this could be just the way to test his electric rifle, and an airship he'd invented as well. "Elephant shooting in Africa!" he exclaims. "My! With my new electric rifle and an airship, what a fellow couldn't do in the dark continent!" Recruiting friends to join him, Tom tells them "With the price of ivory soaring, there's a chance for us all to get a lot of money."

Once in Africa, Tom and his pals are horrified by the natives they encounter there. The reddish hue of the skin of one pygmy tribe makes them resemble "little red apes." A group of taller figures whom they find hideous have "kinky hair stuck full of sticks, bones, and other odd objects." Tom is unafraid, however, confident that his electric rifle will make the natives keep their distance. He does wish Eradicate was at his side. "Maybe he could talk their language," muses Tom, "and tell them we meant no harm."

Long after Tom Swift returned from Africa, his son, Tom Swift Jr., created inventions were even more futuristic than his father's. Swift Sr.'s world was filled with radios, motorcycles, and motorboats. His son's life focused on robots, space travel, and high-tech materials. In this prescient series, Tom Jr. built artificial beings, employed solar energy to power unmanned planes, and invented ways to cope with the radiation and weightlessness that he encountered in his rocket ship *Challenger* (a name the National Aeronautics Space Administration later adopted for its Challenger program).

Deciding what to call his inventions was especially challenging for Tom. "I have a harder job naming some of these things than I do figuring them out," young Tom confessed to a pal. The results were seldom salutary. In *Tom Swift and His Giant Robot* (1954), Tom builds two huge mechanical beings to work in his father's atomic energy laboratory. One is called *Ator* because he is both atomic and robotic. The other is named *Sermek*, to reference the field of "servomechanics" (Tom's adaptation of the existing term *servomechanism*). Both of these seven-footers are coated with a heat-resistant plastic that Tom calls *tomasite*, a substance he later uses to insulate the inside and outside of his rocket ship. The robots themselves are protected from the atomic laboratory's heat by a material combining plastic and asbestos that he dubs *asbestalon*. Tom controls them from a safe distance with radio-waves from a device called a *retrotol*. None of these neologisms made it into the dictionary. On the other hand, the name of the mechanical creatures they referenced already had.

11

Naming the Future

FOLLOWING WORLD WAR I, Czech dramatist Karel Čapek wrote a play set in a future world where work is done by manufactured beings. Čapek couldn't come up with a name for these creatures, however. Striding into the studio of his older brother Josef (a prominent artist and adamant antifascist who later died in the Bergen-Belsen concentration camp), Karel moaned about his problem. Without removing the brush clenched in his teeth, Josef murmured "robot." This spontaneous coinage adapted "robota," a Czech word referring to an involuntary worker. Karel liked Josef's suggestion and gave that name to his mass-produced beings. He called the play itself, which opened in Prague in 1921, *R.U.R.* (for *Rossumovi Univerzální* or "Rossum's Universal Robots"). *R.U.R.* later enjoyed successful runs in London, New York, and elsewhere, leaving the word *robot* behind. Although Karel Čapek's humanlike creations were closer to what today we'd call androids, several generations of the mechanical kind owe their name to the Čapek brothers.

A couple of decades after the Čapeks came up with their name, work involving robots was given the name *robotics*. This term's birth is a classic example of coinage by chance. It first appeared in two stories Isaac Asimov wrote during the early 1940s. In these stories the science fiction writer referred to "robotics" without realizing that this word was his own creation. He'd just assumed this was what the emerging field of robot development was called, in the same vein as, "mechanics," "hydraulics," or "aeronautics." Only when Asimov tried to find "robotics" in a dictionary, more than a decade after his stories were published, did the author realize it was a word of his own invention. Today Isaac Asimov is considered the coiner of "robotics," including by the *OED*.

Speculative writers like Isaac Asimov and Karel Čapek have been an unusually fruitful source of terminology for the modern world. Authors of science fiction

Three "robots" in Karel Čapek's 1921 play *R.U.R.*

in particular imagine future societies with lots of conjured elements that need names. As the contemporary world catches up with their imagined versions, we continually tap neologisms that have appeared in these authors' stories to name new phenomena. Not that this was their intention, necessarily. Such writers are usually more interested in creating intriguing stories that have plausible scenarios depicted with new words than they are in getting readers to adopt those words. In many cases we have nonetheless.

Sci-Fi Semantics

The astonishing idea that not only mechanical robots but lifelike beings could be created in workshops and laboratories fueled the imagination of futuristic writers. Since no existing words other than *Frankenstein's monster* (from Mary Shelley's 1818 novel *Frankenstein*) described this type of being, authors invented their own. In 1936 Sam Fuller—later a successful movie director—published a pulpy novel about an "ectogenetic child" created by artificial insemination. Fuller called his potboiler *Test Tube Baby*. More than four decades later, that phrase went mainstream when the first child conceived by in vitro fertilization was born in 1978 (England's Louise Brown).

Fifteen years after Fuller's novel was published, sci-fi writer Jack Williamson introduced the related term *genetic engineering* in his 1951 novel *Dragon's Island*. This bland phrase referred to an ominous process that was much on our minds and in our nightmares. Four years later Jack Finney tapped into this concern in a 1955 novel he called *The Body Snatchers*. In Finney's dystopian world, sinister aliens bred exact replicas of existing humans in "pods," then replaced the original humans with their hothouse facsimiles. Finney's novel, along with film adaptations in 1956 and 1978 called *Invasion of the Body Snatchers*, contributed the catchphrase *pod person* to our conversations ("He is a real pod person"). Several decades after *The Body Snatchers* was published, the *OED* added this phrase to its lexicon, defined as "a person who is considered to be conformist, unoriginal, or emotionless, or one who lacks personality or individuality." *Pod person* was Oxford's Word of the Day for September 28, 2015.

In Connecticut a group of podlike housewives could be found in the fictional town of Stepford. When not doing housework, these women made themselves available to satisfy their husbands' sexual needs. They were featured in Ira Levin's 1972 novel *The Stepford Wives*, and in two movies based on his book (as well as forgettable sequels with names like *Revenge of the Stepford Wives*, *The Stepford Children*, and *The Stepford Husbands*). Stepford's wives turned out to be androids who were physically identical to the ones whom their husbands had murdered. Although Stepford was actually based on the town of Darien, Connecticut, Levin created its name by grafting "Step" onto the last syllable of the nearby town of Stamford. Not long after *The Stepford Wives* was published, a prophetic book reviewer in Le Mars, Iowa, predicted that "there is a certain kind of woman who, from now on, will be known as a Stepford Wife." Both Levin's novel and its spinoff films captured our imagination so vividly that not only *Stepford wife* but *Stepford* alone has become shorthand for mindless conformity: a Stepford student, a Stepford candidate, or simply "a Stepford" (as in "She's such a Stepford" or "That's so Stepford").

A scarier version of the same phenomenon but with far higher stakes involved what became known as *Manchurian Candidates*. Any time there's even a breath of suspicion that a political leader might be the pawn of a foreign power (Russia, say), this expression gets trotted out. That's because Richard Condon's 1959 novel *The Manchurian Candidate* and the 1962 movie it inspired portray a victim of Chinese brainwashing who's about to become president of the United States. Once in the White House, he will do his brainwashers' bidding.

Condon's novel wasn't the only one to tap into our mind-control anxieties. During the same year that *The Manchurian Candidate* appeared on movie screens, Anthony Burgess's 1962 novel *A Clockwork Orange* introduced a different type of futuristic meddling. In the world portrayed by this book and its 1971 film adaptation, British authorities attempt to control marauding young criminals through behavioral conditioning. (These hooligans use an argot called *Nadsat* that consists of neo-Russian words coined by Burgess.) Burgess's title still alludes to youth run amok and governmental mind manipulation. They exist in a dystopian *clockwork orange* world.

Dystopias or Cacotopias?

Although Anthony Burgess himself preferred the term *cacotopia* to *dystopia* for that type of world, the latter has won naming rights. Both derive from John Stuart Mill's 1868 observation that would-be utopians whose idealistic schemes go awry are "dys-topians, or caco-topians." Mill's concept had lots of buyers in the decades that followed as one attempt after another to create utopian societies produced despotic ones instead. At a time when fascistic and communistic versions haunted our visions of the future, authors who portrayed dystopian worlds had a receptive readership.

One such dystopia was portrayed in Aldous Huxley's 1932 novel *Brave New World*. Huxley's title (which came from a line in Shakespeare's *The Tempest*, "How beauteous mankind is! O brave new world") referred ironically to authoritarian would-be utopias. This phrase took on a life of its own as a way to describe oppressive societies that were meant to be liberated ones. In his 1958 nonfiction follow-up, *Brave New World Revisited*, Huxley said that the actual world had begun to resemble his fictionalized version far more quickly than he'd imagined it would.

Like *Brave New World*, George Orwell's 1949 novel *1984* left behind not only its title but a plethora of neologisms, portmanteaus primarily, that were central to Orwell's nightmarish world of the future. In his book's hyper-supervised society of Oceania, Thought Police fought *thoughtcrime* by monitoring and manipulating citizens' inner lives. The means they employed typically had *think* at the end, *doublethink* in particular, the ability to hold two contradictory beliefs in one's head and believe both of them, which was an essential survival skill in Oceania. *Newspeak*, Oceania's dumbed-down language, permitted only the use of politically approved words. Forbidden terms such as "liberty" and "equality" were considered relics of *oldspeak*. Orwell called the parroting of approved thoughts *duckspeak*. The common use of *speak* as an appendage to all manner of nouns is indebted to this aspect of Orwell's prophetic imagination: *doublespeak, cyberspeak, adspeak, diplospeak,* and *Bushspeak*, to name just a few.

Neo-Utopianism

A more benign world of the future was portrayed by Kurt Vonnegut. In his sci-fi-ish novel *Cat's Cradle*, Vonnegut coined the eponym *Bokononism* for the faith system propagated by a cult leader named Bokonon. (*Bokononism* later showed up as a term in Tom Robbins's novel *Another Roadside Attraction*, and in James Taylor's song "Steamroller Blues.") Bokonon's followers employed an elaborate vocabulary of words invented by the author of *Cat's Cradle*. *Foma* referred to useful lies, *sinwat* to a love-hungry individual, and *zah-mah-ki-bo* to one's destiny. The most successful of Vonnegut's quasi-theological terms was *karass*, referring to a group of people who commune on a spiritual plane. During the Aquarian Age, when a quest for that type of communion was on many minds, *karass* was on many lips.

Even more successful than *karass* was *grok*. Science fiction author Robert Heinlein coined this word for his 1961 novel *Stranger in a Strange Land*, where it appeared 195 times (suggesting that in this case the author did hope readers would adopt his neologism). Heinlein later wrote about this term, one supposedly rooted in a Martian tongue, "Grok means to understand so thoroughly that the observer becomes a part of the observed—to merge, blend, intermarry, lose identity in group experience." No word in English—not "understand," not "sympathize," not "grasp," or "get it"—has ever depicted the same degree of comprehension. That's why, more than half a century after its creation, *grok* remains alive, especially among techies such as the *TechCrunch* reviewer who told readers that a new Apple product was "complicated to grok." Rachel Maddow is also partial to Heinlein's coinage, as when she said about a military matter on her eponymous MSNBC show, "You can even grok this."

Out in Space

Thirteen years before *Stranger in a Strange Land* appeared, Robert Heinlein published a novel called *Space Cadet*. That 1948 book is largely forgotten, but its title, with a subsequent boost from a 1950–55 TV series called *Tom Corbett, Space Cadet*, lives on as a way to describe those considered spacey. They are *space cadets*.

Space itself, referring to the realm beyond our earth's atmosphere, made its debut in John Milton's epic 1667 poem *Paradise Lost*. *Outer space*, for its nether reaches, was introduced by astronomer Alexander von Humboldt in 1845. Half a century later, in H. G. Wells's 1901 novel *The First Men on the Moon*, a character observes that "to go into outer space is not so much worse, if at all, than a polar expedition." The prospect of extraterrestrial travel created new demands for related nomenclature, one filled initially by science fiction writers such as Wells and Jules Verne, who in his 1880 novel *Begum's Fortune* recoined the term *satellite* (which originally referred to human bodyguards, then to smaller planets circling larger ones) as the name of a projectile orbiting Earth. After the Soviet Union launched an earth-orbiting device called Sputnik, Verne's recoinage became the standard way to refer to this type of device. They were, and are, *satellites*, ones launched into space on what came to be known as *rocket ships*.

The term *rocket* had been around for several centuries when a *Popular Science* writer referred to "a rocket-driven 'space ship'" in 1927. Two years later, in Fritz Lang's movie *Woman in the Moon*, the launch of such a rocket-ship is preceded by an on-screen "count down" (spelled out in a title card of this silent movie). Actual spaceship launches later were preceded by such a ritual. TV announcers referred to this as the *countdown*. In time that term became figurative, used to refer to all manner of impending events that involved a degree of suspense, such as an election, or the minutes preceding New Year's Eve. Referring to the outbreak of war in Europe in 1914, historian Margaret MacMillan told an interviewer, "Once you get into a countdown situation, once people begin to think of war as likely, then it becomes that much more likely."

In English-language title cards for *Woman in the Moon*, the countdown is preceded by this comment: "The spaceship *Friede* (peace) is ready for take-off." A decade later *blast off* was introduced in Edward Elmer Smith's 1937 story "Galactic Patrol." In this story one character asks another, "How long do you figure it'll be before it's safe for us to blast off?" Smith's phrase became a standard way to describe rockets being launched into space, until one too many blew up. The National Aeronautics Space Administration (NASA) understandably came to prefer the less alarming *lift off*, and *liftoff*. ("We have liftoff!")

Space Jockeys

After it was founded in 1958, NASA faced the challenge of naming lots of new phenomena. This included its space flight program itself. In late 1958, NASA's twelve-member Space Task Group accepted the suggestion of its Director of Space Flight Programs Abe Silverstein that they call the first version Project Mercury, after the high-flying Roman god who wore winged shoes. (This group played down the fact that Mercury was associated not just with space flight but with thievery and trickery, to say nothing of already being the name of a planet, a record company, and a terrestrial vehicle produced by Ford.)

Figuring out what to call pilots manning Mercury's spaceships was more challenging. On December 1, 1958, the Task Group spent a full day brainstorming possibilities. *Space pilot* was too prosaic. *Mercury* was already taken. Other suggestions that one member scrawled on a blackboard included *spaceman*, *superman*, and, for comic relief, *man-in-a-can*. While leafing through a dictionary, another task group member found *aeronaut*. This turned the conversation to Jason and his Argonauts. The logical next step was to *astronaut*, or "sailor among the stars." Though not in the dictionary, *astronautics* was. They had their word. Not that the pilots themselves liked it. Gus Grissom hated being called an astronaut. "I'm not *ass* anything," Grissom told his fellow space jockeys. "I'm a pilot. Isn't that good enough, for chrissake?"

What no one involved realized was that this apparent neologism had appeared in a futuristic 1880 novel by British author Percy Greg called *Across the Zodiac*. Greg's sci-fi precursor anticipated challenges confronting space travelers such as extreme cold, loss of muscle tone, and food deprivation. Since his characters' spaceship needed a name, like members of NASA's Task Group eight decades later, Greg noodled with Greece's mythological Argonauts. And, like them, he combined the Greek *astro* and *nautes* to name the vehicle in which his space tourists traveled to Mars. Nearly half a century after Greg called his rocket ship *Astronaut*, the *New York Times* published an article in 1928 on "astronautics," which they defined as "the art of voyaging from star to star," calling those who took an interest in this subject *astronauts*. A year later that word made an encore appearance, now referring to actual space travelers in a 1929 *Journal of the British Astronomical Association* article. This article noted the problem of terrestrial gravitation confronting "the would-be 'Astronaut,'" Following another long nap, that term reappeared as part of NASA's glossary.

Other terms that emerged from the American space program include *splashdown*, *go-no-go*, and *soft landing*, an expression that has been repurposed as a way to refer to economic slowdowns that don't become recessions. Another expression imported from the space program is *A-OK*, the phrase members of ground control in Houston used while communicating with Project Mercury astronauts in space. NASA's public information officer Colonel John A. "Shorty" Powers— "the voice of Mercury Control"—used this saying so often that some thought he'd coined it. The fact that Powers's colleagues at ground control considered "A-OK" too Hollywood by half didn't keep it out of the American vernacular. Powers himself never claimed the expression originated with him, however, saying he got it from astronaut Alan Shepard. In fact, *A-OK* was used by aeronautical engineers and merchants long before the first Mercury flight lifted off. A 1952 advertisement for Midvac Steel was titled "A-OK for Tomorrow's Missile Demands."

Another term that made its way from NASA's offices and launching pads into everyday speech is *glitch*, referring to continual problems that delayed getting spaceships ready for lift off. In a 1962 book, John Glenn reported that he and his fellow astronauts originally used "glitch" to refer to a voltage surge, then to minor mishaps of many kinds. For a long time, NASA was thought to be the source of this apparent adaptation of the German term *glitscschig* (meaning slippery). The Austrian-born author Rudolf Flesch speculated that it came from rocket scientist Wernher Von Braun, who went from developing V2 rockets to shoot at London to working on rocket ships for the United States to launch into space. Research by etymologist Ben Zimmer and others has determined that "glitch" was in common use among radio announcers for at least a couple of decades before America's space program got underway. Actor Tony Randall told language maven William Safire that on the eve of World War II, when he and other radio announcers in Worcester, Massachusetts, read the wrong commercial or played the wrong tune, their mistake was entered on a "glitch sheet." Since Yiddish speakers were common in radio at that time, Zimmer thinks that today's *glitch* probably came from yesterday's *glitschen*, the German-derived Yiddish term for "slip."

Terrestrial Tech Talk

Not all of the terms we've adopted from the world of science fiction relate to space travel. Many are more earthly. In his 1914 novella *The World Set Free*, H. G. Wells referred to "three atomic bombs, the new bombs that would continue to explode indefinitely and which no one so far had ever seen in action." Although his prophesy about the nature of such ordnance was a bit off, Wells is the first person known to have used the phrase *atomic bomb*.

No one could beat Isaac Asimov for creating terrestrial techno-talk. *Robotics* wasn't his only contribution to our lexicon. The *OED* also credits Asimov with coining *positronic* (a fictional technology) and *psychohistory*, referring to the psychological interpretation of historical figures and events. Long before there were actual smartphones, Asimov wrote of *pocket computers* in a prescient 1957 story called "The Feeling of Power." This story depicts residents of a future world who have grown so dependent on these devices that they can't perform the most elementary calculations without pulling one from their pocket. (Asimov, who died in 1992, didn't live long enough to see his fantasy come true squared.) In "The Feeling of Power," Asimov was also an early user of the terms *programming* and *programmer*.

William Gibson is another writer who launched a techno-coinage into our lexicon via science fiction. In the early 1980s, friends of Gibson in Seattle who worked in high- tech enterprises told him about the Internet. This gave the writer a story idea involving the setting where human and artificial intelligence converges. While brainstorming names for that setting, Gibson scribbled several possibilities with a red marker on a yellow legal pad. His list included *infospace*, *data space*, and—below them—*cyberspace*. Gibson decided that this one rolled best off his tongue. In 1982 the author auditioned *cyberspace* in a story called "Burning Chrome," then featured this word in his 1984 novel *Neuromancer*. In *Neuromancer*'s pages, Gibson defines cyberspace as "a consensual hallucination experienced daily by billions of legitimate operators, in every nation, by children being taught mathematical concepts . . . A graphic representation of data abstracted from the banks of every computer in the human system. Unthinkable complexity. Lines of light ranged in the nonspace of the mind, clusters and constellations of data. Like city lights, receding." Today Gibson's coinage refers more broadly if less poetically to the electronic settings where Internet users congregate. It also is credited with inspiring the widespread use of *cyber* as a prefix. (More on this in chapter 14.)

Asimov and Gibson are only two of the many, many writers who have created words that became part of the lexicon. Those who write books, plays, and poems are among our most prolific neologizers.

12

Literary Lingo

WHILE SERVING IN World War II, Joseph Heller concluded that war was a farce in which anyone crazy enough to shirk combat was considered sane enough to fight. That became the theme of a novel he wrote several years later. Heller titled his novel *Catch-18*. Just as this book was about to be published in 1961, its editor discovered that an upcoming novel by Leon Uris was called *Mila 18*. "He had stolen our number," the editor, Robert Gottlieb, later recalled. So Gottlieb and Heller began to kick around alternative figures. *Eleven* was out, due to the recent movie *Ocean's 11*. *Fourteen* wasn't funny. *Twenty-six* lacked a certain *je ne sais quoi*. The challenge of finding a new number began to disturb Gottlieb's sleep. One night it came to him: *22*. In the morning he called Heller and said, "I've got it. It's *Catch-22*. It's funnier than 18." Heller agreed. What made 22 funnier than 18? "Who knows," Gottlieb told TV host Charles Osgood. "It just sounds funnier."

Would the title of Heller's novel have become so iconic if it had been called *Catch-18*? Or *Catch-14*? Or *Catch-26*? Certainly those versions sound discordant to ears accustomed to *Catch-22*. Although there are other ways to describe para-doxical experiences—a *no-win situation*; a *double bind*; *damned if you do, damned if you don't*—"Catch-22" is the idiom we use most often. Whom should we credit with coining that concept? Heller? Gottlieb? Both? Call it a co-coinage.

Some of our most useful terms have emerged from the pens and keyboards of authors such as Joseph Heller. Heller's fellow World War II veteran Norman Mailer is another one. Like Heller, Mailer based a first novel on his combat experience: *The Naked and the Dead* (1948). Anticipating censorship, Mailer used the word *fug* in lieu of "fuck" several hundred times in his manuscript. This coinage attracted lots of attention, due partly to a popular anecdote in which the actress Tallulah Bankhead said when meeting Mailer, "So you're the author who doesn't know how to spell 'fuck,'" (Bankhead's biographer and Mailer himself denied that this ever happened. Mailer—who insisted that what Bankhead actually said when greeting him was "Hello"—thought the racier version, which appeared in an April 1950 column called "Edith Gwynn's Hollywood," originated with her press agent.) For some time after *The Naked and the Dead*'s publication, *fug* was our preferred euphemism for fuck, before giving way to "frig," "frick," and "freak" (*friggin', frickin', freakin'*). During the Aquarian Age a rock group called themselves the Fugs.

Factoid was Norman Mailer's other contribution to the postwar lexicon. This coinage first appeared in his 1973 biography of Marilyn Monroe, where Mailer defined it as "facts which have no existence before appearing in a magazine or newspaper." Although *factoid* proved to be an unusually successful neologism, along the way it took on a meaning quite different than the one its coiner had intended. Rather than the subtle, supple notion Mailer had in mind, one that anticipated the era of "alternative facts," over time *factoid* came to refer simply to meager pieces of information.

The fact that authors like Norman Mailer have contributed more than their share of neologisms to the world's word pool is due not only to their hunger for recognition but to the very nature of authorship. As creative users of language, how could they not have a yen to create new terms? Writers who can't come up with the right word to describe something feel no compunction about simply coining a new one.

Miltonisms

John Milton certainly didn't. After diligent scouring of the *OED*, Milton scholar Gavin Alexander of Cambridge University has concluded that the seventeenth-century poet added more than six hundred words to the English language. Alexander's list includes *advantage, complacency, damp, dismissive, fragrance, jubilant, obtrusive, padlock*, and *terrific*. He is just one of many scholars who admire this poet's verbal virtuosity. Creating playlists of Miltonisms seems to be an integral part of assessing his work. A book about Milton by Logan Pearsall Smith featured the author's own favorites: *bannered, liturgical, echoing*, and *Satanic*. In *The Miracle of Language*, Richard Lederer includes on his list *infinitude, all-conquering, smooth shaven*, and *light fantastic*. *Authorisms* author Paul Dickson, who considers John Milton his favorite author-neologizer, told an interviewer that he particularly admires such Miltonisms as *impassive, earthshaking, sectarian*, and *dimensionless*, along with phrases such as *all hell broke loose* and *by hook or by crook*.

Milton lived in a time when the English language was mushrooming, along with scientific and other discoveries. This invited writers to fill gaps in the lexicon with words of their own creation. They did so in diverse ways.

When composing his poetry, writes Logan Pearsall Smith, Milton tapped multiple sources "from old archaic words to the new words he created for himself out of the rags and fragments found in their recesses." Gavin Alexander believes that the freedom Milton felt to tinker with language lay in his commitment to political, religious, and personal liberty. One might also speculate that the poet's blindness (Milton couldn't see for the last two decades of his life, including the period when he dictated all ten volumes of *Paradise Lost* to his daughters and various secretaries) could have contributed to his verbal prowess. Perhaps the imagination called for by a writer who can't easily look up existing words encouraged him to create new ones.

Because the puritanical poet couldn't find a word he considered strong enough to condemn those who engaged in licentious behavior, Milton invented two of his own: *debauchery* and *depravity*. In need of a term for what's perceived through the senses without bringing sex to mind, Milton coined *sensuous* (only to have that word take on erotic overtones anyway). *Love-lorn*—Milton's word for being forsaken by a lover—has also developed a different meaning. So has *terrific*, which Milton used in *Paradise Lost* to mean "terrifying," and *unoriginal* which he created for that epic poem, to refer to being of unknown origin.

According to Gavin Alexander, Milton used several strategies when coining words such as these. One strategy consisted of reformulating existing words (*stunning, space*). Another involved making one word out of two (*self-delusion, arch-fiend*). And—in a strategy Milton relied on for more than a hundred of his neologisms—converting neutral old words into negative new ones by the addition of a prefix: *unprincipled, unaccountable, unintended,* and *irresponsible*. In one case, adding a prefix to a word of his own invention allowed Milton to score a neological twofer: first coining *obtrusive*, then doubling up with *unobtrusive*.

Although many of Milton's neologisms were created by tinkering with existing terms, his most notable contribution to the lexicon was original, if inadvertent. In *Paradise Lost*, Milton called Satan's headquarters *Pandemonium*. This term combined the Greek *pan*, or "all," with the Latin *daemonium*, which referred to demonic spirits. With its first letter lowercased, Milton's name for the devil's chaotic lair left its name behind to refer to a state of chaos in general. In other cases, terms we still use are based on names of fictional characters, and one in particular.

Eponymish Characters

In a book about Miguel de Cervantes's novel *The Ingenious Gentleman Don Quixote of La Mancha*, Amherst College professor Ilan Stavans noted what he called "a single, shocking fact." This fact was that "in all of the western canon, no other novelistic character has ever been adjectivized." Say what? Certainly *quixotic* is a classic case of a fictional character whose name became the basis of an adjective. But the *only* one? Nearly a century before Cervantes's 1605/1615 novel appeared in two parts, François Rabelais's satiric epic *The Life of Gargantua and Pantagruel* (1535) featured a giant and his son whose name inspired the term *gargantuan*. And how about *Faustian*? *Oedipal*? *Gatsbyesque*? To name just a few.

Then there's *Pollyannaish*, referencing the 1913 novel *Pollyanna* whose eleven-year-old protagonist always finds "something to be glad about." In this she resembles *Candide*. Voltaire's 1759 novel by that title features a young man who pursues the philosophy of his mentor Dr. Pangloss, a character based on the German philosopher Gottfried Wilhelm Leibniz whose credo was "All is for the best in this best of all possible worlds." Thus *Panglossian*. And how about the irrepressible clerk Mr. Micawber in Charles Dickens's *David Copperfield* who is ever hopeful that something will "turn up." This type of blind optimism is sometimes referred to as *Micawberesque*.

Dickensian

The works of Charles Dickens feature a treasure trove of characters whose names inspired enduring eponyms. *Micawberesque* is only one. *Scroogish* rivals *quixotic* as a widely used adjective based on an author's name-creation, that of mean and miserly Ebenezer Scrooge in *A Christmas Carol*. *Pecksniffian* has come to describe the type of unctuous hypocrisy displayed by Seth Pecksniff in *Martin Chuzzlewitt*.

But eponyms were not Dickens's only contribution to the English lexicon. He also was an inventive and prolific creator of new words. After years of sniffing out the many neologisms in his work, Knud Sørensen published *Charles Dickens: Linguistic Innovator*. In this 1985 book Sørensen concluded that Dickens was "a large-scale contributor to the vocabulary of English." His close reading of Dickens's canon found some 1059 neologisms in the author's fiction, essays, and letters.

During the years since Sørensen's book was published, diligent etymologists have repeatedly found earlier use of new words once attributed to Dickens. After scouring old publications in the British Library, Michael Quinion discovered how many terms once thought to have originated with Dickens actually predated him. Quinion's list, posted on his *World Wide Words* website, includes *boredom*, *rampage*, *butter-fingers*, *confusingly*, *footlights*, *dustbin*, *squashed*, *spectacularly*, and *tousled* (as *touzled*).

Butterfingers—which Dickens included in *The Pickwick Papers* as *butter-fingers*, referring to a clumsy athlete—had been used more than two centuries earlier (in Gervase Markham's 1615 handbook for housewives who were warned that they "must not be butter-fingered"). Because in *Sketches by Boz* Dickens wrote "put the kye-bosk on her," the author was long thought to have been the source of *kibosh*. Much controversy surrounds this attribution, however, with many other contenders being noted, dating back to at least 1830. In etymologist Anatoly Liberman's droll conclusion, "The number of fanciful etymologies of *kibosh* is rather great."

Although modern search techniques have substantially reduced the size of Dickens's confirmed neologisms, quite a few examples of original word use can nonetheless be found in his writing. According to the *OED*, of 9229 quotations from Dickens's work that appear on their pages, 213 provide evidence of a new word. In his 2011 biography *Becoming Dickens*, Robert Douglas-Fairhurst concluded that without Charles Dickens's many contributions, "the English language would quietly contract, losing more than two hundred words and phrases Dickens brought into print for the first time." *The Oxford Companion to Charles Dickens* concurs. "It is rarely easy to tell if a particular neologism registers an authentic Dickensian coinage or just Dickens's ever-alert ear," they concede, "but in any case—and as in the case of Shakespeare—he exhibits a marvelous facility for being the first to publicize an abundance of striking words and phrases."

Some Dickensisms that Michael Quinion couldn't find in earlier use include *sawbones, whiz-bang, messiness,* and *seediness*. Dickens was the first to use *common* synonymously with vulgar, and *dim* for someone who wasn't too bright. From the theatrical world he borrowed *gag, patter,* and *mug* as a verb. Another verb that came from that world was *make-up*, which became today's noun *makeup* (after Max Factor, in 1920, began to refer to his line of cosmetics as "make-up").

In *Great Expectations* Dickens introduced *doormat* for someone on whom others figuratively wipe their boots. ("She asked me and Joe whether we supposed she was door-mats under our feet.") *David Copperfield* included a passage in which Dickens talked of a woman experiencing *the creeps* ("a visitation in her back which she called 'the creeps'"). *Impossibly, depreciation, aquatic,* and *preventible* (so spelled) also showed up in that novel.

Dickens's childhood love of wordplay survived into adulthood, as when he referred to killing off Little Nell in *The Old Curiosity Shop* as *Nellicide*. *Spoffish* was a term Dickens used in *Sketches by Boz* for a fussy, officious person ("A little spoffish man entered the room"). *Red tapeworm* was his name for an official who adheres slavishly to rules and regulations. In *The Pickwick Papers* the author called a tired person *confoozled*. Someone who over-exclaimed was *ponging*, a piece of slang he borrowed from the theater. Stage prompters to him were *prompterians*. While boating on a lake he might become *sea-sicky*. *Touch-me-not-ishness* was another Dickensism-among-friends. So was *ravenless*, which was Dickens's word for his status after a pet raven died (one he later used in a preface to *Barnaby Rudge*). The author once asked a correspondent who had a black eye, "Did you take it naturally or bacchanalially?" In another letter he wondered if a friend would be drinking port "metropolitaneously," a Dickensism that the *OED* defines as "in metropolitan fashion."

Dickens was fond of converting nouns into adjectives this way, as when he grafted the suffix *-less* onto "care" for *careless*, and created *penniless* from that suffix and *penny*. Less useful were *nephewless, conversationless, fireworkless, pastureless*, and *theatreless*. Other Dickensisms reflected his penchant for creating new words from old ones by appending a *y*. These included lots of self-conscious terms such as *walnut-shelly, pepper-corny, ginger-beery, hearth-broomy, sawdusty, touch-woody*, and *Shakespearianly*. More promising were *fluffy, fruity, frivolity, fearfully, shaky*, and *specialty*. By effective use of the prefix *-un* Dickens gave us *unchangeable, unapproachable*, and *unholy*. Adding the suffix *-al* to "arrive" and "aspiration" produced *arrival* and *aspirational*.

Appending clauses wasn't Dickens's only word-creation technique. In some cases he subtracted them, as when his deletion of "ulent" from "fraudulent" led to *fraud* (with reference to an impostor). More often Dickens expanded rather than contracted, however, commonly creating one word from two (well before Lewis Carroll called such compound terms *portmanteaus*). These Dickensisms included *bodyguard, coffee-shop, featherweight, hothouse*, and *postscript*.

Irving Once More

Dickens didn't just coin neologisms of his own but expressed appreciation for ones introduced by others. Among them was *logocracy*, an obscure term revived and popularized by Washington Irving (adapting the Greek *logos*, for "words," to characterize a political system based on speechmaking and proclamations).

Irving fertilized the English language with multiple new terms. His *History of New York* didn't just add *Knickerbocker* to our storehouse of words but introduced terms such as *bush-whacker, doughnut*, and *stenographer*. In an 1806 letter, Irving Anglicized the Dutch *baas*, or "master," into *boss*. ("I had to return, make an awkward apology to boss, and look like a nincompoop.") His 1836 story "The Creole Village" included the phrase *almighty dollar*. When that story was republished two decades later, the author added a footnote in which he begged forgiveness for giving offense with his coinage. "This phrase," he wrote, "used for the first time in this sketch, has since passed into current circulation, and by some has been questioned as savoring of irreverence. The author, therefore, owes it to his orthodoxy to declare that no irreverence was intended even to the dollar itself, which he is aware is daily becoming more and more an object of worship."

Like Dickens, Twain, and countless colleagues, Irving didn't just use new words and phrases of his own invention but publicized ones he'd come across in his travels. Among them were *sierra, side line, mountaineer, lariat, caballero*, and *cigarillo*. While touring the western frontier during the early 1830s, Irving heard Virginia expats talk of "Lynch's Law." This referred to the drumhead trials of suspected criminals named after Colonel Charles Lynch, a magistrate back home who was notorious for subjecting Tories to extralegal proceedings during the Revolutionary War. In a published account of his western odyssey, Irving said of *Lynch's Law*, "as it is technically termed . . . the plaintiff is apt to be witness jury, judge, and executioner, and the defendant to be convicted and punished on mere presumption."

Kipling

All told, among the 2603 quotations from Washington Irving that can be found in the *OED*, 45 include what they call "first evidence" of a word. Another author on *OED*'s list of prolific word introducers is Rudyard Kipling, the source of 140 first uses of a word among 3134 quotations by him that are included in this dictionary. One such term appeared in a 1904 story by Kipling called "The Army of a Dream." This saga portrayed a fantasy world in which military service is universal and well regarded. At that time, "vet" as a verb referred to the inspection of animals by veterinarians. Such animals were *vetted*. The dream of Kipling's narrator featured a group of unlikely looking recruits assembled on the grounds of a riding school. Responding to a visitor's quizzical look, the soldier who is about to drill these novices assures him, "They've been vetted, an' we're putting 'em through their paces." (In Bertha Croker's 1898 novel *Peggy of the Bartons*, a British military officer says the wives of other officers will "vet" his own wife, suggesting that this recoinage was already military slang when Kipling used it.)

Many of Kipling's contributions to the vernacular drew on his familiarity with military palaver: *bite the bullet*, *hell-for-leather*, and *gadget*, an obscure naval term (also spelled "gadjet") that he escorted into broader usage when referring to "steam gadgets."

Kipling's reference to *traffic lights* in a 1912 story is the first known use of that term (although he used it for signals used to guide aircraft). And long before Dr. Seuss's Grinch began to rival Dickens's Scrooge as a vile Christmas denier, Kipling wrote, "It's woe to bend the stubborn back / Above the grinching quern." According to the *OED*, "grinching," as Kipling used the term, means "to make a harsh grating noise" and could derive from the French verb *grincer* ("to grate, creek, screech").

Kipling's most successful transplant of all occurred when he helped create an eponym based on a character in *Trilby*, an 1894 novel written by the *Punch* cartoonist George du Maurier, wearing his second hat as a writer of fiction (and inadvertently giving us his book's title as the name of narrow-brimmed men's chapeau). Du Maurier's novel featured an Austrian music teacher named Svengali whose magnetic personality helped the book's heroine, Trilby O'Ferrall, win acclaim as a singer. The first known appearance of this name alluding to a disreputable guru came two decades after du Maurier's novel was published, in a 1914 story by Kipling that included a dog named Zvengali. According to the *OED*, Zvengali has a "mesmeric" gaze (referencing eighteenth-century German physician Franz Anton Mesmer who promoted the healing powers of hypnotism).

Kipling gave erotic overtones to the innocuous noun *it* when, in a 1904 short story, he used this two-letter word to refer to a woman with sex appeal ("'Tisn't beauty, so to speak, nor good talk necessarily. It's just *it*. Some women'll stay in a man's memory if they once walked down the street.") The author's racy reassignment reappeared in 1927 as the title of *It*, a novella by Elinor Glyn, and the movie inspired by her book. *It* then was applied to that movie's sultry star, Clara Bow, who became known as "the it girl." Although this phrase faded along with Bow's career, it seems to have made a comeback in the new millennia as many a sultry young actress is again referred to as an "it girl."

Although Rudyard Kipling's main contribution to the English language was as a recoiner, redefiner, escort, transplanter, and popularizer of existing terms, as well as a borrower of words from other languages, along the way the author

Trilby and Svengali played by Marian Marsh and John Barrymore in the 1931 movie *Svengali*.

introduced some original usage of his own. In *Plain Tales from the Hills* (1888), Kipling referred to the "penny-farthing attempts" of an unhappy woman to hide her misery, then of "penny-farthing yarns." *Penny farthing*—1.25 cents—thereafter alluded to woebegone, futile efforts.

An 1892 article by Kipling that appeared in the *London Times* paid tribute to those bold enough to leave the comforts of home and venture abroad. His article was titled "Our Overseas Men." Within its text Kipling said he'd considered writing a book about the breed titled *The Book of the Overseas Club*. According to the *OED* this is the first known use of *overseas* to refer to distant lands across a body of water. Kipling's 1901 novel *Kim* called "down-country men who talked too much" *slack-jawed*. In the same book he referred to "the grass-roots of Evil," the earliest known use of that horticultural term in a figurative sense.

Kipling's 1902 collection of *Just So Stories for Little Children* compiled yarns that dealt with fanciful origins of natural phenomena. In "How the Rhinoceros Got His Skin" he mentioned "the squiggly things on the Parsee's hat," referring to sunrays reflecting off this holy man's headgear. Kipling's adaptation of the existing word *squiggle* (which also appears in the collection) is its first known use as an adjective. *Just-so stories* itself has become an expression scientists use to mock theories that aren't confirmed by evidence.

Not long before he died in 1935, Kipling used "old school tie" as a figurative reference to the apparel, attitudes, and attachments of a certain type of boarding school graduate, leaving that allusion behind in our language.

Kipling's most notable verbal creation was an unfortunate one: *the white man's burden*. This was what he called an 1899 poem that urged the United States to colonize the Philippines. After it appeared in many American newspapers, "The White Man's Burden: The United States and the Philippine Islands" won much acclaim. Theodore Roosevelt considered Kipling's poem bad verse but good policy for U.S. colonial ventures (especially ones in South America).

From Banana Republic *to* Bababadalgharaghtakamminarronnkonnbronntonnerronntuonnthunntrovarrhounawnskawntoohoohoordenenthurnuk

Three years before the publication of Kipling's poem, William Sydney Porter was arrested for embezzling funds from a bank in Austin, Texas. After being released on bail in 1896, Porter fled to Honduras. There, under the pen name O. Henry, the onetime bank clerk wrote a collection of linked stories that was published in

1904 as *Cabbages and Kings* (some of whose content had appeared in magazines two years earlier). Those sagas were set in "Anchuria," a Central American country that resembled Honduras. At the time O. Henry wrote his tales, Honduras's economy was based on bananas. The American companies that grew most of them dominated this country's society and politics. Perforce O. Henry's stories were banana-centric, including continual references to bananas, banana groves, and "banana towns." At one point the author called Anchuria "a small, maritime banana republic." Later he referred to "that banana republic, Anchuria." In time *banana republic* became an enduring way to depict dysfunctional countries (to say nothing of the name of a clothier founded in 1978).*

O. Henry wasn't the only author to leave behind a coinage he'd used in passing. The determined neologizer James Joyce did too. Joyce's works brim with words of his own creation. (Some Joyceans call his passion for coining words "neologeewhiz.") *Ulysses* alone features dozens of terms invented by its author. They include *mrkgnao, diambulist, poppysmick, bullockbefriending, soliloquacity,* and *yogibogeybox*. In *Dubliners* he called being ultra-drunk *peloothered*. The many coinages in *Finnegan's Wake* include not just *quark* but the punny *doublin, pelurious* for hairiness, and—most notably—a word meant to refer onomatopoeically to the sound of an unusually loud thunderclap: *bababadalgharaghtakamminarronnkonnbronntonnerronntuonnthunntrovarrhounawnskawntoohoohoordenenthurnuk.*

For all of his determined coining of new words, Joyce's best contribution to everyday speech was an existing term that he gave a new spin: *epiphany*. In classic Greek this term referred to the appearance of a divinity. In *Stephen Hero*, an autobiographical novel that Joyce wrote in the early 1900s, the author used *epiphany* to refer to an insight prompted by a seemingly minor event. Within that unpublished manuscript, Joyce wrote about the ripple effect of an inconsequential conversation whose consequences lead the author's doppelganger, Stephen Dedalus, to realize that "it was for the man of letters to record these epiphanies with extreme care, seeing that they themselves are the most delicate and evanescent of moments." Later Dedalus said facetiously to a friend that a clock "has not epiphanised yet."

---

* Etymologist Pascal Tréguer has found a December 1, 1901, reference to "banana republics" in a Chicago newspaper. Of course that would follow O. Henry's actual writing of stories incorporating this phrase, which were published in December 1901 and January 1902. This suggests either that *banana republic* was already in use when the author used this phrase in his stories, or that it was he who the newspaper referenced when referring to Latin America's " 'banana republics,' as they are sometimes called."

As with *epiphany*, authors' biggest neological contributions to the vernacular commonly consist of terms that didn't look like *OED* candidates at time of their birth. When Gertrude Stein wrote about her hometown of Oakland "there's no there" (in *Everybody's Autobiography,* 1937), how likely did it seem that that this tautology would become such a common and enduring catchphrase?

Nearly four decades later, in *How the Good Guys Finally Won,* a 1975 book about House Speaker Tip O'Neill's role in getting President Richard Nixon to resign, Jimmy Breslin concluded that political power was based primarily on "mirrors and blue smoke," a phrase he used repeatedly in his book. Shortly after it was published, the *Lowell* (Massachusetts) *Sun* inverted Breslin's wording by referring to "blue smoke and mirrors." In general usage, "blue" soon disappeared and has stayed out of sight. (Pascal Tréguer found a September 1976 comment by Louisiana senator John Johnston about a political proposal that he hoped was substantive, "not just smoke and mirrors.") What remained constitutes one of our most popular catchphrases: *smoke and mirrors.*

Title Talk

The title of an earlier book by Jimmy Breslin inspired another oft-repeated catchphrase. That 1969 novel was called *The Gang That Couldn't Shoot Straight.* Nearly half a century later, an American official said opposition figures in Venezuela constituted a "gang that cannot shoot straight." Before then Rhode Island governor Lincoln Chafee was charged with running a "can't-shoot-straight administration." Breslin's title also provided the basis for a popular mix 'n' match catchphrase, as in the title of a 2006 book *The Gang That Wouldn't Write Straight,* or a 2018 *New York Times* column by Paul Krugman headlined "The Gang That Couldn't Think Straight." Many another book's title has provided similar fill-in-the-blank catchphrases such as *Zen and the Art of____; Fear and Loathing____; Happiness is____*; and *Slouching Toward____.*

In other cases, one clause from a word in a book's title will be taped onto another word to create a new one. Stephen Potter's 1947 treatise *The Theory and Practice of Gamesmanship* didn't just promote the idea of "gaming" situations but inspired tortured mashups such as *grantsmanship, namesmanship,* and *conference-manship.* (*Oneupmanship,* which made a cameo appearance in Potter's book, was already in play.) The most enduring adaptation of Potter's title-word grew out of a 1956 observation by then-secretary of state John Foster Dulles. "The ability to get to the verge without getting into the war is the necessary art," said Dulles in an interview. "If you cannot master it, you inevitably get into war. If you try to run away from it, if you are scared to go to the brink, you are lost." Not long after Dulles touted going to the brink, Adlai Stevenson accused him of "boasting of his brinkmanship, . . . the art of bringing us to the edge of the nuclear abyss." This is the first known use of *brinkmanship*, but hardly the last. When nuclear powers India and Pakistan mass troops and scramble planes during their never-ending conflict over Kashmir, the term *brinksmanship* is used routinely in news coverage.

Then there's whispering. How many "whisperers" have we heard about in the wake of Nicholas Evans's 1995 bestseller *The Horse Whisperer*? Evans's word for trainers who can gently calm skittish horses is not popular in their own ranks. Most prefer "gentler." But *whisperer* has better resonance, and far more versatility. It isn't just Cesar Millan the *dog whisperer* who adopted this word but Tracy Hogg the *baby whisperer* and chef Jeremy Fox who's been called the *vegetable whisperer* (as well as sundry *trout whisperers, tortoise whisperers, tech whisperers,* and *history whisperers*). In Portland, Oregon, a renowned brewmaster is known as a *hop whisperer.*

Although book titles are a rich source of words and phrases, we don't necessarily realize the genesis of these contributions to our discourse. November 24, 1859, was a significant day in this regard. That was when two books of note were published. One was Charles Darwin's *On the Origin of Species.* The other, by a Scotsman named Samuel Smiles, was a paean to self-reliance titled *Self-Help* (an existing but obscure phrase). Darwin himself was among the hundreds of thousands of readers who made *Self-Help* a runaway bestseller. Within a year, reference was being made to "the 'self-help' genre." Over time, the title of Smiles's book became an enduring way to describe that genre, and the type of popular psychology it propagated.

Quite a few titles of pop psychology books have inspired common nomenclature. The birthplace of such terms isn't necessarily apparent to those who use them, however. When George W. Bush called attempts to analyze him as competitive with his father "a typical psychobabble," it would surprise me if the forty-third president realized where that term came from, any more than his brother Jeb would have when he bemoaned the "psycho babble" inflicted on their family. *Psychobabble* first appeared in a 1975 *Boston Phoenix* book review written by journalist R. D. Rosen, then as the title of a *New Times* cover story that Rosen published in the same year. This article was a biting sendup of the touching and feeling and primal screaming of that era, along with its attendant jargon. Two years later Rosen expanded his article into a 1977 book with the same title. It quickly became part of everyday discourse. As the tide of self-helpish programs swelled, ones that incorporated lots of jargony verbiage, *psychobabble* was a word we needed, and still need. So does Rosen get credit for coining this very useful term? Very seldom. More often than he cares to admit, when others use *psychobabble* while chatting with him, Rosen can't resist saying, " 'You know, I invented that term.' "

"It's a claim that's usually, and understandably, met with disbelief," he says. This makes Rosen feel as though his own child has been adopted without his consent. "The life of a word inventor isn't easy," he sighs, adding, "That's the last word I ever invent."

Rosen has also noted how much less success *Psychobabble* has enjoyed as a book than its title has as a word. Not the least reason so many titles become part of common parlance is that one needn't actually read a book with an evocative title to add all or part of it to one's vocabulary. A short list includes *Flow, Doublespeak, Moneyball, Aerobics, Parkinson's Law, The Peter Principle, Other People's Money, Future Shock, Sophie's Choice, The Exurbanites, The Killing Fields*, and my own book *The Post-Truth Era*. Far more people are aware of these titles than have read the books they titled. You don't have to wade through Alexander Solzhenitsyn's hefty novel *The Gulag Archipelago* to be able to call Soviet labor camps *gulags*. A *blackboard jungle* refers to a dicey inner city school even among those who don't know that Evan Hunter published a novel by this title in 1954 (that became a popular 1955 movie with the same title), and a *last hurrah* is commonly used for a final attempt to do something, as seventy-two-year-old Frank Skeffington did when running for one last term as mayor of a Boston-like city in Edwin O'Connor's 1956 bestseller *The Last Hurrah*. The title of William Lederer and Eugene Burdick's 1958 novel *The Ugly American* has become shorthand for boorish Yanks who try to impose their values on native cultures. They're *ugly*

Still from 1955 movie *The Blackboard Jungle*.

Americans. (Ironically, the novel's title refers to the physical homeliness of protagonist Homer Atkins, not his arrogance. This American engineer is actually compassionate toward the residents of a mythical Southeast Asian country whom he tries to help.)

In such cases, title-based terms can take on lives independent of the books on whose cover they appeared. Some, like O'Connor's, even merit an entry in the dictionary. Merriam-Webster defines *last hurrah* as "a final often valedictory effort, production, or appearance." To Merriam, *Catch-22* is "a problematic situation for which the only solution is denied by a circumstance inherent in the problem or by a rule." *Psychobabble*, says Merriam-Webster, is "a predominantly metaphorical language for expressing one's feelings."

But it isn't just book titles like these that become part of the lexicon. Nor are they limited to ones created by mainstream authors. Any number of scholarly books have also been the source of everyday neologisms that appeared in their title, and in their text as well.

13

Ivy-Covered Words

LIKE SO MANY authors, Harvard sociologist Robert Putnam confronted the challenge of coming up with a compelling title for a book he was writing. This book was about declining participation in organizations such as the Rotary, Lions, and League of Women Voters. How could the essence of that decline be captured in a few words? Putnam might have stuck to the standard academic template with a title such as *Civic Anomie: Concepts and Consequences*, but didn't want to. While mulling alternatives, the sociologist ran into a friend who owned a bowling alley. As they discussed Putnam's project, his friend said, "Gosh, Bob, you don't know it but you've stumbled on to the major economic problem facing my industry, because although more Americans are bowling than ever before— bowling leagues, bowling in teams—is off by about sixty percent." Putnam realized immediately that this trend captured in one vivid image the broader syndrome he was trying to portray: bowlers were *bowling alone*.

That's what Putnam called an essay on declining engagement in social groups and the book that followed. His evocative phrase became the well-known title of a little-read book. (Putnam's dense 414-page volume with its many statistics, graphs, and charts along with a hundred pages of addenda and notes, is a tough slog.) Soon after *Bowling Alone* appeared in 2000, its title became shorthand for the type of social isolation Putnam wrote about, as when a *New York Times* essayist alluded to "the decline in civic engagement and social contact known as the 'bowling alone' problem."

Like *bowling alone*, many words and phrases that we use every day originated with members of the academy. A sampling includes *midlife crisis* (Elliott Jaques), *generation gap* (James Coleman), *alpha male* (Rudolph Schenkel), *male bonding* (Lionel Tiger), *personal space* (Robert Sommer), *double bind* (Gregory Bateson), *zero-sum game* (John von Neumann and Oskar Morgenstern), and *broken windows* (James Wilson and George Kelling).

Breaking Windows

The closing decades of the twentieth century were a time of high anxiety about crime in the United States. Americans concerned about being able to walk their streets without getting mugged or to live in homes without fear of being invaded were receptive to proposals for cracking down on criminals. In 1982 political scientist James Q. Wilson and criminologist George L. Kelling made such a proposal. Their long *Atlantic Monthly* article titled "Broken Windows" argued that even petty disorder could lead to serious lawbreaking. A single broken window in a house or building that was left unrepaired, Wilson and Kelling contended, led quickly to other windows being broken in the same structure, then to an increasing sense of disarray. "Window-breaking does not necessarily occur on a large scale because some areas are inhabited by determined window-breakers," they wrote, "whereas others are populated by window-lovers; rather, one unrepaired broken window is a signal that no one cares, and so breaking more windows costs nothing. (It has always been fun.)"

This article caused a sensation. Like "bowling alone," *broken windows* provided a vivid image for a broader perception of social breakdown. To the coauthors who put them on our political agenda, unrepaired windows, graffiti, panhandling, drunkenness, prostitution, and drug use needed to be addressed holistically as part of what they called "order maintenance." This strategy was embraced by big city mayors such as New York's Rudy Giuliani and Michael Bloomberg, who used it as a pretext for flooding high-crime neighborhoods with police officers using tactics such as "stop-and-frisk." Crime rates dropped dramatically in cities that adopted broken-windows law enforcement strategies, but they also dropped dramatically in cities that didn't. On balance, the methods inspired by Wilson and Kelling's 1982 article were at best a wash, at worst a license to harass residents of high-crime areas who'd given no indication that they were breaking the law.

After James Wilson died in 2012, George Kelling himself grew disturbed by the misapplication of their approach to law enforcement. "I wonder if we should back away from the metaphor of broken windows," Kelling told NPR's Shankar Vedantam in late 2016, thirty-four years after the publication of the *Atlantic* article that inspired this metaphor. "We didn't know how powerful it was going to be. It simplified, it was easy to communicate, a lot of people got it as a result of the metaphor. It was attractive for a long time. But as you know, metaphors can wear out and become stale."

A few years after *broken windows* joined the national conversation, another political scientist published an article with a similar impact and arc. In 1995 Princeton professor John Dilulio warned that a wave of unusually violent young criminals was about to crash on our shores. *Super-predators*, Dilulio called them, "the youngest, biggest and baddest generation any society has ever known." This group would soon fill our jails, he predicted, with a type of criminal "who is so impulsive, so remorseless, that he can kill, rape, maim, without giving it a second thought."

Dilulio's article—which appeared in the *Weekly Standard*—was filled with hair-raising forecasts. "Young offenders have been committing more homicides, robberies, and other crimes against adults," he wrote. "There is even some evidence that juveniles are doing homicidal violence in 'wolf packs.'" These super-predators included "boys whose voices have yet to change. We're talking about elementary school youngsters who pack guns instead of lunches. We're talking about kids who have absolutely no respect for human life and no sense of the future. In short, we're talking big trouble that hasn't yet begun to crest." What was worse, the forty million Americans under ten would soon become an adolescent cohort filled with crime-addicted teenagers that was both larger and more vicious than the ones before it. "By my estimate," Dilulio concluded, "we will probably need to incarcerate at least 150,000 juvenile criminals in the years just ahead. In deference to public safety, we will have little choice but to pursue genuine get-tough law-enforcement strategies against the super-predators."

Dilulio's dire warning with its ominous coinage caught the attention of a public still jittery about crime. It certainly impressed Hillary Clinton, who referred to "the kinds of kids that are called superpredators" in a 1996 speech. This notion played an instrumental role in a push to try juvenile offenders as adults, then sentence those convicted to long prison terms, including life without parole. The specter of hordes of *superpredators* terrorizing our communities helped produce decades of get-tough legislation that led to an era of mass incarceration, one that disproportionately affected African Americans.

Dilulio's forecast didn't materialize, however. Quite the opposite. Soon after he issued his jeremiad, the numbers of young lawbreakers began to decline. Five years after Dilulio's article appeared, juvenile crime rates fell by half. Homicides by minors dropped to 1985 rates. A decade later, murders committed by ten- to seventeen-year-olds had been reduced by two-thirds. Dilulio, a devout Catholic, then had what he called an epiphany, one that led him to believe society might be served better by preventing crime than by punishing criminals. He therefore spent years trying to renounce his dire warning and reverse the policies it had helped enact. When the U.S. Supreme Court considered a case that challenged trying minors as adults, Dilulio submitted an amicus brief opposing this practice. In it he and a coauthor admitted that "the predictions by the proponents of the juvenile superpredator myth" were simply wrong.

Although more powerful in its impact, *superpredator* was just one of many neologisms with academic roots that became part of public discourse. The setting where such terms are incubated may be dry, but their origin stories can be intriguing. Scholarly terms don't all originate within ivy-covered walls, of course. One venerable concept that transcended those walls was actually hatched in a Norwegian chicken coop.

Keeping Order

At a home his family rented outside Oslo in the early twentieth century, six-year old Thorleif Schjelderup-Ebbe became fascinated by the interaction among a flock of chickens on the property. What initially seemed like random milling about proved to be a dance of dominance. Thorleif paid particular attention to the way these hens used pecks of their beaks to determine who stood where on the status ladder. Years later, as a university student in zoology, Schjelderup-Ebbe retrieved the notes he'd taken about those chickens and wrote them up in a 1922 paper on the status hierarchy among a group of hens. The Norwegian called it *Hackliste*, a German term later translated as *the peck order*. Three years after Schjelderup-Ebbe's paper appeared, this term was adapted in a book by the German zoologist Friedrich Alverdes as *Hackordnung*. Alverdes's version was translated as "pecking order" in an English edition of his book. This translation informed readers that "'pecking orders' give the society concerned a certain degree of organization." It didn't take long for this concept to be applied to humans as well as hens. Aldous Huxley's 1928 novel *Point Counter Point* featured a man who plans to write a book based on the "almost sacred 'pecking order'" that he observes among church officials, politicians, and various fascists.

Applying the notion of a "pecking order" to human interaction soon became so commonplace that it no longer needed to be set off by quotation marks. In the early 1940s anthropologist Margaret Mead reported that "fifth- and sixth- and seventh-generation Americans lost the zest which came with climbing to the top of the pecking order in their own town or city." A decade later the redoubtable Alsop brothers observed that a Washington official who has no secretary "is at the very bottom of the pecking order."

The great virtue of a concept like *pecking order* is that—like *big bang, bowling alone*, and *broken windows*—it's easy to visualize and grasp. The meaning of such a phrase is virtually self-evident, and can be applied to playground and organizational behavior alike in a way that makes perfect sense to anyone who's ever observed a bunch of human beings pecking at each other like a flock of chickens (which is to say nearly everyone). *Pecking order* is far more satisfying to say than *status ladder* or *dominance hierarchy*.

Alas, not all new terms that emerge from the academy are as accessible as *pecking order*. In fact, few are. I don't know how many times I've seen reference to a word coined by an academic and looked it up eagerly, only to be dismayed by how little sense that term makes outside its point of origin. Though colleges and universities are filled with smart, articulate people who like to invent words, most of the words they invent are virtually incomprehensible outside their walls.

In her novel *Americanah*, Chimamanda Ngozi Adichie's blogger-protagonist tells a Yale professor that she doesn't want to do postgraduate work because "I'm worried that I will leave grad school and no longer be able to speak English. I know this woman in grad school . . . and just listening to her talk is scary. The semiotic dialectics of intertextual modernity. Which makes no sense at all. Sometimes I feel that they live in a parallel universe of academese instead of English." At Columbia University, linguist John McWhorter has observed the same thing. In his book *Doing Your Own Thing*, McWhorter castigates fellow academics for writing prose that's "inaccessible beyond the ivory tower and aesthetically barren even within it."

"It could hardly be said," McWhorter adds, "that the way postmodernist academics have come to write has the slightest resemblance to the way anyone talks." As a case in point, McWhorter cites the prose of University of California professor Judith Butler. Butler is a highly regarded philosopher celebrated by colleagues for her imaginative terminology. The results include terms of her own invention such as *grievability* and *gender performativity* that obviously have great resonance among fellow philosophers. Among everyday speakers of the English language, they are, to put it mildly, puzzling.

In today's academia it almost seems as though the less sense a coinage makes to outsiders, the more acclaim it's likely to win among peers. There is a reason for this, one that's related to the notion of pecking orders. In the first chapter I noted that a common motivation for coining words is to impress others. Nowhere is this more true than within ivy-covered walls. Peer pressure is alive and well there, especially when it comes to monitoring the vocabulary faculty members use among themselves. Choosing the right words is an important way to signal that one belongs. Coining a much-cited term is even better.

One of the most popular concepts among contemporary academics is *intersectionality*. This term made its modern debut in a 1989 article by legal scholar Kimberlé Williams Crenshaw titled "Demarginalizing the Intersection of Race and Sex: A Black Feminist Critique of Antidiscrimination Doctrine, Feminist Theory and Antiracist Politics." (*Intersectionality* was an obscure mathematical term at the time Crenshaw gave it a broader meaning.) Since then, Crenshaw's term for intersecting forms of discrimination has become commonplace in academic circles. *Intersectionality* is defined by Merriam-Webster as "the interconnected nature of social categorizations such as race, class, and gender as they apply to a given individual or group, regarded as creating overlapping and interdependent systems of discrimination or disadvantage." Gulp! A 2015 article in the *Annual Review of Sociology* is aptly titled "Intersectionality's Definitional Dilemmas." Two years later the headline of an article in London's *Telegraph* read "'Intersectional Feminism'. What the Hell Is It? (And Why You Should Care)." The most common Google search about this concept asks how it's defined. Crenshaw herself notes how broadly her term has been applied, and misapplied, leading too easily to the conclusion that issues of discrimination were "complicated." Yes, they are complicated, she concedes; but no, that isn't an excuse for inaction. Yet the opaqueness of Crenshaw's term is one reason for its misuse. As with so many academic neologisms, however, the obscurity of this term may be part of its appeal among those who use it. So is the fact that it works better in print than in person. To those who communicate primarily by reading and writing, this isn't an issue (which helps explain their fondness for terms such as *incommensurability*, *recontextualize*, and *heteronormative*). They are okay with read-only terms.

Obscurity and tongue-twisting don't characterize all academic neologisms. An elite handful leap across the academy's moat and are adopted by the peasantry. Such terms are most likely to come from scholars who try to express themselves in ways that will make their ideas more comprehensible, not less, even when this calls for adopting terminology suggested by others.

The Origin of Survival

In *On the Origin of Species*, Charles Darwin introduced the concept of *natural selection* (a phrase he'd used in a letter two years before his book was published in 1859). Darwin did not, however, refer to *survival of the fittest*. That phrase first appeared five years later, in Herbert Spencer's 1864 book *Principles of Biology*. "This survival of the fittest," wrote Spencer, "which I have here sought to express in mechanical terms, is that which Mr. Darwin has called 'natural selection.'" Darwin liked Spencer's reformulation. In his 1868 book *The Variation of Animals and Plants Under Domestication*, the naturalist wrote, "This preservation, during the battle for life, of varieties which possess any advantage in structure, constitution, or instinct, I have called Natural Selection; and Mr. Herbert Spencer has well expressed the same idea by the Survival of the Fittest. The term 'natural selection' is in some respects a bad one, as it seems to imply conscious choice; but this will be disregarded after a little familiarity."

History has been kinder to Darwin's own coinage than that of Spencer, however, which has developed a bad odor. *Natural selection* is not Darwin's only contribution to the lexicon. Some words that we now use routinely were added to our vocabulary by him. According to the *OED*, Darwin is the earliest known user of 125 terms, including ones he created himself. Some Darwinisms, such as *archaeopteryx, asclepiad, compsognathus*, and *exophthalmos* related directly to his work as a naturalist. Others were more broadly accessible, particularly to those involved with agriculture. *Interbreed* and *cross-fertilize* were coined by Darwin. So were *purebred* and *subgroup*. A long list of Darwin's terminology compiled by Ben Zimmer, who calls the naturalist "a lexical dynamo," includes not just these terms but ones such as *correlated* and *present-day*.

Some words Darwin added to English came from Spanish. In the journal he kept and later published recounting his 1831–36 tour of South America, Darwin referred to Chilean cowboys rounding up cattle in a *rodeo*, the first known use of that word in English. Another Spanish loan word that Darwin included in his journal is *alfalfa*, which he described as "a kind of clover" that he'd seen in Chile. His fellow Victorians took to these words, and made them a lasting part of the English lexicon.

Neurology's Neologizers

During the late Victorian era, a London neurologist named William Gowers was celebrated for his meticulous methodology. Gowers's research methods were so exacting that some think he inspired Sherlock Holmes, the fact-based detective created by his fellow Victorian Arthur Conan Doyle. Like Doyle's detective, Gowers was keen on direct observation. (He taught medical students that diagnosis should begin the moment a patient steps through the door.) One thing Gowers observed among his own patients was the way their knees reflexively jerked upward when tapped with the side of a hand or a small rubber mallet. His colleagues had given this reflex names such as *patellar tendon reflex, knee phenomenon*, and *Westphal phenomenon* (after German physician Carl Friedrich Otto Westphal, who'd studied the phenomenon). In an 1879 lecture, Dr. Gowers said he preferred to call it simply *the knee reflex*. Perhaps thinking that this phrase lacked cachet, Gowers subsequently coined *myotatic* (from the Greek *tatikos*, or "extended"), then appended this Greekish word to *irritability* or *contractions* (*myotatic irritability, myotatic contractions*) to describe the knee's upward jerk. That one hardly suited the plain-spoken neurologist, however. Although "myotatic" and "myotasis" can still be found in medical literature, in his *Manual of Diseases of the Nervous System*, an 1886–88 work considered the "Bible of Neurology," Gowers introduced yet a third descriptive. Two of his own drawings that Dr. Gowers included to illustrate the reflex in question were captioned "the knee-jerk." He described this as "the jerk of the leg which occurs when the patellar tendon is tapped." This vivid, down-to-earth coinage was so compelling that in recent decades it's become allegorical for reflexive responses of many kinds. ("He's such a knee-jerk liberal.")

FIG. 1.—THE KNEE-JERK.
The dotted line indicates the movement
which follows the blow on the patellar
tendon.

FIG. 2.—THE KNEE-JERK.
Method of obtaining it when it
is not readily produced in the
ordinary way.

Sketches of "the knee-jerk" by Dr. William Gowers, in his *Manual of Diseases of the Nervous System,* 1886–88.

Medicine's evolving nature creates a continual demand for new terms. Some physicians work hard to meet that need. During the early 1970s, neurologists Bryan Jennett and Fred Plum thought colleagues could use a better way to describe unresponsive patients. "As our intention was to provide a term that would facilitate communication about this state between doctors and the patient's relatives, moralists and lawyers," Jennett later wrote, "it seemed advantageous to have one that avoided medical jargon." This eliminated the many existing terms that referred to this condition or some aspects of it: *apallic syndrome, akinetic mutism, severe traumatic dementia, post-traumatic dementia, coma vigile,* and *neocortical necrosis. Cognitive death* made more sense, but incorrectly implied that dying was the only possible outcome for unresponsive patients.

Their search for a new term led Jennett and Plum to *vegetate,* which—according to the *OED*—meant "to live a merely physical life, devoid of intellectual activity or social intercourse." *Vegetative,* defined as "an organic body capable of growth and development but devoid of sensation and thought" was promising, having already been used to refer to survivors of severe head trauma, but without a clear definition of their condition. So Jennett and Plum floated *persistent vegetative state* in a 1972 *Lancet* article they titled "Persistent Vegetative State After Brain Damage: A Syndrome in Search of a Name." According to these neurologists, the name they proposed "suggests even to the layman a limited and primitive responsiveness to external stimuli, whilst it reminds the doctor that there is relative preservation of autonomic regulation of the internal milieu of the body."

Their colleagues concurred, adopting Jennett and Plum's way of describing unresponsive patients (though in time "persistent" got dropped because it suggested irreversibility). Not only is "vegetative state" visually evocative, it is ambiguous in a useful way, describing the condition of an unresponsive patient rather than the cause of that condition. Although some think it's demeaning to compare a patient to a vegetable, and efforts have been made to find a better term (including *minimally responsive state* and *minimally conscious state*), none have won more acceptance than *vegetative state*.

Memology

Shortly after *vegetative state* was added to the medical lexicon, a coinage was introduced that took longer to find a home in the English lexicon. Once it did, however, this word became one of our most useful and widely used terms. The neologism first appeared in Richard Dawkins's 1976 book *The Selfish Gene*. In this book Dawkins wrote about social phenomena that replicate themselves: "We need a name for the new replicator, a noun which conveys the idea of a unit of cultural transmission, or a unit of imitation. 'Mimeme' comes from a suitable Greek root, but I want a monosyllable that sounds a bit like 'gene'. I hope my classicist friends will forgive me if I abbreviate mimeme to meme. If it is any consolation, it could alternatively be thought of as being related to 'memory', or to the French word meme. It should be pronounced to rhyme with 'cream.'"

If ever a term took its own sweet time finding an audience, it was this one. That's because the gap it filled in our vocabulary was not evident until the Internet became a fertile incubator of what Dawkins called *memes*. Although Dawkins's coinage antedated the Internet by several years, this revolutionary medium made replicating cultural phenomena so easy and so ubiquitous that we needed a word for the results. Meme was suited up and ready for duty.

A fellow scientist of Dawkins, the physicist John Wheeler, was less successful in creating his own neologism. During a talk he gave on pulsars in the fall of 1967, Wheeler noted that "gravitationally completely collapsed object" was a mouthful. Wasn't there a brisker way to describe collapsing stars? "How about 'black hole'?" someone in the audience called out. As Wheeler later wrote in his autobiography, "I had been searching for just the right term for months, mulling it over in bed, in the bathtub, in my car, wherever I had quiet moments. Suddenly this name seemed exactly right." Users agree. Black hole has become a standard part of the English lexicon (though not the Russian, where it is vulgar slang for vagina; in Russia *frozen stars* is used instead).*

An Academic Rock Star

Wheeler may have had trouble creating a necessary term, but this wasn't a problem for sociologist Robert Merton. Shortly before he died in 2003, at ninety-two, Merton referred to "my enduring engagement with neologisms that are needed to describe newly discovered phenomena and newly emerging ideas." When it came to creating functional terminology, the tall, erudite Philadelphian was an academic rock star. Colleagues applauded his meticulous prose, which usually resulted from multiple manuscript revisions. (Had he not become a college professor, one colleague said, Merton could well have been an editor.) The sociologist paid careful attention to words he used—including ones of his own creation. "Coined words," Merton wrote, "not only need to be striking, they must also 'earn their keep' by providing a name for something that is worth naming."

"A word has to fight for its life," he added. "To survive, a word must claim its place and convince an audience."

Neologisms that emerged from the sociologist's fertile brain included *role model, reference groups, trained incapacity*, and *focused interview*. Lexicographers credit Merton with being the first to use *dysfunction* in the social-psychological sense. (Before that, *dysfunction* and *dysfunctional* referred more broadly to any difficult situation.) Merton's 1936 article "The Unanticipated Consequences of Purposive Action" helped popularize what he and others then called *unintended consequences*.

Merton's most notable contribution to his discipline and our language was the concept of the *self-fulfilling prophecy*. He introduced this concept in a 1948 *Antioch Review* article by that title. "So common is the pattern of the self-fulfilling prophecy," Merton wrote, "that each of us has his favored specimen." His own favorite example involved test takers who are so sure they will do badly that anxiety keeps them from studying, thus confirming their original, flawed, prediction. Such erroneous anticipation, Merton wrote, produces a "reign of error" that ultimately confirms the original false assessment. This can apply not just to test taking but to racial prejudice and even war. Having predicted a bad outcome, we look for evidence to

---

* Wheeler's origin story notwithstanding, "black hole" had already been used to describe collapsing stars by an unnamed commenter at a 1964 meeting of the American Association for the Advancement of Science, conceivably the same person who suggested it to John Wheeler three years later. Be that as it may, when Wheeler died in 2008, his *New York Times* obituary was headlined "John A. Wheeler, Physicist Who Coined the Term 'Black Hole,' Is Dead at 96."

THE SELF-FULFILLING PROPHECY

By ROBERT K. MERTON

IN A SERIES OF WORKS seldom consulted outside the academic fraternity, W. I. Thomas, the dean of American sociologists, set forth a theorem basic to the social sciences: "If men define situations as real, they are real in their consequences." Were the Thomas theorem and its implications more widely known more men would understand more of the workings of our society. Though it lacks the sweep and precision of a Newtonian theorem, it possesses the same gift of relevance, being instructively applicable to many, if indeed not most, social processes.

"If men define situations as real, they are real in their consequences," wrote Professor Thomas. The suspicion that he was driving at a crucial point becomes all the more insistent when we note that essentially the same theorem had been repeatedly set forth by disciplined and observant minds long before Thomas.

When we find such otherwise discrepant minds as the redoubtable Bishop Bossuet in his passionate seventeenth-century defense of Catholic orthodoxy; the ironic Mandeville in his eighteenth-century allegory honeycombed with observations on the paradoxes of human society; the irascible genius Marx in his revision of Hegel's theory of historical change; the seminal Freud in works which have perhaps gone further than any others of his day toward modifying man's outlook on man; and the erudite, dogmatic, and occasionally sound Yale professor, William Graham Sumner, who lives on as the Karl Marx of the middle classes—when we find this mixed company (and I select from a longer if less distinguished list) agreeing on the truth and the pertinence of what is substantially the Thomas theorem, we may conclude that perhaps it's worth our attention as well.

To what, then, are Thomas and Bossuet, Mandeville, Marx, Freud and Sumner directing our attention?

ROBERT K. MERTON is Professor of Sociology and Acting Director of the Bureau of Applied Social Research, Columbia University. His most recent book is *Mass Persuasion* (1946).

First page of "The Self-Fulfilling Prophecy," by Robert Merton, *The Antioch Review,* Summer 1948.

support our prophecy. That in turn makes the prediction come true. During the years following its introduction, Merton's groundbreaking notion inspired hundreds of studies that confirmed its validity. In the process, *self-fulfilling prophecy* became not just a seminal social scientific concept but an everyday truism.

Two decades after introducing *self-fulfilling prophecy*, Merton added *Matthew effect* to the lexicon. This phrase, co-coined with his wife, Harriet Zuckerman, referred to the fact that added advantages accrue to those who already enjoy them. It alluded to Matthew 25:29 in the New Testament: "For unto everyone that hath shall be given, and he will have abundance; but from him who has not, even what he has will be taken away." (Or, as Billie Holiday sang in *God Bless the Child*, "Them that's got shall get. / Them that's not shall lose.") According to this effect, not only do the rich get richer, but those already recognized for their intellectual achievements get credit for work done by others who are more obscure. Malcolm Gladwell—a sometime beneficiary of this syndrome—called the first chapter of his book *Outliers* "The Matthew Effect," attributing this concept to Robert Merton, and helping ensure that it would remain part of our discourse.

Although Merton pioneered research using what he called "the focused interview" in groups, the sociologist didn't call such gatherings "focus groups." That honor goes to motivational research pioneer Ernest Dichter. Dichter was among many who have converted the words of scholars into ones better suited to everyday discourse. Think of them as "interpreters." Unlike those who escort the ideas of others into public discussion with the originators' own terminology, interpreters coin new terms to better convey those concepts.

Interpreters

As a budding anthropologist, Ray Birdwhistell watched a film that portrayed how a Balinese mother and her baby communicated. Afterward he noted how much could be discerned by simply observing the bodily interaction between mother and baby and, by extension, of human beings in general.

From this insight grew Birdwhistell's life work: studying how human beings communicate through physical signals. Based on his research, the anthropologist concluded that no more than a third of communication by humans is accomplished with words. The rest takes place nonverbally, usually in ways that aren't conscious. Birdwhistell called this phenomenon *kinesics*, from the Greek term *kinesis*, referring to movement. In a 1952 monograph titled *Introduction to Kinesics*, Birdwhistell defined his subject as "the study of body-motion as related to the non-verbal aspects of interpersonal communication." These included "facial expression, gestures, posture and gait, and visible arm and body movements." Birdwhistell's neologism spawned *kinesiology*, as well as *kinemes*, and *kinemorphs*. While these were perfectly usable terms, and are still used by those who study body movement (as well as the manufacturer of "kinesiology tape" for athletes), the fact that *kinesics* and its verbal offspring have so little inherent meaning limits their range and utility.

Not so *body language*. This easily comprehensible concept—the title of a 1970 book by writer Julius Fast that introduced the notion of nonverbal communication to a broad audience—quickly became part of the national conversation. Birdwhistell himself didn't care for it. He thought Fast's phrase cheapened his concept, and considered only certain aspects. Nonetheless, without the help of Julius Fast's bestseller, Birdwhistell's insight that we communicate as much with our bodies as with our words might never have achieved the traction that it has. (More than one online dictionary defines kinesics as "study of body language.") When Birdwhistell died in 1994, the *New York Times'* obituary—which was headlined "Prof. Ray L. Birdwhistell, 76; Helped Decipher Body Language"—informed readers that "he did his best-known research in the field of nonverbal communication, or body language."

The seminal ideas of scholars such as Ray Birdwhistell are routinely made available for general discourse with someone else's nomenclature. In one case after another concepts and information generated by scholars have reached a wide audience only after terminology created by an interpreter has helped make their findings more accessible.

At the same time that Ray Birdwhistell's work was being introduced, his fellow anthropologist Edward T. Hall was doing pioneering research on another aspect of human interaction: the amount of distance we need between ourselves and others in order to feel at ease. As Hall established, this varies by culture. Middle Easterners, for example, tend to be comfortable at a closer proximity than those who live in Northern Europe. In 1963 Hall coined a term for the study of how much space people feel they need from other people when interacting: *proxemics.* Like *kinesics*, Hall's coinage won acceptance among his fellow anthropologists. Laypeople, however, needed a term better suited to discussing this topic. That term appeared in a 1969 book by psychologist Robert Sommer titled *Personal Space.* Ever since Sommer's consideration of how much distance from others each of us prefers was published, *personal space* has been the most common name for that phenomenon. During the #MeToo era, Joe Biden was criticized for not respecting the comfort zones of those he touched, hugged, and kissed during public appearances. When confronting those charges, Biden vowed to "be more mindful and respectful of people's personal space."

A few years before *Personal Space* appeared in bookstores, gynecologist Ernst Gräfenberg published a 1950 article in *The International Journal of Sexology* titled "The Role of Urethra in Female Orgasm." In this article Dr. Gräfenberg called attention to areas of unusual sexual sensitivity within the vagina that he called "erotogenic spots." One spot on the vagina's anterior wall, he reported, was particularly easy to arouse by digital stimulation. Although Gräfenberg did not give this location a name, when introducing their own research on extra-clitoral sexual stimulation in 1980, sexologists Beverly Whipple and John Perry called it "the Gräfenberg spot." Two years later, a shortened version of that phrase was highlighted in the title and content of Perry and Whipple's 1982 book *The G-Spot and Other Recent Discoveries About Human Sexuality* (coauthored with Alice Khan Ladas). Their book became an international bestseller. The very notion of an erogenous *G-spot* aroused so much interest that this phrase quickly took hold. In time, it became synonymous with "sweet spot" in a figurative way, as when a British music critic noted that a concert suffered from having too many "musical G-spots whizzing by unnoticed."

Help Wanted

New discoveries call for words and phrases to help us discuss them. The problem is that those who make such discoveries are not necessarily suited to naming them. They need, and often get, help. No better example evidence exists than the gas co-discovered by English clergyman and scientist Joseph Priestley in 1774 that he called *dephlogisticated air*. Today that gas is better known as *oxygen*, a term coined by Anton Lavoisier in 1777.

Albert Einstein needed, and got, similar help. In his 1905 paper "On the Electrodynamics of Moving Bodies," the physicist theorized (essentially) that energy and mass were equivalent, and time relative. Einstein said this theory was one of *invariance* (*invariententheorie* in German). Drawing on its first postulate, *the Principle of Relativity*, his older colleague Max Planck called Einstein's revolutionary insight a *theory of relativity* (*Relativtheorie*).** Einstein himself didn't care for Planck's version, thinking—rightly—that it led too easily to the simplistic notion that "everything's relative." However, *invariance* requires more of an explanation than *relativity* (a term coined by Samuel Coleridge in 1834), so Planck's term for Einstein's theory is the one that caught on. Eventually Einstein himself recognized that this term made his ideas more comprehensible and began to use it himself, even calling a 1916 book *Relativity*. He tried his best to make light of the popular perception of his work, however, once explaining relativity theory by observing that "an hour sitting with a pretty girl on a park bench passes like a minute; but a minute sitting on a hot stove seems like an hour."

Peak Holism

It's not always true that those who make important discoveries are bad namers of their discoveries. Like Robert Merton and Richard Dawkins, some scholars have proved perfectly capable of creating accessible words to describe their findings, terms that in some cases have become part of everyday discourse.

Abraham Maslow was one. This psychologist thought we all have a "hierarchy of needs." This begins with the basic need for safety and peaks with the quest for *self-actualization* (a term psychiatrist Kurt Goldstein had used as a neurological concept several years before Maslow recast it as a psychological need in a 1943 book). *Peak experiences* were an integral part of self-actualization: "rare, exciting, oceanic, deeply moving, exhilarating, elevating experiences that generate an advanced form of perceiving reality." Both *peak experience* and *self-actualization* became an enduring part of popular discourse. *Hierarchy of needs* itself appears regularly in both the scholarly and the popular press, as when a news commentator suggested that personal safety was foremost in gun owners' "hierarchy of needs."

Throughout his long career, Abraham Maslow strived to create a vocabulary that would match his unique take on the human experience. Like most prolific

---

** The phrase *relativity theory* was used in a different context in an 1883 journal article.

neologizers, Maslow failed to get his new words adopted far more often than he succeeded. In a biography of the psychologist, Edward Hoffman devoted five pages to listing his subject's many coinages, virtually all of which died when he did (in 1970). This list included such tongue-twisters as *eupsychian*, *instinctoid*, *aggridant*, and *rubricize*. Another concept of Maslow's that didn't catch on but deserved a second look was that of the *postmortem life*, a phrase he created to characterize the sense of rejuvenation experienced by those who survive a brush with death (as he himself did, after suffering cardiac arrest).

A term that sounds like a Maslow coinage but isn't appeared in a 1947 article he wrote that described his broad-spectrum approach to psychology. Maslow called this article "A Symbol for Holistic Thinking." Although the psychologist helped popularize *holistic*, he didn't coin that word. Who did?

The answer is a jaw-dropper. This popular term—one that sounds like it leaped from the pages of *The Journal of Organic Farming and Alternative Healing* (or some such)—is nearly a century old and comes from an unlikely source. That source was Jan Smuts, the South African author of a 1926 book titled *Holism and*

General Jan Smuts, author of the 1926 book *Holism and Evolution.*

Evolution. An Afrikaner, Smuts was a leading architect of his country's system of racial apartheid and a tormentor of Mahatma Gandhi when the Indian activist lived in South Africa. In his book, the polymath Smuts—who was a botanist, lawyer, military officer, and statesman—wrote, "Holism is the term here coined (from ὅλος = whole) to designate this fundamental factor operative towards making or creation of wholes in the universe." Smuts thought that "this whole-making or holistic tendency is fundamental in nature."

Ironic as it may be that this retrograde figure coined a term so associated with modern progressive thinking, by doing so General Smuts joined the elite club of those who don't just deliberately coin a word, but succeed in getting others to adopt it.

III

Coinage Syndromes

14

Coined with Intent

WHEN NOT PRACTICING medicine in Norwich, Sir Thomas Browne (1605–82) conducted scientific investigations and wrote works of philosophy. In the introduction to one of his books Browne told readers that it had been written during interludes between his *medical* duties. This is the first known use of that word. Other new words he created for colleagues included *incisor*, *follicle*, and *expectoration*.

At a time when the English vocabulary was expanding rapidly, neologizers like Browne fueled that expansion with words of their own invention. Browne's specialty was coining terms that helped him report on his scientific experiments. Some found a home in the lexicon as a whole. Most notably, in his 1646 observation that "Crystal will calefie into electricity" (meaning that rubbing such a material would produce a static charge), the English physician gave us *electricity*. Browne's coinages were not limited to science and medicine, however. Nor were they only technical in flavor. Far from being wooden, or jargony, his neologisms generally pleased the ear. Long after naming one who studies plants a *botanologer*, Browne decided that he preferred the more felicitous term *botanist*.

Botanist was one of many words coined by Browne that appeared in Samuel Johnson's 1755 dictionary. Johnson particularly admired the ability of their creator to add concision to the evolving English language. As the lexicographer put it, Browne "was not content to express in many words that idea for which any language could supply a single term." Browne's prose was so graceful and inventive that his admirers include not only contemporaries like Samuel Johnson but figures such as Herman Melville, Edgar Allan Poe, Ralph Waldo Emerson, Virginia Woolf, Jorge Luis Borges, and, more recently, Stephen Jay Gould. Such fans were particularly impressed by how many of Browne's coined words stood the test of time. Among them are *hallucination*, *deductive*, *suicide*, *anomalous*, *antediluvian*, *carnal*, *coexistence*, *compensate*, *exhaustion*, *ferocious*, *indigenous*, *insecurity*, *locomotion*, *misconception*, and *temperamental*.

According to biographer Hugh Aldersey-Williams, during his prolific career as a doctor, scientist, and writer, Browne coined some 784 words and was an early user of hundreds more. Although his name is not widely known today, Sir Thomas is celebrated by scholars as one of our language's most prolific neologizers. Lexicographers have a particular fondness for Browne. *OED* editor Denny Hilton thinks this is due to the quality of his coinages as much as their quantity. "It's not just neologistic showmanship," Hilton told Aldersey-Williams, "—his words are complicated, minutely detailed, and lovingly created."

New Words Needed

So far, this book has focused on the many words that have been coined inadvertently, in contrast to all the failed attempts to create them intentionally. This doesn't mean that usable, durable words are never coined with intent. As the cases of Browne, Milton, Merton, and others illustrate, quite a few have been. Such neologisms are typically created by combining existing words and clauses, adding prefixes and suffixes, and adapting roots borrowed from other languages.

Greek and Latin figure prominently in such loans, as illustrated by a term Aldous Huxley's grandfather Thomas Huxley invented during the Victorian era. Huxley was such a fierce defender of Charles Darwin's theories of evolution that he became known as "Darwin's bulldog." One reason this distinguished biologist felt free to fly in the face of existing Christian dogma was that he did not believe in the existence of a supreme being, let alone one whose son died for our sins. Nor did he consider himself an atheist.

So what was he? Trying to answer this question bedeviled Huxley. Since he neither thought there was a God nor that there wasn't, unlike his Christian and atheistic colleagues, Huxley lacked even "a rag of a title," as he put it. Huxley felt like the legendary fox who'd lost his tail in a trap and had to go tailless among foxes who still had theirs. After much deliberation, in 1869 Huxley came up with "agnostic," a play on the Greek term *gnostic* (for enlightened believers, ones in the know). His antonym referred to those who professed *not* to know, those with no formal belief system. Having given his spiritual status a name, Huxley paraded this name among fellow members of London's newly formed Metaphysical Society, "to show that I too had a tail, like the other foxes."

As a way to describe those who were neither believers nor atheists, Thomas Huxley's coinage quickly caught on. In time, *agnostic* became the most common way to depict spiritual 'tweeners like him. Bertrand Russell was one. During intake at London's Brixton prison, where the philosopher spent six months in 1918 for adamantly opposing Britain's participation in World War I, Russell was asked by Brixton's warden what his religion was. "Agnostic," he responded. Not having heard this term before, the warden asked how it was spelled. "A-g-n-o-s-t-i-c," responded Russell. His jailer sighed and said, "Well, religions are many, but I guess they all believe in the same God." This observation amused Russell enough to keep his spirits up during the early months of his incarceration.

Sexspeak

Victorian England provided bountiful opportunities to create euphemistic sexual terms, especially ones that depicted same-sex relationships. Victorians were loath to give such relationships an actual name, as if by not calling this tendency anything in particular they could pretend it didn't exist. To some it was a *nameless crime*. Oscar Wilde's lover, Lord Alfred Douglas, called their relationship *the love that dare not speak its name*. Wilde himself considered it *the love of things impossible*. Other circumlocutions included *a wretched illness*, *a perversion*, or *a physical and psychic disease*. In other words, *a crime against nature*. An *unnatural vice*. Those attracted to members of their own sex were *degenerates*. They were *that way*, *like that*, *one of those*. *Unnatural*. *Abnormal*. *Peculiar*. *Uranians*. They had *particular friendships*. A catchall term for some of their sex practices was *sodomy*. To accuse his son's lover of such a crime, Douglas's spelling-challenged father left a calling card at Wilde's club charging him with being a "somdomite." This led to the sensational trial in which Wilde was convicted of *gross indecency* and sent to prison for two years. In a petition requesting early release, the playwright admitted to suffering from "loathsome modes of erotomania," "sensual monomanias," "a strange disease," and an "insanity of perverted sexual instinct."

It wasn't until late in the nineteenth century that English speakers began to refer to *homosexuals*. This term was adapted from *Homosexualität*, an 1868 coinage by German-Hungarian writer Károly Mária Kertbeny that combined the Greek term for "same," *homo*, and one from Medieval Latin, *sexualis*. Although later generations found "homosexual" marginalizing, Kertbeny thought it provided a neutral, non-pejorative way to describe men who were attracted to other men (presumably including himself). As a young man, the writer had been traumatized by the suicide of such a man, a friend who was being blackmailed. Kertbeny vowed to do what he could to normalize the sexual status of men like him. Giving them a nonjudgmental name seemed like a good beginning.

Kertbeny's original coinage made its English-speaking debut in 1891 when John Addington Symonds referred to "homosexual instincts" in his book *A Problem in Modern Ethics*. The sexologist Havelock Ellis was not impressed with this Greco-Roman blend, considering it "a barbarously hybrid word." Ellis preferred *inversion*, adapted from "sexual inverts," a phrase Symonds had used in an 1892 letter to him. Ellis gave the title *Sexual Inversion* to the 1896 volume of his

Studies in the Psychology of Sex. This book was quickly banned. Two years after its publication, the government prosecuted a bookseller because he "sold and uttered a certain lewd wicked bawdy scandalous and obscene libel in the form of a book entitled *Studies in the Psychology of Sex: Sexual Inversion.*"

A subsequent book by Ellis was called *Eonism and Other Supplementary Studies* (1928). Its title referenced a member of the court of Louis XVI named Chevalier D'Eon, who liked to wear women's clothing. Although Ellis thought that *eonism* improved on *cross-dressing*, most English speakers did not. They were, and are, fine with *cross-dressing*, as well as *transvestism*, a word coined by German physician Magnus Hirschfeld in 1910, three years before Ellis floated *eonism*.

Other terms coined by Ellis include *necrosadism*, his word for necrophilia accompanied by mutilation of a corpse, and *auto-erotism* for those who engage in solitary sexual activities such as masturbation. Earlier, he'd referred in an 1898 article to self-pleasurers as *Narcissus-like* (after the Greek god who fell in love with his own reflection in a pool of water). This phrase led to *narcissism*, the English translation of *Narzissismus*, a term coined by German psychiatrist Paul Näcke in 1899 and adopted by Ellis himself. Näcke's coinage was given purchase by Sigmund Freud's 1914 essay *On Narcissism*. In an illustration of the Matthew effect, Freud is often credited with coining "narcissism," although this psychological concept clearly began with the less-renowned Paul Näcke. Freud himself credited Ellis for the coinage, but Ellis conceded that it was co-coined with Näcke. None of them needed to worry. In an 1822 letter Samuel Taylor Coleridge had already referred to self-regard as *narcissism*.

Straight Talk

Linguistically speaking, Havelock Ellis's real forte was using clear, straightforward terminology. To Ellis a penis was a *penis*, not a "male member," and a vagina was a *vagina*, not a "female canal." During his euphemism-rich time, such language was bracing. Although Ellis's straight talk may have shocked staid Victorians, it inspired others to follow suit. One was Margaret Sanger, the outspoken American feminist and champion of contraception. Having read every volume of *Studies in the Psychology of Sex*, when Sanger visited London in 1914 she was keen to meet its author. Over tea at his Brixton flat, the charismatic psychologist and vivacious nurse hit it off. Among other things, they shared a passion for unadorned speech. When discussing their shared conviction that a woman's sexual response was aroused by stimulation of her *clitoris*, they used this taboo word. *Masturbation* was called just that, not *onanism* or *self-abuse*.

Ellis's verbal candor aligned well with Sanger's own. In a sixteen-page pamphlet called *Family Limitation* that was published just before she'd left the

United States for England (fled, actually, using the alias "Bertha Watson," to avoid being prosecuted for obscenity), Sanger didn't just tell readers how to avoid having babies but discussed the act of conception itself. Sanger used *climax* synonymously with "orgasm," noting that "there are few men and women so perfectly mated that the climax of the [sex] act is reached together."* But a woman's ability to climax without anxiety called for being able to effectively prevent pregnancy. "Perhaps the commonest preventive excepting the use of the condom is 'coitus interrupts' [*sic*]," she wrote. This referred to "withdrawal of the penis from the vagina shortly before the action of the semen." That risky form of contraception, Sanger warned, could leave women frustrated and dissatisfied. Sex without satisfaction was little better than prostitution, she contended. Post-coitus douching was therefore better than withdrawal, Sanger wrote, ideally in conjunction with their partner's use of a "cot" (rubber condom).

Due to this type of frankness, *Family Limitation* caused an uproar (which wasn't bad for sales, of 160,000 copies within four years). Nearly a century after its publication, Sanger's pamphlet made a cameo appearance in the TV series *Boardwalk Empire*, illustrating the way its author helped drag the topic of limiting births out of America's conversational closet. One impediment to doing so was the dearth of words available to talk about this topic. "At that time," Sanger wrote later, "there was not even a language in which to discuss these questions. The subject was considered indecent and vulgar. Openly to advocate the prevention of conception—a phrase which the NEW YORK TIMES would not allow in its columns—meant ostracism."

To remedy this vocabulary shortage, Sanger and a group of colleagues gathered in her Greenwich Village apartment to come up with better words for the practice of *contraception* (a term had been around for nearly three decades, combining the Latin *contra*, or "against," with the second clause of *conception*). But that multisyllabic word was rather stuffy, not at all suited to the outreach they had in mind. Worse yet was the eponym *Malthusianism*, named after the Reverend Thomas Robert Malthus—who, more than a century earlier, had called attention to the dangers of overpopulation. *Malthusianism* was even harder to pronounce than contraception, however, in addition to being two syllables longer. Furthermore, Rev. Malthus was no champion of pregnancy prevention, which he considered both immoral and bad for business. In his bleak vision, the best ways to limit population growth were abstinence, starvation, and the plague.

---

* Half a century earlier, the author of a medical journal article had referred more formally to "the climax of coition."

So those two terms were out. Others they considered and rejected included *voluntary motherhood, conscious generation, preventeception, family control*, and, unfortunately, *race control* (Sanger being a committed eugenicist). The only term all could agree on was *birth rate control*. Someone, possibly Sanger herself—who at times took credit and at other times didn't—suggested deleting the word "rate." They had their concept. In July 1914 Margaret Sanger put *birth control* on the verbal map in an article about a "Birth Control League" she was helping organize. When Sanger returned from her trip abroad in October 1915, she was thrilled to pass a newsstand that displayed a magazine whose cover story was titled "What Shall We Do About Birth Control?" That coinage was clearly in play. Sixteen years later Sanger called her 1931 memoir *My Fight for Birth Control*. Four decades after the meeting where this term was conjured, a writer asked Sanger what she'd like him to say about her in his pamphlet on babies. "The fact that I coined the term birth control," she responded.

Verbal Holes

The fact that *birth control* was not a particularly sexy term helped it win acceptance. Successfully coined words catch on not because they are clever, or flatter the coiner, but because they meet a verbal need. None was greater than the need for a way to describe Nazi atrocities during World War II. How do you depict in words the magnitude of this carnage? Existing terms simply weren't up to the task. "Mass murder" didn't have enough scope or weight to describe Hitler's attempt to wipe Jews and others from the face of the earth. Nor did "slaughter," or "massacre." In 1943 New York lawyer Raphael Lemkin—a Polish-Jewish refugee who lost forty-nine relatives to the Nazis—combined *genos* (Greek for *tribe*) with *cide* (Latin for *killing*) and came up with *genocide*. The following year he introduced this term in a magazine article, explaining that it referred to "the destruction of a nation or of an ethnic group."

Lemkin's concept, amplified in his 1944 book *Axis Rule in Occupied Europe*, figured prominently in the postwar prosecution of Nazi war criminals at Nuremberg. As London's *Sunday Times* told its readers, "The United Nations' indictment of the 24 Nazi leaders has brought a new word into the language—genocide. It occurs in Count 3, where it is stated that all the defendants 'conducted deliberate and systematic genocide—namely, the extermination of racial and national groups.'" In short order *genocide* became our standard way of referring the attempted eradication of an entire people, and the name of a crime in international law.

During a more literate time, classically educated coiners like Lemkin turned to Greek, Latin, or both when creating new words. Until relatively recently this was the ore most commonly mined to coin new words. In many cases both of these ancient languages have been tapped for clauses to create one word, as Lemkin did with *genocide*. Purists looked askance at this verbal mongrelization. (Recall that Michael Young at first wouldn't take credit for *meritocracy* from fear of being ridiculed for creating a word that combined elements of Greek and Latin, and that Havelock Ellis thought *homosexual* was a barbarous Greco-Roman hybrid.)

When casting about for resources for a new word to describe the emerging field of artificial intelligence following World War II, MIT mathematician Norbert Wiener stuck to Greek. Number-crunching machines that he and others used were called *computers*, a ho-hum, misapplied term borrowed from an earlier use of that word for "those who compute" (clerks, bookkeepers, and the like). Since early computers were considered good for little more than doing calculations, this term sufficed. Wiener saw far broader applications on the horizon, however. That's why he thought a more expansive term was needed to refer not just to the calculating machines themselves but to the entire apparatus of artificial intelligence that Wiener was sure would one day control our lives. "As happens so often to scientists," he later wrote, "we have been forced to coin at least one artificial neo-Greek expression to fill the gap."

Wiener noodled first with *angelos*, but was concerned that this Greek word for "messenger" might have religious overtones. In any event, the idea of control was more central to his theories than messaging per se. Wiener then came up with *kubērnētes* ("steersman; one who steers"), the Greek name for the helmsmen of ships who appeared often in tales he'd devoured as a child. By adapting this word in its English pronunciation and adding the suffix *-ics*, Wiener created *cybernetics*. According to a popular account, when he floated his coinage among colleagues, one of them—Claude Shannon—advised him, "Use the word 'cybernetics', Norbert, because nobody knows what it means. This will always put you at an advantage in arguments."

Wiener took Shannon's purported advice and in 1948 published a book called *Cybernetics: Or Control and Communication in the Animal and the Machine*. In this book he speculated (among other things) that there might even come a time when computers could play chess with human beings.** Wiener referred often to "what the control engineers call *feed-back*." This referenced the key concept of artificial intelligence: that both natural and electromechanical systems adjust themselves based on information they generate. Wiener's continual reference to

---

** Wiener said that after *Cybernetics* was published he discovered that an existing French word, *cybernétique*, referred to the art of governing.

feed-back when discussing cybernetics was instrumental in introducing this term not just to professional but popular discourse. ("Let me give you some feedback.")

As with so many seminal works, the title of this one gained far greater currency than the book itself did. Not only did *Cybernetics* become the most common way to describe the emerging field of electronic intelligence, its first clause—*cyber*—supplied a prefix for many a coinage to come. In fact, this prefix proved to be far more useful than the entire word itself did. *Cybernetics* itself is seldom heard these days, but *cyber* certainly is. In late 2017 an American government official was said to have "a background in cyber at the Defense Department."

Although tapping Greek and Latin when coining words has faded along with study of those languages, roots from them both made an encore appearance in 2005 when a *San Francisco Chronicle* reporter asked Bay Area activist Jessica Prentice to name a group she was part of that advocated eating food grown locally. Prentice—a wordie as well as a foodie—scoured etymology sites on the Internet in search of inspiration. *Phagein*, Greek for "eat," and the root of *esophagus*, failed to inspire. On the other hand, combining *locus*, Latin for local, and *vorare*, "to swallow" produced *locavore*. This was a little smoother than the more technically correct *localvore*. Prentice also liked the idea of having *loca*, the Spanish word for "crazy woman" embedded in her word. And she saw operatic potential in the fact that *locavore* brings *amore* to mind. So locavore it was, making its debut in the June 1, 2005, edition of the *Chronicle*. Prentice's coinage soon began to appear online. When Barbara Kingsolver used it in her 2007 book *Animal, Vegetable, Miracle*, the deal was sealed. *Locavore* caught on so quickly that Oxford Dictionaries chose it as their word of the year for 2007.

Scratch Words

Most of the deliberately coined words we've considered so far were created by recycling existing words or borrowing elements of other languages. Few neologisms are pure inventions. "The majority of 'coined' words are forms that have been in one way or another created, augmented, cut down, combined, and recombined to convey new needed meanings," linguist Mario Pei wrote in *The Story of Language*. "The language mint is more than a mint; it is a great manufacturing center, where all sorts of productive activities go on unceasingly."

One elite group of word manufacturers don't just tap existing terminology to produce new terms, however, they create them from scratch. The results, which are notable for their scarcity, can be thought of as *scratch words*. Typically such terms come from the fertile imagination of those who are aren't interested in demonstrating familiarity with ancient languages, or impressing others with their intellectual prowess. They just want to please themselves and others.

YES, this is a "BLURB"!

All the Other Publishers commit them. Why Shouldn't We?

MISS
BELINDA
BLURB

IN
THE ACT OF
BLURBING

ARE YOU A BROMIDE?

BY

GELETT BURGESS

Say! Ain't this book a 90-H. P., six-cylinder Seller? If WE do say it as shouldn't, WE consider that this man Burgess has got Henry James locked into the coal-bin, telephoning for "Information"

WE expect to sell 350 copies of this great, grand book. It has gush and go to it, it has that Certain Something which makes you want to crawl through thirty miles of dense tropical jungle and bite somebody in the neck. No hero no heroine, nothing like that for OURS, but when you've *READ* this masterpiece, you'll know what a BOOK is, and you'll sic it onto your mother-in-law, your dentist and the pale youth who dips hot-air into Little Marjorie until 4 Q. M. in the front parlour. This book has 42-carat THRILLS in it. It fairly BURBLES. Ask the man at the counter what HE thinks of it! He's seen Janice Meredith faded to a mauve magenta. He's seen BLURBS before, and he's dead wise. He'll say:

This Book is the Proud Purple Penultimate!!

Cover of Gelett Burgess's book *Are You a Bromide?* (1907)

That was certainly true about the author of *Are You a Bromide?* This 1907 book gave a new meaning altogether to the term *bromide* (a chemical sometimes used as a tranquilizer in patent medicines), applying it to those who communicate with soporific clichés. More than a century later, we still call such pronouncements *bromides*.

For a publishers' convention held during the year it came out, *Are You a Bromide?* was wrapped in a jacket that featured an effusive-looking woman who is holding a cupped hand to her open mouth. According to the jacket's text, this was "Miss Belinda Blurb in the act of blurbing." Beneath that ID the publisher promised, "WE expect to sell 350 copies of this great, grand book. It has gush and go to it. It has that Certain Something which makes you want to crawl through thirty miles of dense tropical jungle and bite somebody in the neck. . . . This book has 42-carat THRILLS in it. It fairly BURBLES. Ask the man at the counter what HE thinks of it! . . . He's seen BLURBS before, and he's dead wise. He'll say *This Book is the Proud Purple Penultimate.*"

In remarks about his book, this author told the gathering that "to 'blurb' is to make a sound like a publisher. . . . A blurb is a check drawn on Fame, and it is seldom honored." Members of his audience apparently were not offended by this sendup of their ways. From the moment *blurb* made its debut, that term became the way publishing puffery is most often described. *Blurbs* tout books on book jackets and ads. Authors *blurb* them. Those books have been *blurbed*.

The author of *Are You a Bromide?* turned out to be none other than Gelett Burgess, the San Francisco humorist who'd already earned lexical fame with his books about the *Goops*. Burgess was a prolific coiner of words. Although few of them caught on, this graduate of MIT deserves more credit than your average neologizer because he didn't just tape together existing terms, add a prefix here and a suffix there, or scour dictionaries for Greek or Latin roots. Burgess created

SPLOOCH

Illustration of *splooch* in *Burgess Unabridged* (1914).

them from scratch. In 1914 he published a compilation of his scratch words called *Burgess Unabridged: A New Dictionary of Words You Have Always Needed*. This book's rationale, he explained, was that "we need so many new words, and we need 'em quick." *Wox* was Burgess's word for "a state of placid, satisfied contentment." *Splooch* meant to fail. An *oofle* was someone whose name escapes you; *oofling* meant trying to figure out that person's name without asking. Although none of these neologisms enjoyed the success of *goop* or *blurb*, they do illustrate the author's verbal dexterity and his moxie in creating coinages from freshly mined ore. In his foreword to *Burgess Unabridged*, Paul Dickson called its contents "an inspiration for those who dared play with and create new words."

De Novo Brands

That would include playwrights George Kaufman and Marc Connelly. In their 1924 play *Beggar on Horseback*, a character tells his daughter's fiancé that he's "in the widget business."

"The widget business?" asks the young man.

"Yes, sir!" replies his father-in-law-to-be. "I suppose I'm the biggest manufacturer in the world of overhead and underground A-erial widgets."

Not long after *Beggar on Horseback* ran on Broadway, the wooden cylinders used to carry messages in pneumatic tubes at the New York Stock Exchange (originally called "tube carriers") were renamed *widgets*. As a way to explain the workings of capitalism, General Motors produced a 1939 film about puppets who make and sell *widgets* in Widget-Land. In addition to being fun to say, this made-up word earned its keep as a generic term for anything in need of naming, hypothetical products especially. Unlike a *doohickey*, say, a *doodad*, *whatsit*, *thingamabob*, *thingamajig*, *thingie*, *gadget*, *gizmo*, or *gewgaw*, a *widget* sounds like it might actually do something or be something. In a *New Yorker* column about the virtues of scale, James Surowiecki pointed out that "the more widgets you produce, the cheaper each widget becomes." Today, of course, *widget* is a multipurpose techno-term that refers to all manner of apps.

Creating a word like *widget*, conveying its meaning, and then getting others to adopt that word is a formidable task. As Donka Minkova and Robert Stockwell observe in their book *English Words*, "Though one might think it an easy matter to create a new word (without basing it on some pre-existing word or part of a word), such creations are rare." The authors' short list of what they call "de novo words" includes older ones such as *flabbergast*, *fandangle*, and *flamdoodle*, along with more recent terms like *grungy*, *dongle*, and *Skype* (both noun and verb). Trademarked terms that Minkova and Stockwell cite as original creations include *Dacron*, *Teflon*, *Kevlar*, and *Kodak*.

The founder of Eastman Kodak, George Eastman, called his product's brand name "a purely arbitrary combination of letters, not derived in whole or in part from any existing word." A 1938 press prelease by Eastman Kodak about *The Origin of the Word Kodak* concluded that "philologically the word 'Kodak' is as meaningless as a child's first 'goo.' Terse, abrupt to the point of rudeness, literally bitten off by ice-cutting consonants at both ends. It snaps like a Kodak shutter." George Eastman's coinage was so successful that for a time it didn't just refer to cameras and film but to photographs themselves. My grandmother liked to call the many snapshots she took "Kodak studies."

Another ubiquitous brand coinage grew out of a morphine-free analgesic that Bayer developed in the late nineteenth century. The German drug company mistakenly thought this painkiller would be nonaddictive. Since its technical name (*diacetylmorphine*) wouldn't work in the marketplace, Bayer queried users about how the new medicine made them feel. "Heroic," was their overwhelming response. That inspired the name for this drug, that Bayer introduced in 1898: *Heroin.* For the next decade, the firm marketed Heroin aggressively as a painkiller and cough suppressant suitable for adults and children alike. Although

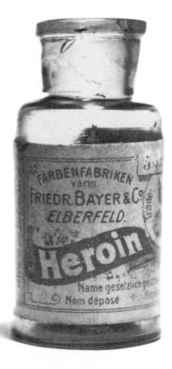

Bottle of "Heroin" analgesic, early twentieth century.

Bayer turned out to be wrong about the nonaddictive part, the word they coined for their medicine has lived on as the street name for a popular narcotic.

Escalator is a comparably durable coinage, and one that's more diverse. This term began life as the brand name of moving stairs invented in 1897 by Charles Seeberger of Otis Elevator. It combined *scala*, Greek for "steps," with the last two syllables of the company's primary product. *Escalator* is a rare commercial coinage that wasn't based on an existing word but did spawn a new one: *escalate*. When this verb joined the lexicon after World War I, one dictionary said it meant "to go up on an escalator." The *OED*'s definition of the new word was "To climb or reach by means of an escalator." *Escalation*, meaning "increase by degree," followed a few years later. Author Herman Kahn put this term on the geopolitical map with his 1965 book *On Escalation*. Soon after that, our need for a word to describe the growing American military presence in Vietnam added *escalation* and *escalate* to war coverage, now shorn of any association with *escalator*. That word itself took on generic meanings such as "escalator clauses," and "on a political escalator."

Another commercial coinage that inspired a generic term apparently came from Bertram Work, the CEO of B. F. Goodrich. After World War I, this rubber products company began selling galoshes called "Mystik Boots." These boots had an innovative tooth-and-hook fastener that was invented in 1917 by one Gideon Sundback. Sundback called his invention a "separable fastener." According to company lore, Work wanted a more active name for this fastener. To show what he meant, the CEO slid the slider of the boot's fastener up and down its teeth, saying, "Zip her up! Zip her up!" From this humble origin emerged *zipper*, which Goodrich trademarked in 1925. *Zipper* soon went generic, describing not just the fasteners on Mystik Boots but any fastener like it (a type of neology triumph that merchants themselves dread because they feel it degrades their brand name) and inspired variations such as *zipless* and *zip it!*

One enduring marketplace neologism has Gallic roots: *cellophane*. A poll conducted on the eve of World War II found that Americans considered *cellophane* to be the third most beautiful word in the English language (after "mother," and "memory"). This clear, crackly wrapping paper was created in 1908 by a Swiss chemist named Jacques Edwin Brandenberger, who named it by combining the French terms *cellulose* and *diaphane* ("transparent / translucent"). Brandenberger's coinage became so deeply embedded in our discourse that one can still hear old-timers use the term *cellophane* for transparent wrapping of any kind.

And The Winner Is . . . .

Two decades after DuPont introduced *cellophane*, its researchers developed a synthetic fiber meant to improve on rayon. Its chemical name was *polyhexamethyleneadipamide*. For the sake of simplicity, those working on this new fabric called it *Rayon 66* (or "66" for short). Since rayon had a reputation for shoddiness, that name didn't fly. DuPonters then took to calling their product *Fiber 66*, which wasn't much better. As an alternative, DuPont's president, Lamott du Pont, proposed *Delawear* (for the company's home state), or *neosheen*. A company vice president added *Duponese*, *pontella*, and *lustrol* to the mix. Another executive suggested *Duparooh*, an acronym for "DuPont Pulls a Rabbit Out of Hat." None caught on.

DuPont employees were then asked to propose some alternatives. An in-house "Name for Fiber 66 Committee" winnowed some four hundred suggestions that poured into DuPont's Wilmington headquarters. They included *Wacara*, a play on the name of *polyhexamethyleneadipamide*'s principal inventor, Wallace Carothers. In her book on *Nylon*, Susannah Handley lists *Amidarn*, *Artex*, *Dusilk*, *Dulon*, *Linex*, *Lasica*, *Morsheen*, *Novasilk*, *Nusilk*, *Ramex*, *Silpon*, *Self*, *Tensheer*, and *Terikon* as other names that were proposed. None of them won DuPont's contest. The new product's naming committee was at an impasse. Its chair then threw *norun* into the mix. This was actually a misnomer. Threads of the new fabric did unravel, or "run." An alternative, *nuron*, brought *moron* to mind. It also sounded like a patent medicine. *Nilon* didn't, but could be pronounced too many ways. *Nylon*, on the other hand, could only be pronounced "neye-lon." So *nylon* won the day, becoming one of the most successful brand name inventions in the history of American commerce. And, incidentally, a scratch coinage, not just a play on existing words.

Despite the failure of DuPont's in-house competition to rename Fiber 66, other corporate naming contests have enjoyed more success. In 1948, for example, thirty-one researchers and executives at the Bell Telephone Laboratories were asked to vote on possible names for a small semiconductor recently developed there. A memo attached to their ballot explained the rationale for six possible names: four variations on *triode*, as well as *icatron* and *transistor*. The latter, apparently suggested by engineer John Robinson Pierce (a sometime writer of science fiction), combined elements of *varistor* and *transconductance*. It won in a landslide.

Competitions to name new products have not been limited to employees of the product's company. When thrown open to the public, coining-by-contest—a prior-day form of crowdsourcing—has produced a notable number of useful neologisms. One such competition was mounted by a Massachusetts prohibitionist named Delcevare King. In 1923 King, a wealthy banker, offered $200 to whoever came up with the best word for "lawless drinkers," those who flouted Prohibition by consuming liquor. A panel of three judges that included the superintendent of the Anti-Saloon League of America, a Boston clergyman, and King himself judged the thousands of entries that poured in from every state. After rejecting suggestions such as "boozocrat" and "boozshevik," the judges chose a winner that King then announced: *scofflaw*. Two contestants from his own state, Henry Dale of Andover and Kate Butler from Dorchester, both submitted that portmanteau. They were awarded $100 apiece. Soon after the winners were declared, on January 24, 1924, a movie studio announced that it planned to produce *The Adorable Scofflaw*, a film about "a young dapper addicted to the cocktail habit."

Extensive research by etymologist Barry Popik has determined how much ridicule this contest-winning word received in the press. One newspaper said it sounded like a dish served under the heading of "German home cooking." Another portrayed a prohibitionist saying "Scofflaw!" to a drinker, who then falls to his knees pleading, "No, No, anything but that." The word had a certain allure, however. Although one detractor pointed out that *scofflaw* could be defined in different ways, this turned out to be a virtue. After the original definition of *scofflaw* died with Prohibition, its broader reference to someone who flouts the law lives on. In terms of durability, Popik has concluded, the word-of-the-year for 1924 should have been *scofflaw*.***

Another naming competition was a bit less structured than Mr. King's. This one resulted from the fact that the George A. Hormel company needed a better name than "spiced ham" for the canned cured pork product it had introduced in 1936. At a New Year's Eve party that year, company president Jay Hormel told guests that whoever proposed an alternative would get a free cocktail. After several improbable names were tossed out, the brother of a Hormel vice president, an actor named Kenneth Daigneau, suggested "Spam."

With the help of its new moniker, this product was enormously popular (except among the many World War II veterans who swore they'd never eat another bite, after consuming so much Spam in the field). Its name became one of the most versatile words in the English vernacular. During the war, GIs called their landing crafts a "Spam fleet." British soldiers in the Gulf War later said those given an unwelcome mission had been "Spammed." In Dr. Seuss's *The Tooth Book* (1981), Pam the Clam said, "No teeth at all. I cannot eat / roast leg of lamb./ Or peanuts! Pizza! Popcorn! SPAM!" Although this line appeared long after the meat medley had disappeared from most American pantries, Theodor Geisel said he could find no better word to replace it. So SPAM! it was. By putting that word in

***Even though this book is primarily about English neologisms, it should be noted that when a Danish newspaper in 1902 asked readers to suggest a better word for *automobil*, its winning entry—*bil*—remains the way cars are referred to not only in Denmark but throughout Scandinavia.

the forefront of young readers, and those who read to them, Geisel helped keep this prize-winning coinage alive in our vocabulary.

Spam was so popular in postwar Great Britain that Uncle Sam was renamed "Uncle Spam" there. In time, however, among Brits this product came to symbolize tedious, low-end food. A 1970 Monty Python routine featured a group of Vikings who storm into a café whose menu is filled with Spam-based dishes, chanting, "Spam, Spam, Spam, Spam, lovely Spam, lovely Spam", making it impossible for anyone else to talk. This routine inspired early programmers and hobbyists (among whom Monty Python was quite popular) to call endless rants by chat room participants "spam," sometimes filling the screen of such bloated posts with "SPAM SPAM SPAM SPAM SPAM." More broadly, masses of data that interfere with online discourse became known as *spam*. Programmer Joel Furr is thought to have first used this word for bulk emails dispatched by *spammers*.

Every winning entry in a word-coining contest doesn't enjoy this much success, of course. In fact, few do. Voting is a far better way to choose political leaders than new words. Neil Howe, who along with coauthor William Strauss gave the *Millennial Generation* its name in their 1991 book *Generations* (which included a chapter about those born after 1981 called "Millennial Generation") later turned to the Internet for help naming those born after 2004. The overwhelming choice was *Homeland Generation*. That appellation disappeared soon after its contest victory in 2005. (The more prosaic *Gen Z* subsequently caught on, begetting *Zoomers* after Zoom became their preferred online gathering place during the Covid-19 pandemic.) So it so often goes. When it comes to word coinage, nonstarters are the norm. They include not just contest winners like *Homeland Generation* but most of the words created by determined neologizers, even ones who have coined neologisms that did become part of the lexicon.

15

Nonstarters

IN THE SPRING of 1940 a stripteaser named Georgia Sothern wrote H. L. Mencken to ask if he could come up with a more suitable name than *stripper* for members of her profession. "Strip-teasing is a formal and rhythmic disrobing of the body in public," Sothern explained. "In recent years there has been a great deal of uninformed criticism leveled against my profession. Most of it is without foundation and arises because of the unfortunate word strip-teasing, which creates the wrong connotations in the mind of the public. I feel sure that if you could coin a new and more palatable word to describe this art, the objections to it would vanish and I and my colleagues would have easier going."

Mencken sympathized with Sothern's plight. He had some thoughts: "It might be a good idea to relate strip-teasing in some way or other to the associated zoological phenomenon of molting. Thus the word moltician comes to mind, but it must be rejected because of its likeness to mortician. A resort to the scientific name for molting, which is ecdysis, produces both ecdysist and ecdysiast."

Sothern liked this suggestion, and so did her press agent. Hardly anyone else did, however. Who could pronounce that term? How was it spelled? What did it mean?

Even Sothern's colleague, Gypsy Rose Lee, had no time for Mencken's coinage. When a *World-Telegram* reporter looked in on Lee as she was about to appear at the New York World's Fair, the stripteaser waved a copy of *Time* magazine that mentioned Mencken's new name for members of her profession. "'Ecdysiast' he calls me!" exclaimed Lee. "Why the man is an intellectual slob. He has been reading books. Dictionaries. We don't wear feathers and molt them off. He makes me think of the girl reporter out in Chicago who asked me if I used zippers when I stripped. Imagine! Zippers! Why I'd catch my—"

The reporter interrupted Lee's soliloquy to ask if she'd ever read anything by Mencken. Indeed she had, said Lee. She was familiar with Mencken's writing.

Poster for 1953 movie *Striporama*, featuring Georgia Sothern (on right).

"What does he know about stripping?" Lee wanted to know. "I hope he comes out to the Fair this summer to see me toss 'em off and that he lets me know he's in the audience. I'll make his hair stand on end!"

It wasn't that Lee objected to a tonier name for stripteasers. She just didn't like Mencken's. Lee thought a new term based on déshabiller, the French word for undressing, made more sense. This proposal got no more play than Mencken's did.

Two decades after it was coined, *ecdysiast* made an encore appearance in the 1959 musical *Gypsy*, where librettist Arthur Laurents had some fun with Mencken's neologism. "Some man called me an ecdysiast," his Gypsy told the audience. "An ecdysiast is one who–or that which–sheds its skin. In vulgar parlance, a stripper. But I'm not a stripper. At these prices, I'm an ecdysiast!"

The problem with so many deliberate coinages such as *ecdysiast* is that the effort shows. As a result, the vast majority are stillborn. Even those that linger for a time seldom stick around. When one searches the word "coined" online, it's striking how many neologisms that at one time looked promising have disappeared. For every coinage that joins the language, even briefly, thousands die a premature death. Some deserved a better fate. Most didn't.

Sniglet Syndrome

In the late 1980s comedian Rich Hall produced a popular series of books devoted to what he called "sniglets," words that don't appear in dictionaries but should. Some were quite clever. They included *frust* ("the small line of debris that refuses to be swept onto the dust pan"), *slurm* ("the slime that accumulates on the underside of a soap bar when it sits in the dish too long"), *hozone* ("the place where one sock in every load of laundry disappears to"), and *narcolepulacy* ("the contagious act of yawning, causing everyone else in sight to also yawn"). None of these neologisms became a lasting part of the vernacular, however. Nor did *sniglet* itself.

Think of this as *sniglet syndrome*: the coining of clever words that have a short life expectancy. This didn't begin with *sniglets*. The invention of witty words that aren't viable has a long history. More than a century ago a London literary journal called *The Academy* held a competition for useful new terms, offering prizes to winners. Submissions included *incompoop* for a tax collector, *glug* for the greasy mud found on streets of large cities at that time, and *gluzy* for something not exactly oily, creamy, or glutinous, but some of each. A catastrophe was given the name *conflumtion*. Trivial irrelevancies were *quinnydingles*, objects of little importance *whifflement*. In their January 14, 1899, issue the *Academy*'s editors announced that they'd awarded a guinea (20 shillings) to Mrs. H. M. Bayne of Blackheath Hill for three submissions they liked: *roofer* (a letter of thanks after staying under someone's roof), *crotion* (an occurrence worth crowing about), and *blue-domer* (one who claims to worship better beneath the blue dome of heaven than in any church). The *Academy*'s editors subsequently said that considerable interest surrounded both *blue-domer* and another winner, *penandincompoop*, referring to a stupid writer. That interest didn't last long.

Nearly three decades later, in 1927, New York's *Forum* magazine asked readers to send them suggestions for new words. Even though H. L. Mencken himself liked some of their submissions, such as *sothers* (brothers and sisters), *hesh* (he and she), and *megaphonia* (talking too loudly), not a one of the *Forum* readers' many proposed neologisms became part of our vocabulary.

With rare exceptions, such as *scofflaw* and *Spam*, this is the usual fate of competitive word coining. Submissions to such competitions are top-heavy with self-conscious neologisms of little lasting utility. When NPR held a contest to come up with a word for almost-sneezing, *snizzle* was the most popular of 2700 entries (being submitted by 328 listeners). Variations on "choo" were also popular: *ischoo, no choo, not choo, deja choo, pseudachoo, missed oppa-choo-nity,* and *about-choo*. So were ones based on gesundheit: *gesundhalt, gesundheist, gesundflight, gesundmight, gesund-less,* and *gesund-ain't*. As their winner NPR's judges chose *sniff-hanger,* a term submitted by four contestants. When was the last time you heard of a sniff-hanger?

Winners of word-coining contests seldom outlive their fifteen minutes of fame. That's because these competitions favor wit over utility. They exist not so much to create a useful word as to see who can be most amusing. This underlies what language maven Barbara Wallraff calls "the Catch-22 of word coining: If a word is clever enough that people will notice it and admire you for coining it, it's too clever to earn a place in our language for real." Based on her many years of judging an *Atlantic* magazine word-creation contest, Wallraff distinguishes between the "actual coining" of usable terms and the "recreational coining" of clever words like most of those that were submitted to her (and provided the basis of her 2006 book *Word Fugitives*). Blogger/author Paul McFedries calls such terms "stunt words." At best they appeal more to neologism devotees than to potential users. McFedries's *Word Spy* website is filled with cute coinages that evoked a chuckle or two when they first appeared, then quickly vanished (e.g., *cord-never*, n., a person who has never subscribed to a cable television package; *adultescent*, n., a middle-aged person who continues to participate in and enjoy youth culture, and *hasbian*, n., a former lesbian who is now in a heterosexual relationship).*

Pop-Ups

The future of many such terms at first looked promising. Some even attracted lots of attention when introduced. After burning brightly for a time, however, they fizzled out. This was the fate of *snowmageddon*, a coinage heard often in late 2008 to describe severe snowstorms that paralyzed the Northeast and Canada. Following its brief vogue, however, *snowmageddon* joined *ecdysiast* and *sniff-hanger* in the neology graveyard. Joining it there was *Frankenstorm*, a term coined by weather forecaster James Cisco as Hurricane Sandy approached America's East Coast in 2012. *Frankenstorm* quickly gave way to *Superstorm Sandy* once that storm reached land. *Superstorm* itself continues to show up now and again, but *Frankenstorm* doesn't. Nor does *snowmageddon*.

Just as a child's precociousness says little about the likelihood that he or she will become a high-achieving adult, the fact that a newly coined word makes a favorable first impression is no guarantee of its long-term viability. Even coinages that are reviewed favorably by journalists, authors, and linguists when they first appear routinely vanish. Like seasonal kiosks, such terms pop up, do some trade,

---

* Mingled among the many nonstarters on *Word Spy*, McFedries's list of the "Top 100" neologisms he's spotted during more than two decades on the job are such success stories as *carbon neutral, social networking, helicopter parenting, gaydar, affluenza, crowdfunding, man cave, chick flick, work-life balance, wardrobe malfunction, bucket list,* and *spin*.

then disappear. To recoin a word—a phrase, actually—they proved to be little more than *pop-ups*.

New words rooted in current events are particularly likely to become pop-ups. Calling closeted gay men *toe-tappers* who have a *wide stance*, as we did for a time during the early twenty-first century, makes no sense to those who aren't familiar with the fact that after being charged with soliciting sex in an airport men's room in 2007, then-senator Larry Craig (R-ID) explained that he tapped his toes beneath adjacent pubic bathroom stalls because he had a wide stance when seated on the toilet.

Terms that are time- and context-specific seldom have lasting utility. None illustrated this syndrome better than those anointed as words-of-the-year. In 1999, for example, the American Dialect Society (ADS) chose *Y2K* for that honor. This term disappeared quickly along with concern about computers being ill-equipped to handle the rollover to a new century. The Society's word for 2000—*chad*—was tied closely to that year's presidential election debacle in which "chads" still hanging on punch-card ballots in Florida made them so hard to re-count. Since punch cards are seldom used in elections anymore, that word has lost its viability. *Plutoed*, ADS's word of the year for 2006—defined as "demoted or devalued"—didn't survive the outrage over that planet's demotion to "dwarf planet." (Pluto has since been reinstated to planet status.) The ADS word of the year for 2007, *subprime*, faded along with the Great Recession. *Occupy*, their word of the year in 2011, was tied too tightly to the anti–Wall Street movement that disappeared along with this recoinage. (Centuries earlier *occupy* enjoyed a long run as a euphemism for sex.)** This is part of the broader syndrome in which coined words lose currency along with their inspiration, especially eponyms based on names-in-the-news.

Spent Coins

On the eve of the Spanish-American War, a group of American soldiers led by naval officer Richmond Hobson took the USS *Merrimac* to Cuba. There they planned to sink this steamship in Santiago's harbor, making it impassable, should the U.S. invade the Spanish colony. Before their plan could be carried out, however, the *Merrimac* came under heavy fire and its crew was captured. A few weeks

---

** In fairness to the ADS, they don't necessarily assume that their words of the year will outlive their prominence. Furthermore, some of their words of the year have proved to be more than pop-ups. They include *9/11* (2001), *weapons of mass destruction* (2001), *red/blue/purple* states (2004), *tweet* (2009), and *app* (2010). App may prove to be not just the word of the year but the word of the decade, or longer.

later they were freed in a prisoner exchange and returned to the United States. There, Lieutenant Hobson was lionized for his heroism and swooned over for his chiseled good looks. As he toured the country promoting America's war with Spain, the sailor was continually accosted by smitten women. Richmond Hobson was the Elvis Presley of his time. As a result, *Hobsonize* became slang for aggressively flirtatious behavior. A 1904 *Baltimore American* article noted that in Atlantic City one could observe lots of "Hobsonizing on the beach."

Although Richmond Hobson stayed in the public eye for a time after being elected to Congress (where he became a champion of women's suffrage, prohibition, and fair treatment of black soldiers), the eponym his name inspired is long forgotten. That's almost inevitable when it comes to neologisms based on the names of celebrities such as Hobson's contemporary Horace Fletcher, aka "The Great Masticator," who was a household name in the late nineteenth and early twentieth centuries. In several popular books, Fletcher touted the benefits of chewing one's food a hundred times per minute. Doing so became known as *Fletcherism*. Before that, *Grahamism* referred to the austere diet recommended by a clergyman named Sylvester Graham in the mid-nineteenth century. Adherents

Lieutenant Richmond P. Hobson, U.S. Navy, ca. 1898.

were called *Grahamites*. (A few decades after Rev. Graham died in 1851, the Graham cracker was named after him.) A century ago such eponyms needed no explanation. Nor did one coined by the epigrammist Elbert Hubbard: *Romeikitis*, referring to habitual reading of news clippings about oneself. Hubbard's coinage was inspired by the name of the founder of America's first news-clipping service, Henry Romeike, who died in 1903. Over time, *Romeikitis* lost its utility for two reasons: (1) who clips papers anymore? and (2) who's Henry Romeike?

The same syndrome can be seen in once-iconic book and movie titles whose relevance has faded with changing times. When *Looking for Mr. Goodbar*, a 1975 novel based on the murder of a New York schoolteacher by a man she'd met in a bar called *Mr. Goodbar*, was popular (as was a 1977 movie it inspired), the name of that bar clearly alluded to perilous assignations. Today *Mr. Goodbar* is more of a "Huh?" type of allusion. So is *Peyton Place*, as the Boomers and pre-Boomers who were so titillated by that 1956 novel, as well as the 1957 movie based on this book, and the 1964–69 TV series it inspired, die off. Calling a community a *Peyton Place* no longer arouses the same steamy imagery that it once did.

No Matter

Whether a new term lives or dies has little to do with factors that might matter in another context. Wittiness has little weight. Literary merit is beside the point. So is the prominence of a neologizer. When she was secretary of state, Madeleine Albright coined *internestic* for matters that combined international and domestic issues. It hasn't been heard from since. Visa founder Dee Hock called complex systems that blend chaos and order *chaordic*; not a bad coinage, but not one many others adopted. Nor did they take to *dontopedalogy*, Prince Philip's word for "the science of opening your mouth and putting your foot in it, a science which I have practiced for a good many years."

The word creations of prominent authors routinely sink from sight no less than any others'. In addition to the many coinages in his plays that became part of the English language, Shakespeare failed to attract users for *pudency* (shyness), *sprag* (clever), *credent* (trusting), or the insulting term *fustilarian*, which Falstaff employed in *Henry V* when he said to Mistress Quickly, "You fustilarian!" William Makepeace Thackeray was no better able to get us to adopt *melophonist*, his attempt to improve on "singer," or *munchet* for a small piece of bread. After novelist James Fenimore Cooper called a woman of his native land an *Americaness*, this word died a quick and well-deserved death. So did J. R. R Tolkien's *eucatastrophe* ("the sudden happy turn in a story which pierces you with a joy that brings tears"). Anthony Trollope's *elsewards* (going elsewhere) went nowhere, as did Graham Greene's *urinoir* for a public toilet, and Thomas

Browne's *retromingent* for urinating backward. Even the celebrated poly-coiner John Milton added many a miss to his hundreds of hits, nonstarters such as *opiniastrous* (opinionated), *quotationist* (one who quotes others), and *intervolve* (to involve one with another). Milton's charming word for silliness—*goosery*—didn't catch on, but perhaps should have.

Obviously an ability to write prose, poetry, or plays doesn't necessarily translate into a flair for coining usable words. This isn't due to lack of effort on the part of writers such as Roald Dahl. Dahl tried hard enough. Even in conversation the author liked to use words of his own making, as when the author told his young daughter that the reason he drank whiskey wasn't because he liked its taste so much as the "nice whizzly feeling it gives you." Dahl's books were a mint of coined words. To celebrate what would have been his hundredth birthday, Oxford published a hefty *Roald Dahl Dictionary* that is filled with hundreds of words he coined, recoined, or popularized. At the same time the *OED* itself added six Dahlisms to its pages. They included *Ooompa Loopa*, *Scrumdiddlyuptious*, and *golden ticket*, like those handed out by eccentric chocolatier Willy Wonka in *Charlie and the Chocolate Factory* (1964). Wonka's name constitutes Dahl's most successful contribution to the vernacular, where it still alludes to eccentrics. ("He's the Willy Wonka of engineering.") But that isolated example paled beside Roald Dahl's many verbal concoctions that did not become part of common parlance, ones such as *lickswishy* (tasty), *chiddler* (child), *sogmire* (quagmire), *cattlepiddler* (caterpillar), *whizzpopping* (farting), and *frobscottle* (a fizzy drink whose bubbles fall rather than rise). Today such words are used primarily by dedicated Dahlites when used at all.

Failure to attract customers is an occupational hazard of peddling neologisms. Even success coining one word doesn't guarantee success coining another. As with bestselling first novels that are followed by meagerly selling second ones, usable neologisms routinely give way to useless terms created by the same neologizer. In the word-coining business, sophomore slump is routine.

Sophomore Slump

After hitting a home run with *cyberspace*, William Gibson struck out with *personal micro-culture* (referring to one's own type of creativity, not one emulating others'). British psychologist David Lewis added *road rage* to the modern lexicon, but couldn't get fellow speakers of English to join him in calling Internet-resisting managers *internots* (an existing if obscure term that he tried to popularize). Another Lewis, Boston College English professor Paul Lewis, found many users for his word *Frankenfood* (genetically modified comestibles), but few for *schoomeoisie* (talkative members of the bourgeoisie), *celebfatigue* (overexposure to news about celebrities), or *likespeak* (teenage argot).

R. D. Rosen tried to capitalize on his success with *psychobabble* by coining *biteability* (the trend to using shorter and shorter pieces of information), *millencholy* (for our mood as the century changed), and *bullcrit* (about the tendency for critics to assess books based on reviews written by others). Although *bullcrit* did get some play here and there for a time, it soon disappeared.

This is a common fate suffered by coiners of multiple words: mingling an occasional hit with many misses. In one case, that fate involved an entire gang of enthusiastic word creators: members of a BBC committee on new words who met during the mid-1930s under the tutelage of Logan Pearsall Smith. In a time of rapid change, Smith thought this task was urgent. When it came to naming their era's many new inventions, processes, and ideas, he said, "If happy words are not found, ugly and awkward ones will take their place."

Initially Smith's committee was charged with recommending terminology for the emerging field of television. In particular the BBC needed a TV-watching counterpart to radio's "listeners." Because he thought television receivers should be called *view-boxes*, Smith liked *view-box gazer*. No one else did. Two members lobbied unsuccessfully for *looker-in*. Other terms the committee's members considered included *viewer-in, auralooker, looker, glancer, optaruist, optovisor, seer, sighter, tele-looker, teleseer, teleserver, televist, teleobservist, televor, visionnaire, visionist, visor,* and *vizior*. Finally, reluctantly, they endorsed a proposal by the BBC's Committee on Spoken English that *televiewer* be adopted until something better came along. Something did. Televiewer was shortened to *viewer*, the term we still use for those who watch television.

Not content to stick to telly technology, Smith's committee then turned its attention to other areas of contemporary life that they thought could use new words, or at least better ones. *Zoological garden* might best be clipped to *zoo*. Members of any military branch should be called *servicemen*. At Smith's behest, the new word committee enjoyed its biggest success recommending that England's traffic circles be called *roundabouts* instead of "gyratory circuses." They soon were, and still are. Their irrepressible chairman then proposed that traffic lights be called *stop-and-goes*. And why not call brain waves *mindfalls*? One member of Smith's committee thought "inferiority complex" could be condensed to *inflex*. Another suggested that Christmas festivities be called *yulery*. What fun!

At this point cooler heads prevailed. Should any of these "ludicrous" terms be broadcast, a BBC official warned, they would cause irreparable harm to the reputation of Britain's official broadcast service. This dampened the committee's ardor. In early 1936 it disbanded. To add insult to injury, decades later some participants in an online discussion about this chapter in BBC history said they liked *gyratory circus* better than *roundabout*.

Word Invention

In 1830 Isaac Pitman introduced a form of abbreviated phonetic writing that he called *Stenographic Sound Hand*. This system enjoyed much success under another name, *Shorthand* (an existing way to describe abbreviated notes). Pitman did no better with *Phonotypy*, the title of his 1844 book about a reformed system of spelling that he called the English Phonotypic Alphabet, one based on *phonography*, the title of an earlier book by Pittman. As Bill Bryson observed in *The Mother Tongue*, Pitman's case illustrates the fact that "inventors are generally hopeless at naming their inventions."

Another inventor, William Fox Talbot, further illustrated Bryson's point. When Talbot invented a picture-taking process during the 1830s, he first called it *sciagraphy* (using shadows to portray objects), then *photogenic drawing*. "Wouldn't 'photography' be a better word?" wondered his colleague John Herschel. After all, *telegraphy* and *lithography* were on many lips at the time. Why not add *photography* to the mix? Those who worked in this field might rather be called *photographers* than *photogenisizers*, he pointed out. And *photographs* certainly improved on *sciagraphs*, or *photogenic drawings*. Herschel's word (Greek for "light drawing") won the day. So did *positive* and *negative*, his subsequent recoinage of those two words for the basis of Talbot's photographic process. (Naming things ran in Herschel's family: his father, William, a noted astronomer, was the first to call space rocks *asteroids*.) Since Talbot's rival Louis Daguerre called his own pictures *daguerreotypes*, friends urged him to call a photoengraving process he developed in the 1840s *talbotypes*. Talbot noodled with that name for a time, even allowing it to be used in the title of a pamphlet, but ultimately stuck with the more modest *calotypes*.

A couple of decades after Talbot invented photography, a Welsh cavalry officer named Walter Clopton Wingfield created a version of tennis to be played on grass. Major Wingfield called his invention *Sphairistikè* (neo-Greek for "ball play"). In 1869 Wingfield demonstrated Sphairistikè to a group of friends that included Arthur Balfour, who later became Britain's prime minister. All agreed that its name was too hard to pronounce. Balfour suggested that Wingfield call his invention *lawn tennis*. Under this name the game took off. Wingfield himself published a book in 1874 titled *The Major's Game of Lawn Tennis*.

Two years later, Alexander Graham Bell patented a device he'd invented that could convey the human voice by electronic signals transmitted on wires through a process he called *electric speech*. Bell couldn't decide whether to call his invention a *speaking telegraph* or a *harmonic telegraph*. How about neither one? asked his wife. At her behest, Bell reluctantly adopted *telephone*, an existing term that combined the Greek words *tele* for "distant," and *phone* for "sound."

Walter Clopton Wingfield, inventor of *Sphairistikè* (aka *lawn tennis*) in 1881. Cover of its rule book, 1874.

Successful inventors such as Alexander Graham Bell routinely prove to be as inept at naming their inventions as they are ept at creating them. If ever a group needed interpreters to help them come up with names for their creations, it's those who invent. Take Dow Chemical's Ralph Wiley. As a young lab assistant, in 1933 Wiley made one of the most important discoveries in modern consumer history as he struggled to clean a laboratory vial. Closer examination determined that it was coated with a solvent-resistant polymer. Thinking that this substance might have commercial prospects, Wiley called it *eonite*, the name of an indestructible material in the comic strip *Little Orphan Annie*. During World War II Dow chemists used Wiley's polymer as the basis for a coating to protect airplane bodies. After the war it became a protective sealant for car seats. In the mid-1950s what Wiley had called *eonite* found its real calling and a better name: as a clingy food wrapping called *Saran Wrap*. That name was created by Wiley's boss at Dow, Jack Reilly. Rather than tap some erudite or pop cultural source for his root, Reilly created *Saran* by combining the names of his wife, Sarah, and daughter, Ann.

Bucky

During the late 1940s Buckminster Fuller designed a modernistic home he called "the 4D House." That terse coinage was based on Fuller's fascination with the notion of a spatial fourth dimension. Abbreviated as "4D," this concept was included in the name of many of his projects, including a "4D House." When that circular dwelling was displayed at the Marshall Field department store in Chicago in 1929, its executives thought a catchier name would be in order. To come up with one, they hired an ad man named Waldo Warren. Warren shadowed Fuller for several days, jotting down terms the inventor liked to use. Since Bucky (his commonly used nickname) was partial to complex words, Warren concluded that the new one should be multisyllabic. Because *dynamic*, *maximum*, and *tension* recurred continually in Fuller's speech, Warren welded them together to create *dymaxion*. This impressive if essentially meaningless term caught Fuller's fancy. He used it repeatedly thereafter, not just for the Dymaxion House on display at Marshall Field with its Dymaxion Bathroom, but his three-wheeled Dymaxion Automobile, a Dymaxion World Map, and Dymaxion Deployment Units, or DDUs (inexpensive dwellings fashioned from circular grain bins that housed radar units during World War II). In a sense, *dymaxion* was a coinage collaboration between Fuller and Warren. Or, one might say, the product of a ghostcoiner.

No inventor was more hapless at naming his own inventions than Buckminster Fuller. Not that he would have agreed. Fuller, who owned 2000 patents, was an avid if uninspired neologizer. Bucky thought that funneling resources toward *livingry* rather than weaponry would help ensure human survival. He and members of his family considered *sunsight* and *sunclipse* an improvement on *sunrise* and *sunset*. Fuller also thought *world-around* was a better term than *worldwide*. *Ephemeralization* was a positive word in the inventor's vocabulary, referring to our increasing ability to do more with less. Fuller's 1951 coinage of the phrase *spaceship earth* did gain a following during the *Whole Earth Catalog* era of the late 1960s. The inventor also adapted the existing words *geodesy*, *geodetic*, and

Only remaining Dymaxion House, Henry Ford Museum, Dearborn, Michigan.

geodetical for the *geodesic dome* that he patented in 1954. This dome was built according to what Fuller called *tensegrity*, using tension and compression rather than supporting components to stabilize structural elements. Fuller is sometimes credited with coining the term *synergy*, but its actual etymology dates back centuries (though Bucky's frequent use of that obscure term did help make it a ubiquitous part of our modern language). Managers in particular adopted this word to describe combined group efforts that produced more than the sum of their parts. Fuller himself used synergy as the basis for *synergetics*, a favorite term of his (referring to the study of systems in transformation). A 1962 compendium of his work was called *Synergetics: Explorations in the Geometry of Thinking*.

When he studied with Buckminster Fuller at Southern Illinois University a half century ago, my brother Gene attended a seminar where Fuller talked of *syntropy*, telling the class that he'd just coined this word. The inventor-professor defined *syntropy* as "a tendency towards order and symmetrical combinations, designs of ever more advantageous and orderly patterns. Evolutionary cooperation. Anti-entropy." Whether or not Fuller actually thought he'd coined *syntropy*, that term had already been used by mathematician Luigi Fantappiè in 1941, nearly three decades before the seminar Gene attended. In this surprisingly common syndrome, many a coinage doesn't catch on when freshly minted, but years later gets excavated, cleaned up, and put back in circulation.

16

Van Winkle Words

ON JANUARY 28, 1754, Horace Walpole wrote a long, chatty letter to his friend Horace Mann. In this letter the political and literary luminary called a recent discovery "of that kind which I call Serendipity." Walpole said this whimsical coinage grew out of a children's tale called *The Three Princes of Serendip* (as Sri Lanka was then known), whose protagonists were forever making accidental discoveries.

Horace Walpole was an incorrigible word coiner. He called early hot air balloonists *airgonauts*, who engaged in *airgonation*. To him, drunkenly maudlin figures were *muckibus*. Any intermediate state was *betweenity*, a coinage that attracted a bit of attention in the early nineteenth century, then disappeared.

Walpole apparently did not consider *serendipity* to be one of his better word creations. In fact, his passing reference to that word when writing Mann was the first and last time Walpole is known to have recorded it on paper. After making its debut this way, *serendipity* took a long nap, one that lasted more than a century. It awoke to reappear in a collection of Walpole's correspondence that was published in 1857. (An earlier collection, in 1833, did not think the letter that contained *serendipity* was worth including.) No known reviewer of the 1857 volume took note of Walpole's neologism, however. It then resumed its slumber before reawakening to make occasional appearances in British literary discourse during the late 1870s. Sporadic uses after that included one by an American magazine columnist who in 1903 reported that a friend had told him, "I've found a new word and a new amusement for you. It's serendipity."

When Walpole's coinage did appear in print, it typically was accompanied by comments about the word's peculiarity. "Curious," it was called, "odd-sounding," "strange-looking," "silly," and "outlandish." During the late Victorian era only a few outliers, like the owner of a London bookstore called the Serendipity Shop, took this word seriously. Even then they didn't always get it right. In 1905 a *New York Times* review of an essay on serendipity called those who make

Horace Walpole, 1754.

accidental discoveries *serendippers*. Seven years later Samuel McChord Crothers, a Unitarian minister in Cambridge, Massachusetts, wrote about his "serendipitaceous" mind. Rev. Crothers then shared the root of this word with Walter Cannon, a prominent scholar at the Harvard Medical School. Dr. Cannon liked it so well that he became a proselytizer for the neologism. In 1932 Cannon called a lecture "Serendipity." After that he used Walpole's coinage repeatedly in his writing and speeches. (Cannon himself coined the phrase *fight or flight* and propagated use of the term *homeostasis*.)

Other scholars also took to *serendipity*, combining as it did elements of chance, luck, and intention in an ear-pleasing way. Writers of many stripes began to use it as well. *Serendipity* showed up not only in works of history written by Hendrik Van Loon but in a detective story by S. S. Dine. James Joyce referred to a *serendipitist* in *Finnegan's Wake* (1939). Fifteen years later, in 1954, a *Detroit Free Press* columnist referred to an acquaintance who'd said, "Serendipity, that's a nice, fancy word—chance and smart fellows." Four years after that, in 1958, a book reviewer wrote in New York's *World Telegram and Sun*, "Then, by a stroke of serendipity (I knew I'd get a chance to use that word some day . . .)."

Serendipity gradually made its way into broader discourse, modestly at first, then ravenously, like a performer demanding attention. By 2001 Google found some 636,000 uses of that word. In late 2019 Google determined that *serendipity* had been used some 42,300,000 times. *Serendipity* now appeared repeatedly in lexicographers' lists of favorite words, sometimes at the top. As its popularity grew, translations were incorporated into languages such as Welsh (*serendipedd*), Italian (*serendipità*), and Spanish (*serendipia*). Even the linguistically possessive French began to refer to *la serendipity*, then *serendipité*. Variations in English included not only the ubiquitous *serendipitous*, but *serendipic, serendipital, serendipitist, serendipper, serendipitiana*, and *inserendipity*.

Two and a half centuries after being coined whimsically by Horace Walpole, *serendipity* was a term whose time had come. Why did it take so long? This question so intrigued Robert Merton that he devoted an entire book to seeking its answer: *The Travels and Adventures of Serendipity*. In this exploration of the history and significance of Walpole's neologism, Merton and coauthor Eleanor Barber pointed out that *serendipity* gained users in conjunction with the growing need of scientists for a way to describe semi-accidental discoveries. Like *ok, paradigm*, and *containment, serendipity* also incorporated a useful ambiguity. This malleable word could be molded to fit users' needs, depending on what point they were trying to make. Last, but not least, it was just fun to say. *Serendipity* emerged playfully from one's mouth. It pleased both the tongue and the ear.

Revival

Serendipity is a classic example of a word that began life in obscurity, went into an extended hibernation, then aroused from its slumber to become one of the most used, and overused, words in the English language. It isn't the only one. Many new words lie dormant for a time, sometimes a long time, and then—like Rip Van Winkle, Washington Irving's character who slept for twenty years before waking up to resume his life—reappear when needed. Even terms that failed to catch on when first introduced, suggested linguist Sol Steinmetz, "are still part of our collective memory and may come up in conversation or writing at any moment." In a book on words, his colleagues David Barnhart and Allan Metcalf compared such terms to seeds in the ground, "waiting for rain and favorable weather to sprout."

Many words that one might think were born recently turn out to have a far longer pedigree. *Cheesiness*, which sounds so contemporary, appeared in Charles Dickens's 1841 novel *The Old Curiosity Shop* (wherein one character refers to another as being in a rather sour state, "beginning to border on cheesiness, in fact"). *Dunno* dates back at least to 1759, *monetize* to 1867. Even some ubiquitous online abbreviations and acronyms have a hidden history. In a 1917 letter to

Winston Churchill, for example, British admiral John Fisher wrote, "I hear that a new order of Knighthood is on the tapis [tapestry]—O.M.G. (Oh! My God!)."

Vegan is another word that feels as fresh as this year's kale crop but isn't. Its coinage dates back some seventy-five years, to the late World War II era when a group of vegetarians who eschewed not just meat but dairy products cast about for a name to identify themselves. One of them, a schoolteacher named Donald Watson, later recalled suggesting "vegan" in the midst of a 1944 brainstorming session. According to Watson's daughter Janet, it was actually her mother, Donald's wife, Dorothy, who had come up with the name, at a dance. Others who may have had a hand in coining *vegan* include Watson's colleagues George and Florence Henderson, who'd proposed that they name their movement *Allvega* and call its publication *Allvegan*. A terser version of this term made its debut in the first edition of *Vegan News*, which appeared in November 1944. There Donald Watson wrote,

WANTED: A NAME

We should all consider carefully what our Group, and our magazine, and ourselves, shall be called. " / 'Non-dairy' / " has become established as a generally understood colloquialism, but like 'non-lacto' it is too negative. Moreover it does not imply that we are opposed to the use of eggs as food. We need a name that suggests what we do eat, and if possible one that conveys the idea that even with all animal foods taboo, Nature still offers us a bewildering assortment from which to choose. "Vegetarian" and "Fruitarian" are already associated with societies that allow the "fruits"(!) of cows and fowls, therefore it seems we must make a new and appropriate word. As this first issue of our periodical had to be named, I have used the title "The Vegan News." Should we adopt this, our diet will soon become known as a VEGAN diet, and we should aspire to the rank of VEGANS. Members' suggestions will be welcomed. The virtue of having a short title is best known to those of us who, as secretaries of vegetarian societies have to type or write the word vegetarian thousands of times a year!

Dozens of suggestions sent by readers included *Total Vegetarian Group* (*T.V.G.*), *neo-vegetarian*, *Non-dairy*, *Dairyban*, *Vitan*, *Benevore*, *Sanivores*, and *Beaumangeurs*. None improved on *vegan*, however, so *vegan* it was, and *vegan* it is.

Another case of born-again food terminology involves uncaged poultry. A chef named Larry Forgione thinks he was the first to call them *free-range*. By his account, while working at the River Café in Brooklyn in the late 1970s, Forgione helped a New Jersey farmer develop a heritage chicken hybrid. Like poultry of yore, the chickens would roam freely, eating food pecked off the ground. But how

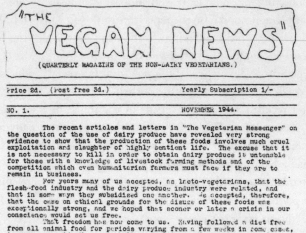

First issue of *The Vegan News*, November 1944.

to identify the unique circumstances in which these chickens were raised? Terms such as "natural" and "farm-fresh" were so overused as to be virtually meaningless. In a book on the history of chickens in America, however, Forgione read about unfenced chickens that foraged on the perimeter of forests. According to this book they "freely ranged." In the fall of 1979 the River Café's menu introduced "Potted free-range chicken with Great Lakes chestnuts, chanterelles and wild rice."

Although Forgione thought *free-range* originated with him, in its consideration of this term the *OED* cites an advertisement for "eggs from pure bred free range hens" that appeared in an Illinois newspaper in 1912. Twenty-four years later, a Pennsylvania newspaper ad touted "free range turkeys." In 1959 a *Times* of London article referred to "free range eggs." It's quite possible that Forgione coincidentally came up with *free-range* two decades later, but even if he had, the chef was hardly its originator. This was a term of long standing waiting to be rediscovered as need for it grew.

Changing circumstances are the alarm clock of slumbering words, waking them up as demand for such terminology mounts. Even though *Ms.* became a popular way to address married and single women alike during the 1970s, centuries earlier it was an abbreviation of "Mistress" in England. In 1901 a Massachusetts newspaper reported that "the abbreviation 'Ms.' is simple, it is easy to write, and the person concerned can translate it properly according to circumstances. For oral use it might be rendered as 'Mizz', which would be a close parallel to the practice long universal in many bucolic regions, where a slurred Mis' does duty for Miss and Mrs. alike."

Then there's *slacker*. Long before the 1990 movie by that name helped add this term to the modern vernacular, it had been used in an English newspaper in 1898. A magazine article that year, written by a "Harvard Man at Oxford," told *Harper's Weekly* readers that while punting on the River Cherwell, "the true slacker avoids the worry and excitement of breakfast parties and three-day cricket matches, and is more apt to conserve his energies by floating and smoking for hours at a time."

Contemporary expressions such as *fiscal cliff* and *credit crunch* languished in obscurity for decades before exploding into headlines under the press of current events. So did *multicultural*, *weapons of mass destruction*, and *regime change*. This is a common fate among newsworthy words. In his 1983 book *Words in Action*, Robert Greenman noted that after figuring prominently in the 1972–74 Watergate hearings, the term *launder*—referring to refurbishing ill-gotten money—had fallen into disuse. "Perhaps it's just a matter of time before another large-scale, shady financial transaction is discovered, and *launder* is recycled," Greenman observed. How little he knew.

Another term that was recycled repeatedly during the late two-thousand aughts was *bomb cyclone*. This is what cataclysmic storms that pounded the Northeast beginning in late 2017 were often called. Members of the press and their readers wondered why. The genesis of this phrase turned out to be a 1980 article in the *Monthly Weather Review* titled "Synoptic-Dynamic Climatology of the 'Bomb.'" In this article, meteorologists Frederick Sanders and John Gyakum discussed the volatile results of a rapid pressure drop in the midst of a cyclone that magnifies its impact, creating the equivalent of a winter hurricane. The two called this process "bombogenesis." A onetime student of Sanders said he'd heard the MIT professor refer to such weather events as "bombs" in 1964. Others say it was common parlance among meteorologists a couple of decades before that. When an actual process of *bombogenesis* occurred in the winter of 2017–18 and ones thereafter, journalists rediscovered this concept, simplified it to "'bomb' cyclone," then made those two words part of their coverage without quotation marks.

A key reason that born-again terms like *bomb cyclone* are in such demand is the fact that so many catastrophic weather events are resulting from a climate in flux. As our concern about this subject has grown, so has our need for terminology to express those concerns.

Eco Words

In a 1907 article, English physicist John Henry Poynting noted one possible consequence of growing air pollution: "the 'blanketing effect' or, as I prefer to call it, the 'greenhouse effect' of the atmosphere." A decade later Alexander Graham Bell took a prophetic interest in this danger. Burning fossil fuels would trap heat in the earth's atmosphere, Bell warned in 1917, leading to "a sort of greenhouse effect." The phrase coined by Poynting and propagated by Bell would languish for several decades and loads of carbon emissions before it rejoined national discourse in 1957. That was when UCLA physicist Joseph Kaplan warned that unless we could limit our use fossil fuels, within fifty or sixty years a "greenhouse" effect could melt polar ice caps, raising sea levels by forty feet or more.

Global warming is a key consequence of the greenhouse effect, of course. Credit for creating that phrase is commonly given to Columbia University geochemist Wallace Broecker, who in 1975 published a paper in *Science* magazine titled "Climatic Change: Are We on the Brink of a Pronounced Global Warming?" As a result of this article, Broecker was long thought to have coined *global warming*. Broecker himself hoped he hadn't. In fact, the prolific author of papers and books was so dismayed by being known primarily for this phrase that in 2010 he offered $250 to whomever could find it being used before his *Science* article was published. A graduate student named David McGee won the prize by locating a 1957 editorial in Indiana's *Hammond Times* that warned of possible "large scale global warming."

"I was happy when David found it," Broecker later told a reporter, "because people think that this is the only thing I did in my life." (When the geochemist died in 2019, many of his obituaries had headlines such as "Scientist Who Coined 'Global Warming' Dies.") Broecker apparently wasn't aware that economists Clifford Russell and Hans Landsberg had referred to "global warming" in a *Science* magazine article that preceded his by four years. And, five years before the *Hammond Times* editorial included this phrase, a 1952 *San Antonio Express* article referred to "scientists who are studying global warming trends."

The phrase "global warming" eventually gave way to "climate change," thanks in part to Republican pollster Frank Luntz. Following George W. Bush's election as president in 2000, Luntz urged members of his administration to use this phrase instead of "global warming" when discussing environmental issues. "'Climate change' is less frightening than 'global warming,'" Luntz wrote in a confidential memo to the White House. "At one focus group participants noted climate change 'sounds like you're going from Pittsburgh to Fort Lauderdale.' While global warming has catastrophic connotations attached to that, climate change suggests a more controllable and less emotional challenge." Although the ubiquity of the phrase *climate change* in political discourse is associated with Luntz, that expression had already been in play for several decades prior to Bush's presidency, referring to changes in our climate caused by human activity. The 1957 *Hammond Times* editorial located by Wallace Broecker's student warned that continued wholesale emissions of carbon dioxide to the earth's atmosphere could result in "a large scale global warming, with radical climate changes."

This illustrates how Van Winkle words enter, exit, and re-enter the lexicon under the press of changing circumstances. Once such terms do reappear, they are typically thought to have been coined recently. This exemplifies what linguist Arnold Zwicky calls *the recency illusion*, "the belief that things YOU have noticed only recently are in fact recent."

The Recency Illusion

In recent years *munchkin* has become the name of a popular card game as well as an insult used by gamers. ("You are such a munchkin!") Apparently many of its millions of players have no idea where that word originated. An online discussion of this subject produced no definitive origin story. One participant thought munchkin was "a derogatory and insulting term coined by elitist gamers." During this exchange, the name L. Frank Baum never came up (Baum having named the diminutive residents of Oz *munchkins*). Nor was a once-popular beverage referenced during a 2017 episode of the TV series *Legion* in which one character says to another, "You've got what the kids these days call 'moxie.'"

In *Flappers to Rappers*, a nifty book on youth slang, Tom Dalzell demonstrates how many terms used by the young are revivals of ones put in play by their ancestors. They include *chill*, *cool*, and *copacetic* (to name just a few). According to Dalzell, *groovy*, *mellow*, and *solid* were popular street terms during the 1940s, lost favor in the 1950s, then resurfaced during the Age of Aquarius. He didn't note, but could have, that "freak" was used in the modern sense more than a century ago when (for example) amateur photographers were called *Kodak freaks*. *Hippie*, *hipster*, and *hip* itself are other revivals. In a 1904 American novel, one character asks another, "Are you hip?" Four years later, a 1908 comic strip included the line "I'm so glad you got hip to yourself at last!"

The 1960s were a hotbed of old coins being circulated as if freshly minted. Long before they became counterculture clichés, *vibe* and *good vibe* were being used at a neo-commune in East Aurora, New York, called the Roycroft Campus. Founded in 1895 by Elbert Hubbard (the same Elbert Hubbard who told Leon Mead he'd coined some four hundred words), Roycroft sold its own furniture, handicrafts, and handbound books written by Hubbard. Roycrofters also had their own lingo, primarily whimsical terms propagated by their leader. *Vibe* was particularly popular, as in "a psychic vibe," and "a good vibe."

During the Aquarian Age, novels by J. R. R. Tolkien that featured hobbits in the Middle Earth enjoyed a renaissance. The diminutive Hobbits were three feet six inches tall, on average. Like *munchkin*, their name is now used synonymously with "smaller person," including members of a pre-human species who once inhabited Indonesia. When *OED* editor R. W. Burchfield asked Tolkien how he'd come up with their name, the Oxford don vaguely recalled scrawling a line during a moment of bored inspiration while grading an exam. That line became the opening sentence of his 1937 novel *The Hobbit*: "In a hole in the ground there lived a hobbit." But was *hobbit* his own coinage? Tolkien himself wasn't sure. The author conceded that he might have "picked it up from a nineteenth century source."

As it turned out, he well might have. After Tolkien died in 1973, *hobbit* was found in a mid-nineteenth-century collection of names for supernatural beings compiled by a Yorkshire folklorist named M. A. Denham. Where Denham got it has never been determined. Nor do we know if Tolkien had seen the word *hobbit* in an 1895 reprint of Denham's work, which was available in an Oxford University library, or if he came up with the word coincidentally. Various other sources have been suggested, including the fact that a type of small cannon used in the early eighteenth century was called a "hobbit." Alternatively, *hobbit* could have been inspired by *hobbit-hoy*, a piece of Yorkshire slang that referred to a clumsy boy. "As all lexicographers know," Tolkien wrote Burchfield, "don't look into things, unless you are looking for trouble: they nearly always turn out to be less simple than you thought.'"

That certainly is true of *muggle*. In her 1997 book *Harry Potter and the Philosopher's Stone*, J. K. Rowling gave this name to feckless individuals who lack magical powers. For a long time afterward, Rowling was thought to have coined their name. This supposition was catnip to etymologists, born debunkers, who determined that *muggle* actually had a long and varied history. In the thirteenth century it referred to a fishlike tail. Four centuries later, *muggle* came to mean "sweetheart." Some seven decades after that, in an 1854 story, Lewis Carroll called

Earliest known mug shot, Belgium, 1843. Mug and photographer unknown.

a villainous character "Muggle." A song recorded by Louis Armstrong in 1928 was titled "Muggles." At that time *muggle* was slang for marijuana (users being *mugglers*), a substance the trumpeter was known to smoke. According to etymologist Angela Tung, *muggle* has also been used for hot chocolate, drinking contests, and restlessness. *Muggle* has a shady precursor in *mug*, a derogatory word for dubious men (think: *mug shot*) which spawned *mug* as a verb for robbing someone with threatened or actual violence. *Mug* can also refer to a type of cup, a man's face ("ugly mug"), and the making of funny facial expressions.

For all of its extensive provenance, J. K. Rowling is clearly the one who gave this Van Winkle word a modern meaning, referring broadly to people with limited powers. They're *muggles*.

On Loan

It isn't just books for children that peddle used merchandise as fresh. Even works of scholarship fall prey to this syndrome. After *Grit: The Power of Passion and Perseverance* appeared in 2016, University of Pennsylvania psychology professor,

MacArthur Fellow, and TED talker Angela Duckworth was sometimes credited with coining the first word of her book's title. Yet, nearly half a century before Duckworth's book was published, the 1968 bestseller *True Grit* was made into a 1969 movie starring John Wayne, who won an Oscar for his portrayal of Rooster Cogburn in that film. (Dr. Duckworth herself was born in 1970.) As a word referring to persistence, the first known appearance of *grit* was in 1808. A weekly national newspaper named *Grit* first appeared in the United States in 1882. Intended to give its mostly rural readers "courage and strength for their daily tasks," *Grit* is still published, on- and offline.

Book titles such as *Grit* are a bountiful source of unacknowledged, or unrealized, Van Winkleism. In 1972, psychologist Irving Janis published another book with such a title: *Victims of Groupthink*. In a *Yale Alumni Magazine* article on how he'd come up with its key word, Janis said that while reading about Kennedy administration members who helped plan the disastrous Bay of Pigs invasion of Cuba in Arthur Schlesinger Jr.'s *A Thousand Days*, he became confounded. How could such a bright and well-informed group of men be lured so easily into such an ill-conceived fiasco? During his Yale seminar on small groups, the psychologist said he'd speculated that perhaps in a case like this, the approval of fellow group members transcended all other goals.

Returning to Schlesinger's book, Janis saw this hypothesis confirmed in case after case during Kennedy's presidency. Broadening his scope, Janis then began to see the same process at work in many another political catastrophe, especially Lyndon Johnson's escalation of the Vietnam War. To name this recurring process, Janis sought a template in George Orwell's notions of "doublethink" and "crimethink." *Groupthink* was the result. This remains one of the most useful terms to wend its way from the academy into general discourse. When Janis died in 1990, the *New York Times* headlined his obituary "Irving Janis Dies at 72: Coined 'Group Think.'"

Except he didn't, at least not exclusively. Two decades before *Groupthink* was published in 1972 (following a 1971 *Psychology Today* article by Janis called "Groupthink"), an article titled "Groupthink" had run in the March 1952 edition of *Fortune,* written by William Whyte. Whyte later wrote *The Organization Man*, a classic book that loaned out its title to generically describe a certain type of conforming executive.

Sebastian Junger is another author of a book whose title inspired an iconic catchphrase: *The Perfect Storm*. According to Junger, the title of his account of a catastrophic 1991 nor'easter originated with a conversation he had with meteorologist Bob Case, who'd been present during that New England storm. Although Junger later recalled Case using the phrase "perfect storm," the meteorologist himself thought he more likely told him that the convergence of warm air from a high pressure system with cool air from a low pressure system and moisture generated by Hurricane Grace created the "perfect situation" for a monumental storm.

Whether or not Junger realized it, the phrase "perfect storm" was in play long before it showed up on the cover of his bestselling 1997 book. That expression had appeared in the British press as early as 1718. Three decades later, in *Vanity Fair*, Thackeray wrote of "a perfect storm of sympathy." As a meteorological term, it was used in a 1936 news account about a flood in Texas that the weather bureau said was due to "'the perfect storm' of its type." Be that as it may, after Junger's book was published, its title quickly became such a popular way to describe all manner of cataclysms caused by a confluence of events that in 2007 it headed the list of overused catchphrases compiled annually at Michigan's Lake Superior State University.

A catchphrase that has yet to appear on a Lake Superior list, despite being nominated by many commenters online, is the title of Malcolm Gladwell's 2000 bestseller *The Tipping Point*. Although this phrase is often attributed to Gladwell, forty-three years before his book was published, a 1957 *Scientific American* article by sociologist Morton Grodzins referred to the moment when whites start fleeing from neighborhoods where blacks are moving in as a *tip point*, and the process itself as *tipping*. Rephrased as *tipping point*, this concept became part of scholarship about racial housing patterns during the early 1960s. A few years later, economist Thomas Schelling referred more broadly to circumstances in which specific events cause rapid change as *tipping points*. When Gladwell borrowed this phrase for his book's title and concept, he noted in passing its use by sociologists during the 1970s but didn't mention Morton Grodzins's 1957 conception of *tip points*, and acknowledged Thomas Schelling only in his endnotes, as the author of two related articles. This left readers free to conclude that *tipping point* originated with Malcolm Gladwell, as many have. Obviously it didn't, any more than *emotional intelligence* was the coinage of Daniel Goleman, who wrote a bestseller by that title. As Goleman noted in his 1995 book, this concept was associated with psychologists Peter Salovey and John Mayer, who'd coauthored a 1990 paper called *Emotional Intelligence*. Five years earlier, "emotional intelligence" was the subject of a 1985 doctoral dissertation by a PhD candidate named Wayne Leon Payne. In an abstract of his dissertation Payne wrote, "This paper introduces the concept of emotional intelligence, a faculty of consciousness heretofore overlooked."

Gen Huh?

On Amazon, one can buy both Daniel Goleman's book *Emotional Intelligence* and *Great Expectations: America & the Baby Boom Generation* by Landon Y. Jones.

The latter is described as "the definitive 1980 book that coined the phrase 'baby boomers.'" According to Jones himself, however, this phrase did not originate with him. It is yet another Van Winkle term enjoying a revival. Referring to a spike in births, *baby boom* made press appearances as early as 1920 (when an article in Ohio's *Conshocton Tribune* headlined "London Baby Boom" reported that "there is a baby boom in London. Births during the first six months of this year have broken all records"). Two decades later, at the beginning of December 1941, *Life* magazine headlined an article "Baby Boom Pushes Up U.S. Birth Rate." One week after that, a December 8 story in *Time* magazine was titled "Baby Boom." *Baby boomer* showed up in the mid-1970s, then achieved widespread currency in *Great Expectations*. Landon Jones had wanted to call his book *The Baby Boomers* but was talked out of this title by his publisher. No one knew what "baby boomers" referred to, the publisher argued. Booksellers therefore were liable to shelve it in their Child Care section. So *Great Expectations* it was, one of six books by that title to appear in 1980, none of which was written by Charles Dickens.

Since *baby boomers* enjoyed so much success as a generational moniker, the offspring of boomers may have thought they deserved a name as good if not better. After several false starts, one finally appeared, as the title of a 1991 novel written by Douglas Coupland: *Generation X: Tales for an Accelerated Culture*. Coupland's account of three post-adolescent Los Angelenos was published to great acclaim, both for its content and its title, which finally gave the post-boomer cohort a viable appellation. The success of this book put *Generation X*, *Gen X*, and *GenXers* on our verbal map (illustrating once again how much power book titles have to expand the lexicon). Not that Coupland took pride in doing so. "I didn't come up with the name for a generation," he later grumbled. "I just came up with a title for a novel."

How had Coupland come up with it? The answer depended on when you asked. As his public profile grew, the Canadian author said he'd been inspired by Paul Fussell's book *Class*, whose last chapter referred to an irreverent, non-status-seeking, convention-flouting cohort that Fussell called "category X." Before citing *Class*, Coupland had told interviewers that his book's title came from a punk rock band fronted by Billy Idol called Generation X. Idol himself said he'd got the band's name from a 1964 book his mother liked that was titled *Generation X*. An early herald of the Swinging '60s, this book had enjoyed enormous success in the U.K. It was based on interviews a London-based journalist named Jane Deverson conducted with young Londoners who described in exciting detail their drug-using, sexually free, gaudily dressed way of life. Since Deverson's interviews were considered too racy for the magazine that commissioned them, a collaborator named Charles Hamblett helped her fashion them into a book. At the suggestion of this veteran journalist, they titled their paperback *Generation X*, and used that term throughout. "It was partly X as in the unknown," Deverson later explained, "—teenagers were a mystery. It was also so shocking at the time, like an X film—because the book interviews pulled no punches."

So there we have it: the earliest use of *Generation X*. Or maybe not. A decade before Deverson and Hamblett's book was published, combat photographer Robert Capa had lamented the anomie he saw among members of the "unknown generation" who were growing up in the aftermath of World War II. According to a 1953 *Holiday* photo essay by Capa, "We named this unknown generation, The Generation X . . ." Since Capa died a year later (after stepping on a land-mine in Indochina), he wasn't around to assert his rights as the probable coiner of *Generation X*. In other cases, those who coined a term, or thought they did, have not been shy about making such claims.

17

Disputation

HALF A CENTURY ago, a Boston journalist named Bill Cardoso complimented his friend Hunter Thompson on a stream-of-consciousness magazine article he'd written about the 1970 Kentucky Derby. According to Cardoso it was "pure gonzo!" In a subsequent letter, Cardoso told Thompson he was "total gonzo, a gonzo journalist."

After that, Hunter Thompson used *gonzo* repeatedly to describe the type of writing he did. "It is not so much 'written' as performed," Thompson explained, "—and because of this, the end result must be experienced instead of merely 'read.'" Colleagues picked up the beat. During Thompson's heyday, he and his writing were seldom referred to without trotting out the word *gonzo*. His outrageous approach to news coverage came to be known as *gonzo journalism*. Today, *gonzo* is applied to any activity that is considered off the wall, if not over the top: *gonzo marketing*, *gonzo filmmaking*, *gonzo engineering*, *gonzo chefs*, and *gonzo pornography* (where a participant records the action).

Gonzo is one of those Humpty-Dumpty words that can mean pretty much whatever you want it to mean, and is also fun to say. Like *Boo yah! Gung ho!* or *Cowabunga!*, it explodes forcefully from one's vocal chords. *Gonzo!* Bill Cardoso basked in the glory of having added this term to the vernacular. When he died in 2006, an obituary in the *San Francisco Chronicle* was headlined—what else?— "Bill Cardoso—Journalist Who Coined the Word 'Gonzo.'"

But did he? Asked where *gonzo* came from, Cardoso initially said that in South Boston *gonzo* referred to the last man standing after a long bout of drinking. On another occasion, the journalist said he thought his claim-to-fame word came from the French-Canadian term *gonzeaux*, or "shining path." Or else it might have been Southie-Irish slang. His explanation varied.

This prompted an Australian professor of journalism named Martin Hirst to do a deep dive into the etymology of *gonzo*. While conceding that Bill Cardoso first applied this term to Thompson's work, Hirst could not determine its provenance. Despite Cardoso's original explanation of its Gallic root, Hirst couldn't locate "gonzeaux" in any of many French dictionaries he consulted. The closest word Hirst found was *gonze*, French slang for "guy" or "bloke." Somewhat more promising were references to *gonzo* in an Italian-English dictionary as "simpleton, dolt, fool," and the Spanish word *ganso*, meaning "idiot, bumpkin." How one made the leap from Italian or Spanish to Canadian French or Boston-Irish slang baffled him. "So far," Hirst concluded in a 2004 account of his search, "I have been unable to confirm beyond reasonable doubt any of the possible explanations outlined here. The central figure in this mystery is Bill Cardoso. What is his source for 'gonzeaux'? How much leg pulling are these experienced jokers engaged in?"

Cardoso's onetime friend Charles Giuliano had an answer for Hirst's questions. He himself was the actual source of *gonzo*. As Giuliano explained in a 2014 article, while visiting Cardoso in the late 1960s he'd told his pal a funny story that included the word "gonzo." According to Giuliano, when hearing this word, Cardoso stopped him.

"'What's that you say Charles?' he said. 'Gonzo! What does that mean?'

"Knowing that he loved baseball I put it in terms he would understand. 'Over the Green Monster (an imposing left field wall of Fenway Park where the Boston Red Sox play). Grand slam. Out of the park. Gonzo man. Total gonzo.'"

Giuliano said a friend of theirs confirmed that he'd used the term *gonzo* when both were together with Cardoso before the latter applied it to Hunter Thompson. In their crowd, "it was gonzo this and gonzo that," Giuliano wrote. When he realized Cardoso was claiming that the word originated with him, Giuliano staked his own claim by including it in a July 3, 1970, Boston *Herald Traveler* article about a rock concert. He told his editor that gonzo was a "hip new term." According to the lead sentence of Giuliano's article, this concert was attended by "some 25,000 gonzo fans." In his 2013 blog post Giuliano charged that Bill Cardoso "stole" *gonzo* from him. "Cardoso took credit for the term which he glommed from me," wrote Giuliano. To him the etymology of *gonzo* is perfectly clear: "I coined the word."

Charles Giuliano was no more the coiner of *gonzo* than Bill Cardoso was, however. As he himself has conceded, that piece of slang was in common use among his peers long before Cardoso applied it to Hunter Thompson. This was confirmed by *Globe* reporter Billy Baker, who did his own investigation of the history of *gonzo* in 2010, four years after Cardoso died. What Baker discovered was that at one time gonzo was common street parlance in South Boston, meaning basically wild and crazy. ("That party was gonzo!") A friend of mine recalls hearing this piece of slang on the streets of Manhattan's Upper West Side during the

1950s. This may have inspired a recording by pianist James Booker called "Gonzo" that was popular in 1960. According to historian Douglas Brinkley, Thompson's friend and literary executor, Booker's song was a favorite of his.

At best, therefore, Bill Cardoso popularized an existing piece of slang that was also the title of a song Hunter Thompson liked. So what is its probable origin? Billy Baker thinks *gonzo* may be little more than "gone" with "zo" added as an intensifier (like creating *nutzo* from *nuts*). But that's just a guess. *Gonzo* apparently is one of those words that circulate on the street before being put in print by someone who then gets credit for coining it. Who first uttered the word, where, and why may never be known.

This illustrates an ongoing problem in trying to ascertain where new words actually originate. It's common to read that X word was coined by Y person, when in fact that word was either coined by someone else or was already being used orally at the time it was introduced to a broader audience by an escort, who then gets coiner's credit. This is one of many reasons that determining original authorship is so problematic. A coinage that has never appeared in print, or can be found only in obscure publications, is susceptible to being claimed by multiple self-proclaimed "coiners," or being attributed to them. That's why someone's claim to have invented a word is such an unreliable source of etymology.

When a new word catches on without a clear point of origin, there is usually no shortage of those willing to say it originated with them. Although Andy Warhol undoubtedly was the herald of "fifteen minutes of fame," once it became popular, others claimed that they'd fed him the line. A fellow artist said he'd once told Warhol that his own early brush with fame "only lasted five minutes." Another artist has been quoted as having said, "Everybody will be famous," before Warhol added a time frame. Forty years after taking pictures of Warhol in 1965, a photographer alleged that when the artist told him that "everybody wants to be famous," he responded, "Yeah, for about fifteen minutes." But in a book published several years earlier, the same photographer said it was Warhol himself who used those words during their shoot.

From Mojo to Bad Hair

While I was researching this book, a friend told me about meeting a man who confided to her that as a hard-drinking serviceman in Germany after World War II, he'd coined the word *mojo*. My friend examined the man's face to try to determine whether he was kidding. He wasn't. The man genuinely believed that *mojo* was his coinage. Other sources report that *mojo* originated one cold night in the early 1960s after an assistant principal at Permian High School in Odessa, Texas (the *Friday Night Lights* school), had asked for "more jo [coffee]" during the third quarter of a football game. This led students in the stands to start chanting "More jo!" Over time, *more jo* became *Mo Jo*, then *MOJO*, which was adopted as their school's nickname and rallying cry.

In fact, as best etymologists can tell, *mojo* was adapted from words related to shamanism that were brought to this country by enslaved Africans. It later became a common term in jazz and blues, such as the 1926 song "My Daddy's Got the Mojo, But I Got the Say So," sung by Butterbeans and Susie. Muddy Waters, Jim Morrison, and the Beatles all referred to *mojo* in songs of their own before Mike Myers gave it the broadest currency of all among white Americans with his Austin Powers character who struggles to get his mojo back.

Fanciful origin stories are common in the annals of word coinage. Lexicographer Kory Stamper says Merriam-Webster's editors (which once included her) routinely get heartfelt messages from users who claim to have coined certain words long before the date cited in their dictionary. As Stamper writes in *Word by Word*,

> They always come with a personal story attached, with brilliant clarity of detail: I coined the term "wuss" in my dorm room in Princeton University in 1969, long before the date you give; you say that "noogie" appeared in 1968, but I grew up with kids getting and giving noogies in grade school, and I was already in graduate school by the time you say the word was created; I was born in Staten Island in 1926, and by 1932 I was ordering ice cream cones with jimmies, and by 1942 I was adding jimmies to ice-cream cones and sundaes as a soda jerk, which proves that your date of 1947 for the word "jimmies" is wrong. People are unswayed, even when we turn up hard evidence of the word in print that antedates their own date. . . .

Consider the case of *bad hair day*. Television personality Jane Pauley believes she conjured this inspired piece of slang during an exchange with her *Today Show* cohost Bryant Gumbel on NBC TV in the early 1980s. (At the time, Pauley was obsessing over many anxieties, such as the prospect of having unkempt hair while on camera.) The earliest appearance cited by the *OED* is in a 1988 *Santa Rosa* (CA) *Press Democrat* column that included the line, "Even those who emerge from the sea to casually braid their shiny wet vines into a thick coil with a hibiscus on the end also have bad-hair days." The author of that column, Susan Swartz, doesn't claim the expression was original to her, however. It clearly wasn't. In the same year that her column ran, a 1988 volume of the *Almanac of the Federal Judiciary*—presumably several years in gestation—included this observation about a judge in Brooklyn: "With the exception of an occasional bad hair day, he's very pleasant, courteous, decent, and kindly."

Such usage suggests that *bad hair day* was a common catchphrase at that time. So where did it originate? Blogger Brent Simmons thinks he knows. As a middle schooler in the late 1970s, Simmons often had to struggle with unruly hair. He therefore began to distinguish "good hair days" from "bad hair days," and tell friends about that distinction. According to Simmons, a girl he knew spread this phrase so widely around school that classmates began to ask if he was having a good hair day or a bad hair day. Whenever he heard "bad hair day" on television in years to come, the blogger marveled that "my little middle-school thing had spread and become part of the culture." Although Simmons conceded it was unlikely that he'd originated this phrase, "still, it had to be someone, right?"

It did indeed, but not him (nor anyone else I've been able to ascertain). Before Simmons was born, a Lansing, Michigan, barber shop advertised in early 1970 that they could help men who were having "bad hair days." Well before that, an English trichologist (hair expert) named Philip Kingsley said he referred to *bad hair days* during a 1957 conversation with London journalist Veronica Papworth. Papworth is said to have repeated Kingsley's expression in an *Express* column that year. (I wish I could find that column.)

The question remains, though: who made the imaginative leap from the use of "bad hair days" for the state of one's hair to the state of one's life? Perhaps it was Jane Pauley.

Hot Dog!

You see why etymology is such a challenging pursuit. Determining the provenance of terms with contested origins is like trying to figure out where the Shroud of Turin originated. *Hot dog*, for example. According to one popular saga, this is how that repast got its name: on a bitterly cold April day in 1901, the New York Giants were playing at the Polo Grounds in New York. An enterprising concessionaire named Harry Stevens had his peddlers hawk frankfurters to shivering fans as "a red-hot dachshund sausage in a roll." Those watching the game included cartoonist Tad Dorgan. The next day Dorgan drew a cartoon that featured a "hot dog" (presumably because he couldn't spell "dachshund"). This origin story dovetailed with Dorgan's reputation as a prolific disseminator of slanguage. The self-promotional cartoonist saw no reason to correct that record. Propagated by the likes of H. L. Mencken, Bill Bryson, and the National Hot Dog and Sausage Council, this recounting of how Tad Dorgan coined "hot dog" became common conventional wisdom.

It's apocryphal. For starters, the first Dorgan cartoons featuring "hot dogs"— two of them—did not appear until late 1906, five years after the Polo Grounds game in question. Furthermore, determined word sleuths have shown that the term *hot dog* was in play long before Dorgan supposedly attended a game there in 1901 (when the cartoonist still lived in San Francisco). A detailed brief against Dorgan's attribution can be found in a book called *Origin of the Term "Hot Dog."* In this etymological tour de force, George Leonard Cohen, David Shulman, and Barry Popik report that during the mid- to late nineteenth century, American consumers of sausage routinely made nervous jokes about its contents. Since dog meat topped the list of suspects, *dachshund, doggie,* and *dog* were popular nicknames for tubes of sausage street vendors sold in rolls. Over time, the suspicion that these so-called frankfurters were filled with chopped canine became a staple of American humor. Cartoons featuring dogs being shoved into sausage-making machines were popular. "Dog eat dog" was the caption of an 1895 *Judge* magazine cartoon that featured a dog consuming a frankfurter.

Since so many sausage vendors plied their trade near colleges, dog-filled-sausage humor was common on campuses. As one composer of doggerel wrote in an 1895 issue of the *Yale Record*, "I delight to bite the dog / When placed inside a bun." The *Record* also published a whimsical fantasy that featured a popular sausage cart Yalies called "the dog wagon" turning up in a packed chapel, where its owner sold his wares to attendees who "contentedly munched hot dogs during the whole service."

Origin of the Term "Hot Dog" shows repeatedly how common this type of badinage was in college humor magazines during the mid-1890s. After that book was published in 2004, even earlier examples turned up. Lexicographer Fred Shapiro found two references to "hot dogs" and "hot dog" in Tennessee newspapers of the mid-1880s. In early 1891, a Nashville news article referred to two men abusing a "'hot dog' vender." According to 1892 press accounts, a sausage vendor in Paterson, New Jersey, named Thomas Francis Xavier Morris was known as "Hot Dog Morris," and "the hot dog man." On the last day of that year, the *Paterson Daily Press* wrote about a local boy who'd recently approached Mr. Morris's wagon:

> "Hey, mister, give me a hot dog quick," was the startling order that a rosy-cheeked gamin hurled at the man as a Press reporter stood close by last night. The "hot dog" was quickly inserted in a gash in a roll, a dash of mustard also splashed on to the "dog" with a piece of flat whittled stick, and the order was fulfilled.

A few months later, the New Jersey beach town of Asbury Park, sixty miles south of Paterson, passed an ordinance regulating "'hot dog' peddlers." In 1913 Coney Island's Chamber of Commerce outlawed the use of "hot dog" on signs at the Brooklyn amusement park. Six decades later Coney Island became the site of Nathan's Hot Dog Eating Contest.

So who actually coined *hot dog*? As with *gonzo*, we will probably never know. It's one of those terms that emerged from someone's mouth somewhere, sometime during the late nineteenth century, and eventually showed up in print. The one thing we can say with confidence is that Tad Dorgan did not coin *hot dog* any more than Bill Cardoso coined *gonzo* or many another claimant has invented terms with comparably complicated origin stories.

Affluenza

In June 2013 a Texas teenager named Ethan Couch killed four pedestrians while driving drunk at twice the speed limit in a town near Dallas. To defend him, Couch's lawyers argued that this product of a privileged upbringing suffered from "affluenza." Testifying for the defense, psychologist G. Dick Miller explained that *affluenza* referred to the status of wealthy individuals who are raised with few limits. Miller was commonly credited with coining this mashup of *affluence* and *influenza*. So was another psychologist, Jessie O'Neill, who's made a specialty of writing, speaking, and consulting on "affluenza" (although O'Neill didn't think it applied to Ethan Couch). Paul Comstock, who writes about private foundations, has also been given credit for coining *affluenza*, as has psychologist John Levy, who used the term in a report on the effects of inherited wealth that he wrote for San Francisco's Whitman Institute. Levy doesn't claim it originated with him, however.

Then where did *affluenza* originate? This portmanteau made its modern debut several years before the Couch trial, in a 1997 PBS program called *Escape from Affluenza*. Its co-producer, John de Graaf, subsequently coauthored a bestselling 2001 book called *Affluenza: The All-Consuming Epidemic*. Affluenza had previously appeared in the American press as far back as 1979. De Graaf himself said he'd first seen this term in a magazine in the 1990s but thought it might have been coined quite a bit earlier, by the head of a foundation that underwrote research on the psychosocial impact of affluence.

That would be Whitman Institute head Fred Whitman. Shortly before he died in 2004, the San Francisco philanthropist told *Chicago Tribune* reporter Marja Mills that he'd coined this word in 1954. Whitman, who said he enjoyed creating playful terms, considered *affluenza* little more than a "giggle" meant to amuse himself and friends. John Levy confirms that this term was used by Whitman, for whom he wrote reports.

But wait; there's more. Garson O'Toole, proprietor of the *Quote Investigator* website, found *affluenza* in a 1908 column in a London newspaper that attributed this term to novelist William Locke. And who knows how often it may have been used before that? As lexicographer Jesse Sheidlower points out, definitively attributing an obvious hybrid like *affluenza* is problematic. Such blend words are particularly susceptible to multiple claims of authorship. Two different people, Sheidlower told Marja Mills, told him they'd coined *mediagenic*, combining "media" and "telegenic." As for *affluenza*, he said, "One of the problems with words like this, this catchy thing formed from other words, is that very often people think they have coined words like this but it was around earlier, despite that."*

When telling me about the death of literary critic Ihab Hassan, a historian said he'd coined the term "postmodern." Sure enough, the headline of a 2015 *Milwaukee Journal Sentinel* obituary for this University of Wisconsin professor read, "Hassan Coined Term Postmodernism for Change in '60s Literature." Ihab Hassan's 1987 book *The Postmodern Turn* was instrumental in putting that term into literary play. But, as the author himself conceded in an interview, it did not originate with him. Hassan thought *postmodern* might have been coined in the 1870s by a British artist named John Watkins Chapman. This attribution apparently originated with British artist Dick Higgins, who in 1978 wrote about the term *postmodern*: "I can recall seeing it in an essay by the English salon painter Chapman who around 1880, wanting to denounce the French impressionists but not wanting (horror!) to sound conservative, used the term to describe himself and his friends." Since Chapman was a popular painter of pictures with titles such as *The Mischievous Model* and *Wooed but Not Won*, but no cultural heavyweight, that vague attribution at best must be regarded with raised eyebrows.

Pointing this out in her book *The Post-Modern and the Post-Industrial*, Margaret Rose concludes that far from being able to attribute the coinage of *postmodern* to Mr. Chapman, "so long as there has been the word modern and the prefix post there has been the possibility of someone speaking of the post-modern." A more tangible appearance of this term can be found in a 1913 theological treatise by the Rev. J. M. Thompson of Magdalen College, Oxford, titled "Post-Modernism." Two decades later, in 1934, the Spanish scholar Federico de Onis said a particular type of poetry was characterized by *postmodernismo*, a term some attribute to him. Others to whom "postmodern" has been credibly attributed include historians Arnold Toynbee and Charles Jencks, design professor Joseph Hudnut, sociologist C. Wright Mills, and philosopher Jean-François Lyotard.

No wonder the warning bells of etymologists ring so insistently whenever they see the words "coined by" following a neologism, especially when the source of that attribution is the reputed coiner.

Booty Call

Comedian Bill Bellamy's claim to have coined *booty call* has enjoyed a favorable press. This harks back to a routine Bellamy first performed a quarter century ago in which he riffed at length about the late-night telephone calls black men

---

* To further complicate matters, *affluenza* is also an Italian word meaning "turnout," or "attendance."

commonly make to women whom they expect to be available for sex on short notice. "Every brother in here done made a booty call," said Bellamy in this 1992 sketch, one that subsequently became part of an HBO special. A year later the hip-hop duo Duice released an album that included a track titled "Booty Call." ("Suddenly you get the urge to make a booty call.") In 1997 the movie *Booty Call* ensured that its title would become a lasting part of the vernacular. Bellamy wishes he'd trademarked the phrase.

If he'd tried, however, the comedian would have had trouble proving that *booty call* originated with him. The coauthor of *Booty Call*'s screenplay, Takashi Bufford, told journalist Elon Green that this movie's title dates back to the early 1980s. That was when he and barhopping friends would make late-night "booty calls" from phone booths. Duice member Anthony Darlington recalled that in 1985 he and his pals commonly relied on pay phones to "call that booty," or, in time, to make what they called "booty calls." Rapper Jesse Weaver (Schooly D) added that in the mid-1980s, when he was still living at home in Philadelphia, his mother and sisters referred to the frequent phone calls he got from female fans late at night as "booty calls." These assertions, ones Elon Green included in a well-reported *Esquire* article on the etymology of *booty call*, raised serious questions about Bill Bellamy's assumption that the phrase originated with him. To muddy the waters even more, during an online discussion of this topic, a military veteran said that he and fellow soldiers used this phrase routinely during the Vietnam War era.

Booty itself derives from *boody*, which was Elizabethan-era slang for genitalia, a play on *body*. *Get some booty* (or *bootie*) has long been man talk for pursuing sex. In 1941 Fats Waller recorded "Come and Get It," a song he co-wrote with his manager Ed Kirkeby, that included the line "I've gotta get myself some booty."

Once again, in a variation on the Matthew effect, we're faced with a street term whose coinage is mistakenly attributed to the most prominent person known to have used it.

Cohort Naming

During the late 1970s, those who studied demographic cohorts identified one as comprising *young professionals*. *New Yorker* cartoonist Roz Chast referenced this commonly used phrase in a 1983 cartoon titled "Attack of the Young Professionals!" After the word "urban" added a welcome vowel, "young urban professional" was condensed into the acronym *yup*.

Columnist Alice Kahn says she was inspired by Chast's cartoon, and by a reference to *yups* in the *Chicago Reader*, to coin *yuppie* in a June 10, 1983, *East Bay* (CA) *Express* column. However, columnist Bob Greene had already used this term in the *Chicago Tribune* a couple of months earlier, on March 23, 1983.

ATTACK OF THE

YOUNG PROFESSIONALS!

Watch in horror as they...

Roz Chast's 1983 cartoon "Attack of the Young Professionals!"

Greene later said he'd overheard someone say "yuppie" in a bar on Chicago's Columbus Avenue. When this prior use of *yuppie* was called to her attention, Alice Kahn responded that she'd had that word in her head before Bob Greene used it in his column.

Both of them were at least three years late in claiming to be the source of *yuppie*, however. That piece of slang had already appeared in a 1980 *Chicago* magazine article about young urban professionals who were moving downtown. The author of this article, Dan Rottenberg, seldom gets proper credit for giving us *yuppie* (perhaps because he's a low-profile writer-editor who now lives in Philadelphia). Rottenberg himself doesn't claim he coined that term, however, saying he'd heard it being used around Chicago during the late 1970s. After he and others committed *yuppie* to print, it didn't take long for this fun word to enjoy an analog version of going viral. Four years after Rottenberg wrote his article, *Newsweek* declared 1984 "The Year of the Yuppie." Over time, that term took on pejorative overtones, then drifted gradually into obscurity. Today *yuppie* is seldom heard, except as a sort of retro reference.

Another cohort needing a name was the one comprising those who are neither black, ethnic, nor Catholic. In his 1964 book *The Protestant Establishment*, sociologist E. Digby Baltzell called this group WASPs, short for White Anglo-Saxon Protestants. For years afterward, Baltzell was credited with coining that acronym. Historian Andrew Hacker begged to disagree. Hacker pointed out, correctly, that he had used it several years before Baltzell did, when referring to "wealthy" Anglo-Saxon protestants in a 1957 *American Political Science Review* article. "They are 'WASPs,'" Hacker wrote, "—in the cocktail party jargon of the sociologists."

For a time, etymologists thought Hacker's reference to WASPS constituted the "earliest use" of this term (in print, anyway; his reference to "cocktail party jargon" suggests that it was already in conversational use). While doing research for the *Yale Book of Quotations*, however, its editor, Fred Shapiro, found an April 17, 1948, *New York Amsterdam News* article by civil rights crusader Stetson Kennedy, himself a white Anglo-Saxon Protestant, who wrote, "In America, we find the WASPs (White Anglo-Saxon Protestants) ganging up to take their frustrations out on whatever minority group happens to be handy—whether Negro, Catholic, Jewish, Japanese or whatnot." Whether this term originated with Kennedy is unknown, but I'm guessing he was more escort than coiner.

What we can safely say is that WASP was not coined by E. Digby Baltzell, nor by Andrew Hacker (and probably not by Stetson Kennedy either). It is yet another term that floated into the national conversation sometime, somewhere, probably after World War II, just begging to be attributed to its most prominent user—in this case, Digby Baltzell. Not only is WASP erroneously attributed to that eminent sociologist because he used it in a book, but the last word of that book's title—*The Protestant Establishment*—has also been the subject of an etymological contretemps.

Establishing Coinage

In 1955, at the peak of the Cold War, it was revealed that two members of Britain's Foreign Office had defected to the Soviet Union four years earlier. The uproar surrounding this revelation dwelled on the fact that the treason of these two Cambridge graduates, Guy Burgess and Donald Maclean was concealed for so long by their upper-class colleagues. In a September 23, 1955, *Spectator* column, British journalist Henry Fairlie proposed a name for that group. "I have several times suggested that what I call the 'Establishment' in this country is today more powerful than ever before," wrote Fairlie. "By the 'Establishment,' I do not mean only the centres of official power—though they are certainly part of it—but rather the whole matrix of official and social relations within which power is exercised."

Fairlie's use of *establishment* thrust that term into the national and international conversation, where it has remained ever since. When the *OED* subsequently cited Fairlie as establishing the *locus classicus*, or standard for use of "the establishment," the journalist said he felt as though he'd been knighted. Like so many durable terms, *establishment* is a word of great range and nuance. (I've even seen reference in print to a man's "Establishment good looks.") It's also been a source of opprobrium since the 1960s, when left-wing protestors vilified targets of their ire as members of *the establishment*. Several decades later, right-wing populists railed against "establishment Republicans." A most useful, diverse word indeed.

Henry Fairlie, a Tory, was not pleased to see *establishment* become such a common way for activists to identify groups whom they were attacking. In fact, Fairlie was put off by the odor of paranoia and whiff of conspiracy theory that had attached itself to what he considered his verbal progeny.

But was it? Soon after Fairlie's 1955 column put *the establishment* in modern play, questions were raised about his assumption that this term originated with him. As its provenance was debated, any number of Englishmen stepped forward to claim that they'd referred to *the establishment* long before Henry Fairlie did. And so they had. Two years before Fairlie's column appeared, the historian A. J. P. Taylor had referred to "the governing classes, the Establishment," in a 1953 book review. A few years earlier, Douglas Golding's 1945 book *The Nineteen Twenties* referred to what author Ford Madox Ford "used to call the Establishment." Nearly a decade before that, biographer Hesketh Pearson used this term repeatedly in a 1936 biography of the prominent Victorian-era political figure Henry Labouchère.

Clearly *establishment* had been around long before Henry Fairlie used it in 1955. As others pointed out, and he eventually acknowledged, at one time this word referred to the hierarchy of the Church of England, and to other hierarchies as well. In an 1841 lecture called "The Conservative," Ralph Waldo Emerson referred to the subject of his talk as "an upholder of the establishment." Although the way Emerson used it suggests familiarity with this term among members of his audience in Boston, Emerson's reference remains the earliest known appearance of "the establishment" in its contemporary sense. After being made aware of the Yankee philosopher's lecture, Henry Fairlie conceded that "the palm, I think, has to be given to Emerson."

Brits vs. Yanks

This raises the question of who gets credit for a coinage when competing claims are made on both sides of the Atlantic. Because he used the phrase "pursuit of the almighty dollar" in an 1871 novel, British novelist-politician Edward Bulwer-Lytton is sometimes thought to have introduced the last two words as a phrase. As we've seen, however, Washington Irving had already referred to the *almighty dollar* some four decades before Bulwer-Lyton did. So credit the Yank. But hang on. Whether or not Irving realized it, in a 1599 letter, and again in a 1616 poem, the English poet and playwright Ben Jonson had mentioned "almighty gold."

Another term with disputed trans-Atlantic origins became part of the international conversation when, during a 1946 speech in Fulton, Missouri, Winston Churchill warned about an "iron curtain" surrounding the Soviet Union. That memorable allusion was widely assumed to have originated with him. It didn't. *Iron curtain* originally referred to the fireproof curtains installed in late-eighteenth-century theaters to protect members of the audience should a fire break out onstage. It subsequently was applied figuratively to all manner of impermeable borders. In his 1915 book *A Mechanistic View of War and Peace*, George Washington Crile asked his fellow Americans to imagine how they'd react if Mexico were a nation "with a deep-rooted grievance, and an iron curtain at its frontier."

Controversy over whether to attribute specific neologisms to a Yank or a Brit is common, and understandable. Since *brunch* has achieved its greatest circulation in the United States, this coinage is widely assumed to be an Americanism. In fact, that portmanteau originated during the late nineteenth century among Oxford students (who also called breakfast *brekkers*) before being exported to the U.S., where it won great popularity after World War II. During the same period, a comedy program called *The Goon Show* was introduced on BBC Radio in 1951, leading many Brits to assume that *goon* originated on their shores. But not only had *goon* appeared in the comic strip *Popeye* long before *The Goon Show* made its debut, that show's creator, Spike Milligan, said that Popeyes's Goon family inspired his own program's name.

Another coinage whose country of origin is a matter of Anglo-American debate is *fashionista*. Although Stephen Fried is generally credited with coining that term in his 1993 book *Thing of Beauty*, the *OED* has an earlier citation: "R.W. Conway (title) *Vague: Violet Pea, a fashionista*: *a girl with her own take on fashion.*" This odd reference caught the attention of American word sleuths. Since *Vague* could not be found in any U.S. library, Yale's Fred Shapiro had a copy sent to him from one in Dublin. *Vague* turned out to be a self-published tome with no copyright date. Linguist Ben Yagoda then contacted its author, Richard Conway-Jones. This one-time habitué of London's fashion scene told Yagoda that he'd self-published the novella around 1991, in photocopied form, before turning it into an actual book the following year. Although *fashionista* did appear in its pages, Conway-Jones didn't claim to be that word's originator. *Vague*'s author told Yagoda that the term had been circulating in London's fashion scene long before he put it in print. Once again the common phenomenon of new words being spoken before they were written came into play, as did Jesse Sheidlower's advisory about hybrid words being especially susceptible to multiple claims of coinage. In this case, Yagoda concluded, the early appearance of *fashionista* in two different settings at about the same time most likely was "a case of (almost) simultaneous discovery."

This type of transatlantic confusion is part of a broader and longlasting edginess that characterizes Anglo-American relations when it comes to neologizing. "Edginess" is actually a polite way of putting it. "Combat" is a more accurate way to describe the conflict about language that pits Brits against Yanks, and sometimes against each other as well.

18

Word Wars

SOON AFTER THEY arrived in America, English colonists got busy with an important task: reinventing their language. This called for giving new meanings to old words and creating new ones altogether. "The new circumstances under which we are placed," explained Thomas Jefferson in a letter to his grammarian friend John Waldo, "call for new words, new phrases, and for the transfer of old words to new objects." In the process, he and his fellow colonists displayed a playful, utilitarian approach to word creation that would persist throughout America's history.

Settlers called the plump, smelly rodents they encountered in wetlands *muske rats*. A type of feline known as a lynx back home to them looked like a *bobcat*. Other forms of wildlife were named *katydids*, *catfish*, and *whippoorwills*. To these colonists, *sleigh* sounded more graceful than "sledge," and *the help* reflected their values better than "servants." The easy-to-grasp quality of terms such as *rattlesnake*, *timberland*, and *hillside* were a boon to the increasing numbers of immigrants whose native language wasn't English. *Frostbite* is more clear than *chilblains*, *eggplant* than *aubergine*, *sidewalk* than *pavement*. *Doghouse* defined itself; *kennel* did not. Such were the many virtues of New World neologisms.

When they caught wind of this irreverent attitude toward their common language, self-appointed guardians of the King's English back home took umbrage. To them, creating words willy-nilly this way was tantamount to schoolchildren inventing their own vocabulary rather than adopting that of their parents. After Jefferson used the word *belittle* in his 1785–87 book *Notes on the State of Virginia*, a British reviewer exclaimed, "*Belittle!* What an expression! It may be an elegant one in Virginia, and even perfectly intelligible; but for our part, all we can do is, to *guess* at its meaning. For shame, Mr. Jefferson!" Little daunted, Jefferson proceeded to coin *Anglophobia*.

The swamp rodents that early American settlers called *muske rats,* as portrayed by John James Audubon.

The third president of the United States was a proud and prolific coiner of words. "I am a friend to neology," Jefferson wrote John Adams. In his letter to John Waldo, Jefferson said that, "Necessity obliges us to neologize." According to the *Oxford English Dictionary,* this is the first appearance of *neologize.* All told, the *OED* includes 108 quotations from Jefferson that involve the earliest known use of a word. Other new words that the *OED* attributes to Jefferson include *indescribable, pedicure,* and *electioneer. Stump-orators* is another term he introduced, referring to those who address crowds while standing on tree stumps. This one eventually spawned derivatives such as *stump speakers, stump speech, a stump* (a rote speech), and *stumps* (rote oration). *Stump* also became a verb, as when campaigning politicians are said to be *stumping.*

Jefferson and Adams both believed that developing an American version of English was an essential part of asserting their independence from the mother country. "As an independent Nation We have as good a Right to Coin Words as well as Money as the English have or ever had," Adams wrote his fellow revolutionary Benjamin Rush. "We are no more bound by Johnsons Dictionary, than by the common or Statute or Cannon Law of England. . . . We ought to have an American Dictionary; after which I Should be willing to lay a Tax of an Eagle [$10] a Volume upon all English Dictionaries that Should ever be imported."

This would include Samuel Johnson's *Dictionary of the English Language*. Not that its compiler would have cared. His 1755 opus eschewed words coined in the North American colonies. Johnson considered those who lived there to be little more than rascals, robbers, and pirates who "ought to be thankful for any thing we allow them short of hanging." In case we missed his point the lexicographer added, "I am willing to love all mankind, except an American." Perforce, the new lexicon being created across the Atlantic was of little interest to him.

It did interest others. To hear for themselves, beginning in the early eighteenth century, English travelers toured the colonies, recording linguistic abominations they heard while there. According to them the American version of their language was characterized by brazen vulgarity, rampant mispronunciation, and unbridled "innovations." After visiting Georgia in 1735 Francis Moore reported to his countrymen that the village of Savannah stood on a flat hill overlooking a river that residents "in their barbarous English call a *bluff*." *Foothill* was another term colonists used that raised hackles back home. So did *eel grass* and *skunk*.

Historically, self-appointed British guardians of the English language (in the absence of an official oversight body there is no other kind) have looked upon words created in America with all the enthusiasm of an architect examining an outhouse. "Motley gibberish" as one British journalist called them in 1787. An 1810 review of Aaron Bancroft's biography of George Washington in the *British Critic* noted "with regret rather than with astonishment, the introduction of several *new* words, or *old* words in a new sense, a deviation from the rules of the English language." To New Worlders, *truthful* was as good as *honest*, but not to Old Worlders, many of whom considered that term an odious Americanism. Nor were they pleased by the recoining of *mad* to mean angry instead of insane, and the use of *clever* to describe anything from an amiable person to an appealing house or a rewarding voyage. All were considred *clever.*

Barbarisms were what outraged Englishmen most often called such linguistic deviations. Those who used them *barbaric*. They were *barborous*. "The foulest vice in language is to speak barbarously," George Puttenham had written in *The Arte of English Poesie* (harking back to the ancient Greeks who considered those who didn't speak their language to be primitive babblers who made sounds like *bar-bar*). Samuel Johnson routinely dismissed any term he disapproved of as "barbarous." *Banter* to Johnson was "a barbarous word." *Extraordinary* was "a colloquial barbarism." "Barbarizing" was the process by which such loathsome words were created. After touring the United States in 1833, a retired British army officer named Thomas Hamilton (a Scot) lamented that in this country, "the privilege of barbarizing the King's English is assumed by all ranks and conditions of men." Captain Hamilton likened the American version of English to a "massacre of their mother tongue." Yet this version was used even by members of the country's better classes, he found.

They included Noah Webster who, in 1828, had published *An American Dictionary of the English Language.* When announcing his intention to create this tome, which would include many a New World neologism, the Connecticut lexicographer had defended their inclusion by saying that "new circumstances, new modes of life, new laws, new ideas of various kinds give rise to new words." Webster agreed with Jefferson and Adams that just as the United States had developed its own form of government, it should create its own version of English. "As an independent nation," he wrote soon after the War of Independence had ended, "our honor requires us to have a system of our own, in language as well as government. Great Britain, whose children we are, and whose language we speak, should no longer be our standard, for the taste of her writers is already corrupted, and her language is on the decline." To blindly adopt the terminology of the old country, Webster added, "would be to stamp the wrinkle of decrepit old age upon the bloom of youth." For that reason, he added, "New words will be formed, if found necessary or convenient without a license from Englishmen."

As far as Webster was concerned, the more new words the better, if they found users. While conceding that "some writers indulge a licentiousness in coining words," Webster wrote in the introduction to his 1828 dictionary, nonetheless, "the lexicographer is not answerable for the bad use of the privilege of coining new words." Nor would it "be judicious to reject all new terms; as these are often necessary to express new ideas." In any event, he pointed out, the actual addition of words to the lexicon "must depend on public taste or the utility of the words." As if to illustrate this point, Webster unapologetically included in his dictionary's 70,000 entries domestic inventions such as *squash, moose, tomato, chowder, skunk,* and *succotash.* Who was he to exclude such commonly used terms?

Reviewers of Noah Webster's work in the old country considered this attitude impudent. Presumptuous. Insulting to the King's English. One visitor from abroad, a former British Army officer named Basil Hall, made this case in person. While touring Connecticut in 1827, Captain Hall looked in on the lexicographer, who was then completing his dictionary. During their meeting Hall said he was dismayed by all the unfamiliar words he'd heard Americans use. Webster defended the verbal inventions of his countrymen. If a new word proved useful, why not add it to the vocabulary?

"Because there are words enough already," responded Hall, "and it only confuses matters, and hurts the cause of letters to introduce such words."

Language Tourism

Throughout the nineteenth century, a steady stream of British tourists like Basil Hall and Thomas Hamilton made a hobby of compiling the many barbaric new words they'd noted while visiting America. Frances Trollope (Anthony's mother) bemoaned the "strange uncouth phrases and pronunciation" that filled the air during several years she spent in America after moving there in 1827. While touring the United States twice in the early 1840s, Charles Dickens was both amused and appalled by the language he heard there. A talkative man was *tongue-y*. Autumn days began with *a snap of cold weather*. *Fix* could be a verb synonymous with fetch ("fix the luggage"), getting dressed ("fix yourself"), and setting a table ("fix the table"). The noun *fixin'* was a culinary term ("all the fixin's"). Dickens introduced his British readers to these and other Americanisms, such as *breakdown* for a dance, *chawed up* for demolished, and the vivid names Americans gave to the drinks they called *cocktails* (an archaic Britishism): *Gin-slings*, *Mint Juleps*, and *Timber Doodles*. Much as he enjoyed such colorful palaver, like so many of his countrymen, the author was disturbed by how many "vulgarisms" Americans used. Being asked continually where he *hailed from* stuck particularly hard in Dickens's craw.

Some residents of the United States shared such concerns. When the Scottish-born clergyman John Witherspoon (who headed what became Princeton University) called uniquely American words *Americanisms*, he was not being complimentary. Rather, Reverend Witherspoon explained, his coinage referred to "vulgarisms" and "improprieties" in the American vernacular. (A 1781 collection of Witherspoon's writing was titled *Essays on Americanisms: Perversions in the English Language in the United States, Cant Phrases, etc.*) Witherspoon was just one of many appalled Americans who joined English counterparts in bemoaning all the new words being used by their countrymen. Despite being a sometime neologizer himself, Benjamin Franklin urged Noah Webster to join him in suppressing verbs such as *advocate, notice, progress,* and *opposed* that had assaulted his ears after he returned to the United States following nine years spent in France. Joseph Dennie, editor of the Tory *Gazette of the United States*, wrote that instead of planting invasive verbal seedlings in the garden of proper English, the neology-friendly lexicographer "would be much better employed in rooting out the noxious weeds than in mingling them with the flowers." (Dennie filled his *Gazette* with spurious letters to Webster, such as one from "Dermot O'Grabble" who wrote, "I hereby certify that my wife Martha has the best knack at coining new words of any I ever knew—& with the aid of a comforting drop she'll fill you two dictionerys in an hour if you please.") Warren Dutton, editor of the *New England Palladium*, went even further, arguing in an 1801 commentary that a language so exalted as English "requires no introduction of new words."

When he compiled a glossary of New World terms (such as *deputize, package,* and *graduate*) in 1816, New England jurist John Pickering took pains to point out that the words he'd included shouldn't be considered "correct English." Pickering had plenty of company in this conviction. A few years before he published his compilation, a book critic wrote in the *Edinburgh Review* (in 1807) that the American lexicon was cluttered with "a great multitude of words which are radically and entirely new, and as utterly foreign as if they had been adopted from Hebrew or Chinese." Fifteen years later Samuel Taylor Coleridge (the coiner of *pedoeuvre* for acts performed by feet) charged in 1822 that Americans had "stolen" their language from its actual owner. Truth be told, the poet concluded, Americans were "a people without a language."

John Ruskin was particularly acerbic in his disdain for the American branch of English. In 1873 the British man of letters warned that "England taught the Americans all they have of speech, or thought, hitherto. What thoughts they have not learned from England are foolish thoughts; what words they have not learned from England, unseemly words: the vile among them not being able even to be humorous parrots, but only obscene mocking-birds." (This from the man who hoped English speakers would adopt neologisms of his own invention such as *illth* for misspent wealth, *aesthesis* for sensual perceptions, and *chromolithotint* for a tinted lithograph.)

Three decades after Ruskin issued his jeremiad, the English grammarians Henry and Frank Fowler advised readers of their 1906 book *The King's English* that terms coined in America should be considered "foreign words." Two years later, British writer Charles Whibley published an essay in which he expressed horror at such Americanisms as *transportation*, *commutation*, and *proposition* as well as *locate*, *operate*, and *antagonize* used as verbs. Words like these, wrote Whibley in 1908, "if words they may be called, are hideous to the eye, offensive to the ear, meaningless to the brain." More than a century after that, echoes of this attitude could still be heard among those who consider themselves guardians of the English language. When she Googled "Americanism," well after the turn of the twenty-first century, Lynne Murphy, an American linguist who teaches at England's University of Sussex, found that term was paired with unflattering ones in a 30:1 ratio. Her survey found *Americanism* accompanied by the modifier "lovely" 227 times, "useful" 100 times, and "apt" 73 times, compared with "ugly" 7780 times, "horrible" 4780 times, "vile" 3610 times, "awful" 1700 times, and "dreadful" 963 times. In her book *The Prodigal Tongue: The Love-Hate Relationship Between American and British English,* Murphy calls this condition *amerilexicosis*: "a pathologically unhinged reaction to American English." According to Prince Charles, Americans "invent all sorts of nouns and verbs and make words that shouldn't be." Grammarians Patricia O'Conner and Stewart Kellerman, who included the prince's lament in their book *Origins of the Specious: Myths and Misconceptions of the English Language,* say they routinely hear from subjects of the prince who share his concerns. "Why do you refer to 'American English' and

'British English'?" asked one. "Surely it should be 'American English' and 'proper English.'"

But who decides what's proper?

What's Proper?

Although pitched battles about the American version of English have provided the most active field of combat regarding "proper" usage in recent centuries, wars were being fought about the English language well before the *Mayflower* set sail. These wars involved grammar, spelling, punctuation, pronunciation, and, of course, word coinage. Since its mongrel birth some fifteen centuries ago, English has always been an anarchic language, filled with helter-skelter spellings and inconsistent grammar, along with a constant flow of neologisms that appear and disappear with little rhyme or reason. In 1553 the rhetorician Thomas Wilson pointed with alarm at "affected" and "outlandish" new words being used in England, ones such as *capacity*, *celebrate*, *confidence*, *fertile*, and *relinquish*. Four decades later British author Thomas Nashe complained about the "pathetic" terms *negotiation*, *notoriety*, and *ingenuity* that had invaded his country's language during the Elizabethan era.

For centuries ferocious conflict has taken place between those who think new words debase the language and those who believe they enrich it. New words annoy those who prefer old ones, or at least think they should be adopted only after being approved by the proper authorities. Yet many a neologism that aroused ire when it was introduced over time has come to seem quite ordinary. During the 1870s, for example, the American poet and newspaper editor William Cullen Bryant compiled a list of recent dictionary entries that he thought should be deleted. On Bryant's list were *pants*, *taboo*, *loafer*, *ovation*, *raid*, *talented*, *reliable*, and *standpoint*.

Beginning some four centuries ago, determined efforts were made to bring order to this verbal chaos. Calls were issued to create an academy like ones in Italy and France that would supervise the evolution of England's language and certify proper usage. Such a body, Daniel Defoe argued in 1702, could rid English of its many "Irregular Additions." Defoe thought that a group of thirty-six worthies appointed by the king—divided evenly among noblemen, gentlemen, and men of "meer merit"—should have the authority to "Correct and Censure the Exorbitance of Writers." Under their supervision, Defoe was sure, "no Author wou'd have the Impudence to Coin without their Authority." Then, he concluded, "'twou'd be as Criminal then to *Coin Words, as Money.*"

Defoe's colleague Jonathan Swift shared his concerns. Swift, who feared and loathed the appearance of "new conceited Words" such as *bamboozle, banter, bully,* and *sham,* was appalled by the way the English lexicon changed so routinely and unpredictably. Too many neologisms relied on "corruptions" such as abbreviations and contractions, he thought. The satirist was particularly vexed by *mob,* a clip of *mobile vulgus* (Latin for "fickle crowd"). When asked by a woman what word she should use instead for unruly hordes, Swift responded, "The rabble, to be sure."

In 1712 Swift published *A Proposal for Correcting, Improving and Ascertaining the English Tongue.* This tract echoed Defoe's call for an academy to oversee the English language. Under the supervision of its members, English could be "refined to a certain Standard," Swift thought. Ideally, ways would be found to "fix it for ever." In Swift's opinion even an imperfect but stable language was better than one in constant flux. This did not mean that new words should never be added. (The *OED* credits Swift with introducing 139 of them himself.) When needed, however, such words would have to be evaluated by the proper authorities before being approved for general use.

There was no consensus on this point among those who wanted to standardize the English language. Although at one time Samuel Johnson believed that a learned academy should supervise the evolution of English, the lexicographer ultimately decided that any attempt to regulate its growth was futile, like trying to "lash the wind." The "spirit of liberty" that permeated his countrymen, Johnson realized, would always undermine such efforts. By the time his *Dictionary of the English Language* was published, Johnson had concluded that it wasn't his prerogative to try to dictate which words should be used by his countrymen. Such evaluation would be left up to users themselves. His duty was simply to record and define words already in use. (This didn't stop Johnson from railing against ones he considered barbaric or mere cant, ones such as *budge, coax, fib, fun, fuss, swap, volunteer,* and *wobble.*)

In time, Johnson's usage-tolerant view prevailed among his fellow lexicographers, and even became a way to compare the creativity of English speakers favorably with rules-bound counterparts across the Channel. A language-supervising academy like those on the continent, concluded Joseph Priestley in 1761, was "unsuitable to the genius of a *free nation.*" Better, he thought, that usage itself determine the winners of attempts to coin new words. According to Priestley, a grammarian as well as a scientist, "it is better to wait the decisions of *Time,* which are slow and sure, than to take those of *Synods,* which are often hasty and injudicious."

To those like Joseph Priestley who had no use for language supervision, the need for authoritative dictionaries was another matter. Within such works of reference words could be vetted without the heavy hand of government fiat. Well before Swift, Defoe, and others issued their calls for a language academy, in 1665 the scholar John Evelyn had called instead for a book compiling "all the pure English words," one that would both record and evaluate the many "exotic words such, as are daily minted."

Coinage Conflict

Some two centuries later a group of dedicated, ambitious Englishmen undertook the monumental task of compiling such a book. They quickly discovered that deciding which words to include and which ones to exclude from what became the *Oxford English Dictionary* was no easy task. After sifting through the *OED*'s archives while researching *Lost for Words*, her fascinating history of this dictionary, Lynda Mugglestone discovered that its founding editors initially chose not to include many terms that in time found a proper home in our lexicon. They included now-common ones such as *landscaping, limeade, radium, pacifist,*and *forsythia*.

The choices made by these editors reflected their taste and values. Americanisms were out, of course. So were words considered slang, ones coined by journalists. and neologisms introduced by authors of popular fiction. Terms found in scientific or technological publications had to fight their way into the dictionary. *Appendicitis* was excluded as mere medical jargon, an omission that glared when King Edward VII's 1902 coronation was delayed because he had to have his appendix removed and the public needed a vocabulary to discuss his condition. Although it had been in circulation since the late nineteenth century, *appendicitis* did not appear in the *OED* until 1933. In that same year *electronic* made its *OED* debut, defined as "Of or pertaining to an electron or electrons."

Literary terms received more favorable treatment in the *OED*. Words attributed to Shakespeare, Milton, and other literary luminaries were well represented on the dictionary's pages, perhaps over-represented. Samuel Taylor Coledridge's *linguipotence* (meaning mastery of languages) was included. So was Algernon Swinburne's *harvestry*, even though the poet himself told the *OED*'s editors that he couldn't recall when or why he'd coined that term, or exactly what it meant. Mugglestone calls the favoritism shown by the *OED*'s creators for literary over scientific or technological language "linguistic apartheid."

Despite its controversial birth, one scientific neologism that the *OED* did include was *scientist* itself. Three decades earlier, after being rebuked for coining that word in 1834, William Whewell reintroduced it in an 1840 book called *Philosophy of the Inductive Sciences*. *Physicist* was another neologism Whewell included in that book. Because *physician* was already taken, he wrote, perhaps those who study physics could be called *physicists*. This coinage, Michael Faraday told the author, was "to my mouth and ears so awkward that I think I never shall be able to use it." Half a century later, Lord Kelvin (William Thomson) said he still considered *physicist* "un-English, unpleasing, and meaningless."

"Un-English" is the key idea here. Like Lord Kelvin, many guardians of the King's English were (and are) less concerned about new words being added to the lexicon than about ones being added that come from dubious sources. No source is more dubious than the United States, of course. Nothing proper about the English spoken there. "Proper" English is whatever a would-be language guardian considers proper, of course. And their convictions have as much to do with fashion, and snobbery, as lexicography. "Class biases have shown up over and over again throughout the history of proper English," points out Jack Lynch in *The Lexicographer's Dilemma*. (Lynch didn't put "proper" in quotes, but could have.) Henry Hitchings adds morality to class biases as a driver of what's assumed to be proper English. So is a heavy investment in the verbal status quo, Hitchings adds in his book *The Language Wars*, "or, more often, in a fantasy of the status quo."

One reason *serendipity* took so long to find a place in English discourse, Robert Merton concluded, was resistance to adopting new words among members of the upper class, who thought using existing forms of speech confirmed their status, and new ones would threaten it. This led the sociologist to ask, "To what extent did (or does) upper-class language tolerate the use of neologisms?"

That question returns us to the birth of the *Oxford English Dictionary*. Members of England's upper classes were well represented among its founders, of course. In the words of one, the dictionary was intended for "The English of educated people in England." The concept of *Anglicity* was to guide their work, said founding editor James Murray (a coinage of his own). Racial bias is implicit in such an attitude, not just in the continual use of *barbarisms* to denigrate any terms considered beyond the pale (adapting a term Greeks used to disparage non-Greeks), but more nakedly, too, as when an early *OED* editor proposed that *white man* be defined as "A man of honourable character such as one associates with a European (as opposed to a negro)."

American language snobs were no less likely than their British counterparts to indulge in such linguistic bigotry. One domestic critic of Noah Webster's coinage-friendly dictionary thought its contents were so "foul and unclean" that the lexicographer might as well "adopt at once the language of the *aborigines*." Among the spurious letters to Webster that appeared in the *Gazette of the United States* was one from a correspondent named "Cuffee" who wrote, "Masa Webser plese put sum HOMMANY and sum GOOD POSSUM fat and sum two tree good BANJOE in your new what-you-call-um Book for your fello Cytsen."

The Academy of Users

In the end, protecting one's ethnic privilege and national franchise has proven to be more important than preserving linguistic purity (whatever that is) in the face of incursions from outsiders.

Ironically, many so-called Americanisms that have outraged British purists over the years are actually preserved Britishisms. *Fall*, for example, was synonymous with *autumn* in both countries before British purists mistakenly concluded that it was a colonial barbarism. Overlooking the fact that *scientist* had been coined by a Cambridge professor, because this word achieved greater currency in the United States than in Great Britain, a (London) *Daily News* writer in 1890 denounced this neologism as "an ignoble Americanism," a "cheap and vulgar product of transatlantic slang." When she assessed a BBC list of the fifty "Most Noted" Americanisms more than a century later, Lynne Murphy found that seventeen of them were actually long-forgotten Britishisms. They included *transportation, expiration, oftentimes,* and *alphabetize.*

In the ultimate irony, *stiff upper lip*, a phrase synonymous with British resolve, made its first known appearance in *Reif's Philadelphia Gazette and Daily Advertiser*. As discovered by Pascal Tréguer, a correspondent for that American newspaper advised his readers in 1811 that bellicose posturing toward England was merely an attempt to "look big and keep a stiff upper lip." Subsequent references cited by the *OED* during the following half century are all North American, including a line in *Uncle Tom's Cabin*: "'Well, good-by, Uncle Tom; keep a stiff upper lip,' said George." In 1874 an American poet named Phoebe Cary published a poem called "Keep a Stiff Upper Lip." The earliest British use of this phrase that the *OED* could find was in an 1887 issue of the *Spectator.* If Brits had realized its country of origin, would *a stiff upper lip* be considered so central to their national identity?

Contempt for Americanisms isn't universal in the land where English was born. When William Archer toured the United States at the turn of the last century, in addition to George Ade's slang, the London drama critic was charmed by such Americanisms as *elevator* for lift, *scrap* for quarrel, and *scoop* for a newspaper's exclusive story. Archer was not enamored with every Americanism he heard, of course. But overall he broke ranks with his many countrymen who had little but contempt for Yankee verbal innovations. "The idea that the English language is degenerating in America is an absolutely groundless illusion," Archer advised readers of the *Pall Mall Gazette.* "As American life is far more fertile of new conditions than ours, the tendency towards neologisms cannot but be stronger in America than in England." Far from the back of their hand, Archer concluded, his fellow Brits should offer a grateful handshake to American innovators for the many new words and phrases they'd invented.

Virginia Woolf concurred. The English novelist wrote in 1925, "When we want to freshen our speech, we borrow from American—*poppycock*, *rambunctious*, *flip-flop*, *booster*, *good mixer*. All the expressive, ugly, vigorous slang which creeps into use among us, first in talk, later in writing, comes from across the Atlantic." A decade later Alistair Cooke estimated that by 1935 the average Brit was using as many as forty Americanisms a day. That figure is undoubtedly higher today, far higher. (When watching contemporary British television productions, I used to try to keep track of all the American expressions characters used in their speech but gave up because there were too many of them.) In *The Secret Life of Words*, Henry Hitchings flags terms such as *advisory*, *badlands*, *bandwagon*, *curvaceous*, *haywire*, *isolationism*, *law-abiding*, *mileage*, *slapstick*, *split-level*, *squatter*, *stampede*, *stunt*, and *unshakeable* as Americanisms whose dubious roots are seldom realized among his fellow Brits, who use them regularly. After migrating from the U.S. to the U.K., they lost their American accent.

Establishment, as we now use that term, made this journey too, one Henry Fairlie concluded was helmed by Emerson in 1841, a century before he himself escorted this word into general usage. How did the British journalist feel about the results? Not so good, it turns out. "I tried to wriggle away from the success of the word almost as soon as I first used it in print," Fairlie wrote several years after he'd done so. "I wish the language could be rid of it."

That type of sentiment is far from uncommon on the part of both word coiners and word revivers like Henry Fairlie. Coiner's remorse abounds.

19

Coiner's Remorse

WHEN HE WAS the secretary of the Treasury, Alan Greenspan gave a speech that called attention to a stock market he considered overvalued. This was due, Greenspan said, to "irrational exuberance." Those two words caused the manic-depressive market to dip. Yet "irrational exuberance" described the bubbly investment climate so well that it has become a lasting part of American discourse, even inspiring the title of a 2000 book. A decade after Greenspan gave his memorable speech in 1996, *Fresh Air* host Terry Gross asked him how he'd come up with this influential phrase. Her guest sighed, then said, "I wish I hadn't."

Neologizers beware: terms you create can come back to haunt you. Adapting the old saw about marriage, coin in haste, repent at leisure. Alan Greenspan wasn't the first to discover the perils of neology, and certainly won't be the last. Mixed feelings are commonly experienced by those who dare to add a word or phrase to our lexicon. Such ambivalence can be felt for a variety of reasons: the attitudes of word coiners change, they develop reservations about their coinage, or they don't like the way others use and misuse it. Over time, neologizers may find they simply no longer care for a term of their own invention. By then it's too late, however. Neologisms can't be shed easily by remorseful coiners. "Words are like harpoons," observed Fred Hoyle of his regretted *big bang* coinage. "Once they go in, they are very hard to pull out."

Coining in Public

Uttering words one comes to regret is an occupational hazard of working in the public eye. Those who make speeches, are interviewed regularly, or testify before government bodies have continual opportunities to use words they wish they hadn't. When those words are ones of their own creation, this regret is amplified.

That's what Republican senator Trent Lott discovered in 2003 when filibuster threats by Democrats were keeping President Bush's judicial nominees from being confirmed. A frustrated Lott, who was the Senate's majority leader, threatened to change Senate rules so that some presidential appointments could be approved by a fifty-one-vote majority rather than the sixty votes needed under threat of a filibuster. Lott acknowledged that this would constitute a radical tinkering with hallowed Senate traditions. One might even consider it "nuclear." *New Republic* correspondent Michael Crowley asked, "What might Lott's 'nuclear' option be?" Crowley's emendation of Lott's threat stuck to the Mississippi senator like super-glue. Lott pleaded that instead of the *nuclear option*, we should call his proposed change of Senate rules the *constitutional option* (or at least did before Senate Democrats actually exercised that option). We didn't heed his call. During the years after it was hatched, the Lott-Crowley coinage took on a life of its own, not just in politics but in many another context where any radical course of action is subject to being called a "nuclear option." The *OED* defines this option as "the most drastic of the possible responses to a situation."

As Michael Crowley's role in the coinage of "nuclear option" suggests, it isn't just public figures themselves who coin terms they later regret. Those swimming in their wake—speechwriters, ghostwriters, journalists—also create words and expressions, then wish they hadn't.

Moonbeam Retracted

As a colorful way to depict Jerry Brown, *Chicago Daily News* columnist Mike Royko observed in 1976 that if California's unconventional governor ran for president, he'd be likely to attract "the moonbeam vote." In gritty Chicago, *moonbeam* was a term used to mock notions considered flaky, off-the-wall, or pie-in-the-sky. Brown's proposals to create a state space academy, launch a communications satellite, and develop renewable sources of energy certainly qualified. These notions had made California's governor the target of mocking nicknames such as *flake*, *snowflake*, and *Governor Mork* (for the character from planet Ork played by Robin Williams in *Mork and Mindy*). As "Governor Moonbeam," Royko's epithet played an important role in keeping Jerry Brown from being taken seriously on the national stage.

Four years after sticking the "moonbeam" label on Brown, Royko heard him speak at the 1980 Democratic convention. Brown gave by far the best-informed, most thoughtful speech Royko heard there. Had he unjustly maligned this man?

A decade later, the two met for coffee as Brown was considering another run for the White House in 1990. Toward the end of their chat, Brown looked Royko in the eye and said about his long-shot candidacy, "I'd have to deal with the, uh ... the ..."

After an uncomfortable silence Royko interjected, "The moonbeam factor."

Brown nodded. Royko squirmed. Surely the impact of that unfortunate label had faded, he said hopefully.

"No," Brown responded, shaking his head. "It's still there."

"What a guilt trip," Royko later told his readers. "You see, I have the dubious distinction of being the author of the phrase 'Governor Moonbeam.'

"Even worse, I don't even remember when I wrote it or in what context. But I do know that that column appeared in several California papers and, to my amazement, 'Governor Moonbeam' became part of the political vocabulary."

In a 1991 column Royko called his phrase an "idiotic, damn-fool, meaningless throw-away line," one that indelibly burdened Jerry Brown "because a guy in Chicago was stringing some words together one evening to earn his day's pay and tossed in what he thought was an amusing phrase. And if he had it to do over again, he sure as hell wouldn't." *Governor Moonbeam* was a term Royko now renounced as "unfair, inappropriate and outdated."

"So enough of this 'Moonbeam' stuff," Royko pleaded. "As the creator of this monster, I declare it null, void and deceased."

Truthful Hyperbole, Fake News, and Deep States

Mike Royko is only one of many neologizers who have tried to retract terms of their own creation. Such remorseful word coiners sometimes plead for redemption years after they added terms to public discourse. Frank Luntz is one of them. Nearly two decades after successfully urging Republicans to stop talking about *global warming* and start talking about *climate change*, the GOP pollster admitted that he'd made a mistake. During mid-2019 testimony before the Senate's Special Committee on the Climate Crisis, Luntz told members, "I'm here before you to say that I was wrong in 2001. Just stop using something that I wrote 18 years ago, because it's not accurate today."

Tony Schwartz feels every bit as repentant as Luntz about a phrase he added to public discourse. Schwartz's remorse isn't about a coinage credited to him but one he put in the mouth of someone else: Donald Trump. To supplement his work as a journalist, Schwartz ghostwrote Trump's 1987 bestseller, *The Art of the Deal*. In that book the real estate developer boasted about engaging in "truthful hyperbole." This was a phrase Schwartz had conjured to put a positive gloss on Trump's serial mistruths. Trump loved Schwartz's concept and used it repeatedly. Schwartz says the developer told him that *truthful hyperbole* described perfectly what he considered to be innocent exaggeration while negotiating business deals. When Trump made continual fact-free assertions while running for president in 2016, Schwartz confessed that it was he who'd created this rationale for doing so. Unlike its beneficiary, Schwartz came to feel that misleading others with his euphemism for lying was inherently dishonest. "'Truthful hyperbole' is a contradiction in terms," he told the *New Yorker*'s Jane Mayer mid-campaign. "It's a way of saying, 'It's a lie, but who cares?'" Schwartz didn't try to duck the role he played in helping Trump become president. "I put lipstick on a pig," the writer concluded. "I feel a deep sense of remorse that I contributed to presenting Trump in a way that brought him wider attention and made him more appealing than he is."

During his presidential campaign, then as president, Donald Trump continually disparaged press coverage he didn't like as *fake news*. This was a phrase that Canadian journalist Craig Silverman introduced in a 2014 tweet: "Fake news site National Report set off a measure of panic by publishing fake story about Ebola outbreak." Although initially used primarily by progressives to describe fabrications by conservatives, after Trump began using the phrase as a cudgel to attack journalists it became a predominantly right-wing charge. In retrospect, Silverman came to see that in a hyperpartisan climate, assuming the expression *fake news* would refer to manufactured reportage of any political stripe had been naïve. Instead, it was "weaponized," becoming one more bludgeon to use against enemies real and perceived. Following the election of 2016, *fake news* had been reduced to an "empty slogan," Silverman concluded, one that pushed aside the actual issue of fictionalized news. Toward the end of Trump's first year in office, he wrote, "Three years after that tweet about National Report, I cringe when I hear anyone say 'fake news.'"

Another phrase Donald Trump and other conspiracy-minded conservatives used continually was *deep state*. From Trump's perspective, this referred to a cabal of unelected civil servants and other behind-the-scene officials whose swamp he intended to drain. It was introduced to contemporary American discourse by onetime congressional aide Mike Lofgren in a widely read 2014 essay that he called "Anatomy of the Deep State." Lofgren later expanded his essay into a 2016 book titled *The Deep State: The Fall of the Constitution and the Rise of a Shadow Government*. Its publisher touted this book as a "gripping portrait of the dismal swamp on the Potomac and the revolution it will take to set us back on course." Although Lofgren didn't claim to have originated his book's title (he'd seen the phrase in a 2013 novel by John le Carré, echoing earlier use of that term in the Middle East), he did escort *deep state* into modern domestic palaver.* Ironically, although that concept first won plaudits from progressive followers of Bill Moyers, whose website published Lofgren's original essay, the notion of

---

* The notion that a group of unelected figures are conspiring behind the scenes to manipulate the American government has a long history. During the early twentieth century this supposed cabal was called an "invisible government," or "invisible empire." In their 1964 book *The Invisible Government*, David Wise and Thomas B. Ross referred to a secretive group of CIA-dominated individuals and agencies as a "shadow government."

a *deep state*—a sinister cousin of *the establishment*—gained its greatest usage among right-wing conspiracy theorists. Lofgren—a moderate Republican—was appalled by this development. He compared his two little words to a virus. "Once it gets out into the environment it mutates, you've totally lost control over it," Lofgren told Joseph Bernstein of *BuzzFeed News*. Reaching for other ways to describe how he felt about adding *deep state* to the political agenda, Lofgren said it came to seem like a species of animal he'd introduced into the wild. Or else a Frankenstein monster. Whatever the best analogy might be, he lamented, "what it does is not within my control."

This is a common sentiment among word introducers like Craig Silverman, Mike Lofgren, and Tony Schwartz. When they innocently add terms to public discourse, it is hard to anticipate that these words can take on a life of their own. And it's not just political phrases that come back to haunt their creators. Management terms can too.

Nonprofit Centers

During his six-decade career, Peter Drucker was among the most influential of postwar management consultants. One of the most important concepts attributed to him is that of *profit centers*, a term he coined soon after World War II. It referred to those parts of a company that reliably generate income. According to Drucker, managers could best improve the bottom line of their business as a whole by giving particular support to its most profitable divisions.

For decades this was a hallowed corporate concept. Taking Peter Drucker's advice, companies strived to convert "cost centers" into "profit centers" by laying off employees, shrinking the size of money-losing divisions, and in some cases spinning them off into what they hoped would be autonomous sources of revenue. Over time, Drucker realized that this was a mistaken notion of how businesses make money. Profitability had less to do with the way an enterprise was organized than with its appeal to customers. The consultant therefore came to regret both the concept and phrase describing it that helped make the notion of "profit centers" so central to the corporate ethos. "Many, many years ago," Drucker explained in 2002, "I coined the term *profit center*. I am thoroughly ashamed of it now, because inside a business there are no profit centers, just cost centers. Profit comes only from the outside. When a customer returns with a repeat order and his check doesn't bounce, you have a profit center. Until then you have only cost centers."

Drucker's second thoughts had less to do with his coinage per se than the way it misrepresented his evolving views. Like many another neologizer, Drucker didn't regret his coined concept per se; only the fact that he no longer believed it to be valid. This is among the most common forms of coinage remorse.

Evolution

As insurrections spread through the Middle East during early 2011, political scientist Marc Lynch contributed an article to the blog of *Foreign Policy* magazine titled "Obama's Arab Spring." In his subsequent book *The Arab Uprising* (2012), Lynch called *Arab Spring* "a term that I may have unintentionally coined in a January 6, 2011 article." In this book and in subsequent comments Lynch conceded that the phrase misrepresented Middle Eastern insurrections. When these uprisings descended into chaos that led to the rise of authoritarian leaders who promised to restore order, Lynch said he was sorry he'd given them such a benign designation. This wasn't because of any flaw in the phrase *Arab Spring*, which echoed the name given earlier insurrections in Poland, Czechoslovakia, and South Korea (Polish Spring, Prague Spring, Seoul Spring), but because the promise of a political renaissance faded so quickly after uprisings were crushed in Egypt, produced near anarchy in Libya, and led to a savage civil war in Syria. As a result, the notion of an *Arab Spring* took on a bitterly ironic tone. In addition to being inaccurate, Lynch realized it implied that the Middle East had been frozen until the 2011 movements caused that region's politics to thaw. "It's not like the Arabs just woke up," the author told an interviewer. "They've been awake for a long time. They've just been struggling against these authoritarian repressive regimes that they couldn't defeat." (Lynch's regret about coining *Arab Spring* was misplaced; this phrase had been in play for years before he used the term.)

John Gyakum could sympathize with Lynch's change of heart. Nearly four decades after he helped coin *bomb cyclone* in 1980, when that coinage became a weathercaster's commonplace, the meteorologist stopped using it himself. In terrorist times, casual use of a word such as *bomb* was ill-advised, Gyakum concluded. "When I talk about these explosively developing storms, I go through the trouble of mouthing the terms 'explosively developing,' and I don't use 'bomb,'" Gyakum told *HuffPost* in early 2018. "It's somewhat inappropriate when you consider other aspects of the world right now."

Unlike remorseful word coiners such as Alan Greenspan and Trent Lott, the remorse of ones such as Gyakum and Lynch had more to do with the march of events and their own changing views than regret about their coinage itself. In the current argot, their thinking "evolved." Like them, many other neologizers found that as times change, so does their perspective. Terms they coined years earlier may no longer reflect their outlook.

Pop Penitents

In his review of the 2007 movie *Elizabethtown*, film critic Nathan Rabin called the character played by Kirsten Dunst a "Manic Pixie Dream Girl," or MPDG for short. Dunst's character was just one of many "adorably daffy" young women in contemporary movies whose main role was to lift the spirits of depressed young men, he explained. Rabin conceded that this was purely a male fantasy, one so compelling that many a man in the audience wanted to find himself an MPDG to marry posthaste. Although the critic never thought that *MPDG* would out-live his 2007 coinage, one year later a colleague created a list of "16 films featur-ing Manic Pixie Dream Girls." Joining Kirsten Dunst on that list were Natalie Portman in *Garden State*, Goldie Hawn in *Butterflies Are Free*, and Diane Keaton in *Annie Hall*. Ukulele-strumming Zooey Deschanel subsequently portrayed a quintessential MPDG in the 2009 movie *500 Days of Summer*. In time, the con-cept of a *Manic Pixie Dream Girl* became ubiquitous enough to merit a lengthy Wikipedia page. In 2015 it was added to Oxford Dictionaries. An article pub-lished online in early 2020 was titled "How to Avoid Becoming Your Partner's 'Manic Pixie Dream.'"

Four years after Nathan Rabin reviewed *Elizabethtown*, that movie's director, Cameron Crowe, told an interviewer about the MPDG trope, "I dig it . . . I keep thinking I'll run into Nathan Rabin and we'll have a great conversation about it." This blew the critic's mind. Rabin had no idea that his casual coinage would attract so much attention. In a *Salon* column that appeared seven years after he introduced the phrase *Manic Pixie Dream Girl*, Rabin wrote, "The archetype of the free-spirited life-lover who cheers up a male sad-sack had existed in the cul-ture for ages. But by giving an idea a name and a fuzzy definition, you apparently

Manic Pixie Dream Girl Kirsten Dunst, in the movie *Elizabethtown*, 2005.

also give it power." This notion was inherently sexist, he'd come to believe, since the primary purpose of an MPDG is to be a human antidepressant for gloomy men. Rabin apologized for giving a name to an archetype he now regarded as a male-fantasy stereotype.

Pop culture no less than any other branch of cultural life includes neologisms whose premise gets out of step with changing times. This was the experience of Joe Boyd, an American expat who'd become part of Britain's recording industry during the mid-1960s. In 1987 Boyd joined a group of London music moguls who met in a pub to discuss how to market recorded music from settings such as Senegal, Cape Verde, Brazil, and Cuba that was growing increasingly popular. At a time when CDs ruled, there was a particular need for a category whose name would help record store owners decide where to shelve albums of music from around the world. Suggestions were made; votes were cast. "Roots" was already taken. "Ethnic" sounded too scholarly. "Worldbeat" left out music that had no bass or percussion. Boyd (as he recalls) finally suggested "world music." This label won the day, and has endured for more than three decades. "Our ambition was very modest," said Boyd on the thirtieth anniversary of this coinage. "We had no real desire to change the music world or our end of it. We just wanted a little category."

Over time, however, a growing number of world musicians objected to being categorized this way. Talking Heads founder David Byrne called it "a way of dismissing artists or their music as irrelevant to one's own life. It's a way of relegating this 'thing' into the realm of something exotic and therefore cute, weird but safe." As the Internet brought the world itself to computer users' doorsteps, three decades after *world music* was coined Boyd concluded that this term had outlived its usefulness. "Probably the sooner we put a stake through its heart the better," he said (on PRI's *The World*, appropriately).

Aspies

Lorna Wing wished *Asperger's syndrome* would enjoy that fate. Before the English psychiatrist gave mild autism this name, that condition had had unfortunate designations such as *dementia infantilis* and *schizoid personality of childhood*. In 1944 Viennese psychiatrist Hans Asperger completed a PhD thesis titled "Autistic Psychopathy in Childhood." Asperger's work was not well known outside Austria before Wing described it in a 1981 paper titled "Asperger's Syndrome: A Clinical Account." Although German psychiatrist Gerhard Bosch had already referred to "the differences between Asperger and Kanner syndromes" fourteen years earlier (referencing child psychiatrist Leo Kanner of John Hopkins University, who studied what he called "early infantile autism"), Wing is generally credited with popularizing *Asperger's syndrome* to describe those on the mild end of the autism spectrum. In 1988 a London conference titled "Asperger's Syndrome" confirmed its acceptance.

Over time, Dr. Wing began to have second thoughts about the name she'd given this condition. She'd come to feel that labeling psychiatric conditions limits our ability to grasp their complexity. "I wish I hadn't done it," Wing said about coining this way of identifying mild autism, in an interview with Adam Feinstein for his 2010 book *A History of Autism*. "I would like to throw all labels away today, including Asperger's syndrome."**

Far from being thrown away, however, this label is more widespread than ever, as speculation abounds about socially inept success stories such as Bill Gates and Mark Zuckerberg. Might they be *aspies*? That's the contraction introduced by educator Liane Holliday Willey in her 1999 memoir *Pretending to Be Normal: Living with Asperger's Syndrome*, and several subsequent books. Although Willey's hope was to offer the mildly autistic a friendlier name for their condition than Asperger's syndrome, the author sometimes heard from readers who thought this appellation trivialized their status. "I regret this is so," said Willey. That regret did not keep Willey from naming her website *aspie.com*.

Willey is not the only word coiner to be ambivalent about a coinage: expressing remorse about coining it, yet wanting credit for doing so. While taking pride in his coinage of *gobbledygook*, a year before he died in 1954 Maury Maverick wrote to a friend, "I do hope that when I kick the bucket that they will do something else than say I originated that word."

Another neologizer, Columbia University law professor Tim Wu, has decidedly mixed feelings about a term he added to public discourse in his 2003 article "Network Neutrality, Broadband Discrimination." As Wu came to realize, *network neutrality* is not among the crisper coinages of our time (even in its abbreviated form of *net neutrality*). Nor is it easy to grasp. What exactly does this expression refer to? Ever since it became a prominent topic of political discussion, Wu has struggled to explain the concept of *network neutrality* in plain English. The law professor realizes better than anyone that a livelier, more vivid term would make it easier to consider the idea that broadband access to the Internet should be available to everyone on the same terms. When NPR's Laura Sydell noted how dull the term was, Wu responded, "Oh, God, I know, I know." Wu then pointed out that his coinage had nonetheless remained in play ever since he introduced it, and helped generate substantial public engagement. When asked point-blank

---

** Since it has come to light that some of the children whom Hans Asperger diagnosed as mildly autistic were later euthanized by the Nazis, many feel his name should no longer be used to describe those with mild autism.

whether he regretted coining *network neutrality*, Wu told another interviewer, "I don't regret it all."

Of course if Wu had come up with something snappier than *net neutrality*, he might have regretted this coinage even more. That's been true of any number of neologizers among his fellow scholars who coined terms to make their work accessible to a broader public, then felt those terms trivialized that work.

Scholarly Second Thoughts

In his 1986 book *Engines of Creation: The Coming Era of Nanotechnology*, Eric Drexler called self-replicating molecular machines *gray goo*. Later he wished he hadn't, feeling that the colloquial, slangy quality of this phrase kept his warning about the negative impact of micromachinery from being taken more seriously. "I wish I had never used the term 'gray goo,'" Drexler told *Nature* magazine. The engineer also regrets using *nanotechnology* in the subtitle of his book, which he thought made it too easy to confuse molecular manufacturing with miniaturized technology in general. (Although some think this term was coined by Drexler, in 1974 Tokyo Science University professor Norio Taniguchi had titled a 1974 paper "On the Basic Concept of 'Nano Technology.'")

Another title that has caused heartburn for its scientist-author is *The God Particle*. This was the name of a 1993 book on particle physics that Nobel laureate Leon Lederman coauthored with science writer Dick Teresi. Its title refers to the subatomic particle known as Higgs boson (after Peter Higgs, who during the 1960s had postulated its existence). In a speech he gave before writing the book, Lederman whimsically called the elusive Higgs boson a "God particle." Teresi suggested they use this as their book's working title. Publishers never adopt working titles, he assured Lederman. Theirs did. "The rest is history," Lederman and Teresi wrote in the preface to the 2006 edition of *The God Particle*. "The title ended up offending two groups: 1) Those who believe in God, and 2) those who do not. We were warmly received by those in the middle."

The *God Particle* resonated broadly in a way *Higgs boson* never did, or could. A moniker meant to be tongue-in-cheek hardly represented the complexity of Lederman's thinking on this subject, however. (The physicist liked to joke that if his publisher had consented he'd have called his book *The Goddamn Particle* because pursuing the Higgs boson was such an ordeal.) Rather than referring to holy creationism, Lederman had meant *God Particle* to suggest the difficulty of determining how particles acquire mass, leading to the birth of the universe itself. Instead, particularly to all of those who have heard about this book but haven't read it, the title implies that its author thinks a supreme being created our world one particle at a time (leading a Christian woman to ask Lederman if there might be a Satan particle as well as a God one). Physicists' disdain for Lederman's way of depicting *Higgs boson* has only grown over time. "Leon needed a catchy title for his book," his colleague Nicholas Soloney told a reporter two decades after *The God Particle* was published. "I know he regrets it."

Like Leon Lederman, Richard Dawkins has gnawing doubts about the title he gave his bestseller *The Selfish Gene*. In that book's thirtieth anniversary edition, Dawkins lamented the way this phrase became part of the debate surrounding evolution, even among those who hadn't read his book. He had no one to blame but himself. A British publisher had urged him to change the word "selfish" in his title because it was too negative, and too easy to misinterpret. Why not call his book something more positive; *The Immortal Gene*, say? Dawkins stuck to his guns. Three decades later he wished he hadn't. Many of those who criticize a work like his, Dawkins came to see, "prefer to read a book by title only. No doubt this works well enough for *The Tale of Benjamin Bunny* or *The Decline and Fall of the Roman Empire*, but I can readily see that 'The Selfish Gene' on its own, without the large footnote of the book itself, might give an inadequate impression of its contents." Because *The Selfish Gene* had as much to do with altruism as selfishness, Dawkins felt that the title he'd insisted on misrepresented not only his book but his take on evolution in general. Based on *The Selfish Gene*'s title alone, its author was indelibly, if inaccurately, branded as a bard of selfishness, a zoological Ayn Rand.

As for his most successful neologism of all, *meme*, Dawkins doesn't regret having coined that term, nor been sorry about its application to Internet replications. He does have reservations about the many ways that term is misinterpreted and misapplied, however. Cute cat videos, presidential tweets, and deep fake doctored photos (to say nothing of computer viruses) that are created with the intention of "going viral" don't exemplify a concept he'd meant to be analogous to natural selection.

Like Dawkins, some coinage penitents don't regret a term they created as much as the uses to which it's been put, and the many ways it's misconstrued. It isn't that their neologism was such a bad one, they feel. In some ways it was too good, too malleable, too easy to misinterpret and use in ways the coiner never intended.

After his neologism *factoid* developed a more prosaic meaning than the one he'd intended, referring more to trivia than to dubious data, Norman Mailer felt betrayed. He felt similarly about his other noted coinage: *fug*. "The word has been a source of great embarrassment to me over the years," said Mailer while taking part in a 1968 panel discussion, two decades after he introduced this euphemism in *The Naked and the Dead*. The apocryphal story about Tallulah Bankhead's saying he coined *fug* because couldn't spell fuck caused him particular pain. Mailer said this urban myth had caused him to become a "sort of household joke. . . . And I regretted it." (For all of that, Mailer liked to greet new acquaintances by growling, "Who the fug are you?")

Mailer's fellow novelist Erica Jong experienced similar chagrin about her own F-word (or Z-F-word, to be precise). *Zipless fuck* was not only taken seriously by readers of *Fear of Flying*, she found, but was assumed to be based on her own experience. Jong tried repeatedly to explain that the notion of a *zipless fuck* was meant to be a fantasy shared by author and reader, not an endorsement of spontaneous coupling, let alone a thinly disguised portrayal of her own sexual activity. "People so misinterpreted 'zipless,' " Jong told a reporter in 2015, more than four decades after her novel titillated readers with its imaginary coupling between strangers. "I say in *Fear of Flying* that it's a Platonic ideal and a fantasy, and I have never had one, but people seem to overlook that."

Beverly Whipple came to second-guess making reference to a specific *spot* rather than to an "area" of the vagina that was unusually erogenous. Calling that area a "spot" prompted as much frustration as arousal among too many of the women and their partners who searched in vain for an orgasmic button to push. Whipple herself knew that this was misleading, but those who read, or heard, about her book, did not. (Would a book called *The G-Area* have attracted as much attention as one called *The G-Spot?*)

Like unruly offspring, neologisms can go their own way, and in the process develop meanings their parents never intended. Linguists take this process for granted. They assume that the meaning of new words will grow, diversify, and take off in directions never intended by their creator. The more users a coinage attracts, the greater number of meanings it will acquire along the way. This is small consolation to those who introduced such terms, however. They're far more likely to be perturbed than reassured by this inevitable process of definition diffusion. Certainly that was the way George Kennan felt about *containment*, Thomas Kuhn about *paradigm*, and Clayton Christensen about *disrupt*. Kimberlé Crenshaw compares the way her term *intersectionality* has acquired an ever-growing range of definitions to a bad game of "telephone:" (in which a message gets more and more garbled as one person whispers it to another).

Neologizers like Crenshaw have a lot of company in feeling that their verbal offspring were mistreated once they left the nest. That's exactly how Lin Farley feels. This onetime AP reporter introduced the phrase *sexual harassment* during a hearing about women in the workplace held by New York's Human Rights Commission in April 1975. At first Farley was gratified by the way press coverage of that expression helped facilitate discussion of this topic. "Working women immediately took up the phrase, which finally captured the sexual coercion they were experiencing daily," she wrote in a 2017 *New York Times* op-ed. "No longer did they have to explain to their friends and family that 'he hit on me and wouldn't take no for an answer, so I had to quit.' What he did had a name."

Over time, however, as media chatter trivialized this concept, corporations hired "sexual harassment" officers (then ignored their counsel), and sexual exploitation in the workplace continued unabated, Farley wondered if naming that syndrome had had the impact she'd hoped it would. More likely this concept had been sapped of its vigor by overuse and misuse. "'Sexual harassment' was never meant to be a term that the corporate world would feel comfortable tossing around," Farley wrote in her *Times* column. "It is a vicious practice—one that flourishes because men hold authority over women at work, and they use it to extract sex and to humiliate. If the price of popularizing the notion of sexual harassment has been to dampen its impact, it's now time to reclaim and redefine the term as the ugly thing it is—to imbue it with its initial power."

Although common, regret is far from the most typical response to being known as the source of a term in widespread use. A quarter century after he coined *cyberspace*, William Gibson compared being identified with that word to having a tattoo. Yet when asked whether he was sick of having the phrase "coined cyberspace" appear so prominently in his bio, Gibson responded, "I think I'd miss it if it went away."

20

You Too Can Coin a Word

WHAT LITERATE PERSON hasn't dreamed of creating a word that would join the lexicon and stake their claim to posterity? Put somewhat differently, who has never enjoyed a pleasant fantasy of seeing the phrase "coined by" preceding their name? Converting this fantasy into reality is a tough go, however. Creating a neologism is hard. Getting others to adopt it is even harder.

As we approach the end of this book, let's look more closely at both of these challenges: how to best coin a word, and how to enhance its chances of actually being used.

Creation

Although it isn't always clear why one coinage succeeds in being adopted and another does not, when creating a new word there are ways to improve its odds of success. Here are some guidelines: (1) go short; (2) have fun; (3) please the ear; (4) create word pictures; (5) evoke feeling; (6) use good letters.

1. Go Short

Winston Churchill had no time for jargony, tongue-twisted prose. "Let us not shrink from using the short, expressive phrases," he advised staff members in a 1940 memo. Instead of tapping Latin and Greek for obscure, multisyllabic terms, Churchill recommended communicating with terse, forceful words rooted in Anglo-Saxonisms. "Old words are best," he said while accepting a literary award in 1949, "and old short words best of all."

Especially when it comes to word creation, Churchill had it right. *Gobbledygook* and *serendipity* notwithstanding, when coining new words, brevity is generally a virtue (*blurb*, *blog*, *meme*, *spam*). Short words are easier to remember than long ones. Most are easier to spell. A pithy neologism that is easy to remember and spell is more likely to catch on.

As Paul McFedries points out, an added virtue of short words is that their pronunciation is usually clear. *Sitcom*, for example, is a portmanteau whose succinctness and obvious pronounceability enhances its appeal. By contrast, the pronunciation of *democrazy* is not at all clear (to say nothing of the fact that our brain routinely auto-corrects this to "democracy"). A neologism that needs a coiner's help to pronounce it is unlikely to catch on. Similarly, a new word that works visually but not orally (or vice versa) is a nonstarter. *Urbs* isn't a bad nickname for those who live in cities, but using this word in conversation would require explaining that it doesn't refer to plants used for seasoning. Linguist Erin McKean adds that coining a word whose spelling has no apparent sound is not a good strategy. Including silent letters is particularly problematic. (Think: *limn*.) To make this point, McKean, founder of the website *wordnik*, cites an old joke: "Q: How Do you pronounce Hen3ry? A: HEN-ree. The '3' is silent."

2. Have Fun

Among the least appreciated traits of promising new words is playfulness. "Not only children but our whole species is given to play," pointed out Swedish linguist Nils Thun in a dissertation on the appeal of what I call conjoined terms, and what linguists call "reduplicative" words (e.g., *flim-flam*, *zig-zag*, *shilly-shally*, *hurly-burly*, and thousands more). "An element of playfulness is to be found also in language, mankind's most specific characteristic. There is play with language as well as with objects."

One reason children's authors have contributed so many words to the adult lexicon is that they tend to have a keen awareness of the fun-hunger that characterizes readers of all ages. Think *twitter* and *tweet*, *bling* and *blog*, *piffle* and *pooh-bah*.

That term was coined by playwright William S. Gilbert for Gilbert and Sullivan's 1885 operetta *The Mikado*, in which a Lord-High-Everything-Else named *Pooh-Bah* tries to manage everything in sight. This name caught on quickly, at first referring to self-important bureaucrats, then to puffed-up figures of many kinds. ("He's a real pooh-bah.") Well over a century later, Gilbert's playful term is still in play—literally—even generating *poobahism*.

The fun factor helps explain why—despite being a mouthful—*gobbledygook* has been so durable. In that case, the appealing phonics of this word obviate its length. The same thing is true of *discombobulate*, *flibbertigibbet*, *copasetic*, *boondoggle*, and *serendipity*. When assessing new words, the ear is as important as the eye. Neologisms are judged as much by how they sound as what they say.

Gilbert and Sullivan's Pooh-Bah, as portrayed on Player's Cigarette card, 1927.

3. Please the Ear

It's a subtle difference, but the key reason *yuppie* beat out *yappie* in their neology bakeoff was that it sounded better. *Yappie*, an acronym coinage based on Young Aspiring Professionals, brought annoying little dogs to mind. *Yuppie* built on the affirmative word *yup*. Another ear-pleasing term is *bleep*, the euphemism for censorship that simply spells out the sound made by this technological censor. Its felicitous onomatopoeic quality has helped keep this techno-term in our vocabulary since it was introduced in the late 1960s. Ditto *cha-ching*, another popular term that makes a word from a sound (albeit one seldom heard these days). This slang term for money was introduced in a 1992 ad for the Rally's fast food chain that featured actor Seth Green ringing up charges on a cash register at a more expensive rival chain while saying "Cha ching! Cha ching! Cha ching!"

One reason *baby boomer* has been such a successful generational moniker is its semi-onomatopoetic allusion to the explosive impact of this huge cohort. According to that group's chronicler, Landon Jones, "The words have a playful, alliterative rhythm to them. They are bouncy iambic duometers." Perhaps that's why it's the only name of a generation to achieve broad international usage, as *babyboomers* (German), *de babyboomers* (Dutch), and *les baby-boomers* (French).

Alliteration is generally a neological plus. A coinage that alliterates is likely to catch on and linger longer in the lingo. Think: *Ping Pong*, *hip-hop*, *heebie jeebies*, *chump change*, *road rage*, *meter maid*, and *ticky tacky*. *Slippery slope* combines a nice alliterative quality with a bonus of being easy to visualize.

4. Create Word Pictures

When it comes to neologizing, vivid imagery is always in order, a clear plus factor (e.g., *bowling alone*, *black holes*, *broken windows*, *pecking order*, *knee-jerk*). The main reason *Whac-a-Mole* has enjoyed so much success as a metaphor is that it's easy to picture (as well as being applicable to multiple misadventures). *Whisperer* owes its popularity in no small measure to the agreeable image it creates in our mind of being whispered to.

Radio has been a particularly fruitful source of lasting neologisms because, as Fred Hoyle realized when conjuring *big bang* for the BBC, its broadcasters are so dependent on verbal imagery. While announcing basketball games, pioneering sportscaster Marty Glickman relied on word pictures of his own creation, easy-to-visualize terms such as *lane* and *key* (for those parts of a basketball court). The sportscaster called a basketball that doesn't touch the rim as it sails through the net a *swish* (actually a verb—*swish!*). The opposite of a swish is an *air ball*. That's how Los Angeles Lakers announcer Chick Hearn referred to a basketball that touches neither rim nor net after being shot. Hearn also coined *slam dunk* to describe a ball being slammed assertively through the net by a swooping player. That phrase didn't just enrich basketball's nomenclature but is used routinely to describe anything at all that's easy; what we used to call a lead pipe cinch. Complemented by an exclamation mark, Hearn's coinage doesn't just evoke vivid imagery but strong feeling: "It's a *slam dunk!*"

5. Evoke Feeling

In early 1941 Western observers noted a slogan of Chinese worker-soldier teams that sounded to them like "*gung* ho" (an Anglicization of *kung*, meaning "work," and *ho* for "together"). After America joined China's fight against Japanese

invaders, U.S. Marine colonel Evans Carlson borrowed that motto for his soldiers. In 1943, their success on the battlefield was celebrated in a movie titled
Gung Ho! That title inserted this explosive, evocative expression into public discourse. It has remained there ever since, becoming a bit of a cliché in the process.
("I find Laura a bit too gung ho.")

Terms that evoke feeling make a beeline for the reptilian part of our brain,
its most emotive center, where they get stuck and are hard to unstick. In time,
these terms grow clichéd. An active word such as *disrupt* has become a buzzword
as much because of the feelings it arouses as any conceptual value. "Buzzwords
feed off their emotional resonances, not their ideas," noted the linguist Geoffrey
Nunberg. "And for pure resonance, 'disruptive' is hard to beat."

In addition to its other virtues, *contraband* evoked exciting images of night-
time smuggling, sword-wielding pirates, and armed battles at sea. More recently
neologisms such as *bomb cyclone* and *blast off!* have stirred our blood. On the
positive end of the arousal spectrum is *climax*. At the other end is *superpredators*,
a buzzword whose success was rooted in the fear it aroused.

Buzzword itself is a word that arouses affect. It has other merits as well. This
term—which apparently originated among students at the Harvard Business
School following World War II—doesn't just evoke the sense of a word humming
about our ears like a bumblebee, or penetrating our brain like a circular saw, but
benefits from incorporating some of our favorite letters.

6. Use Good Letters

Certain letters—*b*, *g*, *k*, and *z*—punch above their weight in the fight for survival
among coined words.

B

When Research in Motion was developing a radically new type of mobile phone
in the late 1990s, this Canadian company hired a California branding firm called
Lexicon to create an alluring name for their product. Several dozen possibilities
suggested by that Sausalito firm included Vacation, OutRigger, Byline, and Blade.
Lexiconers were partial to the letter *b*, whose sound, their research showed, was
unusually appealing. Lexicon's CEO therefore scribbled *blackberry* on a white
board. Although members of RIM's sales force preferred *Blade*, founder Mike
Lazaridis chose *BlackBerry* as their phone's name.

Not the least reason that BlackBerrys revolutionized the cell phone industry
was the appeal of their perky name, which had not just one but two *b*'s (with
the second one capitalized for emphasis). A study of "sound symbolism" once
determined that the alphabet's second letter suggested speed and efficiency. It is
a potent letter.

B's potency is illustrated by a rare exception to the perishability of words based on names in the news: *bork*. That verb, meaning to fail catastrophically, originated as the eponym *Bork* after the messy rejection of Robert Bork's 1987 nomination to be a Supreme Court justice. With its first letter lowercased, this term took on a life of its own, even among those unlikely to have heard of Mr. Bork (as when a British newspaper reported that an aborted space capsule launch in late 2019 had been *borked*). The venerability of this eponym is almost entirely due to its *b*-based harmonics. Had Robert Bork been named Robert Jones, his surname is not likely to have become part of our vernacular. Could one be *Jonesed?*

B is an assertive letter that bursts from one's pursed lips like a pellet shot from a BB gun. *Bah! Bunk! Bull! Baloney!* It has been argued more or less seriously that part of the reason Britons voted to exit the European Union was the vigor of the word *Brexit*. (Its antonym, *remain*, had no such panache.) *B* is the basis for many another popular term, including ones with multiple *b*'s: *baby, boob, blob, bub, bombast, bimbo, bamboo, bamboozle, blockbuster,* and *bebop*. One reason that *bobo* did somewhat better than David Brooks's many other neologisms might be the double-*b* factor. In his introduction to *The Annotated Snark*, Martin Gardner paid tribute to "that remarkable four-letter word *bomb*," noting that it both began and ended with a *b* (yet another reason that *bomb cyclone* has done better than *Frankenstorm* in weather reporting). The first edition of the *OED* noted how many newly created words featured one or more *b*'s: *bamboozle, bang, bilk, blab, blare, blear, blight, blizzard, blob, blot, blotch, blunder, blunt, blue, blurt, bluster, bogus, boom, bore, bosh, bother, brash, brunt, bub, bum, bump, bunch, bungle, burr, bustle,* and *buzz,* to name just a few.

Words with multiple *b*'s such as *blabber, blubber, bumblebee, hubbub,* and *bubble* have that letter's appeal squared. *Bubble* is also unusually diverse (soap bubble, investment bubble, speech bubble, quarantine bubbles, etc.) As a verb, *bubble* and *bubble up* perform well in both the traditional and post-pandemic sense. According to one news account, "in 2020, back-to-school shopping means frantically searching for other families to 'bubble up' with."

G

Gelett Burgess tapped the added-value of double-*b*'s for his wonderful word *blurb*. When creating neologisms, Burgess himself was particularly partial to the letter *g*. The prolific coiner thought this letter "applies spuzz to a word that can hardly be obtained elsewhere in the alphabet." (*Spuzz* was Burgess's coinage for "mental energy, an aggressive intellect.") The humorist-neologist may have been on to something. Consider *geek, goop, goon, grok,* and *grinch*. *Gobbledygook* benefits from having two *g*'s (along with its two *b*'s), as do *gag, gig, giggle, gong, gaga,* and *boondoggle*. One reason that *google* has resurfaced so often so long and in so

many iterations is the fact that its double *g*'s help make this word a pleasure to say. Though hardly pleasurable, *gulag* is another term that gains power by having forceful *g*'s at the beginning and end. All-purpose words such as *gadget*, *gimcrack*, *gizmo*, and *gewgaw* rely heavily on *g*, as do *thingie*, *thingamajig*, *thingamabob*, and *widget*.

In some cases, *g* needs no other letters at all, as when it represents a thousand dollars (short for "grand"), *g-force* in space flight (*g* being short for gravity), *G-men* (Depression-era slang for "government men," FBI agents especially), *G-string*, and, of course, the *G-spot*.

<h1 style="text-align:center">K</h1>

Another letter that can stand on its own is *k* (when referring to a thousand dollars, or a baseball strikeout). Allan Metcalf is particularly high on this letter. He thinks that "the power of *k*" lends vigor to terms such as the venerable OK. *K* is our alphabet's most conspicuous letter, the linguist points out, not just orally but visually. In conjunction with *O* it makes for a pleasing dialectic. As Metcalf puts it, "*O* is a satisfying oval, all curves; *K* is all straight lines, a collection of sticks."

Other words that Metcalf believes gain strength from their *k* power include *strikeout*, and *knockout* with its double *k*'s. *Kodak*'s neological success was due in part to the *k*'s George Eastman included at the beginning and end of his company's brand name. The photo mogul found this letter to be "strong and incisive . . . firm and unyielding." Double *k*'s also contribute to the appeal of *Kokomo*, one of our favorite place names, along with *Kankakee*, which has not just two but three *k*'s.

Americans have long loved to playfully replace hard *c*'s with *k*'s—*kitchen kabinet*, *Keystone Kops*, *Krazy Kat*. "I'd rather be a 'Kat' alive instead of a 'Kop' what ain't," said Krazy a century ago. He also referred to "the kwaint confines of the kalabozo del kondado de Kononino."

In a paper she wrote nearly a century ago called "The Kraze for K," linguist Louise Pound pointed out that even Walt Whitman succumbed to the temptation to respell our northern neighbor Kanada, and call its residents Kanadians. Merchants had a particular predilection for *k* when naming their enterprises, Pound noted. Just a few of the examples she collected in the early 1920s included Kwality Kut Klothes, Kut Kwik Razor Strops, Klose Kloset Hamper, and Klever Klippers for Hairkutters. "All in all," Pound concluded, "there is no mistaking the kall of 'k' over our country, our kurious kontemporary kraving for it, and its konspicuous use in the klever koinages of commerce." A century later, that kall is alive and well in the form of Kwik Kleen, Krispy Kreme, Kitchen Kaboodle, Marina's Kafe, and many another *k*-based business name.

Catskill comedians thought words that contained a *k* were unusually funny. A list of humorous *k*-words compiled by Roy Blount, Jr. includes *cockamamie*,

kooky, tickly, picky picky, Pickwickian, kerplunk, okey-dokey, hunky-dory, cracker-jack, chockablock, lickety-split, muck, stuck, clunk, and *schlock.* In his introduction to Jesse Sheidlower's book *The F Word,* Blount also notes how many sex words are based on a forceful *k* or hard *c*: *bonk, poke, stick, kink, carnal, canoodle,* and scores more. At one time *canoe* was a euphemism for erotic activity because this vessel was a popular getaway vehicle where couples could engage in some discreet hanky-panky. ("Would you like to go canoeing?") Strategies for canoodling in a canoe are a popular form of Canadian humor.

Z

Another entry on Blount's list of funny *k*-words is *kazoo.* This benefits not just from its introductory *k* but an inner *z.* The last letter of our alphabet has quite a following. Tom Robbins was particularly fond of it. "Every time I type or pen the letter *Z,*" the novelist explained, "I still feel a secret tingle, a tiny thrill." Before it was absorbed by Tanzania, Zanzibar was Robbins's favorite country, the Zuiderzee his favorite body of water, ZZ Top his favorite band. And just imagine, he noted, how much fun we could have had referring to Zsa Zsa Gabor if the actress had married rocker Frank Zappa and become Zsa Zsa Zappa.

Many of Gellett Burgess's fanciful neologisms relied on *z*'s for their zip. Not just *spuzz* but *zeech* ("a monologist; one who is lively, but exhausting"), *zobzib* ("an amiable blunderer, one displaying misguided zeal"), and *huzzlecoo* ("an intimate talk, a confidential colloquy").

No one made better use of *z*'s than Burgess's acolyte Theodor Geisel. *Z* provided Geisel's Dr. Seuss with some of his most inspired word creations: *zong, zifft, zamp, zatz, zans, zaks, zeds, zuks, zooks, zodes, zobbels, zlocks, ziffs, zuffs,* and *zummers.* To illustrate the alphabet's last letter in his ABC book, Geisel created a genial creature he called a *Zizzer-Zazzer-Zuzz.* His character *Zaxx* invented a product he called *Zaxx-ma-Taxx.* Like Dr. Seuss, contemporary pop culturists have a particular penchant for *Z*-based words. *Zombies. 'Zines. The Kidz Network. Boyz N the Hood.*

What makes *z* such a seductive letter? I think it has something to do with the buzzing-bee-ness of its harmonics. The ear appeal of this letter is especially evident when words with *z*'s are spoken aloud: *jazz, razz, fizzle, dazzle, razzle-dazzle, snazzy, tizzy, wazoo, zig-zag, zap, zip, zipper, zap, zing, zoom,* and *zounds.* Get some *zzzzz*'s. *Amazon. Zoot suit. Shazam!* Such words have pizzazz. They've got razzamatazz.

As a building block of enjoyable new words, *z* is hard to beat. Despite their penchant for *b*-based words, the branding firm Lexicon has changed its name to Zinzin. I would not be surprised if the ubiquity of the telemeeting service *Zoom,* especially among Covid-19 social isolates, had something to do with its

HUZZLECOO

Illustration of *huzzlecoo* in *Burgess Unabridged* (1914).

crisp, forceful, *Z*-based name. *Gen Z*, the pedestrian name for post-millennials, may give way to *Zoom Generation*, one comprising *Zoomers* who gathered on that platform during the pandemic that defined their early life. (A 2018 Pentagon war game simulating a mid-2020s "Zbellion" by members of *Gen Z* was later said to involve *Zoomers*.) *Zoom* has multiple assets. It's terse, fun to say, begins with an engaging *z,* and includes double *o*'s. Its ubiquity throughout the pandemic transformed this agreeable term into a lower-cased noun ("Let's have a zoom"), a verb ("I'm busy zooming"), and even a fashion statement ("I've got to put on my zoom shirt.")

Not the least reason for the popularity of Frank Baum's word "Oz" was its second letter. Imagine if it were "The Wonderful Wizard of Om," or "Op," or "Os," or "Ot." Would *gonzo* have become so popular with one letter's difference: *gondo*, say, *gonvo*, or *gonyo*? Would *pizza* be such a culinary hit if it was called *pivva*? How many steaks would be sold with a *siddle*, instead of a *sizzle*?

Sizzle is a hallowed word in the marketing lexicon. "Science of Selling the Sizzle," reads the headline of an article about restaurants. "Supermarkets Add a Little Sizzle," reports an article in *Parade*. The prevalence of this term goes back to 1938 when sales guru Elmer Wheeler introduced five *Wheelerpoints*, the first of which was "Don't Sell the Steak—*Sell the Sizzle!*" Whether or not he realized it, Wheeler had stumbled on a truism of effective coinage: new words that incorporate one or more z's have added zip. He undoubtedly had a good marketer's ear for the onomatopoeic appeal of a term such as *sizzle*. Wheeler did not actually coin this word of course (it's an emendation of "fizzle," which originally referred to a slow, protracted fart) but gave sizzle such an entirely new spin that it became a recoinaage if not an actual neologism. When *Forbes* asks about the company producing Lexus automobiles, "Can It Keep the Sizzle Alive?," no further explanation is needed.

As the ubiquity of "sizzle" reminds us, why some terms strike our fancy and others don't can be an enigma. In its case, the double z's were clearly an asset. But they didn't help Dr. Seuss's *Zummzian Zuks, his Zumble-Zays*, or the *Yuzz-a-ma-Tuzz* become everyday terms. As we've seen throughout this book, predicting which neologisms will be hits and which will strike out is no easy task. Which isn't to say it can't be done.

Adoption

From his perch as chair of the American Dialect Society's new words committee, Ben Zimmer has had an unrivaled opportunity to assess the traits that help a neologism survive, and those that don't. In particular, says Zimmer, a new word's prospects of survival is undercut by being "too self-consciously clever, too ephemerally trendy, too difficult to say or spell, or too restricted to a particular niche or subculture." As far as what does help a word win favor, Allan Metcalf, the longtime ADS secretary and the author of *Predicting New Words*, cites frequency of use, diversity of users, and, especially, unobtrusiveness.

Unobtrusiveness

In her book *Word Fugitives*, Barbara Wallraff agrees with Metcalf that unobtrusiveness was the most important predictor of a successful new word. Henry Hitchings concurs. When it comes to the survival prospects of a neologism, Hitchings writes in *The Language Wars*, "unobtrusiveness helps a word's chances more than gaudiness." That certainly was true of Charles Dickens's multitude of successfully coined words. In his book on Dickens's verbal innovations, Knud Sørensen points out how many of them were quite ordinary terms such as *casualty ward, allotment garden, cool customer, acquired taste, right-hander*, and *sawbones*. "Most neologisms are unspectacular," concludes Sørensen.

The best new words don't necessarily *sound* new. This relates to the "naturalness" that University of South Florida linguists Constantine Lignos and Hilary Pritchard say characterizes the most successful "blend" words (aka portmanteaus), naturalness and "understandability." These qualities are what the linguists think have made words such as *brunch, guesstimate*, or *mockumentary* a lasting part of our lingo, while puzzling, clunky nonstarters like *fozzle* (fog drizzle) and *brinkles* (bed wrinkles) have disappeared. Marketing terms that rank high in understandability but low in naturalness—*beerstro, croissandwich*, or *coatigan*, for example—have also failed to win an audience. Lignos and Pritchard are developing a "blendometer" algorithm to assess the prospects of blended neologisms. Whether this algorithm will be able to take account of the myriad vagaries of word adoption remains to be seen. "It's like the challenge of predicting what might go viral," they concede; "some blends have a certain *je ne sais quoi* that escapes our model because it's hard to quantify."

Versatility

Versatility is a major asset for a freshly minted term. Like professional athletes who play many positions, words that can be used in multiple ways are more likely to make the team. Consider the humble *bug*. Aside from high tech's *bug* and *debug*, there's the lower tech *someone put a bug in my phone*. More generically we speak of being *bug-eyed*, and *cute as a bug* (or a *bug in a rug*). *Don't bug me*, we say, *bug out, bug off. Buggery*, synonymous with sodomy in Great Britain, might also be included on this list. Those caught engaging in this practice risked being sent to the *bug house. Bug* is also an integral part of the coinage *jitterbug* that Cab Calloway popularized in the 1930s, and its cousin *litterbug*.

Despite its political connotations, *comrade* is another word of great versatility. As a character in Amor Towles's novel *A Gentleman in Moscow* notes, this salutation can be used to address anyone, "be they male or female, young or old, friend or foe." Similarly, one key to the popularity of *serendipity* is its chameleon-like quality. Depending on who's using it and how it's used, *serendipity* can mean many different things. The same thing is true of *Catch-22, zipless, paradigm*, and *postmodern*. Due to their flexibility, such terms can be used rather promiscuously, and are.

Speaking of promiscuity, *hookup* is another term whose appeal is rooted not just in its versatility but its vagueness. One challenge facing those who want to study this branch of sexual activity is determining what *hookup* actually means to those whom they're studying. A *hookup* is someone with whom one *hooks up*, obviously. But what's involved in this practice? For some, it refers simply to a bit of groping and kissy-face (what once was called *petting*). To others, it suggests something more advanced, various levels of foreplay (yesterday's *heavy petting*). Hooking up can also include *intercourse*, of course, a word that was once synonymous with innocent human interaction until it was pressed into service as a cool term for a hot subject. Sexual discourse is in constant need of bland repurposed words to replace more provocative ones. *Score*, for example, *shag, party,* and *it. Do,* it's been suggested, has become so lascivious that nowadays this verb may need a parental advisory.

The realm of sex is a fruitful one for neologizing, to accommodate the high demand for euphemistic terms that can help us discuss this touchy topic. In sex-casual times, we needed not only *hookup* to depict informal liaisons but *friends-with-benefits* as well. Since sex is such a visceral activity, and so subject to changing mores, a continual demand exists for new words we can use when discussing its standards and practices.

Gap Filling

Before journalism professor James Gorman coined the word *uptalk* in 1993, there hadn't been much need for such a term because ending sentences with a rising intonation wasn't that common. Today it is, and Gorman's way to describe this manner of speaking has become a modest success, appearing both in the press and on the street. ("She's quite an uptalker.") Like so many useful coined terms, it filled a gap.

Naming a current concern or phenomena is one of the most fruitful ways to get one's coinage adopted. If no term exists to compete with a new one, its odds of survival improve exponentially. (The durability of *genocide* has more to do with our ongoing need for that word than any inherent quality.) Then, even the ear-pleasing requirement can be waived. I would not have predicted that a sterile term such as "Type A" would catch on, but, in the absence of any better way to describe a contemporary breed of frenzied, stressed-out workaholic, this phrase became ubiquitous after cardiologists Meyer Friedman and Ray Rosenman published *Type A Behavior and Your Heart* in 1974. Those who merit this moniker typically consider it a badge of honor, perhaps assuming that the *A* component of *Type A* refers to a good grade. "Type B" probably wouldn't have made the cut, and certainly not "Type F," or even "Type H" (which brings Preparation H to mind).

Even though the coronavirus pandemic that began in early 2020 generated few original words (at this writing), our desperate need for a vocabulary to discuss it led to the recoining of some existing terms and escorting of others from esoteric to widespread use: *epicenter, self-isolate, droplets, incubation period, herd immunity, flatten the curve, contact tracing, social distancing,* and *PPE* (*personal protective equipment*). Words like *petri dish* and *incubator* experienced a semantic shift, moving from labs and maternity wards into *hotspots* where the virus flourished.

Although a gap in our vocabulary provides a first-rate opportunity for successful coinage, some new words simply sound better than old ones already in use. *Bunk* improves on *nonsense, climax* on *orgasm, roundabout* on *gyratory circus. Carousel* is a perfectly good word, but *merry-go-round* creates a better word picture. *Table tennis* is a more than adequate name for that game: clear, direct, descriptive. It even is alliterative. But table tennis isn't as enjoyable to say and hear as the onomatopoeic and equally alliterative *Ping Pong*. After being trademarked by London's John Jaques and Son in 1901 (when previous names such as *Whiff Waff, Pom-Pom, Pim-Pam, Netto, Clip-Clap, Gossima,* and *Tennis de Salon* didn't catch on), *Ping Pong* has become so ubiquitous as both a noun and verb that it now can refer to anything at all being *ping-ponged* back and forth. ("He ping-ponged between LA and New York on a regular basis.") When the table tennis teams of China and the U.S. played each other in 1971, this diplomatic thaw was called the *Ping Pong Spring*.

Familiarity

In semiliterate times like ours, erudition is basically a nonfactor when it comes to successful word creation. Clauses from Greek or Latin, or allusions to ancient mythology count for little in today's neology marketplace. A public that's embraced *booty call, bling,* and *cha-ching* would probably have reacted with "Huh?" to *Achilles heel* or *Trojan horse* if these allusions had been introduced during the new millennium.

Allusions depend on familiarity with what's being alluded to. This is true not just of Greco-Roman mythology. Idioms such as *logroll* and *full steam* established themselves in the nineteenth century when sure-footed loggers spun logs on bodies of water and steamboats raced at maximum energy, but would not have done well in the twenty-first century. *Mrs. Robinson* was an excellent allusion to older women pursuing younger men among those familiar with the character portrayed by Anne Bancroft in *The Graduate* more than half a century ago. Current generations prefer *cougar*.

Allusions aside, terms that are easy to grasp generally have an edge when jostling for acceptance in the neology marketplace. Vivid, self-defining words such as *armrest, footstool, bedroom, breadwinner, beachcomber, firefighter, cheerleader, runaway, skyscraper, sawdust, toothpick, corkscrew, gunfighter, lackluster, pickpocket, loudmouth, numbskull, scatterbrain, scarecrow, sunup, sundown, woodpecker, trailblazer, takeout, takedown, headscratcher, heartburn, handshake, earthquake, landslide, lawmaker, lawbreaker, troublemaker,* and *wrongdoer* have a running start in the word adoption competition. Some of our most popular modern neologisms—*humblebrag, cringeworthy, side-eye, bromance,* and *mansplain*—tell you what they mean. So does *painkiller.* There's nothing wrong with the term *analgesic,* but it's not nearly as vivid as that self-explaining term.

Metaphorical terms like *cherrypicking* and *helicopter parents* that combine allusion with clarity and imagery do especially well. By contrast, coined words whose meaning needs to be explained (Richard Dawkins's *dundridge* comes to mind, as does Edward Hall's *proxemics*) are at a disadvantage. If instead of *disruption* Clayton Christensen had written of "type 1 innovation," and "type 2 innovation," as the Harvard professor wished he had (so that we'd need to read his book to make sense of them), he would probably have ended up teaching Business Practices 101 instead of giving lucrative speeches to corporate gatherings. I speak from painful experience. In a book on risk-taking (*Chancing It: Why We Take Risks*), I made the spectacular mistake of calling those who take short- or long-term risks "Level I" and "Level II' risk-takers. Referring to them as *sprinters* and *marathoners* would have made the same point far more vividly, in a way that was clear, visual, and easy to discuss.

Clarity and imagery is what made *big bang* such a neological hit. After he coined this phrase as a taunt, Fred Hoyle watched with dismay as it became the preferred term for cataclysmic universe creation. To make matters worse, the astronomer's coinage for his own preferred theory of how the universe expanded—*C-field* (for "creation field")—languished in obscurity. Who knew what it referred to? Decades after coining that term Hoyle ruefully told a lecture audience, "If only I had chosen a more user-friendly or memorable term I might yet have been credited as the originator of the inflationary universe."

Words Needed

The universe of "needed words" is vast. As aging baby boomers become increasingly forgetful, we need a better word for the *mnemonic* devices that help us remember things. How do you pronounce this term, let alone spell it? *Onomatopoeia* is another word whose pronunciation and spelling are problematic. (My own clumsy attempts defy even autocorrect's estimable powers.) In a speech to London's Philological Society, its president, James Murray, said that *onomatopoeia* "had neither associative nor etymological application to words imitating sounds." As a replacement he suggested *echoism,* and *echoic.* These terms certainly improve on *onomatopoeia* and *onomatopoeic* but have never achieved widespread usage. Perhaps they should have. *Onomatopoeia* remains a word in desperate need of an user-friendly synonym.

Other hard-to-spell-and-say words on my personal list include *amanuensis, opprobrium, legerdemain, encomium,* and *perspicacious* as well as Swift's *brobing-dangnian* and Poe's *tintinnabulation. Schadenfreude* is not only difficult to spell but—since it's German—has no self-evident meaning to English speakers. *Schadenfreude* leads an extensive glossary of words that we borrow from other languages because nothing comparable exists in English. Others include *simpatico, frisson,* and *chutzpah.* Yiddish provides a cornucopia of delicious words like *chutzpah* that have no real English equivalent. Others include *klutz, kosher, kvetch, mensch, maven, nosh, nudge, schlock, schmooze, schlep, schlemiel, shtick,* and *zaftig.* Yiddish also has a number of useful words for kin by marriage, such as *machetayneste* for the mother of your child's spouse, and *machuten* for his/her father. Russian speakers call that father a *svat,* that mother a *svakha.* In Spanish, both parents are *consuegros;* in Italian, *consuoceri.* Everyday English has no comparable words. It should. *

Other languages are not a bad place to seek fodder for English variations, as we've done by translating the French phrase *à pleine gorge* into *full-throated* (a bit of a Van Winkleism that's been around for decades but has gained popularity in these raucous times). We could also use an English version of Diderot's apt phrase *esprit de l'escalier* (literally "staircase words," comments we wish we'd made but think of only when it's too late) and its Yiddish counterpart *trepverter* as well as the German *Treppenwitz.*

Blessings will be upon whoever can successfully create friendlier synonyms for the many user-hostile terms that clutter today's verbosphere. Medicine is a particular thicket of needlessly complicated, tongue-twisting terminology that works better for physicians than their patients. In recent years I've been treated by an *otolaryngologist* (an ear specialist who's trained in *otolaryngology*) and been handed a pamphlet titled "Managing Laryngopharyngeal Reflux." No matter how meaningful such terms may be to health professionals, they are virtually meaningless to the laity. And it isn't just patients who are confounded by medical tongue-twisters. A friend of mine recently had a sinus procedure called "functional endoscopic sinus surgery with image guidance." When my friend asked his surgeon how to pronounce this, the man replied "Roto Rooting." (That, in fact, is what he and colleagues call the procedure among themselves.)

---

* This is a two-way street, of course. Terms such as *flaky, hinky, heebie-jeebies,* and *booty call* are nearly impossible to translate. So is *d'oh!*

New technology always generates and will continue to generate a need for entire new vocabularies to describe its presence in contemporary life. Meeting that need produces a new one: for updated words born of technology we no longer use. A wide range of terms related to landline telephones are fast becoming obsolete, especially ones left over from rotary dial days: *dial up*, *dial down*, *dialed in*, *dial for dollars*, *dial tone*, *redial*, and *pocket dial* (for accidentally calling someone when the phone in one's pocket is jostled). We've yet to replace such verbal fossils with cell phone analogs.

In the realm of relationships, there must be a better term than the pedestrian *partner* to describe someone with whom we have a lasting connection. Those older than forty need something more age-appropriate than *boyfriend* and *girlfriend* to refer to their significant other. And, as gender identities grow more fluid, surely we can do better than LGBTQ to describe those who don't fit conventional categories. (How many more initials can this abbreviation tack on before it collapses under its own weight?)** Despite the increasing acceptance of same-sex relationships, and open discussion of this topic, we continue to have a paucity of words to help us out. I've seen this firsthand. When visiting with a recently married lesbian couple, our talk turned to their relationship. One of them described how some of her parents' straight friends still had trouble accepting . . . She groped for a word but couldn't come up with one. Finally, the young woman resorted to waving a finger between her wife and herself like a windshield wiper, saying "this."

As organized religion declines, our need grows for an antonym to *atheist* that describes those who, unlike *agnostics*, believe in a supreme being but aren't affiliated with any formal faith group. (Simply *believers*?) As political affiliations grow more amorphous, we could use a word like *mugwump* to describe political outliers. Or perhaps *mugwump* could be revived, become a Van Winkleism. Why not? I doubt that we could improve on that delightful term.

When it comes to pronouns, we desperately need a plural of *you* that's better than youse, you'ns, and y'all. Ditto a gender-neutral pronoun. Although for their 2015 word of the year the American Dialect Society chose *they* as an acceptable term for members of both sexes, as did Merriam-Webster four years later, linguists still consider the holy grail of neology to be a gender-neutral term that improves on *they*, *he or she*, or *s/he*, as well as one to replace *guys*. Three-quarters of a century ago, in 1943, the Canadian author Stephen Leacock observed, "We are always hard up for neutral words to mean 'just a person,' each new one gets spoiled and

---

** Since writing this line, I've been apprised of two such run-on coinages: *LGBTQPAN*, referring to "lesbian, gay, bisexual, transgender, queer/questioning, pansexual, asexual, and/or nonbinary," and *LGBTQIAPK* for "lesbian, gay, bisexual, transgender, queer or questioning, intersex, asexual, and pansexual."

has to be replaced. Hence the need for 'guy,' which will gradually rise from ridicule to respectability." Leacock was prescient. Two decades after he made his prediction, language arbiter Rudolf Flesch announced in his 1963 book *Lite English* that it was now perfectly respectable to use this term. In the years since then, its usefulness has grown as *guys* is routinely used to refer to mixed-gender groups. ("So, you guys ready to order?") Surely we can do better.

In Conclusion . . .

Here's a question: what if Guy Fawkes had been called Guido Fawkes, as he wished? Would a generic man now be called a *Guido*, and mixed groups *Guidos*?

If a newspaper editor hadn't coined *OK* as a puerile joke two centuries ago, how would we signify assent without affirmation?

Suppose Frank Baum's filing cabinet had had four drawers instead of three, one of which was labeled U–Z. Would his Wizard have joined Job in the Land of Uz?

Had Winston Churchill suggested that the world's leaders gather at the "peak," or "the apex," would we now be holding *peak conferences* or *apex meetings*?

Imagine that the judges of Hormel's product-naming contest considered *Hamloaf* a better submission than *Spam*. Would mass emails today be called *hamloaves*?

If Thomas Kuhn had written about *exemplars* rather than *paradigms*, as he later wished he had, would we call major social changes *exemplar shifts*?

Such questions take us back to this book's central theme: the unpredictability of word coinage. Their absurd tenor illustrates the fact that ultimately it's not always clear how usable words get created, or which ones will win the adoption sweepstakes. The little-known stories surrounding them constitute a bouillabaisse of fluke, mistakes, and happenstance. And thank goodness. Its endless vagaries are what make the hidden history of coined words such a fascinating subject.

Bibliography

THE FOLLOWING BIBLIOGRAPHY lists sources I've consulted extensively as well as ones I've relied on for general background. (Works specific to a particular entry are cited in the endnotes.)

A word about *Wikipedia*. Like so many researchers, I find this crowdsourced encyclopedia a valuable resource. At the same time, I am wary of its contents overall which vary so much in quality and reliability. As I advise students, *Wikipedia* is a better place to begin one's research than to complete it. That is the way I have used *Wikipedia* and comparable online resources in researching *The Hidden History of Coined Words*.

Among online dictionaries, the *OED* is the gold standard, though hardly infallible, and often incomplete (especially when it comes to American references). *Merriam-Webster Online* is also quite helpful. The crowdsourced *Urban Dictionary* is a great compendium of contemporary slang, though quite a sprawling mishmash. Among the many online sites devoted to various aspects of word origins, the *Online Etymology Dictionary* is quite good, as is *The Phrase Finder*, *word histories*, and *World Wide Words*, but perforce Anglocentric. On the other side of the Atlantic, unusually useful sites include *The Big Apple*, *Grammarist*, *Grammarphobia*, *Language Log*, *Quote Investigator*, *Visual Thesaurus*, *Wiktionary*, *Wordnik*, and *wordorigins.org*.

Algeo, John, ed. *Fifty Years Among the New Words*. Cambridge: Cambridge University Press, 1991.

Allen, Irving Lewis. *The City in Slang: New York Life and Popular Speech*. New York: Oxford University Press, 1993, 1995.

American Heritage editors. *Word Histories and Mysteries: From Abracadrabra to Zeus*. Boston: Houghton Mifflin, 1986.

Ammer, Christine, ed. *The American Heritage Dictionary of Idioms*. Boston: Houghton Mifflin, 1997.

Archer, William. *America To-Day: Observations and Reflections*. Carlisle, MA: Applewood, 1899, 2007.

Ayto, John, ed. *Arcade Dictionary of Word Origins: The Histories of More Than 8,000 English-Language Words.* New York: Arcade/Little, Brown, 1990.

Babcock, Clarence Merton, ed. *The Ordeal of American English.* Boston: Houghton Mifflin, 1961.

Barnhart, David K. *Neo-Words: A Dictionary of the Newest and Most Unusual Words of Our Times.* New York: Collier/Macmillan, 1991.

Barnhart, David K., and Allan A. Metcalf. *America in So Many Words.* New York: Houghton Mifflin Harcourt, 1997, 1999.

Baron, Naomi S. *Alphabet to E-Mail: How Written English Evolved and Where It's Heading.* London: Routledge, 2000.

Bernard, André. *Now All We Need Is a Title: Famous Books Titles and How They Got That Way.* New York: Norton, 1995.

Bolinger, Dwight. *Forms of English: Accent, Morpheme, Order.* Cambridge, MA: Harvard University Press, 1965.

Bolinger, Dwight, and Donald A. Sears. *Aspects of Language,* 3rd ed. New York: Harcourt Brace Jovanovich, 1981.

Brewer, E. Cobham. *The Dictionary of Phrase and Fable.* New York: Avenel, 1894, 1978.

Brdar, Mario. *Metonymy and Word-Formation: Their Interactions and Complementation.* Newcastle-upon-Tyne, UK: Cambridge Scholars, 2018.

Bryson, Bill. *Made in America: An Informal History of the English Language in the United States.* New York: Avon, 1994, 1996.

Bryson, Bill. *The Mother Tongue: English and How It Got that Way.* New York: Morrow, 1990.

Burgess, Gelett. *Burgess Unabridged: A New Dictionary of Words You Have Always Needed.* New York: Walker, 1914, 2007.

The Cambridge History of the English Language, Vol. 3, Roger Lass, ed. Cambridge: Cambridge University Press, 2000.

The Cambridge History of the English Language, Vol. 6, John Algeo, ed. Cambridge: Cambridge University Press, 2001.

Carver, Craig M. *A History of English in Its Own Words.* New York: HarperCollins, 1991.

Chapman, Robert L., ed. *New Dictionary of American Slang.* New York: Harper & Row, 1986.

Chatfield, Tom. *Netymology: From Apps to Zombies: A Linguistic Celebration of the Digital World.* London: Quercus, 2013.

Ciardi, John. *A Browser's Dictionary: A Compendium of Curious Expressions & Intriguing Facts.* New York: Harper & Row, 1980.

Ciardi, John. *Good Words to You: An All-New Browser's Dictionary and Native's Guide to the Unknown American Language.* New York: Harper & Row, 1987.

Clute, John, and Peter Nicholls, *The Encyclopedia of Science Fiction.* New York: St. Martin's, 1993.

Claiborne, Robert. *Loose Cannons and Red Herrings: A Book of Lost Metaphors.* New York: Norton, 1998.

Cole, Sylvia, and Abraham H. Lass. *The Facts on File Dictionary of Modern Allusions.* New York: Checkmark Books, 1991, 2001.

Considine, John. *Adventuring in Dictionaries: New Studies in the History of Lexicography.* Newcastle-upon-Tyne, UK: Cambridge Scholars, 2010.

Cousineau, Phil. *Painted Word: A Treasure Chest of Remarkable Words and Their Origins.* New Dehli: Viva, 2012.

Cousineau, Phil. *Wordcatcher: An Odyssey into the World of Weird and Wonderful Words.* New Dehli: Viva, 2010.

Crystal, David, ed. *The Cambridge Encyclopedia of the English Language.* Cambridge: Cambridge University Press, 1995.

Crystal, David. *The Story of English in 100 Words.* New York: St. Martin's, 2012.

Dalzell, Tom. *Damn the Man! Slang of the Oppressed in America.* Mineola, NY: Dover, 2010.

Dalzell, Tom. *Flappers 2 Rappers: American Youth Slang.* Springfield, MA: Merriam-Webster, 1996.

Dalzell, Tom, and Terry Victor, eds. *The New Partridge Dictionary of Slang and Unconventional English.* London: Routledge, 2006.

D'Ammassa, Don. *Encyclopedia of Science Fiction.* New York: Facts on File, 2005.

de Vere, M. Schele. *Americanisms: The English of the New World.* New York: Scribner, 1872.

Dickson, Paul. *Authorisms: Words Wrought by Writers.* New York: Bloomsbury, 2014.

Dickson, Paul. *Words from the White House: Words and Phrases Coined or Popularized by America's Presidents.* New York: Walker, 2013.

Dickson, Paul. *The Dickson Baseball Dictionary*, 3rd ed. New York: Norton, 2009.

Dickson, Paul. *A Dictionary of the Space Age.* Baltimore: Johns Hopkins, 2009.

Dickson, Paul. *Family Words: A Dictionary of the Secret Language of Families.* Oak Park, IL: Marion Street, 2007.

Dickson, Paul. *Slang: The Topical Dictionary of Americanisms.* New York: Walker, 2006.

Dickson, Paul. *War Slang: American Fighting Words and Phrases from the Civil War to the Gulf War.* New York: Dover, 1994, 2011.

Dillard, J. L. *All-American English: A History of the English Language in America.* New York: Random House, 1975.

Dillard, J. L. *American Talk: Where Our Words Came From.* New York: Vintage, 1976, 1977.

Dixon, R. M. W. *Making New Words: Morphological Derivation in English.* Oxford: Oxford University Press, 2014.

Dohan, Mary Helen. *Our Own Words.* New York: Penguin, 1974, 1975.

Ehrlich, Eugene. *What's in a Name? How Proper Names Became Everyday Words.* New York: Holt, 1999.

Erard, Michael. *Um . . . : Slips, Stumbles, and Verbal Blunders, and What They Mean.* New York: Anchor, 2007, 2008.

Ewart, Neil. *Everyday Phrases: Their Origins and Meanings.* Poole, Dorset, UK: Blandford, 1983.

Farkas, Anna, ed. *The Oxford Dictionary of Catchphrases.* Oxford: Oxford University Press, 2002.

Flavell, Linda, and Roger Flavell. *The Chronology of Words and Phrases: A Thousand Years in the History of English.* Enderby, Leicester, UK: Silverdale/Bookmart, 1999.

Flesch, Rudolf. *Lite English: Popular Words That Are OK to Use No Matter What William Safire, John Simon, Edwin Newman, and the Other Purists Say!* New York: Crown, 1983.

Flexner, Stuart Berg. *Listening to America: An Illustrated History of Words and Phrases from Our Lively and Splendid Past.* New York: Simon & Schuster, 1982.

Flexner, Stuart Berg. *I Hear America Talking: An Illustrated History of American Words and Phrases.* New York: Touchstone, 1976, 1979.

Forsyth, Mark. *The Horologicon: A Day's Jaunt Through the Lost Words of the English Language.* New York: Berkley, 2012, 2013.

Forsyth, Mark. *The Etymologicon: A Circular Stroll Through the Hidden Connections of the English Language.* New York: Berkley, 2012.

Fraser, Edward, and John Gibbons. *Soldier and Sailor Words and Phrases.* London: Routledge, 1925.

Freeman, Morton S. *Even-Steven and Fair and Square: More Stories Behind the Words.* New York: Plume/Penguin, 1993.

Funk, Charles Earle. *2107 Curious Word Origins, Sayings & Expressions.* New York: Galahad, 1993.

Garrison, Webb. *Why You Say It: The Fascinating Stories Behind over 600 Everyday Words and Phrases.* New York: Routledge/MJF, 1992.

Gooden, Philip. *Name Dropping: An A to Z Guide to the Use of Names in Everyday Language.* New York: St. Martin's, 2008.

Gorrell, Robert. *Watch Your Language: Mother Tongue and Her Wayward Children.* Reno: University of Nevada Press, 1994.

Greenman, Robert. *Words in Action.* New York: Times Books, 1983.

Grose, Francis. *A Classical Dictionary of the Vulgar Tongue.* Edited by Eric Partridge. New York: Barnes & Noble, 1785, 1963.

Hendrickson, Robert. *American Talk: The Words and Ways of American Dialects.* New York: Viking, 1986.

Hendrickson, Robert, ed. *The Facts on File Encyclopedia of Word and Phrase Origins,* 3rd ed. New York: Checkmark/Facts on File, 2004.

Hitchings, Henry. *Defining the World: The Extraordinary Story of Dr. Johnson's Dictionary.* New York: Farrar, Straus and Giroux, 2005.

Hitchings, Henry. *The Language Wars: A History of Proper English.* New York: Picador, 2012.

Hitchings, Henry. *The Secret Life of Words: How English Became English.* New York: Picador, 2008, 2009.

Hughes, Geoffrey. *Words in Time: A Social History of the English Vocabulary.* Oxford: Blackwell, 1988.

Humes, James C. *Churchill: Speaker of the Century.* New York: Scarborough/Stein and Day, 1980.

Humez, Alexander, Nicholas Humez, and Rob Flynn. *Short Cuts: A Guide to Oaths, Ring Tones, Ransom Notes, Famous Last Words, & Other Terms of Minimalist Communication.* New York: Oxford University Press, 2010.

Jack, Albert. *It's a Wonderful Word: The Real Origins of Our Favourite Words, from Anorak to Zombie.* London: Random House, 2011.

Jones, Paul Anthony. *The Accidental Dictionary: The Remarkable Twists and Turns of English Words*, 2nd ed. London: Elliott & Thompson, 2016, 2019.

Jones, Paul Anthony. *Word Drops: A Sprinkling of Linguistic Curiosities.* Albuquerque: University of New Mexico Press, 2016.

Jones, Paul Anthony. *Haggard Hawks and Paltry Poltroons: The Origins of English in Ten Words.* London: Constable & Robinson, 2013.

Keyes, Ralph. *Euphemania: Our Love Affair with Euphemisms.* New York: Little, Brown, 2010.

Keyes, Ralph. *I Love It When You Talk Retro: Hoochie Coochie, Double Whammy, Drop a Dime and the Forgotten Origins of American Speech.* New York: St. Martin's, 2009

Keyes, Ralph. *The Quote Verifier: Who Said What, Where, and When.* New York: St. Martin's, 2006.

Keyes, Ralph. *The Wit and Wisdom of Oscar Wilde.* New York: HarperCollins, 1996.

Keyes, Ralph. *"Nice Guys Finish Seventh": False Phrases, Spurious Sayings, and Familiar Misquotations.* New York: HarperCollins, 1992.

Kirkpatrick, E. M., and C. M. Schwarz. *The Wordsworth Dictionary of Idioms.* Ware, Hertfordshire, UK: Wordsworth, 1993.

Knowles, Elizabeth, ed. *The Oxford Dictionary of Phrase, Saying, and Quotation.* Oxford: Oxford University Press, 1997.

Korach, Myron. *Common Phrases and Where They Come From.* Guilford, CT: Lyons/ Globe Pequot, 2002.

Langworth, Richard. *Churchill by Himself: The Definitive Collection of Quotations.* New York: Public Affairs, 2008.

Lederer, Richard. *The Miracle of Language.* New York: Gallery/Simon & Schuster, 1999.

Lee, Laura. *The Name's Familiar: Mr. Leotard, Barbie, and Chef Boyardee.* Gretna, LA: Pelican, 1999.

Lepore, Jill. *A Is for American: Letters and Other Characters in the Newly United States. New York: Knopf,* 2002.

Lepore, Jill. *These Truths: A History of the United States.* New York: Norton, 2018.

Lerer, Seth. *Inventing English: A Portable History of the Language.* New York: Columbia University Press, 2007.

Liberman, Anatoly. *A Bibliography of English Etymology.* Minneapolis: University of Minnesota Press, 2009.

Liberman, Anatoly. *An Analytic Dictionary of English Etymology.* Minneapolis: University of Minnesota Press, 2007.

Liberman, Anatoly. *Word Origins and How We Know Them: Etymology for Everyone.* New York: Oxford University Press, 2005.

Lighter, J. E., ed. *Random House Dictionary of American Slang*, Vol. 1. New York: Random House, 1994.

Lighter, J. E., ed. *Random House Dictionary of American Slang*, Vol. 2. New York: Random House, 1997.

Lynch, Jack. *The Lexicographer's Dilemma: The Evolution of "Proper" English, from Shakespeare to South Park.* New York: Walker, 2010.

Lynch, Jack, ed. *Samuel Johnson's Dictionary: Selections from the 1755 Work That Defined the English Language.* New York: Levenger/Walker, 2002.

Macrone, Michael. *Brush Up Your Shakespeare*, 2nd ed. New York: HarperResource, 1990, 2000.

Makkai, Adam, Maxine T. Boatner, and John E. Gates. *Handbook of Commonly Used American Idioms*, 3rd ed. Hauppauge, NY: Barron's, 1995.

Malless, Stanley, and Jeffrey McQuain. *Coined by God: Words and Phrases That First Appear in the English Translation of the Bible.* New York: Norton, 2003.

Manchester, William. *The Last Lion: Winston Spencer Churchill: Visions of Glory, 1874– 1932.* Boston: Little, Brown, 1983.

Manchester, William, and Paul Reid. *The Last Lion: Winston Spencer Churchill: Defender of the Realm, 1940–1965.* New York: Little, Brown, 2013.

Mann, Leonard. *A Bird in the Hand: And the Stories Behind 250 Other Common Expressions.* New York: Prentice Hall, 1994.

Markham, Gervase. *The English Housewife,* reprint of 1615 edition. Kingston, ON: McGill-Queens University Press, 1986.

Martin, Peter. *The Dictionary Wars: The American Fight over the English Language.* Princeton, NJ: Princeton University Press, 2019.

Mathews, Mitford M., ed. *A Dictionary of Americanisms: On Historical Principles*, Vol. 1. Chicago: University of Chicago Press, 1951.

Mathews, Mitford M., ed. *A Dictionary of Americanisms: On Historical Principles*, Vol. 2. Chicago: University of Chicago Press, 1951.

McArthur, Tom, ed. *The Oxford Companion to the English Language.* New York: Oxford University Press, 1992.

McFedries, Paul. *Word Spy: The Word Lover's Guide to Modern Culture.* New York: Broadway, 2004.

McKean, Erin, ed. *Totally Weird and Wonderful Words.* New York: Oxford University Press, 2006.

McQuain, Jeffrey. *Never Enough Words: How Americans Invented Expressions as Ingenious, Ornery, and Colorful as Themselves.* New York: Random House, 1999.

McQuain, Jeffrey, and Stanley Malles. *Coined by Shakespeare: Words & Meanings First Penned by the Bard.* Springfield, MA: Merriam-Webster, 1998.

McWhorter, John. *Doing Your Own Thing: The Degradation of Language and Music and Why We Should, Like, Care*. New York: Gotham, 2003.

Mead, Leon. *Word-Coinage: Being an Inquiry Into Recent Neologisms and a Brief Study of Literary Style, Slang, and Provincialisms*. New York: Crowell, 1902.

Mencken, H. L. *The American Language*, 4th ed. New York: Knopf, 1936, 1957.

Mencken, H. L. *The American Language, Supplement I*. New York: Knopf, 1945.

Mencken, H. L. *The American Language, Supplement II*. New York: Knopf, 1948.

Merriam-Webster. *The Merriam-Webster New Book of Word Histories*. Springfield, MA: Merriam-Webster, 1991.

Merton, Robert K., and Eleanor Barber. *The Travels and Adventures of Serendipity: A Study in Sociological Semantics and the Sociology of Science*. Princeton, NJ: Princeton University Press, 2004.

Metcalf, Allan. *From Skedaddle to Selfie: Words of the Generations*. New York: Oxford, 2015.

Metcalf, Allan. *OK: The Improbable Story of America's Greatest Word*. New York: Oxford University Press, 2012.

Metcalf, Allan. *Predicting New Words: The Secrets of Their Success*. Boston: Houghton Mifflin, 2002.

Metcalf, Allan. *The World in So Many Words: A Country-by-Country Tour of Words That Have Shaped Our Language*. Boston: Houghton Mifflin, 1999.

Minkova, Donka, and Robert Stockwell. *English Words: History and Structure*. New York: Cambridge University Press, 2001.

Moore, John. *You English Words*. London: Collins, 1945.

Morris, Evan. *From Altoids to Zima: The Surprising Stories Behind 125 Famous Brand Names*. New York: Fireside/Simon & Schuster, 2004.

Morris, Evan. *The Word Detective: Solving the Mysteries Behind Those Pesky Words and Phrases*. New York: Plume/Penguin, 2001.

Morris, William, and Mary Morris. *Morris Dictionary of Word and Phrase Origins*, 2nd ed. New York: HarperCollins, 1988.

Morris, William, and Mary Morris. *Harper Dictionary of Contemporary Usage*, 2nd ed. New York: Harper & Row, 1985.

Mugglestone, Lynda. *Lost for Words: The Hidden History of the Oxford English Dictionary*. New Haven, CT: Yale University Press, 2005.

Murphy, Lynne. *The Prodigal Tongue: The Love-Hate Relationship Between American and British English*. New York: Penguin, 2018.

Nunberg, Geoffrey. *Going Nucular: Language, Politics, and Culture in Confrontational Times*. New York: Public Affairs, 2004.

Nunberg, Geoffrey. *The Way We Talk Now: Commentaries on Language and Culture*. Boston: Houghton Mifflin, 2001.

O'Conner, Patricia, and Stewart Kellerman. *Origins of the Specious: Myths and Misconceptions of the English Language*. New York: Random House, 2009.

Ostler, Rosemarie. *Dewdroppers, Waldos, and Slackers: A Decade-by-Decade Guide to the Vanishing Vocabulary of the Twentieth Century*. New York: Oxford University Press, 2003.

Partridge, Eric. *Partridge's Concise Dictionary of Slang and Unconventional English: From A Dictionary of Slang and Unconventional English by Eric Partridge*. Edited by Paul Beale. New York: Macmillan, 1989.

Partridge, Eric. *A Dictionary of Catch Phrases*. Edited by Paul Beale. New York: Dorset Press, 1988.

Partridge, Eric. *A Dictionary of Slang and Unconventional English*. New York: Macmillan, 1961.

Partridge, Eric. *Origins: A Short Etymological Dictionary of Modern English*. New York: Macmillan, 1958.

Partridge, Eric. *Here, There and Everywhere: Essays upon Language*. London: Hamilton, 1950.

Pei, Mario. *Words in Sheep's Clothing*. New York: Dutton, 1969.

Pei, Mario. *The Story of Language*. Philadelphia: Lippincott, 1949, 1965.

Pinker, Steven. *The Stuff of Thought: Language as a Window into Human Nature*. New York: Penguin, 2007, 2008.

Pinker, Steven. *The Language Instinct: How the Mind Creates Language*. New York: HarperPerennial, 1994, 1995.

Pound, Louise. *Selected Writings of Louise Pound*. Westport, CT: Greenwood, 1949, 1971.

Prucher, Jeff, ed. *Brave New Words: The Oxford Dictionary of Science Fiction*. New York: Oxford University Press, 2007.

Pyles, Thomas. *Words and Ways of American English*. New York: Random House, 1952.

Quinion, Michael. *Gallimaufry: A Hodgepodge of Our Vanishing Vocabulary*. Oxford: Oxford University Press, 2006.

Quinion, Michael. *Port Out, Starboard Home: And Other Language Myths*. New York: HarperCollins, 2004.

Quinion, Michael. *Ballyhoo, Buckaroo, and Spuds: Ingenious Tales of Words and Their Origins*. Washington, DC: Smithsonian, 2004.

Raymond, Eric S. *The New Hacker's Dictionary*, 3rd ed. Cambridge, MA: MIT, 1996.

Read, Allen Walker. *Milestones in the History of English in America*. Durham, NC: Duke University Press, 2002.

Redfern, Walter. *The Dead and the Quick: Clichés and Neologisms in the Written, Spoken and Visual Cultures of Britain, the United States and France*. London: Academica, 2010.

Redfern, Walter. *Clichés and Coinages*. Cambridge, MA: Blackwell, 1989.

Rees, Nigel, ed. *Cassell's Dictionary of Word and Phrase Origins*. London: Cassell, 1996, 2002.

Rees, Nigel, ed. *Dictionary of Popular Phrases*. London: Bloomsbury, 1990.

Rogers, John. *Origins of Sea Terms*. Mystic, CT: Mystic Seaport Museum, 1985.

Rosten, Leo. *The New Joys of Yiddish*. New York: Three Rivers, 2003.

Safire, William. *Safire's Political Dictionary*, rev. ed. New York: Oxford University Press, 2008.

Savan, Leslie. *Slam Dunks and No-Brainers*: *Pop Language in Your Life, the Media, and Like . . . Whatever*. New York: Vintage, 2006.

Shapiro, Fred, ed. *The Yale Book of Quotations*. New Haven, CT: Yale University Press, 2006.

Shipley, Joseph, ed. *Dictionary of Word Origins,* 2nd ed. New York: Philosophical Library, 1945.

Smith, Logan Pearsall. *The English Language*. London: Oxford University Press, 1912, 1966.

Smith, Logan Pearsall. *Milton and His Modern Critics*. Boston: Little, Brown, 1941.

Smith, Logan Pearsall. *Words and Idioms*: *Studies in the English Language*. Boston: Houghton Mifflin, 1925.

Smith, Stephanie A. *Household Words: Bloomers, Sucker, Bombshell, Scab, Nigger, Cyber*. Minneapolis: University of Minnesota Press, 2006.

Sørensen, Knud. *Charles Dickens: Linguistic Innovator*. Aarhus, Denmark: Aarhus Universitetsforlag, 1985.

Soukhanov, Anne H. *Word Watch: The Stories Behind the Words of Our Lives*. New York: Holt, 1995.

Stamper, Kory. *Word by Word: The Secret Life of Dictionaries*. New York: Pantheon, 2017.

Steinmetz, Sol. *There's a Word for It: The Explosion of the American Language Since 1900*. New York: Harmony, 2010.

Steinmetz, Sol. *Semantic Antics*: *How* and *Why Words Change Meaning*. New York: Random House, 2008.

Steinmetz, Sol, and Barbara Ann Kipfer. *The Life of Language: The Fascinating Ways Words Are Born, Live and Die*. New York: Random House, 2006.

Taylor, Anna Marjorie. *The Language of World War II: Abbreviations, Captions, Quotations, Slogans, Titles and Other Terms and Phrases*. New York: Wilson, 1948.

Thun, Nils. *Reduplicative Words in English: A Study of Formations of the Types Tick-tick, Hurly-burly and Shilly-shally*. Uppsala, Sweden: Uppsala University Press, 1963.

Tuleja, Tad. *Marvelous Monikers: People Behind More than 400 Words and Expressions*. New York: Harmony, 1990.

Urdang, Laurence. *A Fine Kettle of Fish, and Other Figurative Phrases*. Detroit: Visible Ink/Gale, 1991.

Urdang, Laurence. *The Whole Ball of Wax and Other Colloquial Phrases: What They Mean & How They Started*. New York: Perigree/Putnam, 1988.

van der Sijs, Nicoline. *Cookies, Coleslaw, and Stoops: The Influence of Dutch on the North American Languages*. Amsterdam: Amsterdam University Press, 2009.

Vanoni, Marvin. *Great Expressions*: *How Our Favorite Words and Phrases Have Come to Mean What They Mean*. New York: Morrow, 1989.

Wallraff, Barbara. *Word Fugitives: In Pursuit of Wanted Words*. New York: Collins, 2006.

Wallraff, Barbara. *Your Own Words.* New York: Counterpoint/Perseus, 2004.

Wallraff, Barbara. *Word Court: Wherein Verbal Virtue Is Rewarded, Crimes Against the Language Are Punished, and Poetic Justice Is Done.* New York: Harcourt, 2000.

Webber, Elizabeth, and Mike Feinsilber. *Grand Allusions: A Lively Guide to Those Expressions, Terms and References You Ought to Know but Might Not.* Washington, DC: Farragut, 1990.

Webber, Elizabeth, and Mike Feinsilber. *Merriam-Webster's Dictionary of Allusions.* Springfield, MA: Merriam-Webster, 1999.

Williams, Raymond. *Keywords: A Vocabulary of Culture and Society.* New York: Oxford University Press, 1976, 1983.

Wilton, David. *Word Myths: Debunking Linguistic Urban Legends.* New York: Oxford University Press, 2004.

ONLINE

The Big Apple, https://www.barrypopik.com/

Dictionary.com, https://www.dictionary.com/

Fritinancy, https://nancyfriedman.typepad.com/away_with_words/

Grammarphobia, https://www.grammarphobia.com/

Grammarist, https://grammarist.com/

IMDb, https://www.imdb.com/?ref_=nv_home

Language Log, https://languagelog.ldc.upenn.edu/nll/

Lexicon Valley, https://slate.com/podcasts/lexicon-valley

The LINGUIST List, https://new.linguistlist.org/

Merriam-Webster Online, https://www.merriam-webster.com/

Online Etymological Dictionary, https://www.etymonline.com/

Oxford English Dictionary, https://www.oed.com/

The Phrase Finder, https://www.phrases.org.uk/

Phrases.com, https://www.phrases.com/

Quote Investigator, https://quoteinvestigator.com/

Snopes.com, https://www.snopes.com/

Urban Dictionary, https://www.urbandictionary.com/

Visual Thesaurus, https://www.visualthesaurus.com/

Wikipedia, http://www.wikipedia.org/

Wiktionary, https://en.wiktionary.org/wiki/Wiktionary:Main_Page

word histories, https://wordhistories.net/

Word Spy, https://www.wordspy.com/

Wordnik, https://www.wordnik.com/

Wordorigins.org, http://www.wordorigins.org/

World Wide Words, http://www.worldwidewords.org

Notes

IN THE GOOGLE era, books and other publications increasingly rely on Casey Stengel's approach to source citation: you could look it up. Isn't that what search engines are for? Well, partly yes, but mostly no. Yes, you could probably find the sources authors have consulted by doing an online search. But no, even in the Google era I think readers are entitled to a clear indication of where an author found his or her information. That is what these endnotes are for.

Here I cite my primary sources and suggest leads for those of you who would like to pursue further the origins of specific neologisms. Within them you will find plenty of paths to follow if you are interested. In the process you might find additions and corrections, which I would certainly like to hear about via www.ralphkeyes.com. Don't assume these notes are just a dry listing of source material: quite often I elaborate on matters discussed in the text, and certain aspects of my source materials as well.

Books listed in these notes are referred to by the author's last name and book title. Page numbers are given from books cited, as well as their publisher, edition, and the date of their original publication if earlier, for those not included in the bibliography. Where available, volume, issue number, and page numbers are given for citations from periodicals (the pages of the entire article, followed by the specific pages cited). When online sources are cited, a URL is also included, as well as the date it was accessed. Well-known online publications such as *Salon, Slate, Politico, The Hill,* and *Wikipedia* are cited without a URL. Since *The Oxford English Dictionary* is now used primarily online, wherein its editions and supplements are merged and content is continually updated, I merely note "*OED*" when citing it as a source. (In this case you *could* look it up.) Other frequently cited sources are abbreviated by these initials:

AL—*The American Language* by H. L. Mencken
ATL—*The Atlantic*
BG—*Boston Globe*
IMDb—International Movie Database
LAT—*Los Angeles Times*
M-W—*The Merriam-Webster New Book of Word Histories*
NPR—National Public Radio

NYer—New Yorker
NYT—New York Times
PRI—Public Radio International
SFC—San Francisco Chronicle
SPD—Safire's Political Dictionary
WP—Washington Post
WSJ—Wall Street Journal
UD—Urban Dictionary

Without further ado, my sources:

A WORD WITH THE READER . . .

Zimmer: Ben Zimmer, "Spreading the Word," *Forbes.com*, April 23, 2009, https://www.forbes.com/2009/04/23/how-language-made-options-books-zimmer.html#79fa42bb2f46, accessed January 18, 2016.

supermodel: John Green, "Who Claims to Have Invented the Word 'Supermodel'?," *classroom*, https://classroom.synonym.com/claims-invented-word-supermodel-11092.html, accessed April 19, 2019; Barry Popik, "Superman; Superstar; Supermodel," *The Big Apple*, July 25, 2004, https://www.barrypopik.com/index.php/new_york_city/entry/superman_superstar_supermodel/, accessed April 19, 2019.

Jefferson, *neologize*: See notes for Chapter 18. **Asimov,** *robotics*: See notes for Chapter 11.

Metcalf, Steinmetz: Metcalf, *Predicting New Words*, 168; Steinmetz, *There's a Word for It*, 237.

google: Gene Weingarten, "Take This™ and Google It!," *WP*, February 13, 2012; **Dickens**: Charles Dickens, *A Child's History of England*, in *The Works of Charles Dickens*, Vol. 30, London: Chapman and Hall, 1898, 359; Mathews, *A Dictionary of Americanisms*, Vol. 1, 716. For more on *google*, see notes for Chapter 10.

Snoop Dogg: See notes for Chapter 2.

blurb **misattributed**: "blurb (n.)," *Online Etymology Dictionary*, https://www.etymonline.com/word/blurb, accessed February 10, 2018; Brdar, *Metonymy and Word-Formation*, 7; Brander Matthews, "A Round-Up of Blurbs," *NYT*, September 24, 1922; Brander Matthews, "The Art of Making New Words," *The Unpopular Review* 9, no. 17, January–March 1918, 58–89, 64.

tweed: "tweed," https://en.oxforddictionaries.com/definition/tweed, accessed March 15, 2019; "James Locke & Tweed," *Crombie Chronicle*, https://www.crombie.co.uk/crombie-chronicle/james-locke-tweed/, accessed March 15, 2019; Fiona Anderson, *Tweed*, London: Bloomsbury Academic, 2017, 7–8. **Rouse**: Joshua Olsen, *Better Places, Better Lives: A Biography of James Rouse*. Washington, DC: Urban Land Institute, 2003, 46.

Stamper: Stamper, *Word by Word*, 191.

Pinker: Pinker, *The Stuff of Thought*, 16.

hashtag coinages: *#BlackLivesMatter* was introduced in 2012 by UCLA sociologist Marcus Anthony Hunter (and adopted the next year by Alicia Garza, Patrisse Cullors, and Opal Tomet, the founders of a movement against police brutality). *#MeToo* is actress Alyssa Milano's 2017 hashtag of a phrase coined eleven years earlier by Tarana Burke for her movement against sexual abuse. In 2016 a Donald Trump supporter named Gene McVay began tweeting with the hashtag *#MAGA*, an acronym for Make America Great Again, the phrase Trump borrowed from Ronald Reagan as his 2016 campaign slogan. See "The 2010s: Hashtags and Social Movements," *Weekend Edition Saturday*, NPR, December 28, 2019, https://www.npr.org/2019/12/28/792022266/the-2010s-hashtags-and-social-movements, accessed June 9, 2020; Marcus Anthony Hunter, "How Does L.A.'s Racial Past Resonate Now?," June 8, 2020, https://www.latimes.com/entertainment-arts/books/story/2020-06-08/six-writers-on-l-a-and-black-lives-matter, accessed June 9, 2020.

Ngram: Corroborating my own experience is that of Sarah Zhang: Sarah Zhang, "The Pitfalls of Using Google Ngram to Study Language," *Wired*, October 12, 2015, https://www.wired.com/2015/10/pitfalls-of-studying-language-with-google-ngram/, accessed May 26, 2018. **think tanks**: Leonard Zwilling, *A TAD Lexicon*, Rolla, MO: Gerald Cohen, 1993, 82. **tipping point**: *Oakland Tribune*, June 30, 1910.

Shakespeare: McQuain and Malless, *Coined by Shakespeare*. Paul Dickson's compilation of varying estimates of Shakespeare's coinages overlaps with my own in some cases: Dickson, *Authorisms*, 197–204. Dickson's reviewer: Henry Hitchings, "'Authorisms' by Paul Dickson," *WSJ*, April 20, 2014; Macrone, *Brush Up Your Shakespeare*, 193; Michael Blanding, "Plagiarism Software Unveils a New Source for 11 of Shakespeare's Plays," *NYT*, February 7, 2018, citing work by Dennis McCarthy and June Schlueter; Ammon Shea, "You Didn't Invent That: Shakespeare's Spurious Neologisms," *dictionary.com*, April 22, 2015, is a good survey of this subject, https://www.dictionary.com/e/spurious-neologisms-shakespeare/, accessed March 27, 2019.

holy neologisms: Malless and McQuain, *Coined by God*.

1. ZEN AND THE ART OF WORD CREATION

Churchill's muffled typewriters: Manchester and Reid, *The Last Lion*, 11–12; Andrew Roberts, "Winston Churchill: America's Enduring Love for Winnie and His Words," *Telegraph*, August 4, 2012. **klop**: Manchester, *The Last Lion*, 32; Langworth, *Churchill by Himself*, 38–39. (Langworth's book is a definitive and reliable collection of Churchill utterances.) Langworth **quoted**: Ibid., 32. Ibid., 41. **bottlescape**: Ibid., 34; Humes, *Churchill*, 141. **Winstonian**: *OED*; Langworth, *Churchill by Himself*, 46.

queutopia: Ibid., 32, 42; Manchester, *The Last Lion* 32; Manchester and Reid, *The Last Lion*, 993–94. **fearthought, afterlight**: Langworth, *Churchill by Himself*, 37, 32. **social security, fly-in, seaplane, under-employed, terminological inexactitude**: *OED*. **Battle of the Bulge**: Langworth, *Churchill by Himself*, 33. **Home Guard**: Manchester, *The Last Lion*, 30; Langworth, *Churchill by Himself*, 275; BBC, "Fact File: Formation of the Home Guard," http://www.bbc.co.uk/history/ww2peopleswar/timeline/

factfiles/nonflash/a1057303.shtml accessed January 4, 2019. ***ready-made***: Manchester, *The Last Lion*, 30; Langworth, *Churchill by Himself*, 68; Brett and Kate McKay, "The Winston Churchill Guide to Public Speaking," https://www.artofmanliness.com/articles/guide-to-public-speaking/, accessed January 4, 2019; (footnote) **Duchamp**: "Ready-Made: Style of Art," https://www.britannica.com/art/ready-made, accessed January 4, 2019. ***jaw, jaw***: Richard Langworth, " 'Jaw to Jaw' versus 'Jaw, Jaw,' " *Richard M. Langworth*, December 14, 2010, https://richardlangworth.com/jaw-jaw accessed January 15, 2020. ***summit***: Langworth, *Churchill by Himself*, 441, 482; Manchester and Reid, *The Last Lion*, 994–95; Safire, *NYT*, October 15, 1989; Ben Zimmer, " 'Summit' Has a Peak Moment: Where the Term Comes From," *WSJ*, June 15, 2018.

ancient Romans, Horace: Redfern, *Clichés and Coinages*, 2, 183; Hitchings, *The Secret Life of Words*, 12; *The Epistles of Horace*, Cambridge: Cambridge University Press, 1888, 62; Basil Dufallo, "Words Born and Made: Horace's Defense of Neologisms and the Cultural Poetics of Latin," *Arethusa* 38, no. 1, 2005, 89–101; William Michael Short, *Sermo, Sanguis, Semen: An Anthropology of Language in Roman Culture*, a dissertation submitted in partial satisfaction of the requirements for the degree of Doctor of Philosophy in Classics in the Graduate Division of the University of California, Berkeley, 2007, 66–70. ***sesquipedalian***: "Defenestration, 'Kerfuffle,' & Other Greatest Hits: People's Top 10 Favorite Words," *Words at Play, Merriam-Webster*, https://www.merriam-webster.com/words-at-play/top-10-peoples-favorite-words/defenestration accessed January 18, 2020.

Puttenham, Puttenhamisms: *OED*; Steinmetz and Kipfer, *The Life of Language*, 166; George Puttenham, *The Art of English Poesie*, ed. Gladys Doidge Willcock and Alice Walker, London: Cambridge University Press, 1936, 1970, xxxvii–xxxix, lxxxvii–lxxxix, xc–xciii; George Puttenham, *The Art of English Poesie by George Puttenham: A Critical Edition*, ed. Frank Whigham and Wayne A. Rebhorn, Ithaca, NY: Cornell University Press, 2007, 58, 336–38. At times Puttenham is referred to as "Richard Puttenham."

Shakespeare, *Coine words*: *Coriolanus*, Act III, Scene 1. **Homemaking book**: Markham, *The English Housewife*, 53.

French, Flaubert: Redfern, *Clichés and Coinages*, 182. **Algeo**: Neology Forum in *Dictionaries: Journal of the Dictionary Society of North America*, November 16, 1995, 1–2.

D'Israeli: Hitchings, *The Secret Life of Words,* 279. **Balzac**: Maryam Monalisa Gharavi, "Neologism: How Words Do Things with Words," *The White Review*, Online Exclusive, June 2013, https://www.thewhitereview.org/feature/neologism-how-words-do-things-with-words/, accessed February 10, 2020. **Mead**: Mead, *Word-Coinage*, vii–viii, 15–16, 79, 87–88, 97, 106–7, 116–18, 124–25, 147, 150–52, 157–59.

Theodore Roosevelt's words and phrases: *AL*, 174; *SPD*, xv; Keyes, *The Quote Verifier*, 184–86; Gamaliel Bradford, *The Quick and the Dead*, Boston: Houghton Mifflin, 1931, 31. ***weasel words***: *SPD*, 799–800; Pascal Tréguer, "Meaning and Origin of the Phrase 'Weasel Word,' " *word histories*, February 22, 2019, https://wordhistories.net/2019/02/22/weasel-word-origin/, accessed January 8, 2020.

Gross about Wu: *Fresh Air*, NPR, October 17, 2016.

Kameny: Jose Antonio Vargas, "Signs of Progress: Franklin Kameny Keeps Mementos of His Activism in the Attic, Not the Closet," *WP*, July 23, 2005.

obituaries: *New York Times*' obituaries of Oates, Freudenberger, and Weinberg, October 26, 1999, December 5, 2009, March 22, 2017. William Safire noted the obituary-prestige factor in his "On Language" column, *NYT*, January 2, 2000.

Grexit/Brexit: See notes for Chapter 2 and Chapter 20.

Barrett: Grant Barrett, "Putting in a Good Word," *Forbes*, April 22, 2009, https://www.forbes.com/2009/04/23/new-words-survival-opinions-books-barrett. html#57d7ad630da5, accessed January 7, 2019; Grant Barrett, "Which Words Will Live On?," *NYT*, December 31, 2011.

Brooks, *bobos*: David Brooks, *Bobos in Paradise: The New Upper Class and How They Got There*, New York: Simon & Schuster, 2000; *NYT*, April 29, 2008; October 14, 2000; *The Guardian*, May 31, 2008. ***odyssey years***: *NYT*, October 9, 2007. ***orchid generation***: *NYT*, August 30, 2016. ***organization kids***: David Brooks, "The Organization Kid," *ATL*, April 2001, 40–54. ***manly upscale proles***: *NYT*, October 4, 2003. ***amphibians***: *NYT*, February 15, 2018.

Friedman: Ian Parker, "The Bright Side," *NYer*, September 10, 2008, 52–63, 55. ***petropolitics***: *NYT*, May 1, 2006. ***Fayaadism***: *NYT*, April 23, 2013. ***electronic herd***: Thomas Friedman, *The Lexus and the Olive Tree: Understanding Globalization*, New York: Farrar, Straus and Giroux, 1999, 101, 112. **MIDS (*Microchip Immune Deficiency Syndrome*)**: Ibid., 76. **Great Inflection**: *NYT*, January 29, 2013. ***flat world***: Ian Parker, "The I.D. Man," *NYer*, 26–34, 29; Thomas L. Friedman, *The World Is Flat: A Brief History of the Twenty-First Century*, New York: Farrar, Straus and Giroux, 2005, 5; Daniel H. Pink, "Why the World Is Flat," *Wired*, May 1, 2005, https://www. wired.com/2005/05/friedman-2/, accessed January 8, 2019. ***Pottery Barn Rule***: Bob Woodward, *Plan of Attack*, New York: Simon & Schuster, 2004, 150; *WP*, April 28, 2004; *Fresh Air*, NPR, June 3, 2004; *Weekend Edition*, NPR, September 7, 2002; *NYT*, February 12, 2003; William Safire, *NYT Magazine*, October 17, 2004, 24.

Wallraff: Joshua J. Friedman, "Sniglets and Slithy Toves," *ATL*, March 2006, https://www.theatlantic.com/magazine/archive/2006/03/sniglets-and-slithy-toves/ 304756/, accessed January 8, 2019.

Dawkins, dundridge: Richard Dawkins (@Richard Dawkins), Twitter post, November 3, 2013, https://twitter.com/richarddawkins/status/396956105869250561? lang=en, accessed January 8, 2019, February 9, 2020; Richard Dawkins, *An Appetite for Wonder: The Making of a Scientist*, New York: ECCO, 2013, 39–40; *Telegraph*, November 4, 2013; *The Guardian*, June 9, 2015.

Menand: Louis Menand, "Words of the Year," *NYer*, January 8, 2018, 15.

Baum, Oz: L. Frank Baum, *The Annotated Wizard of Oz: The Wonderful Wizard of Oz*, ed. Michael Patrick Hearn, New York: Potter, 1973, 103.

Elvismania: Pascal Tréguer, "The Authentic Origin of the Phrase 'Elvis Has Left the Building,'" *word histories*, October 7, 2018, https://wordhistories.net/2018/10/07/

elvis-left-building/, accessed February 9, 2020; Associated Press, "Horace Logan, 86; Coined Elvis Catchphrase," *NYT*, October 16, 2002.

boondoggle: *NYT*, August 15, 1957, April 4, 1935; *SPD*, 74; *M-W*, 58–59; Mathews, *A Dictionary of Americanisms*, Vol. 1, 163; Barnhart and Metcalf, *America in So Many Words*, 230–31. Alternative origins of this term in the Ozark Mountains and British Isles were suggested in the *Literary Digest* in 1935, with little supporting evidence: "The Lexicographer's Easy Chair," *The Literary Digest*, June 1, 1935, 3; John Algeo, "Etymologies Unknown: Boondoggle," *American Speech* 59, no. 1, 1984, 93–95. See aso "boondoggle," *wordwizard*, July 15–22, 2011, http://www.wordwizard.com/phpbb3/viewtopic. php?t=23019, accessed February 10, 2020; Ben Zimmer, "The Story of 'Boondoggle': A Useful Word for Useless Work," *Visual Thesaurus*, September 22, 2015, https://www. visualthesaurus.com/cm/wordroutes/the-story-of-boondoggle-a-useful-word-for-useless-work/, accessed September 20, 2019; Michael Quinion, "Boondoggle," *World Wide Words*, accessed February 28, 2017; Garson O'Toole, "Further Antedating of 'Boondoggle,'" *The LINGUIST List*, January 24, 2016, http://listserv.linguistlist.org/pipermail/ads-l/2016-January/140527.html, accessed February 12, 2020.

Whac-a-Mole: Peter Rugg, "The Man Who Made the Whac-a-Mole Has One More Chance," *Popular Mechanics*, February 3, 2016, https://www.popularmechanics.com/technology/gadgets/a18927/the-man-who-made-the-whac-a-mole-has-one-more-chance/, accessed January 8, 2019; *WP*, July 7, 2015; *NYT*, October 29, 2006; Benjamin Mueller, "'Whac-a-Mole' Against Virus Sounds Reasonable, Unless You're the Mole," *NYT*, July 9, 2020; Ed Yong, "How the Pandemic Will End," *ATL*, March 23, 2020, https://www.theatlantic.com/health/archive/2020/03/how-will-coronavirus-end/608719/, accessed June 13, 2020.

2. COINED BY CHANCE

wardrobe malfunction: *Wikipedia* has extensive coverage of this episode on its "Wardrobe Malfunction . . . Super Bowl XXXVIII Halftime Show Controversy" page. See also "Janet Jackson's Wardrobe Malfunction," *NBC.com*, http://www.nbcnews.com/id/4147857/ns/msnbc-countdown_with_keith_olbermann/t/janet-jacksons-wardrobe-malfunction/, accessed March 25, 2007.

Mead: Mead, *Word-Coinage*, 53.

schooner: *OED*; Liberman, *Word Origins*, 129; "The History of Gloucester Fishing," April 7, 1923, https://www.downtosea.com/1901-1925/fishist.htm, accessed March 15, 2019.

OED re chance: Bryson, *The Mother Tongue*, 71. **ghost words**: Mugglestone, *Lost for Words*, 51-3, 173. **blunderful**: Redfern, *Clichés and Coinages*, 203, 249, 252. (The *OED* records *blunderful* being used as early as 1881.) **Proust**: Ibid., 200.

family language: Ralph Keyes, "Family Spoken Here," *Good Housekeeping*, April 1986, 72, 74; Dickson, *Family Words*, 6–15; Wallraff, *Word Fugitives*, 6, 46–49, 95–96, 146, 177. **Allen Walker Read**: Dickson, *Family Words*, 7. **Gladstone,**

Glynne, Baring: Merton and Barber, *The Travels and Adventures of Serendipity*, 12; Christopher Stray, "'Mrs Gladstone's Drawers': Language and Identity in Victorian Families," *Australasian Victorian Studies Journal* 9, 2003, 172–87, 179; Christopher Stray, ed., *Contributions Towards a Glossary of the Glynne Language By a Student* (*George William, Lord Lyttleton*), Newcastle-upon-Tyne, UK: Cambridge Scholars, 1851, 2008, vii–xiv.

wiffle ball: Marc Santora, "What's 50, Curvy and Full of Air?; It's the Wiffle Ball, Still Popular, Holes and All," *NYT*, August 14, 2003; Ethan Trex, "A Brief History of the Wiffle Ball," *Mental Floss*, June 29, 2014, https://www.mentalfloss.com/article/24609/it-curves-brief-history-wiffle-ball, accessed March 8, 2019; (footnote) **Bernice the Whiffle Hen**: "Bernice," *Popeye the Sailorpedia*, https://popeye.fandom.com/wiki/Bernice, accessed January 13, 2020.

Smurf: "Smurf," *UD*; "Etymology of Smurf," *irregarret.ess* magazine, March 30, 2015, http://www.irregarret.essmagazine.com/articles/etymology-of-smurf/. accessed January 8, 2019; *NYT*, December 2, 2002.

Bolinger and Sears: Bolinger and Sears, *Aspects of Language*, 235.

quark: American Heritage editors, *Word Histories and Mysteries*, 230–31; *M-W*, 183; "What Does 'Quark' Have to Do with Finnegan's Wake? How a Word Used by James Joyce Became the Name for an Elementary Particle of Matter," *Merriam-Webster.com*, https://www.merriam-webster.com/words-at-play/quark, accessed February 19, 2018; Dot Wordsworth, "Mind Your Language: Quark," *The Spectator*, May 14, 2011; Lee Edson, "Two Men in Search of the Quark," *NYT Magazine*, October 8, 1967, 54; David Herreby, "The Man Who Knows Everything: Murray Gell-Mann," *NYT Magazine*, May 8, 1994, 24; Murray Gell-Mann, *The Quark and the Jaguar: Adventures in the Simple and the Complex*, New York: Freeman, 1994, 180–81; George Johnson, *Strange Beauty: Murray Gell-Mann and the Revolution in Twentieth-Century Physics*, New York: Vintage, 1999, 2001, 18–21, 212–18, 233–36, 239, 275, 290, 299, 351–52, 366–67, 388–92; Harald Fritzsch, *Quarks: The Stuff of Matter*, New York: Basic, 1983, 62–64, 73–75.

Bushisms: *SPD*, 64; Mark Crispin Miller, *The Bush Dyslexicon: Observations on a National Disorder*, New York: Norton, 2001; Jacob Weisberg, "The Complete Bushisms: Updated Frequently," *Slate*, March 20, 2009; O'Conner and Kellerman, *Origins of the Specious*, 51–52; Erard, *Um . . .* , 11–12, 224–32; "Top 'Bushisms' of 2006 Released," UPI, https://www.upi.com/Top-Bushisms-of-2006-released/96421168230119/. accessed May 7, 2019. *decider*: "Bush: 'I'm the Decider' on Rumsfeld," *CNN*, April 18, 2006, http://www.cnn.com/2006/POLITICS/04/18/rumsfeld/, accessed May 6, 2019; *Time* **cover**: *Time,* June 18, 2012; *Newsweek* **cover**: *Newsweek*, September 17, 2007; *NYT* **columnist**: Timothy Egan, "Clueless-in-Costco," *Opinionator Blog*, https://opinionator.blogs.nytimes.com/2009/12/16/clueless-in-costco/, accessed December 17, 2009. (footnote) **early use of "decider"**: *OED*.

decision-maker: Leo Rosten letter to William Safire in William Safire, *Quoth the Maven: More on Language from William Safire*, New York: Random House, 1993, 11–12.

misunderestimate: "'Misunderestimate' Tops List of Notable 'Bushisms,'" *New York Daily News*, January 8, 2009; Metcalf, *Predicting New Words*, 115–20; *SPD*, 64. Franken: "Franken: I Received a 'Doctorate in Megalomania at Trump University,'" *The Hill*, July 25, 2016. ***strategery***: Metcalf, *Predicting New Words*, 120; Dave Itzkoff, "'SNL' Begins a New Season with Alec Baldwin as Donald Trump," *NYT*, October 2, 2016.

***wee-weed* up**: *Daily Mail*, August 21, 2009; Dan Amira, "What Does 'All Wee-Weed Up' Mean, President Obama?," Daily Intelligencer, *New York*, http://nymag.com/intelligencer/2009/08/what_does_wee_weed_up_mean_pre.html, accessed October 4, 2016.

likeable enough: "Likeable Enough?" *Time* (cover), April 18, 2016. ***deplorable***: Katie Reilly, "Read Hillary Clinton's 'Basket of Deplorables' Remarks About Donald Trump Supporters," *Time.com*, September 10, 2016, https://time.com/4486502/hillary-clinton-basket-of-deplorables-transcript/, accessed October 31, 2019; T-shirts and posters boasting about being *deplorable* can be found on many Internet sites.

bigly: "Did Trump Say 'Bigly' or 'Big League'?," *Merriam-Webster.com*, https://www.merriam-webster.com/news-trend-watch/did-trump-say-bigly-or-big-league-20160927, accessed January 6, 2017; Liam Stack, "Yes, Trump Really Is Saying 'Big League,' Not 'Bigly,' Linguists Say," *NYT*, October 24, 2016; Gorsuch: Ryan Teague Beckwith, "Neil Gorsuch Used the Word 'Bigly' at His Confirmation Hearing," *Time*, March 23, 2017, https://time.com/4709790/neil-gorsuch-confirmation-bigly/, accessed February 10, 2020; *bigly* around since Middle Ages: *OED*.

eggcorns: Katy Steinmetz, "This Is What 'Eggcorns' Are (and Why They're Jar-Droppingly Good)," *Time*, May 30, 2015, http://time.com/3902230/what-is-an-eggcorn/, accessed May 6, 2019; *OED*; "eggcorn," *Merriam-Webster.com*, https://www.merriam-webster.com/dictionary/eggcorns, accessed May 6, 2019; Mark Memmott, "'Eggcorns': The Gaffes That Spread Like Wildflowers," *Weekend Edition Saturday*, NPR, May 30, 2015; Mark Liberman, "Egg Corns: Folk Etymology, Malapropism, Mondegreen???," *Language Log*, September 23, 2003, http://itre.cis.upenn.edu/~myl/languagelog/archives/000018.html, accessed May 6, 2019; Ben Zimmer, "Eggcorn Makes the OED," *Language Log*, September 16, 2010, http://languagelog.ldc.upenn.edu/nll/?p=2633, accessed May 6, 2019.

mondegreen: *OED*; Sylvia Wright, "The Death of Lady Mondegreen," *Harper's Magazine* 209, no. 1254, November 1954, 48–51; Cousineau, *Wordcatcher*, 186–87; Wallraff, *Word Fugitives*, 66–67; William Safire, *On Language*, New York: Avon, 1980, 1981, 166–72. "Laid him on the green" comes from an old Scottish ballad called "The Bonnie Earl O'Moray."

Dogg, Rogen: Lizzie Dearden, "Snoop Dogg Explains to Seth Rogen Where the Word 'Chronic' Comes From," *MTV News*, http://www.mtv.com/news/1842999/snoop-dogg-seth-rogen/, accessed March 1, 2016; "Snoop Dogg Reveals What 'The Chronic' Means While Getting High with Seth Rogen," *The Independent*, June 11, 2014.

Sacks: Oliver Sacks, "Mishearings," *NYT*, June 5, 2015; "Filter Fish," *NYer*, September 7, 2015.

button-hole: *OED*; McFedries, *Word Spy*, 25; Hendrickson, *The Facts on File Encyclopedia of Word and Phrase Origins*, 120; Pascal Tréguer, "Origin of 'To Buttonhole' (To Detain in Conversation)," *word histories*, September 30, 2017, https://wordhistories.net/2017/09/30/origin-of-buttonhole/, accessed December 13, 2019.

Bryson: Bryson, *The Mother Tongue*, 71.

Americanisms: See notes for Chapter 18.

Smith, *raccoon*: *AL*, 104; Mathews, *A Dictionary of Americanisms*, Vol. 2, 1345–46; Hitchings, *The Secret Life of Words*, 154; Crystal, *The Story of English in 100 Words*, 117.

Erard: Erard, *Um . . .*, 55.

negawatt: *OED*; Elizabeth Kolbert, "Mr. Green," *NYer*, January 22, 2007, 36; "The 'Soft Path' Solution for Hard-Pressed Utilities," *Business Week*, July 23, 1984, 96L; "The Negawatt Revolution—Solving the CO2 Problem—Keynote Address by Amory Lovins at the Green Energy Conference," Montreal 1989; email from Rocky Mountain Institute librarian, March 22, 2013; The Association négaWatt: https://negawatt.org/en, accessed February 10, 2020.

derring-do: *OED*; Hitchings, *The Secret Life of Words*, 136; Funk, *2107 Curious Word Origins, Sayings & Expressions*, 309.

court-packing: Geoffrey C. Ward, *Closest Companion: The Unknown Story of the Intimate Friendship Between Franklin Roosevelt and Margaret Suckley*, New York: Houghton Mifflin Harcourt, 1995, 96; Geoffrey C. Ward, *The Roosevelts: An Intimate History*, New York: Knopf, 2014, 345.

Silicon Valley: Good accounts of the history of the term "Silicon Valley" can be found in David Laws, "Who Named Silicon Valley?," *Computer History Museum blog*, January 4, 2015, https://www.computerhistory.org/atchm/who-named-silicon-valley/ and Alan J. Weissberger's report of a lecture by Paul Wesling, "Who Coined the Term Silicon Valley?," *SIGCIS blog*, August 31, 2013, https://www.sigcis.org/node/422, accessed May 6, 2019. See also Carolyn E. Tajnai, "Fred Terman, the Father of Silicon Valley," *Stanford Computer Forum*, May 1985, http://forum.stanford.edu/carolyn/terman, accessed May 7, 2019; **Hoefler obituary**: *Spokane Chronicle*, April 16, 1986.

jitterbug: Shapiro, *The Yale Book of Quotations*, 740; Justin di Paola, "What Is the Jitterbug?," *Sydney Swing Katz logo*, November 5, 2010, http://sydneyswingkatz.com.au/blog/2010/11/jitterbug-historical/, accessed December 28, 2019; "Jitterbug," *h2g2*, March 22, 2006, https://h2g2.com/edited_entry/A8240438, accessed December 28, 2019: D.C. Copeland's JITTERBUG!, https://www.jittrbug.net/jitterbug-song-writing-team--creative-directors.html, accessed December 28, 2019.

Moral Majority: Michelle Norris interview with Paul Weyrich, *All Things Considered*, NPR, May 15, 2007.

Joe-Six-Pack: Martin Nolan, "After the Soul of Joe Six-Pack," *BG*, August 28, 1970; William Safire, "On Language; The Return of Joe Six-Pack," *NYT Magazine*, May 3, 1998, 30.

Astroturf: *NYT*, August 18, 2009; *Politico*, February 10, 2017; *The Hill*, February 11, 2017.

Murray, *aphesis, nonce*: *OED*; *M-W*, 19–20; James Murray, "Ninth Annual Address of the President to the Philological Society, Delivered at the Anniversary Meeting, Friday, 21st of May, 1880," *Transactions of the Philological Society* 18, no. 1, May 1881, 117–76; Considine, *Adventuring in Dictionaries*, 235–36; James D. Alexander, "Aphesis in English," *Word* 39, no. 1, 1988, 29–65; Mugglestone, *Lost for Words*, 98–101.

bully: Archer, *America To-Day*, 245–46; Mathews, *A Dictionary of Americanisms*, Vol. 1, 217; H. W. Boynton, "The American Language," *The Bookman* 27, March 1908, 63–71, 64. **bully pulpit**: *SPD*, 88; *Taegan Goddard's Political Dictionary*, https://politicaldictionary.com/words/bully-pulpit/, accessed April 8, 2020. **hearts and minds**: *SPD*, 667; Randall B. Woods, *Shadow Warrior: William Egan Colby and the CIA*, New York: Basic, 2013, 153. **binge watch**: Steven Poole, "From Woke to Gammon: Buzzwords by the People Who Coined Them," *The Guardian*, December 25, 2019. **Brexit**: Ibid.

3. *CASUAL COINAGE*

contraband: Kate Masur, "A Rare Phenomenon of Philological Vegetation: The Word 'Contraband' and the Meanings of Emancipation in the United States," *Journal of American History* 93, no. 4, March 2007, 1050–84; "Slaves Declared Contrabands of War," *American Antiquarian Society Online Resource*, 2006, https://www.americanantiquarian.org/Freedmen/Intros/contrabands.html accessed April 16, 2019; Rick Beard, "Grant's Contraband Conundrum," *NYT*, November 14, 2012, https://opinionator.blogs.nytimes.com/2012/11/14/grants-contraband-conundrum/, accessed April 11, 2018; Benjamin F. Butler, *Butler's Book: Autobiography and Personal Reminiscences*, Boston: Thayer, 1892, 256–64; Hans L. Trefousse, *Ben Butler: The South Called Him BEAST!*, New York: Twayne, 1957, 53–54, 75–79, 82–83; Howard P. Nash Jr., *Stormy Petrel: The Life and Times of General Benjamin F. Butler*, Rutherford, NJ: Fairleigh Dickinson, 1969, 104–11; Michael Thomas Smith, "Benjamin F. Butler (1818–1893)," *Encyclopedia Virginia*, https://www.encyclopediavirginia.org/Butler_Benjamin_F_1818-1893, accessed October 16, 2015; "General Butler and the Contraband of War," *NYT*, June 2, 1861; "The Slave Question.; Letter from Major-Gen. Butler on the Treatment of Fugitive Slaves," *NYT*, August 6, 1861. **three slaves**: Adam Goodheart, *1861: The Civil War Awakening*, New York: Knopf, 2011, 312–15, 324–33, 339, 342–43; **McPherson**: James McPherson, *The War That Forged a Nation: Why the Civil War Still Matters*, New York: Oxford University Press, 2015, 99–100; Andrew Ward, *The Slaves' War: The Civil War in the Words of Former Slaves*, Boston: Houghton Mifflin, 2008, 111, 184–91. **Butler's dilemma**: Butler-Cary meeting: Butler, *Butler's Book*, 256–58; Nicolay-Hay: John G. Nicolay and John Hay, *Abraham Lincoln: A History*, Vol. 4, New York: Century, 1904, 389. **Nott**: Kate Masur, "A Rare Phenomenon of

Philological Vegetation," 1051. **McPherson**: McPherson, *The War That Forged a Nation*, 100. *contraband* **etymology**: *OED*. **Butler's use of *contraband***: James Oakes, *Freedom National: The Destruction of Slavery in the United States, 1861–1865*, New York: Norton, 2013, 514. **Douglass**: L. Diane Barnes, *Frederick Douglass: Reformer and Statesman*, New York: Routledge, 2013, 89. **northern newspaper reporter**: Nash, *Stormy Petrel*, 108; Edward L. Pierce, "The Contrabands of Fort Monroe," *ATL*, November 1861, http://www.drbronsontours.com/bronsonedwarret.piercecontrabandsnov1861.html, accessed October 19, 2015. **cultural references to contrabands**: Eleanor Jones Harvey, *The Civil War and American Art*, New Haven, CT: Yale University Press, 2012, 199–203, 211, 214–15, 267; "Civil War Contraband Art," *lunchcountersitin*, September 18, 2015, https://jubiloemancipationcentury.wordpress.com/2015/09/18/civil-war-contraband-art/, accessed April 16, 2019; "Zouave Contraband Art: The White View of the Black Exodus," *lunchcountersitin*, October 23, 2018, https://jubiloemancipationcentury.word-press.com/tag/zouave/, accessed April 16, 2019; "Jubilo! The Emancipation Century African Americans in the 19th Century: Slavery, Resistance, Abolition, the Civil War, Emancipation, Reconstruction, and the Nadir," https://jubiloemancipationcentury.wordpress.com/category/contraband/, accessed April 11, 2018; Fiona McWilliam, "Louisa May Alcott's 'My Contraband,' and Discourse on Contraband Slaves in Popular Print Culture," *Studies in American Fiction* 42, no. 1, Spring 2015, 51–84.

Masur: Masur, "A Rare Phenomenon of Philological Vegetation."

Cary's confirmation: Butler, *Butler's Book*, 262–63. **Butler's memoir, "poor phrase"**: Ibid., 259–64.

containment: U.S. Department of State, Office of the Historian, "Milestones: 1945–1952, Kennan and Containment, 1947," https://history.state.gov/milestones/1945-1952/kennan, accessed December 4, 2015; Jon Thurber, "Diplomat Was Architect of U.S. Cold War Policy," *LAT*, March 18, 2005; John Lewis Gaddis, *George F. Kennan: An American Life*, New York: Penguin, 2011, 235, 245–46; "X" (George F. Kennan), "The Sources of Soviet Conduct," *Foreign Affairs* 25, no. 4, July 1947, 566–78, 580–82; William G. Hyland, "Containment: 40 Years Later: Introduction," *Foreign Affairs* 65, no. 4, Spring 1987, 827–30; George F. Kennan, "Containment Then and Now," *Foreign Affairs* 65, no. 4, Spring 1987, 885–90. **Kennan, "light-heartedly"**: Ibid. **Herken**: Gregg Herken, *The Georgetown Set: Friends and Rivals in Cold War Washington*, New York: Knopf, 2014, 40. **Kennan on containment**: Gaddis, *George F. Kennan*, 249–50, 260–61, 274–75, 309–11, 342, 477, 605, 625, 697. **Different interpretations of containment**: "Containment," *SPD*, 145–47; Gaddis, *George F. Kennan*, 477–78, 485–88, 658, 672, 680–83, 694; Nicholas Thompson, "A War Best Served Cold," *NYT*, July 31, 2007; Nicholas Thompson, *The Hawk and the Dove: Paul Nitze, George Kennan, and the History of the Cold War*, New York: Holt, 2009, 77; Henry A. Kissinger, "The Age of Kennan," *NYT*, November 10, 2011; Louis Menand, "Getting Real: George F. Kennan's Cold War," *NYer*, November 14, 2011, 76–83, 81, 82, 83. ***Safire's Political Dictionary***: *SPD*, 145. **Kennan told 1996 interviewer**: "Kennan on the Cold War: An Interview on CNN TV," *johndclare.net*, May–June 1996, http://www.johndclare.net/

cold_war7_Kennan_interview.htm, accessed February 12, 2020. **Kennan on how concept made him feel**: Thompson, *The Hawk and the Dove*, 77.

paradigm shift **cartoon**: *NYer*, December 9, 1974, 48. *paradigm, paradigm shift*: Robert Fulford, "The Word 'Paradigm,'" (Toronto) *Globe and Mail*, June 5, 1999; Darin Hayton, "The Use and Abuse of Kuhn's 'Paradigm Shift,'" blog post, January 23, 2016, http://dhayton.haverford.edu/blog/2016/01/23/the-use-and-abuse-of-kuhns-paradigm-shift/, accessed June 17, 2017; Tania Lombrozo, "What Is a Paradigm Shift, Anyway?," *Cosmos & Culture*, NPR, July 18, 2016, https://www.npr.org/sections/13.7/2016/07/18/486487713/what-is-a-paradigm-shift-anyway, accessed January 22, 2018. **Kuhn**: Steve Fuller, *Thomas Kuhn: A Philosophical History for Our Times*, Chicago: University of Chicago Press, 2000; "Thomas Kuhn," *Stanford Encyclopedia of Philosophy*, 2004, 2018, https://plato.stanford.edu/entries/thomas-kuhn/, accessed April 15, 2019; John Naughton, "Thomas Kuhn: The Man Who Changed the Way the World Looked at Science," *The Guardian*, August 18, 2012; John Horgan, "Profile: Reluctant Revolutionary: Thomas S. Kuhn Unleashed 'Paradigm' on the World," *Scientific American* 264, no. 5, May 1991, 40–49; John Horgan, "What Thomas Kuhn Really Thought About Scientific 'Truth,'" *Scientific American Blog Network*, May 23, 2012, https://blogs.scientificamerican.com/cross-check/what-thomas-kuhn-really-thought-about-scientific-truth/, accessed January 19, 2018; John Horgan, "Did Thomas Kuhn Help Elect Donald Trump?," *Scientific American Blog Network*, May 25, 2017, https://blogs.scientificamerican.com/cross-check/did-thomas-kuhn-help-elect-donald-trump/, accessed April 15, 2019. *The Structure of Scientific Revolutions*: Thomas Kuhn, *The Structure of Scientific Revolutions*, 3rd ed., Chicago: University of Chicago Press, 1996; Thomas Kuhn, *The Structure of Scientific Revolutions*, 50th anniversary ed., introductory essay by Ian Hacking, Chicago: University of Chicago Press, 2012, xvii–xxii; Thomas Kuhn, "Second Thoughts on Paradigms," in *The Structure of Scientific Theories*, ed. Frederick Suppe, Urbana: University of Illinois Press, 1974, 459–82. **Kuhn's regret**: Benjamin A. Elman, "It Took a Scientist to Historicize One!," *Historical Studies in the Natural Sciences*, 42, no. 5, November 2012, 500–503.

conventional wisdom: John Kenneth Galbraith, *The Affluent Society*, Boston: Houghton Mifflin, 1958, 7–20.

Christensen, *disrupt*: http://claytonchristensen.com/, accessed April 15, 2019; https://www.christenseninstitute.org/clayton-m-christensen/, accessed April 15, 2019; Joseph L. Bower and Clayton M. Christensen. "Disruptive Technologies: Catching the Wave," *Harvard Business Review* 73, no. 1, January–February 1995, 43–53; Clayton M. Christensen, *The Innovator's Dilemma*, Boston: Harvard Business School, 1997.

disruptive innovation: http://claytonchristensen.com/key-concepts/, accessed April 15, 2019; Rosamund Hutt, "What Is Disruptive Innovation?," *World Economic Forum*, June 25, 2015, https://www.weforum.org/agenda/2016/06/what-is-disruptive-innovation/, accessed May 26, 2017. *Webster's*: This remains Merriam-Webster's basic definition of *disrupt*. https://www.merriam-webster.com/dictionary/disrupt, accessed

February 12, 2020.: Jill Lepore, "The Disruption Machine," *NYer*, June 23, 2014, 30–36; Lepore, *These Truths,* 736; **revival-style meetings**: Ibid., 31. **festival of disruption**: "What Disruptive Innovation Means," The Economist Explains, *The Economist*, January 25, 2015, https://www.economist.com/the-economist-explains/2015/01/25/what-disruptive-innovation-means, accessed May 26, 2017. **Tech Crunch conferences**: Geoff Nunberg, "From TED Talks to Taco Bell, Abuzz with Silicon Valley-Style 'Disruption,'" *Fresh Air*, NPR, April 27, 2015. **Taco Bell, etc.**: Ibid., Alexis C. Madrigal, "Meet Taco Bell's 'Resident Disruptor,'" *ATL*, June 20, 2014, https://www.theatlantic.com/technology/archive/2014/06/meet-taco-bells-resident-disruptor/373153/, accessed April 16, 2019. **Disruptive toothbrush**: "9 Reasons So Many Dentists Recommend This Disruptive Toothbrush," *locker dome*, https://lockerdome.com/quip, accessed April 15, 2019. **theory "coined"**: "Disruptive Innovation," Christensen Institute, https://www.christenseninstitute.org/key-concepts/disruptive-innovation-2/, accessed April 15, 2019.

  innovation: Jill Lepore, "The Disruption Machine," 32; Lepore, *A Is for American,* 58, 187, 195, Lepore, *These Truths,* 52; Emma Green, "Innovation: The History of a Buzzword," *ATL*, June 20, 2013, https://www.theatlantic.com/business/archive/2013/06/innovation-the-history-of-a-buzzword/277067/, accessed February 23, 2018; Benoit Godin, "Innovation: A Conceptual History of an Anonymous Concept," Working Paper No. 21, 2015, Montreal: Project on the Intellectual History of Innovation, http://www.csiic.ca/PDF/WorkingPaper21.pdf, accessed April 15, 2019; Benoit Godin, *Innovation Contested: The Idea of Innovation over the Centuries*, Abingdon, UK: Routledge, 2015. Noah Webster: "Innovation," *American Dictionary of the English Language*, Webster's Dictionary, 1828, http://webstersdictionary1828.com/Dictionary/innovation, accessed February 12, 2020. **Schumpeter**: Lepore, *These Truths,* 735-36; Richard Alm and W. Michael Cox, "Creative Destruction," *EconLib, https://www.econlib.org/library/Enc/CreativeDestruction.html*, accessed September 14, 2020; Sharon Reier, "Half a Century Later, Economist's 'Creative Destruction' Theory Is Apt for the Internet Age: Schumpeter: The Prophet of Bust and Boom," *NYT*, June 10, 2000.

  Christensen's second thoughts: Clayton M. Christensen and Michael Overdorf, "Meeting the Challenge of Disruptive Change," *Harvard Business Review* 78, no. 2, March–April 2000, 66–76; Clayton M. Christensen, Michael Raynor, and Rory McDonald, "What Is Disruptive Innovation?," *Harvard Business Review* 93, no. 12, December 2015, 44–53; Ilan Mochari, "The Startup Buzzword Almost Everyone Uses Incorrectly," *Inc.com*, November 19, 2015, https://www.inc.com/ilan-mochari/clayton-christensen-disruptive-innovation-cheatsheet.html, accessed January 29, 2020; Oliver Staley, "Innovation Guru Clayton Christensen's New Theory Is Meant to Protect You from Disruption," *Quartz*, October 12, 2016, https://qz.com/801706/innovation-guru-clayton-christensens-new-theory-will-help-protect-you-from-disruption/, accessed June 1, 2017.

4. JUST KIDDING

missionary position: Albert Kinsey, Wendell B. Pomeroy, Clyde E. Martin, *Sexual Behavior in the Human Male*, Bloomington: Indiana University Press, 1948, 1998, 373. **Malinowski, "missionary fashion"**: Bronislaw Malinowski, *The Sexual Life of Savages in North-Western Melanesia: An Ethnographic Account of Courtship, Marriage and Family Life Among the Natives of the Trobriand Islands, British, New Guinea*, New York: Reader's League, 1929, 478–79. **Priest**: Robert J. Priest, "Missionary Positions: Christian, Modernist, Postmodernist," *Current Anthropology* 42, no. 1, February 2001, 29–68, 30–31. **Alan Dundes, French sexologist**: Ibid., 49–50. See also Gershon Legman, *Rationale of the Dirty Joke*, New York: Simon & Schuster, 1968, 2006, 545–46. **Burridge**: Robert J. Priest, "Missionary Positions: Christian, Modernist, Postmodernist," 47. **Priest's rejoinder:** Ibid. 58–63; Priest email to author, March 18, 2016. **Translations of "missionary position"**: Priest, "Missionary Positions: Christian, Modernist, Postmodernist," 31. **Lesley**: Craig Lesley, *River Song*, New York: Picador, 1989, 55.

Read, "jubilance": McFedries, *Word Spy*, 11; Michelle Stacey, "At Play in the Language," *NYer*, September 4, 1989, 51–74, 56, 74; Allen Walker Read, "Coast to Coast," *Voice of America*, October 23, 2002, https://learningenglish.voanews.com/a/a-23-a-2002-10-23-3-1-83111172/117929.html, accessed April 17, 2019.

"play spirit": Read, *Milestones in the History of English in America*, 314–17; "The Play Spirit as a Motivation in Semiotic Behavior," 1980, and "The Play Spirit in English," 1982, in Allen Walker Read Papers, The State Historical Society of Missouri. **Mencken**: Mencken, *The American Language, Supplement II*, 647.

Warhol, fifteen minutes of fame: *Time*, October 13, 1967; *Andy Warhol*, Boston: Boston Book and Art, 1968 (reprint of catalog, Andy Warhol exhibition at Moderna Museet, Stockholm, February–March 1968); Victor Bockris, *The Life and Death of Andy Warhol*, New York: Bantam, 1989, 147; "What's the Exact '15 Minutes of Fame' Quote?," *The Warhol: Museum Info*, http://www.warhol.org/museum_info/faq.html, accessed April 18, 2005; email to author from assistant archivist Matt Wrbican, The Warhol Museum, May 3, 2005; Garson O'Toole, "In the Future Everyone Will Be Famous for 15 Minutes," *Quote Investigator*, April 4, 2012, https://quoteinvestigator.com/category/andy-warhol/, accessed January 23, 2017. On his website *Warholiana*, Blake Gopnik compiles sightings of various versions of this Warholism, most recently the artist's observation in 1965 that in the future we'd all be famous for a week. Blake Gopnik, "In the Future, Everyone Will Be World-Famous for 15 Minutes," *Warholiana*, http://warholiana.com/post/81689862604/in-the-future-everyone-will-be-world-famous-for, accessed April 18, 2019.

rope-a-dope: Angelo Dundee, *My View from the Corner*, New York: McGraw-Hill, 2009, 172. Ali biographer Michael Ezra questions how central rope-a-doping was to Ali's victory over Foreman. See Michael Ezra, "How Muhammad Ali's Rope-a-Dope Myth Suckered America," *Deadspin*, October 30, 2014, https://deadspin.

com/how-muhammad-alis-rope-a-dope-myth-suckered-america-1652932623, accessed November 13, 2019.

CNN correspondent: Aaron Brown, *CNN*, October 8, 2001; **financial commentator**: Chuck Butler, "Backing Away from the Treasury Auction Window!," *FXStreet,* January 18, 2018, https://www.fxstreet.com/analysis/backing-away-from-the-treasury-auction-window-201801181247, accessed April 19, 2019.

Read: Read, *Milestones in the History of English in America*, 316.

mugwump: *OED*; *AL*, 106–7; *SDP*, 445–46; Mathews, *Dictionary of Americanisms*, Vol. 2, 1098; Lighter, *Random House Dictionary of American Slang*, Vol. 2, 615–16; Forsyth, *The Horologicon*, 68; Mead, *Word-Coinage*, 178.

Mencken: H. L. Mencken, "The American Language," *The Yale Review* 25, no. 3, March 1936, 538–52, 544, reprinted in Babcock, *The Ordeal of American English*, 53–57, 55.

bunk: Pyles, *Words and Ways of American English*, 165–66; Steinmetz and Kipfer, *The Life of Language*, 209; *SDP*, 89; *M-W*, 73. **Haliburton**: Thomas Chandler Haliburton, *The Attaché*, New York: Stringer & Townsend, 1856, 143. **Woodward**: W. E. Woodward, *Bunk*, New York: Harper, 1923, 2, 4–6.

bug, debug: Raymond, *The New Hacker's Dictionary*, 94–95; Walter Isaacson, "Grace Hopper, Computing Pioneer," *The Harvard Gazette*, December 3, 2014, https://news.harvard.edu/gazette/story/2014/12/grace-hopper-computing-pioneer/, accessed April 18, 2019; Elizabeth Dickason, "Remembering Grace Murray Hopper: A Legend in Her Own Time," June 27, 2011, https://www.doncio.navy.mil/chips/ArticleDetails.aspx?ID=2389, accessed April 18, 2019; Fred Shapiro, "You Can Quote Them," *Yale Alumni Magazine* 73, no. 3, January/February 2010; "The First Computer Bug," *James S. Huggins' Refrigerator Door*, http.//ww.jameshuggins.com/h/tek1/first_computer_bug.html accessed December 6, 2012; "Moth in the Machine: Debugging the Origins of 'Bug,'" *Computerworld*, September 3, 2011, https://www.computerworld.com/article/2515435/moth-in-the-machine--debugging-the-origins-of--bug-.html, accessed January 16, 2017; "The First Computer Debug Bug," *Anomalies Unlimited*, undated, http://www.anomalies-unlimited.com/Science/Grace%20Hooper.html, accessed February 10, 2008; "Computing History Displays: Fifth Floor—Harvard Mark 1: Letter by Grace Hopper Describing the Bug," University of Auckland (New Zealand), https://www.cs.auckland.ac.nz/historydisplays/FifthFloor/LogicAndSwitching/HarvardMark1/HarvardMark1Pictures.php, accessed December 8, 2014; "Log Book with Computer Bug," National Museum of American History, https://americanhistory.si.edu/collections/search/object/nmah_334663, accessed April 18, 2019.

Wiki: American Heritage editors, *Word Histories and Mysteries*, 318–19; Daven Hiskey, "Where the World 'Wiki' Comes From," *Today I Found Out*, October 15, 2010, http://www.todayifoundout.com/index.php/2010/10/where-the-word-wiki-comes-from/, accessed August 20, 2015; "The Honolulu Airport Welcomes You!," http://www.hawaii-vacation-fun.com/honolulu-airport.html, accessed January 31, 2018.

Bluetooth: Elyse Wanshel, "The Mysterious Origins of 21 Tech Terms," January 8, 2015, *Gizmodo*, https://gizmodo.com/the-mysterious-origins-of-21-tech-terms-1678246145 accessed January 16, 2017.

software: Chatfield, *Netymology*, 219–21; Metcalf, *Predicting New Words*, 104–5; Jeremy Norman, "The Origins of the Term 'Software' Within the Context of Computing," *History of Information.com*, August 4, 2014, http://www.historyofinformation.com/detail.php?entryid=936, accessed January 31, 2018.

Niquette: Paul Niquette, "Softword: Provenance for the Word 'Software,'" 2006, http://www.niquette.com/books/softword/tocsoft.html, accessed January 9, 2013; "Part 6, Challenger: John Wilder Tukey," http://www.niquette.com/books/softword/part6.htm, accessed July 8, 2011; "Appendix B—Challenger References," http://niquette.com/books/softword/AppB.htm, accessed April 18, 2019; David Leonhardt, "John Tukey, 85, Statistician; Coined the Word 'Software,'" *NYT*, July 28, 2000.

weblog, blog: *OED*; "Weblogs Rack up a Decade of Posts," *BBC News*, December 17, 2007, http://news.bbc.co.uk/2/hi/technology/7147728.stm, accessed April 18, 2019; Declan McCullagh and Anne Broache, "Blogs Turn 10—Who's the Father?," *CNET News*, March 20, 2007, https://www.cnet.com/news/blogs-turn-10-whos-the-father/, accessed April 18, 2019; Paul McFedries, "blog," *Word Spy*, November 17, 2003, https://wordspy.com/index.php?word=blog, accessed April 18, 2019.

Merholz: Peter Merholz, "Play with Your Words," *peterme.com*, May 17, 2002, https://www.peterme.com/archives/00000205.html, accessed July 8, 2011. **Graham**: Bil Browning, "Gay Blogger Who Invented the Term 'Blogosphere' Dies," *The Bilerico Project*, January 5, 2010, http://bilerico.lgbtqnation.com/2010/01/gay_blogger_who_invented_blogosphere_dies.php, accessed July 8, 2011; Jeff Jarvis, "The Man Is Gone, but Long Live the Blogosphere," *All Things Considered*, NPR, January 6, 2010.

crowdsource: William Safire, "Fat Tail," *NYT*, February 8, 2009; Jeff Howe, "The Rise of Crowdsourcing," *Wired* 14, no. 6, June 2006, 1–4; Howe email to author, July 16, 2014; Jeff Howe, *Crowdsourcing*, New York: Crown Business, 2008, 1–4.

zipless: Erica Jong, *The Fear of Flying*, New York: Holt Rinehart and Winston, 1973, 11; **Douthat**: Ross Douthat, "The Sterile Society," *NYT*, December 2, 2017; **Friedel:** Robert Friedel, *Zipper: An Exploration in Novelty*, New York: Norton, 1994, 214 **"zipless coup"**: Jon Lee Anderson, "A Man of the Shadows," *NYer*, January 24 and 31, 2005, 64.

fashionista: Stephen Fried, *Thing of Beauty: The Tragedy of Supermodel Gia*, New York: Pocket, 1993; Stephen Fried, "I Apologize for Inventing the Word 'Fashionista' 20 Years Ago," *ATL*, April 17, 2013, https://www.theatlantic.com/entertainment/archive/2013/04/i-apologize-for-inventing-the-word-fashionista-20-years-ago/275048/, accessed May 15, 2015; Rebecca Moss, "Why the Term 'Fashionista' Is Misunderstood: The Origin Story of Fashionista," *Elle*, April 18, 2013, https://www.elle.com/culture/news/a16864/stephen-fried-fashionista/, accessed May 25, 2015; Ben Yagoda, "Local Boy Makes Word?," *Lingua Franca—The Chronicle of Higher Education*, August 20, 2014, https://www.chronicle.com/blogs/linguafranca/2014/

08/20/local-boy-makes-word/, accessed October 14, 2015; Penelope Green, "Mirror, Mirror: How Stylish People Don't Describe Themselves," *NYT*, July 4, 1999; *OED*.

scientist: "How the Word 'Scientist' Came to Be," *Talk of the Nation*, NPR, May 21, 2010; Sydney Ross, "Scientist: The Story of a Word," *Annals of Science* 18, no. 2, June 1962, 65–85, 71–75; Sydney Ross, *Nineteenth-Century Attitudes: Men of Science*, Dordrecht, Netherlands: Kluwer, 1991, 1–39; Richard Holmes, *The Age of Wonder: How the Romantic Generation Discovered the Beauty and Terror of Science*, New York: Pantheon, 2008, 449–50. **Ross**: Sydney Ross, *Nineteenth-Century Attitudes*, 10. **Sedgwick**: Holmes, *The Age of Wonder*, 449–50. **Huxley**: Sydney Ross, *Nineteenth-Century Attitudes*, 21.

OK: The most comprehensive source on the history of "OK" is Allan Metcalf's book *OK*. See also: *Cambridge History of the English Language*, Vol. 3, 196–97; *M-W*, 329–31; Hitchings, *The Secret Life of Words*, 303; Bryson, *The Mother Tongue*, 164; Crystal, *The Story of English in 100 Words*, 183–86; "How 'OK' Took Over the World," *BBC News Magazine*, February 18, 2011, https://www.bbc.com/news/magazine-12503686, accessed February 22, 2011.

Andrew Jackson: Allen Walker Read, "Could Andrew Jackson Spell?," *American Speech* 38, no. 3, October 1963, 188–95; John William Ward, *Andrew Jackson: Symbol for an Age*, New York: Oxford University Press, 1955, 84–87; Richard Shenkman, *Legends, Lies & Cherished Myths of American History*, New York: HarperCollins, 1993, 33–35; Metcalf, *Predicting New Words*, 140–43; Metcalf, *OK*, 59–67, 71. **Other etymologies:** Ibid, 87–90.

Read: Metcalf, *OK*, ix–xi; Read, *Milestones*, 123–247; Michelle Stacey, "At Play in the Language," 51–74, 5158; "Allen Walker Read / 'O.K.,'" *Coast to Coast*, Voice of America, October 24, 2002, https://learningenglish.voanews.com/a/a-23-a-2002-10-23-3-1-83111172/117929.html, accessed April 17, 2019.

5. PRANKERY

Irving, Knickerbocker: Mary Weatherspoon Bowden, *Washington Irving*, Boston: Twayne/Hall, 1981, 34; Edwin G. Burrows and Mike Wallace, *Gotham: A History of New York City to 1898*, New York: Oxford University Press, 1998, 417–18; Andrew Burstein, *The Original Knickerbocker: The Life of Washington Irving*, New York: Perseus, 2007, 3–4, 70–87; Brian Jay Jones, *Washington Irving: An American Original*, New York: Arcade, 2008, 89–100; Washington Irving, *The Complete Works of Washington Irving in One Volume*, Paris: Baudry's European Library, 1834, 133. **knickerbocker, knickers, Knicks**: *OED*; *M-W*, 263–65; Christine Palm, "What's Up with the 'Witches' Knickers'?," *Hartford Courant*, July 2, 2006; Joe Schwarez, "Witches Knickers: The Plastic Bag Crisis," *McGill Office for Science and Society*, March 20, 2017, https://www.mcgill.ca/oss/article/environment-quirky-science-science-science-everywhere-you-asked/what-environmental-problem-referred-witches-knickers-ireland, accessed December 17, 2019; "What's a Knickerbocker?," *The Official Site of the*

New York Knicks, https://www.nba.com/knicks/history/whatsaknickerbocker.html, accessed October 17, 2016.

Knickerbocker was actually an established surname among Dutch-descended residents of the Hudson River Valley, including Rep. Herman Knickerbocker, who served in the U.S. Congress from 1809 until 1811 and later was friendly with Washington Irving. See "Herman Knickerbocker [1779–1855] US Congressman," *New Netherland Institute*, https://www.newnetherlandinstitute.org/history-and-heritage/dutch_americans/herman-knickerbocker/, accessed February 14, 2020; "List of People Associated with Albany County, New York, 'Herman Knickerbocker,'" *revolvy*, https://www.revolvy.com/page/Herman-Knickerbocker, accessed March 9, 2020; Andrew Burstein, *The Original Knickerbocker*, 72.

miscegenation: *Miscegenation: The Theory of the Blending of the Races, Applied to the American White Man and Negro*, New York: H. Dexter, Hamilton, 1864; "The Miscegenation Hoax," *The Museum of Hoaxes*, http://hoaxes.org/archive/permalink/the_miscegenation_hoax, accessed June 10, 2015; John C. Waugh, *Reelecting Lincoln*, New York: Crown, 1997, 317–21; Sidney Kaplan, "The Miscegenation Issue in the Election of 1864," in *Interracialism: Black-White Intermarriage in American History, Literature, and Law*, ed. Werner Sollers, New York: Oxford University Press, 2000, 219–65. Kaplan's long essay, which originally ran in the July 1949 issue of *Journal of Negro History*, is an unusually detailed review of this episode and is the primary source of the following citations. **Abolitionist, antislavery publications**: Ibid., 230–31. **Polish expat** (Adam Gurowski): Ibid., 237. **"Miscegenation Proclamation"**: Ibid., 245. **Cincinnati Enquirer**: Ibid., 244. **New Hampshire newspaper**: Ibid., 242. **Locke/Nasby**: Ibid. 240–41. **New York World**: "The Miscegenation Hoax," ibid., 256–57. **Barnum**: P. T. Barnum, *The Humbugs of the World*, New York: Carleton, 1866, 273–83. **Redfern**: Walter Redfern, *Clichés and Coinages*, 246. **Croly's widow**: Sidney Kaplan, "The Miscegenation Issue in the Election of 1864," 261. **Croly's continued use of "amalgamation"**: Ibid.

moxie: The best single source of information about Moxie is Q. David Bowers's well-researched book *The Moxie Encyclopedia*, Vestal, New York: Vestal Press, 1985. See esp. 25–41, 306. See also Jim Baumer, *Moxie: Maine in a Bottle*, Camden, ME: Down East Books, 2012, 4–16; Frank N. Potter, *The Moxie Mystique*, Virginia Beach–Norfolk, VA: Donning, 1981, 1, 4, 6, 17–19; "Moxie Facts," Marietta Soda Museum, http://mariettasodamuseum.com/moxie_facts.htm, accessed March 31, 2006; Paul Dickson, *The Dickson Baseball Dictionary*, 559–60; Morris, *The Word Detective*, 131, 134.

tank: *OED*; Sir Albert G. Stern, *Tanks, 1914–1918: The Log-book of a Pioneer*, London: Hodder and Stoughton, 1919, 8–13, 18, 31–33, 37–39, 50, 52–57, 59–60, 89, 93–102 (see esp. 39); John Glanfield, *The Devil's Chariots*, Stroud, UK: Sutton, 2001, 121–24, 320–21; Winston S. Churchill, *The World Crisis 1911–1918*, New York: Free Press, 2005, 304, 306, 308, 732; "The Battlefield Debut of the Tank, 1916," *Eyewitness to History.com*, http://www.eyewitnesstohistory.com/tank.htm, accessed April 12, 2018.

gobbledygook: *OED*; *SPD*, 281–82; Barry Popik, "Gobbledygook," *The Big Apple*, December 23, 2006, https://www.barrypopik.com/index.php/new_york_city/entry/gobbledygook_maury_maverick_wwii_term, accessed July 5, 2011; Richard B. Henderson, *Maury Maverick: A Political Biography*, Austin: University of Texas Press, 1970, 239–40; Maury Maverick, "The Case Against 'Gobbledygook,'" *NYT Magazine*, May 11, 1944, 11, 35–36. ***gobbledygoo***: Lighter, *Random House Dictionary of American Slang*, Vol. 1, 912; Ayto, *Twentieth Century Words*, 279. **Maverick's salty tongue**: Henderson, *Maury Maverick*, 33–35, 65, 71–73. https://siteresources.worldbank.org/TRANSLATIONSERVICESEXT/Resources/Translation_Style_Guide_English.pdf, accessed April 23, 2019. (footnote) **Samuel Maverick**: Paula Mitchell Marks, "Maverick, Samuel Augustus," *The Handbook of Texas Online*, Texas Historical Association, https://tshaonline.org/handbook/online/articles/fma84, accessed April 4, 2007; David Dary, "Mavericks and Mavericking," Ibid.; *M-W*, 298–89; Alex Frankel, *Wordcraft: The Art of Turning Little Words Into Big Business,* New York: Three Rivers, 2004, 17–19; John Schwartz, "Who You Callin' a Maverick?," *NYT*, October 4, 2008; Maury Maverick, *A Maverick American*, New York: Covici Friede, 1937, 77–80.

bigfoot: Joshua Blu Buhs, *Bigfoot: The Life and Times of a Legend*, Chicago: University of Chicago Press, 2009, 66–87; Blaine McCarty, "The Legends of Bigfoot: Or How I Regained My Manhood," MA thesis, *DigitalCommons@Kennesaw State University*, Winter 2015, 4–6; Mike McPhate, "The Legend of Bigfoot Turns 60 This Month," *California Sun*, August 7, 2018; Ben Cair, "Why Do So Many People Still Want to Believe in Bigfoot?," *Smithsonian*, September 2018, 11–13; "Digging into the Enduring Mythology of Bigfoot," Shereen Merisol Meraji interview with Laura Krantz, *All Things Considered*, NPR, October 14, 2018. ***bigfootology***: Rhettman A. Mullis Jr., "About—Bigfootology," *bigfootology.com*, accessed October 15, 2018. ***bigfootologist***: Wiktionary. **high-powered figures, *bigfoot* as verb**: *SPD*, 51.

sasquatch: Joshua Blu Buhs, *Bigfoot*, 51–58; Nicki Thomas, "Sasquatch," *The Canadian Encyclopedia*, January 21, 2007, https://www.thecanadianencyclopedia.ca/en/article/sasquatch, accessed October 18, 2018; Hammerson Peters, "How the Sasquatch Got Its Name," *Mysteries of Canada*, July 12, 2018, https://www.mysteriesofcanada.com/bc/how-the-sasquatch-got-its-name/, accessed March 2, 2020; Martin J. Clemens, "Sasquatch by Any Other Name . . . Is Just a Man?" *Daily Mail*, January 26, 2016.

Keely: Mead, *Word-Coinage*, 1; Daniel W. Herring, "The Keely Motor Hoax," from Daniel W. Herring, *Foibles and Fallacies of Science*, New York: Van Nostrand, 1924, reprinted at https://www.lockhaven.edu/~dsimanek/museum/keely/keely-h.htm, accessed November 16, 2015; Brian Taylor, "How John Keely Screwed Investors and Tricked the World with His Perpetual Motion Machine," *Business Insider*, December 10, 2013, https://www.businessinsider.com/john-keelys-perpetual-motion-machine-2013-12, accessed January 17, 2017; Theo Paijmans, *Free Energy Pioneer: John Worrell Keely*, Lilburn, GA: IllumiNet Press, 1998, 9, 85–87, 162–63, 176–83.

grunge: Rick Marin, "Grunge: A Success Story," *NYT*, November 15, 1992; "Grunge Speak," *The Museum of Hoaxes* http://hoaxes.org/archive/permalink/grunge_speak, accessed June 10, 2015; Sam Kim, "Swingin' on the Flippity Flop: The Grunge Speak Hoax," *The World*, PRI, September 20, 2018; Paul de Barnes, "Meet the Punk Who Saved Sub Pop," *Seattle Times*, January 13, 2016.

mountweazels: Jones, *Haggard Hawks and Paltry Poltroons*, 245–50; Henry Alford, "Not a Word," *NYer*, August 29, 2005, 62; Patricia T. O'Conner and Stewart Kellerman, "In Search of the Wild Mountweazel," *Grammarphobia*, September 15, 2011, https://www.grammarphobia.com/blog/2011/09/mountweazel.html, accessed January 13, 2016; Michael Quinion, "Nihilartikel," *World Wide Words*, November 7, 2009, http://www.worldwidewords.org/weirdwords/ww-nih1.htm, accessed February 1, 2018.

funistrada: Steinmetz and Kipfer, *The Life of Language*, 240: Paul Dickson, *Chow: A Cook's Tour of Military Food:* New York, Plume, 1978. "Providing Leelanau County with a Taste of Italy," Trattoria Funistrada, https://trattoria-funistrada.com/, December 29, 2017.

Gothamites, Gotham: *OED*; *M-W*, 264; Allen, *The City in Slang*, 241, 256; Mead, *Word-Coinage*, 2; Andrew Burstein, *The Original Knickerbocker*, 56, 268; Carmen Nigro, "So Why Do We Call It Gotham, Anyway?," *The New York Public Library Blogs*, January 25, 2011, https://www.nypl.org/blog/2011/01/25/so-why-do-we-call-it-gotham-anyway, accessed October 11, 2016; Barry Popik, "Gothamist (inhabitant of Gotham)," *The Big Apple*, December 20, 2011, https://www.barrypopik.com/index.php/new_york_city/entry/gothamist_inhabitant_of_gotham/, accessed October 11, 2016. **Lamb**: Charles Lamb, *The Complete Works of Charles Lamb in Prose and Verse*, London: Chatto & Windus, 1901, 241; Edwin G. Burrows and Mike Wallace, *Gotham*, 416. ***Times* obituary**: Margalit Fox, "Janet Wolfe, Gleeful Gothamite on a First-Name Basis with Her Era, Dies at 101," *NYT*, December 7, 2015.

6. TAUNT TERMS: EURO

big bang, c-field: *OED*; Fred Hoyle, *The Nature of the Universe*, rev. ed., New York: Harper, 1960, 124; Fred Hoyle, *Home Is Where the Wind Blows*, Mill Valley, CA: University Science, 1994, 255–56, 353, 401–6, 412–14; Simon Mitton, *Conflict in the Cosmos: Fred Hoyle's Life in Science*, Washington, DC: Joseph Henry, 2005, 124–25, 134–36, 139–40, 146–47, 208–9, 238, 356; Nicholas Bakalar, "Ripples of the Big Bang Are Seen Through 'The Times.'" *NYT*, November 17, 2014; Helge Kragh, "Big Bang: The Etymology of a Name," *Astronomy & Geophysics* 54, no. 2, April 2013, 2.28–2.30, https://doi.org/10.1093/astrogeo/att035, accessed April 29, 2019; "Hoyle on the Radio: Creating the 'Big Bang,'" *Fred Hoyle: An Online Exhibition*, https://www.joh.cam.ac.uk/library/special_collections/hoyle/exhibition/radio, accessed April 26, 2016. **Hoyle obituaries**: "Sir Fred Hoyle; Coined 'Big Bang,'" *LAT*, August 23, 2001; Walter Sullivan, "Fred Hoyle Dies at 86; Opposed 'Big Bang' but Named It," *NYT*, August 22, 2001; Bernard Lovell, "Sir Fred Hoyle," *The Guardian*, August 23, 2001; Cormac

O'Raifeartaigh, "Fred Hoyle, the Brilliant Man Who Lost the Big Bang Debate," *Irish Times*, October 29, 2015; Greg Demme and Jonathan Sarfati, "Big Bang Critic Dies (Fred Hoyle)," *Journal of Creation* 15, no. 3, December 2001, 6–7. **Renaming contest**: Metcalf, *Predicting New Words*, 137; "New Name for the Big Bang? Contest Judges Can't Find Anything Better in the Universe," *Seattle Times*, February 4, 1994; "Still the Big Bang," *Baltimore Sun*, February 7, 1994; Henry M. Morris, "The Big Bust," Institute of Creation Research, May 1, 1994, https://www.icr.org/article/750/, accessed April 29, 2019; "Bagging the Universe," *Salient*, May 28, 2007, http://salient.org.nz/2007/05/bagging-the-universe/, accessed December 18, 2012.

namby-pamby: *OED*; *M-W*, 314–15; "Namby-Pamby: or, A Panegyric on the New Versification," *Representative Poetry Online*, University of Toronto Libraries, https://rpo.library.utoronto.ca/poems/namby-pamby-or-panegyric-new-versification, accessed April 29, 2019; American Heritage editors, *Word Histories and Mysteries*, 187; Michael Quinion, "Namby-pamby," *World Wide Words*, October 29, 2005, http://www.worldwidewords.org/weirdwords/ww-nam1.htm, accessed April 29, 2019; "The Meaning and Origin of the Expression: Namby Pamby," *The Phrase Finder*, https://www.phrases.org.uk/meanings/namby-pamby.html, accessed May 14, 2018.

impressionism: "About Impressionism," http://www.impressionism.org/teachimpress/browse/aboutimpress.htm, accessed June 9, 2015; Linda Nochlin, *Impressionism and Post-Impressionism: Sources and Documents*, Englewood Cliffs, NJ: Prentice-Hall, 1966, 10–14.

bureaucracy: "Jacques-Claude-Marie Vincent, Seigneur de Gournay, 1712–1759," *The History of Economic Thought Website*, http://www.hetwebsite.net/het/profiles/gournay.htm, accessed October 17, 2016; Williams, *Keywords*, 49; "Bureaucracy" Becomes a Four-Letter Word," William H. Starbuck, *Harvard Business Review* 83, no. 10, October 2005, 17.

silhouette: *OED*; Mead, *Word-Coinage*, 56; Charles Frederick Partington, *The British Cyclopaedia of the Arts, Sciences, History, Geography, Literature, Natural History, and Biography*, London: Orr, 1838, 688. Alternative suggestions for the origin of *silhouette* based on different aspects of Etienne de Silhouette's life and practices can be found at Matthew Dennison, "The Art of the Silhouette," *Country Life*, May 31, 2016, https://www.countrylife.co.uk/luxury/art-and-antiques/the-art-of-the-silhouette-90279, accessed October 14, 2016; Simon Kemp, "Great French Lives: Etienne de Silhouette," September 23, 2015, https://bookshelf.mml.ox.ac.uk/2015/09/23/great-french-lives-etienne-de-silhouette/, accessed October 14, 2016; *Online Etymology Dictionary*, https://www.etymonline.com/word/silhouette, accessed January 14, 2016; "What Is the Origin of the Word 'Silhouette'?," https://en.oxforddictionaries.com/explore/what-is-the-origin-of-the-word-silhouette/, accessed April 30, 2019.

guillotine: *OED*; *M-W*, 206–7; Richard Cavendish, "Death of Joseph-Ignace Guillotin," *History Today* 64, no. 3, March 2014, https://www.historytoday.com/archive/months-past/death-joseph-ignace-guillotin, accessed March 18, 2016; "Biography of Joseph Ignace Guillotin," *TheBiography*, https://thebiography.us/en/

guillotin-joseph-ignace, accessed March 18, 2016; J. D. Thomas, "The Fate of Doctor Guillotin," March 28, 2011, *Accessible Archives*, https://www.accessible-archives.com/2011/03/the-fate-of-doctor-guillotin/, accessed March 18, 2016; "Biography of Joseph Ignace Guillotin," *Whonamedit? A Dictionary of Medical Eponyms*, https://www.whonamedit.com/doctor.cfm/2275.html, accessed March 18, 2016; "Joseph Ignace Guillotin—Biography," *Chambers Edinburgh Journal* (1844), in *Today in Science History*, https://todayinsci.com/G/Guillotin_Joseph/GuillotinJoseph-Bio(1844).htm, accessed March 18, 2016.

ideology: Steinmetz, *Semantic Antics*, 110; Williams, *Keywords*, 153–57; Robert J. Richards, "Ideology and the History of Science," *Biology and Philosophy* 8, no. 1, 1993, 103–8; Radhika Sanghani, "Why Wonder Woman's 'Feminist Ideology' Is No Mistake," *The Telegraph*, June 1, 2017.

tabloid: Ciardi, *Good Words to You*, 277–78; Flavell, *Dictionary of Word Origins*, 232–33; Keyes, *I Love It When You Talk Retro*, 108–9. **Hands**: Vicki Lee Brumagin, *A Study of Women in American Journalism from 1696 to 1972*, MA thesis, California State University, Northridge, June 1972, 71; Helen Moyes, Interview, "Oral Evidence on the Suffragette and Suffragist Movements," The Women's Library, London University: London School of Economics, Videocassette (VHS); Charles E. Hands, "The Lady War Correspondent," *Sydney Morning Herald*, December 3, 1898. **suffragette**: *OED*; Elizabeth Crawford, *The Women's Suffrage Movement: A Reference Guide 1866–1928*, London: Routledge, 1999, 452; Ray Strachey, *The Cause*, London: Virago, 1928, 1978, 302; Dame Christabel Pankhurst, *Unshackled*, London: Hutchinson, 1959, 62; Lisa Tickner, *The Spectacle of Women: Imagery of the Suffrage Campaign 1907–14*, Chicago: University of Chicago Press, 1998, 8, 277.

lumpectomy: "The Word 'Lumpectomy' Was a Surgeon's Insult," *Medical Innovation Bill*, April 9, 2014, http://medicalinnovationbill.co.uk/the-word-lumpectomy-was-a-surgeons-insult/, accessed June 3, 2015; Leslie Wise, "The Role for Mastectomy Is Very Limited: Lumpectomy Is the Usual Choice," in *Breast Cancer: Controversies in Management*, ed. Leslie Wise and Houston Johnson Jr., Leander, TX: Futura, 1995, 105–25; Geoffrey Keynes, *The Gates of Memory*, London: Oxford University Press, 1983, 212–17; Siddhartha Mukherjee, *The Emperor of All Maladies*, New York: Scribner, 2010, 193–201; Jane Brody, "New Treatment Views Scored," *NYT*, May 20, 1971.

meritocracy: Michael Young, *The Rise of the Meritocracy*, New Brunswick, NJ: Transaction, 1958, 1994, xi–xvii, 11; Michael Young, "Meritocracy Revisited," *Society* 31, no. 6, September–October, 1994, 87–89; Michael Young, "Down with Meritocracy," *The Guardian*, June 28, 2001. (footnote) **Fox**: Alan Fox, "Class and Equality," *Socialist Commentary*, May 1956, 11–13, cited in Jo Littler, "Meritocracy as Neoliberal Mantra," *DiscoverSociety*, October 2, 2018, https://discoversociety.org/2018/10/02/meritocracy-as-neoliberal-mantra/, accessed May 1, 2019.

Iron Lady: Will Stewart, "Revealed: Red Army Colonel Who Dubbed Maggie the Iron Lady . . . and Changed History," *Daily Mail*, February 24, 2007; Max Fisher,

"'Irony Lady': How a Moscow Propagandist Gave Margaret Thatcher Her Famous Nickname," *WP*, April 8, 2013; Robert Evans, "Witness: 'The Iron Lady'—My Part in Her Ascent," *Reuters*, April 8, 2013.

7. TAUNT TERMS: U.S.

gerrymander: "The Gerry-mander," *Boston Gazette*, March 26, 1812, 2. Although there are various accounts of how the term *gerrymander* the originated, *Columbian Centinel* editor Benjamin Russell himself vouched for the one involving James Ogilvie in his office. Many believe that the unsigned engraving of a "Gerry-mander" was drawn by Gilbert Stuart, but stronger evidence points to the less prominent Elkanah Tisdale as its actual creator. On both these points, see John Ward Dean, "The Gerrymander," *Potter's American Monthly* 2, 1873, 276, and Henry F. Griffin, "The Gerrymander," *Outlook* 97, January 28, 1911, 186–93. See also *M-W*, 195–96; Metcalf, *Predicting New Words*, 195–96; Elmer Cummings Griffith, *The Rise and Development of the Gerrymander*, Chicago: Scott Foresman, 1907, 17–20; Kenneth C. Martis, "The Original Gerrymander," *Political Geography* 27, no. 8, November 2008, 833–39; Kenneth C. Martis, "Gerrymandering," http://pages.geo.wvu.edu/~kmartis/index.php/gerry-mandering/, accessed April 24, 2019; Eric Trickey, "Where Did the Term 'Gerrymander' Come From?," *AskSmithsonian*, July 20, 2017, https://www.smithsonianmag.com/history/where-did-term-gerrymander-come-180964118/#ucr7Te1zkpKyz7S6.99, accessed May 1, 2019; "The Birth of the Gerrymander," *Massachusetts Historical Society*, September 2008, https://www.masshist.org/object-of-the-month/objects/the-birth-of-the-gerrymander-2008-09-01, accessed May 1, 2019; "Tisdale, Elkanah—Portrait of a Man," *American Miniature Portraits*, http://americanminiatures.blogspot.com/2007/11/tisdale-elkanah-portrait-of-man.html, accessed May 23, 2011.

Hoosiers: Mead, *Word-Coinage*, 199; *M-W*, 224–26; *Indiana State Facts*, https://www.in.gov/auditor/files/State_Facts.pdf, accessed May 2, 2019; Jeffrey Graf, "The Word *Hoosier*," unpublished, http://www.indiana.edu/~librcsd/internet/extra/hoosier.html, accessed October 12, 2016. For a fuller report by Graf, see https://libraries.indiana.edu/sites/default/files/The%20Word%20Hoosier-Revised-and-Expanded-2018.pdf, accessed May 2, 2019; Katie Mettler, "'Hoosier' Is Now the Official Name for Indiana Folk. But What Does It Even Mean?," *WP*, January 13, 2017.

Indianapolis: Although the daughter of a colleague of Judge Sullivan's named Samuel Merill later claimed that her father came up with this name, historians generally give the nod to Sullivan. See William Robeson Holloway, *Indianapolis: A Historical and Statistical Sketch of the Railroad City, a Chronicle of Its Social, Municipal, Commercial and Manufacturing Progress, with Full Statistical Tables*, Indianapolis: Indianapolis Journal Print, 1870, 10; Jacob Platt Dunn, *Greater Indianapolis: The History, the Industries, the Institutions, and the People of a City of Homes*, Vol. 1, Indianapolis: Unigraphic, 1910, 26–27; Jacob Piatt Dunn, *Indiana and Indianans: A History of Aboriginal and Territorial*

Indiana and the Century of Statehood, Chicago: American Historical Society, 1919, 363–65; Lisa Lorentz, "Welcome to Suwarrow, Indiana," November 8, 2013, *Historic Indianapolis.com*, https://historicindianapolis.com/friday-favorites-naming-this-city/, accessed October 11, 2016; *Indianapolis Star*, December 9, 1923; *A Biographical History of Eminent and Self-made Men of the State of Indiana*, Cincinnati: Western Biographical, 1880, 48; Joseph Herman Schauinger, "Jeremiah C. Sullivan, Hoosier Jurist," *Indiana Magazine of History* 37, no. 3, September 1941, 217–36.

The Lily: Anne C. Coon, *Hear Me Patiently: The Reform Speeches of Amelia Jenks Bloomer*, New York: Praeger, 1994, 25. *The Lily* was revived in 2017 in homage to America's first female-owned publication; in further homage, the *WP* has a section called "The Lily." **Bloomer**: D. C. Bloomer, *Life and Writings of Amelia Bloomer*, New York: Schocken, 1895, 1975, x–xii, 7–14, 65–74, 82, 163–64; Margaret Farrand Thorp, *Female Persuasion: Six Strong-Minded Women*, New Haven, CT: Yale University Press, 1949, 107–42; Coon, *Hear Me Patiently*, 2–25, 34–36, 62; Ellen Carol DuBois, ed., *Elizabeth Cady Stanton, Susan B. Anthony: Correspondence, Writing, Speeches*, New York: Schocken, 1981, 15–16, 37–40, 54–55; Elizabeth Cady Stanton, *Eighty Years and More: Reminiscences of Elizabeth Cady Stanton*, New York: Source Book Press, 1898, 1970, 200–203; Charles Neilson Gattey, *The Bloomer Girls*, New York: Coward-McCann, 1967, 56–79, 111–14, 170; Smith, *Household Words*, 1–34, 173–74; *OED*.

semantic shift/change: Elizabeth Closs Traugott, "Semantic Change," Linguistics, Oxford Research Encyclopedias, http://oxfordre.com/linguistics/view/10.1093/acrefore/9780199384655.001.0001/acrefore-9780199384655-e-323, accessed April 25, 2019. Jones, *The Accidental Dictionary*, includes many examples of such a shift.

guy: *M-W*, 208; Mathews, *Dictionary of Americanisms*, Vol. 1, 761; Lighter, *Random House Dictionary of American Slang*, Vol. 2, 1003–4; Wallraff, *Word Court*, 63–65; Metcalf, *From Skedaddle to Selfie*, 163–65; Roz Young, "'Guy Attains Respectability,'" *Dayton Daily News*, January 3, 1998; "9 Things You Never Knew About Guy Fawkes," *The Telegraph*, October 31, 2017; **Chesterton**: Mencken, *The American Language*, 254; G. K. Chesterton, *On Lying in Bed and Other Essays by G. K. Chesterton*, ed. Alberto Manguel, Calgary, Alberta: Bayeux Arts, 2000, 416. After this manuscript was largely completed, Allan Metcalf published a thorough exploration of the word *guy*: Metcalf, *The Life of Guy*. A summary of his findings can be found in Allan Metcalf, "The Surprising Origins of the Phrase 'You Guys,'" *Time*, September 30, 2019, https://time.com/5688255/you-guys/, accessed December 19, 2019.

muckraker: *OED*; *SPD*, 443–35; Keyes, *I Love It When You Talk Retro*, 109–10. Theodore Roosevelt referenced "The Man with the Muck Rake," John Bunyan, *Pilgrim's Progress*, New York: Collier, 1909, 205.

spread, Gould: Stephen Jay Gould, *Hen's Teeth and Horse's Toes: Further Reflections in Natural History*, New York: Norton 2010, 276; Mead, *Word-Coinage*, 5; *OED*.

Mencken, monkey trial, Bible Belt: "Bible Belt," *Dictionary of Christianese*, July 17, 2012, https://www.dictionaryofchristianese.com/bible-belt/, accessed March 25, 2016; *Full Text of "Coverage of the Scopes Trial by H. L. Mencken,"* https://archive.org/stream/

CoverageOfTheScopesTrialByH.l.Mencken/ScopesTrialMencken.txt, accessed March 25, 2016; "Mencken Epithets Rouse Dayton's Ire," *NYT*, July 17, 1925.

whistlestop: Mathews, *A Dictionary of Americanisms*, Vol. 2, 1860; Elyse Bruce, "Whistle-Stop Campaign," *Historically Speaking*, June 9, 2015, https://idiomation. wordpress.com/tag/whistle-stop-campaign/, accessed October 13, 2016; Philip White, *Whistlestop: How 31,000 Miles of Train Travel, 352 Speeches, and a Little Midwest Gumption Saved the Presidency of Harry Truman*, Lebanon, NH: ForeEdge/ UPNE, 2014, 61; "How the Term 'Whistle Stop' Originated," http://www.krohm. com/tewsp/kv/whistle.html, accessed October 13, 2016; John Barbour, "Bound for Victory: Truman's Whistle-Stop Swing Aided Come-from-Behind Win," *LAT*, September 13, 1992; Allen, *The City in Slang*, 254; Barnhart and Metcalf, *America in So Many Words*, 229–30; Robert Underhill, *FDR and Harry: Unparalleled Lives*, Westport, CT: Greenwood, 1996, 65; Clark M. Clifford, with Richard Holbrooke, *Counsel to the President: A Memoir*, New York: Random House, 1991, 202.

pollster: Lindsay Rogers, *The Pollsters: Public Opinion, Politics, and Democratic Leadership*, New York: Knopf, 1949. Political scientist Amy Fried has written extensively on polling and those who poll. See especially Amy Fried, "The Forgotten Lindsay Rogers and the Development of American Political Science," *The American Political Science Review* 100, no. 4, 2006, 555–61 and Amy Fried, *Pathways to Polling*, New York: Routledge, 2012, 81–82. See also Jean Converse, *Survey Research*, New York: Routledge, 2017, 254–55. **Lepore**: Jill Lepore, "Politics and the New Machine," *NYer*, November 16, 2015, 36; Lepore, *These Truths*, 542–43, 546, 852; "Polling Is Ubiquitous, but Is It Bad for Democracy?," interview with Jill Lepore, *Fresh Air*, NPR, February 11, 2016; Cynthia Crossen, *Tainted Truth: The Manipulation of Fact in America*, New York: Simon & Schuster, 1994, 7, 100, 105, 106, 235, also uses the term "poller."

Best and Brightest: David Halberstam, *The Best and the Brightest*, New York: Random House, 1972; *Smithsonian*, December 2015.

Cartoons, Leech drawing in Punch: 1843 London exhibit: "Substance and Shadow," *The Victorian Web*, http://www.victorianweb.org/art/illustration/leech/101. html, accessed June 9, 2015; Mark Bryant, "The First Cartoon," *History Today* 55, no. 11, November 2005, 58–59; "John Leech: The Cartoonist Who Gave Us Christmas Past," *The Conversation*, December 14, 2017, https://theconversation.com/john-leech-the-cartoonist-who-gave-us-christmas-past-88977, accessed May 8, 2019.

8. COINS IN BUBBLES

curate's egg: Michael Quinion, "Curate's Egg," *World Wide Words*, June 17, 2000, http://www.worldwidewords.org/qa/qa-cur1.htm, accessed November 12, 2015; Pascal Tréguer, "Meaning and Origin of 'Curate's Egg,'" *word histories*, February 20, 2017, https://wordhistories.net/2017/02/20/curates-egg/, accessed January 31, 2020; Hugo Vickers's review of "The Crown," *Daily Mail*, October 15, 2016.

bedside manner: Although George du Maurier is widely credited with coining *bedside manner*, an earlier appearance has been reported by Pascal Tréguer on his *word histories* website: https://wordhistories.net/2018/08/01/bedside-manner-origin/, accessed May 18, 2019. In an 1870 novel, *Stepping Heavenword* by American author Elizabeth Prentiss, a character says of a doctor, "He had such 'sweet bed-side manners,'" Elizabeth Prentiss, *Stepping Heavenward*, New York: A.D.F. Randolph, 1870, 237.

Inge: M. Thomas Inge, *Comics as Culture*, Jackson: University Press of Mississippi, 1990, 17–27. **Bryson**: Bryson, *Made in America*, 199. **Mort Walker**: Walker, *The Lexicon of Comicana*, Port Chester, NY: Museum of Cartoon Art, 1980, 46.

Churchill's observation: Winston Churchill, *Thoughts and Adventures*, New York: Norton, 1990, 1932, 11–22.

Nast, Uncle Sam, Tweed: "Famous Cartoonist Made Donkey and Elephant the Symbols of Political Parties," *WP*, January 27, 2012; *M-W*, 483–84; O'Conner and Kellerman, *Origins of the Specious*, 107; Fiona Deans Halloran, *Thomas Nast: The Father of Modern Political Cartoons*, Chapel Hill: University of North Carolina Press, 2012, 60, 105; Albert Bigelow Paine, *Thomas Nast: His Period and His Pictures*, New York: Chelsea, 1904, 1980, 164, 197; Leo Hershkowitz, *Tweed's New York: Another Look*, Garden City, NY: Anchor/Doubleday, 1978, xviii; Kenneth D. Ackerman, *Boss Tweed: The Rise and Fall of the Corrupt Pol Who Conceived the Soul of Modern New York*, New York: Carroll & Graf, 2005, 7–8, 371.

teddy bear: *OED*; "The Real Teddy Bear Story," *Theodore Roosevelt Association*, https://www.theodoreroosevelt.org/content.aspx?page_id=22&club_id=991271&module_id=333084, accessed June 5, 2020; "Happy Birthday, Teddy Bear!," *The History Blog*, http://www.thehistoryblog.com/archives/40698/comment-page-1, accessed June 5, 2020. Despite the ubiquity of the Michtoms' origin story, at least one teddy bear historian questions its veracity: "The Teddy Bear," *factoids*, http://www.faktoider.nu/teddybear_eng.html, accessed June 20, 2011.

McCarthyism: In his memoir *A Cartoonist's Life* (New York: Macmillan, 1993, 133), Herbert Block wrote, "The word 'McCarthyism' originated—with no thought of creating a new term—in a cartoon in March 1950." Four decades earlier, in *The Herblock Book* (Boston: Beacon, 1952, 144), Herblock was more circumspect, writing of *McCarthyism*, "That word seems to have originated in the elephant-and-smear-buckets cartoon." Noting that the March 28, 1950, *Christian Science Monitor* editorial titled "Choice for Republicans" that mentions *McCarthyism* is dated a day before Herblock's cartoon, historian Simon Appleford concludes this is unlikely to be coincidental. Appleford thinks that the cartoonist probably used it as his inspiration for including *McCarthyism* in his March 29 cartoon, but concedes that we will never know if this is the case or not. He notes that via syndication, Herblock's cartoon certainly gave the term wider circulation than the *Christian Science Monitor* editorial did. See Simon Appleford, "Offensive Weapons: Herblock and the Visual Rhetoric of Postwar Liberalism," PhD dissertation, University of Illinois at Urbana–Champaign, 2014, 112–16, https://core.ac.uk/download/pdf/29175088.pdf, accessed May 9, 2019. Joseph McCarthy himself made an unsuccessful attempt to co-opt the term, titling a 1952 book of his *McCarthyism: The Fight for America*, New York: Devin-Adams, 1952.

DeBeck: Mort Walker, *Barney Google and Snuffy Smith*, Wilton, CT: Comicana, 1994, 78. **Feiffer**: Jules Feiffer, *The Great Comic Book Heroes*, New York: Dial, 1965, 4.

Dorgan: Even though it was written without the benefit of modern search tools, by far the most comprehensive and reliable resource on Tad Dorgan's contributions to the English vernacular is Leonard Zwilling's *A TAD Lexicon* (see above). See also Hendrickson, *Word and Phrase Origins*, 703; Partridge, *A Dictionary of Catch Phrases*, 289–90; "'Tad,' Cartoonist, Dies in His Sleep," *NYT*, May 3, 1929; W. L. Warner, "Tad Dorgan Is Dead," *American Speech* 4, no. 6, August 1929, 430; *AL*, 561; S. J. Perelman, "How I Learned to Wink and Leer," *NYT Magazine*, April 23, 1978, 16, 80, 82–83.

duck soup: Zwilling, *A TAD Lexicon*, 34; Lighter, *Random House Dictionary of American Slang*, Vol. 1, 668. Marx Brothers' movie *Duck Soup*: Matthew Coniam, *The Annotated Marx Brothers: A Filmgoer's Guide to In-Jokes, Obscure References and Sly Details*, Jefferson, NC: McFarland, 2015, 92–101, 100–101.

nobody home: Zwilling, *A TAD Lexicon*, 59. **bonehead**: Ibid., 19; *OED*. **bum's rush**: Zwilling, *A TAD Lexicon*, 21. **misattributions**: Ibid., 11. **yes-man**: *OED*; Mencken, *The American Language*, Supplement 2, 647, 701; Barry Popik, "Yes Man," *The Big Apple*, May 14, 2012 (citing its use in the *Fort Wayne* [IN] *Sentinel* on March 11, 1911), https://www.barrypopik.com/index.php/new_york_city/entry/yes_man, accessed May 13, 2019.

gate-crasher: Barry Popik, "(Gate) Crasher," *The Big Apple*, June 15, 2005, https://www.barrypopik.com/index.php/new_york_city/entry/gate_crasher, accessed February 17, 2020; Zwilling, *A TAD Lexicon*, 39. **horsefeathers**: Ibid., 46; "The Meaning and Origin of the Expression: Horse Feathers," *The Phrase Finder*, https://www.phrases.org.uk/meanings/horse-feathers.html, accessed February 17, 2020; claimed by DeBeck: Michael Quinion, "Horsefeathers," *World Wide Words*, May 17, 2006, http://www.worldwidewords.org/qa/qa-hor1.htm accessed February 17, 2020; Lighter, *Random House Dictionary of American Slang*, Vol. 2, 163 (citing DeBeck's response to an inquiry, *American Speech* 4, no. 2, December, 1928, 98).

DeBeck: Inge, *Comics as Culture*, 69–76; Walker, *Barney Google and Snuffy Smith*, 77–100 (on DeBeck's terms, see especially 78, 90, 115, 127–28); R. C. Harvey, "Barney Google and Snuffy Smith: Billy DeBeck, Fred Lasswell, and John Rose," *The Comics Journal*, February 23, 2012, http://www.tcj.com/barney-google-and-snuffy-smith-billy-debeck-fred-lasswell-and-john-rose/, accessed April 10, 2017; Anthony Harkins, "From 'Sweet Mamas' to 'Bodacious' Hillbillies: Billy DeBeck's Impact on American Culture," *Studies in American Humor*, n.s., 3, no. 13, 2006, 55–72; Judith O'Sullivan, *The Great American Comic Strip: One Hundred Years of Cartoon Art*, Boston: Bulfinch/Little, Brown, 1990, 158; Brian Walker, *The Comics Before 1945*, New York: Abrams, 2004, 148. **google**: Inge, *Comics as Culture*, 20–21. **Sweet Mama**: Ibid., 72; Walker, *The Comics Before 1945*, 78; R. C. Harvey, "Barney Google and Snuffy Smith," 90. **heebie-jeebies**, **hotsy-totsy**: Walker, *The Comics Before 1945*, 78, 90; Michael Quinion, "Heeby-jeebies,"

World Wide Words, May 21, 2006, http://www.worldwidewords.org/qa/qa-hee1.htm, accessed June 16, 2017; Ben Zimmer, "How Did We Get the Heebie-Jeebies?," *Visual Thesarus*, July 29, 2015, https://www.visualthesaurus.com/cm/wordroutes/how-did-we-get-the-heebie-jeebies/, accessed May 13, 2019. **Vance Rudolph**: Inge, *Comics as Culture*, 72. **Mountaineer vocabulary**: Ibid., 70–75, especially 75; Walker, *The Comics Before 1945*, 115, 127–28. **DeBeck's pride**: Moira Davison Reynolds, *Comic Strip Artists in American Newspapers*, *Comic Strip Artists in American Newspapers, 1945–1980*, Jefferson, NC: McFarland, 2003, 38.

    Capp, *Li'l Abner*: Maurice Horn, ed., *100 Years of American Newspaper Comics*, New York: Gramercy, 1996, 176–77; Miss Celania, "The Enduring Legacy of Li'l Abner," *Mental Floss*, July 14, 2011, http://mentalfloss.com/article/28236/enduring-legacy-lil-abner, accessed April 13, 2017; E. J. Kahn, "OO!!! (SOB) EEP'!!. (GULP!!) ZOWIE!!!," *NYer*, November 29, December 6, 1947, 45–52, 54–57; 46–50, 52, 54–58, 61; Al Capp, *My Well-Balanced Life on a Wooden Leg: Memoirs*, Santa Barbara, CA: John Daniel, 1991; Arthur Asa Berger, *Li'l Abner: A Study in American Satire*, Independence, KY: Twayne, 1969, Jackson: University Press of Mississippi, 1994; Alexander Theroux, *The Enigma of Al Capp*, Seattle: WA: Fantagraphics, 1999; Michael Schumacher and Denis Kitchen, *Al Capp: A Life to the Contrary*, New York: Bloomsbury USA, 2013. **John Steinbeck**: Al Capp, *The World of L'il Abner*, intro. by John Steinbeck, New York: Farrar, Straus and Young, 1953, ii. ***druthers***: *OED* cites uses of "druther" by Mark Twain, and in this line in an 1895 issue of *Dial*: "Bein's I caint have my druthers . . ."; **names of characters, expressions**: Kahn, "OO!!!," 46; Theroux, *The Enigma of Al Capp*, 24–29, 34; Schumacher and Kitchen, *Al Capp*, 81–82, 88–90. ***skunk works*, Lockheed**: Webber Feinsilber, *Merriam-Webster's Dictionary of Allusions*, 502–3; Michael Quinion, "Skunk Works," *World Wide Words*, August 10, 2002, http://www.worldwidewords.org/qa/qa-sku1.htm, accessed December 24, 2006; "Skunk Works® Origin Story," *lockheedmartin.com*, https://www.lockheedmartin.com/en-us/who-we-are/business-areas/aeronautics/skunkworks/skunk-works-origin-story.html, accessed May 14, 2019; "Skunk Works® Legal Notice," *lockheedmartin.com*, https://www.lockheedmartin.com/en-us/who-we-are/business-areas/aeronautics/skunkworks/skunk-works-legal-notice.html, accessed May 14, 2019; Lynn Feigenbaum, "Report to Readers; Got a Kleenex?® We're Skunked," *The Virginian Pilot*, April 26, 1998. ***Shmoos***: Berger, *Li'l Abner*, 114–19; Theroux, *The Enigma of Al Capp*, 26–28; Schumacher and Kitchen, *Al Capp*, 136–39; Denis Kitchen, "The Shmoo from Al Capp's Li'l Abner: Shmoo (not Schmoo) Facts & Trivia," *deniskitchen.com*, http://www.deniskitchen.com/docs/new_shmoofacts.html, accessed August 25, 2006. A good summary of the many neologisms *shmoo* has inspired and other ways it has become a cultural icon can be found in Wikipedia's "Shmoo" page. See also "Shmoos," *medical-dictionary*, https://medical-dictionary.thefreedictionary.com/Shmoo, accessed October 25, 2016; Andrew Murray, "How to Shmoo and Find a Mate," February 8, 2012, lecture, https://www.youtube.com/watch?v=TfpOKWdOolM, accessed October 25, 2016. **Capp's methodology**: Kahn, "OO!!!," 56. **Joe Btfsplk**: "Joe Btfsplk," *Revolvy*, https://www.revolvy.

com/page/Joe-Btfsplk, accessed May 14, 2019; Ed Raymond, "The Resurrection of Al Capp's Joe Btfsplk," *Duluth* (MN) *Reader*, November 1, 2012, http://duluthreader. com/articles/2012/11/02/1129_the_resurrection_of_al_capps_joe_btfsplk, accessed May 14, 2019; "Supervisor Candidates Team Up Even Before Getting Elected," *SFGate*, September 25, 2016, https://www.sfgate.com/politics/article/SF-supervisor-candidates-team-up-even-before-9283803.php, accessed October 25, 2016; Garrison Keillor, "When the Peril of Prominence Morphs into Naked Embarrassment," *Chicago Tribune*, June 8, 2016, https://www.chicagotribune.com/opinion/commentary/ct-garrison-keillor-column-election-20160607-story.html, accessed May 14, 2019. **Evil-Eye Fleegle**: *OED*; John H. Elliott, "The Fear of the Lear: The Evil Eye from the Bible to Li'l Abner," *Forum* 4, no. 4, December 1988, 42–70, 42; "Evil-Eye Fleegle," *Comic Vine*, https://comicvine.gamespot.com/evil-eye-fleegle/4005-67696/, accessed October 25, 2016. Evil-Eye Fleegle was apparently based on an actual boxer known as "Evil Eye Finkle" (Benjamin Finkle), who fought during the 1920s and was said to put a hex on opponents with his "evil eye." See Pat Putnam, "Evil Eye Finkle: Two Parts Voodoo and One Part Fraud," *The Sweet Science*, June 14, 2005, http://tss.ib.tv/boxing/articles-of-2005/2245-evil-eye-finkle-two-parts-voodoo-and-one-part-fraud, accessed December 23, 2006; "Benjamin (Evil Eye) Finkle," *Box Rec*, http://boxrec.com/media/index.php/ Benjamin_(Evil_Eye)_Finkle, accessed May 14, 2019. Finkle was said to put a whammy on opponents with a chronically bloodshot eye, and sometimes even a double whammy. See Pascal Tréguer, "History of the Terms 'Whammy' and 'Double Whammy,'" *word histories*, February 13, 2019, https://wordhistories.net/2019/02/13/double-whammy-origin/, accessed May 14, 2019. **whammy, double whammy**: Ibid.; "The Meaning and Origin of the Expression: Double Whammy," *The Phrase Finder*, https://www.phrases. org.uk/meanings/119750.html, accessed May 23, 2018; Mark Liberman, "Higher Order Whammying," *Language Log*, December 21, 2004, http://itre.cis.upenn.edu/~myl/ languagelog/archives/001738.html, accessed December 23, 2006. In his book *Fighting Talk*, Bob Jones says *whammy* was a slang term commonly used by prewar pugilists and that it originated in rural America before World War I, where "hexes and spells" were called *whammies*. Bob Jones, *Fighting Talk:: Boxing and the Modern Lexicon*, Auckland, NZ: Penguin Random House, 2013. **double whammy strips**: Al Capp, *Li'l Abner: Dailies. Volume 21, 1955*, Northhampton, MA: Kitchen Sink Press, 1995, 113–29.

   Popeye: Bud Sagendorf, *Popeye: The First Fifty Years*, New York: Workman, 1979; Fred M. Grandinetti, *Popeye: An Illustrated History*, Jefferson, NC: McFarland, 1994, 2004; Horn, *100 Years of American Newspaper Comics*, 371–73; Walker, *The Comics Before 1945*, 238; Inge, *Comics as Culture*, 86–96. ***Jeep***: *OED*; Sagendorf, *Popeye*, 87–89; Grandinetti, *Popeye*, 2004, 186, 188; Ayto, *Twentieth Century Words*, 282; *M-W*, 249; O'Conner and Kellerman, *Origins of the Specious*, 63–64. ***I yam what I yam***: Sagendorf, *Popeye*, 120–21; Inge, *Comics as Culture*, 94. ***goon***: Sagendorf, *Popeye*, 102–3; Grandinetti, *Popeye*, 2004, 185–86; Lighter, *Random House Dictionary of American Slang*, Vol. 1, 933; Liberman, *Word Origins and How We Know Them*, 135; Mathews, *A Dictionary of Americanisms*, Vol. 1, 933–35; Frederick Lewis Allen, "The Goon and His Style,"

Harper's Weekly, 1921, 123–24. As the *OED* points out, in various iterations, "goon" (as well as "gooney") has a long history of English usage, but its use in Popeye was unique and put that word on the modern language map. ***doofus***: *OED*; Sagendorf, *Popeye*, 113.

milquetoast: *OED*; Webber and Feinsilber, *Merriam-Webster's Dictionary of Allusions*, 360–61; Horn, *100 Years of American Newspaper Comics*, 375–76; Merrill Perlman, "The Origin of the Word 'Milquetoast,'" *Columbia Journalism Review*, April 16, 2018, https://www.cjr.org/language_corner/milquetoast.php, accessed May 17, 2019; H. T. Webster, *The Timid Soul: A Pictorial Cccount of the Life and Times of Caspar Milquetoast*, New York: Simon & Schuster, 1931; H. T. Webster, *The Best of H. T. Webster: A Memorial Collection*, New York: Simon & Schuster, 1953, 7–13, 158. ***New Yorker* writers** (Dorothy Wickenden, Idrees Kahloon): *NYer*, May 22, 2006, 27; March 9, 2020, 78.

Sad Sack: Horn, *100 Years of American Newspaper Comics*, 335–36; Walker, *The Comics Before 1945*, 304; "Inspection," http://sadsack.hypermart.net/SSyank9.htm, accessed May 17, 2019.

Baker: "sad sack," *Phrases*, https://www.phrases.com/phrase/sad-sack_26430, accessed May 17, 2019. The root of "a sad sack of shit" may be found in the fact that during the late seventeenth century, *shit sack* referred to religious dissenters and other miscreants. This referenced a popular yarn involving a nonconformist clergyman who preached to some vagrants in a barn while suspended above them in a sack tied to a beam. As the preacher warned his listeners that they'd be called to judgment by the call of a trumpet, a prankster hidden nearby blew on such a horn, causing the startled sermonizer to foul his sack. Thereafter, unfortunates like him were commonly known as *shit sacks*. See Grose, *A Classical Dictionary of the Vulgar Tongue*, 307–8. Other antecedents can be found in "What's This Sack of Shit?," *Strong Language*, January 3, 2017, https://stronglang.wordpress.com/2017/01/03/whats-this-sack-of-shit/, accessed May 17, 2019. ***sadsack***: Kirk Michael, "Film Review: 'The Girl on the Train,'" *Sonoma Index-Tribune*, October 13, 2016.

nebbish: Alan Waldman, "Tribute to Herb Gardner," *Films for Two*, http://www.films42.com/tribute/herb_gardner.asp, accessed May 2, 2006; Buce, "Nebbish?," *Underbelly*, http://underbelly-buce.blogspot.com/2009/03/nebbish.html, accessed February 5, 2018. **Early nebbish cartoons**: *Antioch Record*, undated, Antiochiana, Olive Kettering Library, Antioch College. **Gardner about nebbishes**: "The Rise of the Nebbishes: A Tribute to Herb Gardner," *Media Funhouse*, July 6, 2016, http://mediafunhouse.blogspot.com/2016/07/the-rise-of-nebbishes-tribute-to-herb.html, accessed February 5, 2018. **Knotts**: Nick Gillespie, "Not a Doofus: Donald Trump's Collapse Gives Gary Johnson an Opening," *The Daily Beast*, https://www.thedailybeast.com/donald-trumps-collapse-gives-gary-johnson-an-opening, accessed October 20, 2016.

Peanuts: Inge, *Comics as Culture*, 18–20, 104–5; Horn, *100 Years of American Newspaper Comics*, 237–38; Reinhold Reitberger and Wolfgang Fuchs, *Comics: An Anatomy of a Mass Medium*, trans. Nadia Fowler, Boston: Little, Brown, 1972, 54–57;

Jonathan Franzen, "The Comfort Zone: Growing Up with Charlie Brown," *NYer*, November 29, 2004, 61–89. **Lucy and football**: Horn, *100 Years of American Newspaper Comics*, 238; Jeff Greenfield, "Thinking the Unthinkable: What if Trump Succeeds?," *Politico Magazine*, May 2, 2018. **security blanket**: Inge, *Comics as Culture*, 18–20, 104; Horn, *100 Years of American Newspaper Comics*, 238; Lee Mendelson in association with Charles M. Schulz, *Charlie Brown and Charles Schulz*, New York: World, 1970, 75.

    Larson: Gary Larson, *The PreHistory of the Far Side: A 10th Anniversary Exhibit*, Kansas City, MO: Andrews McMeel, 1989. **Luposlipaphobia**: Sara Latta, *Scared Stiff: Everything You Need to Know About 50 Famous Phobias*, New York: Houghton Mifflin Harcourt, 2014, 97. **Analidaephobia**: Larson, *The PreHistory of the Far Side*, 89.

    Thagomizer: Ibid., 137; Gil Namur, "The Thagomizer!," *Life as a Human*, February 15, 2013, https://lifeasahuman.com/2013/our-human-experience/things/the-thagomizer/, accessed June 9, 2015. **Larson namesakes**: Larson, *The PreHistory of the Far Side,* 170–71; "The Far Side," *All The Tropes*, https://allthetropes.fandom.com/wiki/The_Far_Side, accessed January 18, 2016; Stephen Pincock, "Use the Force, Bacteria," *The Scientist*, December 1, 2006, comment by Alex O'Neal, https://www.the-scientist.com/notebook-old/use-the-force-bacteria-46984, accessed January 18, 2016. **Larsonesque**: "Larsonesque," *Wiktionary*.

9. INK-STAINED WORD COINERS

Archer, Artie: Archer, *America To-Day*, 211, 234, 250–52. **Artie Blanchard**: George Ade, *Artie: A Story of the Streets and Town*, Chicago: Stone, 1896, 4, 147.

    Ade: Willard Thorp, *American Humorists*, Minneapolis: University of Minnesota Press, 1964, 29; Edd Applegate, "George Ade," in *Literary Journalism: A Biographical Dictionary of Writers and Editors*, Westport, CT: Greenwood, 1996, 5–8; Kalman Goldstein, "Ade, George," in *Encyclopedia of American Humorists*, ed. Stephen H. Gale, New York: Garland, 1988, 4–7; Fred C. Kelly, *George Ade: Warmhearted Satirist*, Indianapolis: Bobbs-Merrill, 1947; Fred C. Kelly, *The Permanent Ade: The Living Writings of George Ade*, Indianapolis: Bobbs-Merrill, 1947; Jean Shepherd, *The America of George Ade (1866–1944): Fables, Short Stories, Essays*, New York: Putnam's, 1960; Ronald D. Staub, *George Ade's Fiction: A Critical Survey of His Stories and Fables*, MA thesis, Oxford, OH: Miami University, 1962; George Ade, *Chicago Stories*, Chicago: Regnery, 1963; Lee Coyle, *George Ade*, New York: Twayne, 1964; Terence Tobin, ed., *Letters of George Ade*, West Lafayette, IN: Purdue University Studies, 1973. **Ade's admirers**: E. F. Bleiler, introduction to Dover Edition, *Fables in Slang and More Fables in Slang*, by George Ade, New York: Dover, 1960, v–xi, vii; Staub, *George Ade's Fiction*, 3, 20–21, 39–40, 87, 169; Kelly, *George Ade*, 158. **White's comment**: Ibid., 144; "George Ade, the Aesop of Indiana," Indiana Historical Society, https://indianahistory.org/wp-content/uploads/George-Ade-Essay.pdf, accessed June 24, 2019.

    gladhand: George Ade, *Artie*, 4, 147. **date**: Ibid., 65; Moira Weigel, *Labor of Love: The Invention of Dating*, New York: Farrar, Straus and Giroux, 2016, 12; Beth L. Bailey, *Front*

Porch Back Seat: Courtship in Twentieth-Century America, Baltimore: Johns Hopkins, 1989, 17; E. W. Howe's 1885 novel *The Mystery of the Locks* (reprinted in 2016 by Amazon's Palala Press) included this exchange between two men about a third man: "If he'll make a date with me, I'll exchange stories with him" (p. 187). **all dated up**: George Ade, *The Girl Proposition: A Bunch of the He and She Fables*, New York: Russell, 1902, 70. **tightwad**: George Ade, "The Fable of the Honest Money-Maker and the Partner of His Joys, Such as They Were," in George Ade, *More Fables*, Chicago: Stone, 1900, 30. **panhandler**: George Ade, *Doc Horne*, Chicago: Stone, 1899, 255; *OED*. **bunk**: George Ade, *More Fables*, 15. **Ade's use of ok**: Allan Metcalf, *OK*, 135–37. **Ade on his colloquial writing**: George Ade, "They Simply Wouldn't Let Me Be a High-Brow," *American Magazine*, December 1920, 50–51, 197–99, 197. **Ade's list**: Kelly, *George Ade*, 153. **Other terms**: Staub, *George Ade's Fiction*, 170; Coyle, *George Ade*, 47, 2; Tobin, *Letters of George Ade*, 3; Jonathan Green, "Green's Heroes of Slang: 2. George Ade," *The Dabbler*, July 2, 2011, http://thedabbler.co.uk/2011/06/george-ade/, accessed February 23, 2016. **London theater glossary**: Kelly, *George Ade*, 195–98. **sidestep**: George Ade, *Fables in Slang*, Chicago: Stone, 1899, 56. **asphalt jungle**: George Ade, *Handmade Fables*, Garden City, NY: Doubleday, Page, 1920, 83. **Mencken, Funk on Ade**: H. L. Mencken, *Prejudices: First Series*, New York: Knopf, 1919, 122; "Press: Doctor & Duke," *Time*, January 15, 1934. **Ade on slang-slinging**: Ade, "They Simply Wouldn't Let Me Be a High-Brow." **Ade's letter to Runyon**: Kelly, *Letters of George Ade*, 180.

Runyon, surname: Jean Wagner, *Runyonese: The Mind and Craft of Damon Runyon*, Paris, France: Stechert-Hafner, 1965, 13; Patricia Ward D'Itri, *Damon Runyon*, Boston: Twayne, 1982, 17; Clark Kinnaird, foreword to *Runyon First and Last*, by Damon Runyon, Philadelphia: Lippincott, 1945, 12; Pete Hamill, introduction to *Guys and Dolls and Other Writings*, by Damon Runyon, New York: Penguin, 2008, viii–ix; Christy Smith, "Damon Runyon: Pueblo's Storied Man," *The Pulp*, September 1, 2015, https://pueblopulp.com/damon-runyon-pueblos-storied-man/, accessed June 20, 2017. **Runyon's Broadway beat**: William R. Taylor, "Broadway: The Place That Words Built," in *Inventing Times Square: Commerce and Culture at the Crossroads of the World*, ed. William R. Taylor, New York: Russell Sage, 1991, 212–232, 221–31; Daniel R. Schwarz, *Broadway Boogie Woogie: Damon Runyon and the Making of New York City Culture*, New York: Palgrave Macmillan, 2003, 57, 141, 148, 249, 260; Adam Gopnik, "Talk It Up: Damon Runyon's Guys and Dolls," *NYer*, March 2, 2009, 66–71. **"Personally, I always take a gander"**: Damon Runyon, "The Brakeman's Daughter," in *Damon Runyon Favorites*, New York: Pocket, 1942, 133–47, 133. **"Cried all the way to the bank"**: Long before Liberace famously said in 1953 that after being lambasted by critics he'd "cried all the way to the bank," *New York Post* columnist Leonard Lyons reported that a boxing manager had heard Damon Runyon (who died in 1946) use this phrase. See Pascal Tréguer, "Meaning and History of to 'Laugh/Cry All the Way to the Bank,'" *word histories*, July 24, 2017, https://wordhistories.net/2019/03/21/laugh-cry-way-bank/, accessed March 4, 2020. **Argot used by Runyon's characters, their nicknames**: La Rocque Du Bose, "Damon Runyon's Underworld Lingo," *The University of Texas Studies in*

English 32, no. 1, 1953, 123–32; Jean Wagner, *Runyonese*, 22, 31–32, 48–49, 51, 86, 89, 103–8; Daniel R. Schwarz, "Essays and Annotations," in Runyon, *Guys and Dolls and Other Writing*, 617–19. **moolah, Chuck Green:** Pei, *The Story of Language*, 169; William Safire, *NYT*, June 8, 2003. Stephen Goranson found "moola" used as slang for money in a 1937 newspaper column titled "Moola Prospects (?), or No," *The LINGUIST List*, http://listserv.linguistlist.org/pipermail/ads-l/2010-August/101614.html, accessed August 16, 2019. **longshot:** Jean Wagner, *Runyonese*, 89, 107; **photo-finish:** Ibid.; Damon Runyon, "Blonde Mink," *Colliers Weekly*, August 4, 1945, 11–12, 75, 11. **Hoorah Henry:** "Hooray Henry," *The Phrase Finder*, February 26, 2018, https://www.phrases.org.uk/meanings/hooray-henry.html, accessed February 26, 2018; "Hooray Henry," *Wikipedia*, accessed June 19, 2020; Rees, *Cassel's Dictionary of Word and Phrase Origins*, 123–24. **Roaring Forties:** Jimmy Breslin, *Damon Runyon: A Life*, Boston: Ticknor & Fields, 1991, 198. **Runyonese, Runyon's coinages:** Jean Wagner, *Runyonese*, 87–99, 108; William R. Taylor, *Broadway*, 222–23; Schwarz, *Broadway Boogie Woogie*, 57, 141, 148, 249, 260. **Runyon's neologisms in "Butch Minds the Baby":** Jean Wagner, *Runyonese*, 91; Damon Runyon, "Butch Minds the Baby," in *Damon Runyon Favorites*, 1–15.

Winchell: Neal Gabler, *Winchell: Gossip, Power and the Culture of Celebrity*, New York: Random House, 1995. **make whoopee:** *OED*; Paul Robert Beath, "Winchellese," *American Speech* 7, no. 1, October 1931, 44–6, 44; *AL*, 560–61; Barry Popik, "'Makin' Whoopee' (1928)," *The Big Apple*, July 11, 2006, https://www.barry-popik.com/index.php/new_york_city/entry/makin_whoopee_1928, accessed January 15, 2008. **Winchell's surname:** Neal Gabler, *Winchell*, 26–27. **Winchell's three-dot journalism:** Ibid., 80; Thivanka Perera, "5 Facts About Beloved Journalist Herb Caen," *The Culture Trip*, https://theculturetrip.com/north-america/usa/california/articles/5-facts-about-herb-caen/, accessed July 1, 2019. **Winchellese, Winchellisms:** Paul Robert Beath, "Winchellese," *American Speech* 7, no. 1, October 1931, 44–46; "Newspaperman," *Time*, July 11, 1938; *AL*, 560–61; Gabler, *Winchell*, xxii, 71–72; "15 Terms Popularized by Walter Winchell," *howstuffworks*, https://people.howstuffworks.com/15-terms-popularized-by-walter-winchell.htm, accessed January 15, 2008. **blessed event:** Gabler, *Winchell*, 80. **yada yada:** Linda Shrieves, "Phrase Has History . . . Yada, Yada, Yada," *Orlando Sun-Sentinel*, June 14, 1997. **frienemies:** *OED*; Elyse Bruce, "Frenemy," *Historically Speaking*, August 20, 2010, https://idiomation.wordpress.com/2010/08/20/frenemy/, accessed June 30, 2015.

Pegler: Finis Farr, *Fair Enough: The Life of Westbrook Pegler*, New Rochelle, NY: Arlington, 1975; David Witwer, *Shadow of the Racketeer: Scandal in Organized Labor*, Urbana: University of Illinois Press, 2009. **bleeding hearts:** Ibid., 15; *OED*; *SPD*, 81, 352; Finis Farr, *Fair Enough*, 149; "Origins of 'Bleeding Heart Liberal,'" *Tom Paine's Ghost*, September 3, 2013, http://www.tompainesghost.com/2013/09/origins-of-bleeding-heart-liberal.html, accessed October 31, 2016; "Bleeding Heart Yard," *Chambers Journal* 63, no. 2, October 9, 1886, 653–55, 654. **double-domes:** *SPD*, 352; David Witwer, *Shadow of the Racketeer*, 15. **Old Weenie, Bubblehead, Moosejaw the First:** Frank J. Krompak, "A Wider Niche for Westbrook Pegler," *American Journalism*

1, no. 1, December 1983, 31–45, 37. *la Boca Grande*: Ibid.; Farr, *Fair Enough*, 209.
Peglerized: David Witwer, *Shadow of the Racketeer*, 1, 5.

    Caen, *Berserkely, Baghdad-by-the-Bay*: Michael Y. Ybarra, "Herb Caen, 80,
San Francisco Voice Dies," *NYT*, February 2, 1997; Nick Furgatch, "Investigating
the Origins of 'Berserkley,'" the *Daily Californian*, October 2, 2020. *beatniks*: Jesse
Hamlin, "How Herb Caen Named a Generation," *SFC*, November 26, 1995; Herb
Caen, "Pocketful of Note," *SFC*, April 2, 1958, reprinted in *SFC*, February 8, 1997;
Metcalf, *Predicting New Words*, 8; Dalzell, *Flappers 2 Rappers*, 94–96. **Kerouac con-
fronted Caen**: Ibid.; Tom Dalzell, "The Origins of 'Beat' and 'Beatnik,'" *Oxford Words
Blog*, March 11, 2015, http://blogoxforddictionaries.com/2015/03/beat-beatnik-jack-
kerouac, accessed January 24, 2017. **Caen later said**: Ibid.; Dalzell, *Flappers 2 Rappers*,
96. **bagel shop**: Hamlin, "How Herb Caen Named a Generation." **Ginsberg**: Allen
Ginsberg, *The Letters of Allen Ginsberg*, ed. Bill Morgan, Boston: DaCapo, 2008, 222–
23. **Mailer**: Norman Mailer, *Advertisements for Myself*, New York: Putnam's, 1959, 372.
Caen's 1961 confession: Dalzell, *Flappers 2 Rappers*, 95–96; Tom Dalzell, "The Origins
of 'Beat' and 'Beatnik.'"

    southern strategy: Stewart Alsop, "Can Goldwater Win in 64?," *The Saturday
Evening Post*, August 31, 1963, 19–25; *SPD*, 682–83; Goldwater's 1971 letter to *Business
Week*, ibid., 734. *missile gap*: Gregg Herken, *The Georgetown Set*, 241–42. **Alsops**: Ibid.,
157–59, 241–43, 277–85, 298, 302–5. *daddyknowsbestism*: *Tyrone* (PA) *Daily Herald*,
March 4, 1955. *Waltermittyization, the Clothespin Vote, degringolade*: *Newsweek*,
March 30, 1970, 100; April 17, 1972, 108; April 1, 1974, 88. *Irish mafia*: *SPD*, 354–
55. *hawks* and *doves*: Stewart Alsop and Charles Bartlett, "In Time of Crisis," *The
Saturday Evening Post*, December 8, 1962, 15–21. *domino theory*: *SPD*, 191–92;
William C. Effros, ed., *Quotations, Vietnam: 1945–1970*, New York: Random House,
1970, 46–51; Keyes, *The Quote Verifier*, 110–11, 124, 235. *light at end of tunnel*: Ibid.,
235; *OED*; "The President's News Conference of December 12, 1962," *Public Papers of
the Presidents*, Washington, DC: National Archives, 870; *Time*, September 28, 1953,
22; Montagu Norman, "One Step Enough," *Living Age*, December 1932, 316. *WASP*
ascendancy: Gregg Herken, *The Georgetown Set*, 35; Joseph W. Alsop and Adam Platt,
"The WASP Ascendancy," *New York Review of Books*, November 9, 1989, 48–56. **egghead**: Joseph and Stewart Alsop, *The Reporter's Trade*, New York: Reynal, 1958, 188–90;
Arthur Schlesinger Jr., *The Letters of Arthur Schlesinger, Jr.*, ed. Stephen C. Schlesinger,
New York: Random House, 2013, 54–56, 471–72; *SPD*, 209; Allen, *The City in Slang*,
220; Lighter, *Random House Dictionary of American Slang*, Vol. 1, 698–99. **Sandburg's
letter**: Ibid., 699; *OED*; *SPD*, 209. *Hallelujah, I'm a Bum*: IMDb.

10. KIDDIE LIT

nerd: *OED*; David Anderegg, *Nerds: Who They Are and Why We Need More of Them*,
New York: Tarcher, 2007, 25; Ben Zimmer, "Birth of the Nerd," *BG*, August 28, 2011;
Andrew Boyd, "The Etymology of 'Nerd,'" *Engines of Our Ingenuity*, February 6, 2014,

https://www.uh.edu/engines/epi2926.htm, accessed July 2, 2019; Michael Quinion, "Nerd," *World Wide Words*, March 24, 2012, http://www.worldwidewords.org/qa/qa-ner1.htm, accessed, June 29, 2015.

Seuss: E. J. Kahn Jr., "Children's Friend," *NYer*, December 17, 1960, 47–93; Judith Morgan and Neil Morgan, *Dr. Seuss & Mr. Geisel*, New York: Random House, 1995; Charles D. Cohen, *The Seuss, the Whole Seuss, and Nothing but the Seuss: A Visual Biography of Theodor Seuss Geisel*, New York: Random House, 2002; Philip Nel, *Dr. Seuss: American Icon*, New York: Continuum, 2004; Philip Nel, *The Annotated Cat: Under the Hats of Seuss and His Cats*, New York: Random House, 2007; Donald E. Pease, *Theodor SEUSS Geisel*, New York: Oxford University Press, 2010. *meticulosity*: Judith Morgan and Neil Morgan, *Dr. Seuss & Mr. Geisel*, 247; Donald E. Pease, *Theodor SEUSS Geisel*, 150. *vug*: Morgan and Morgan, *Dr. Seuss & Mr. Geisel*, 225. **Zillow**: Julian Hebron, "Is Zillow Named After a Dr. Seuss Character?," *The Basis Point*, April 8, 2011, https://thebasispoint.com/is-zillow-named-after-a-dr-seuss-character/, accessed July 2, 2019; Adam Lang, "Why Is It Called Zillow?," *Rewind&Capture*, January 26, 2014, https://www.rewindandcapture.com/why-is-it-called-zillow/, accessed January 5, 2018. **Yertle**: Nancy Friedman, "Name in the News: Yerdle," *Fritinancy*, March 3, 2017, https://nancyfriedman.typepad.com/away_with_words/2017/03/name-in-the-news-yerdle.html, accessed February 26, 2018. **Nook**: Court Merrigan, "Why B&N Called It the Nook: Maybe Because They're Dr. Seuss Fans," *TeleRead.com*, October 23, 2009, http://teleread.com/why-bn-called-it-the-nook-maybe-just-because-theyre-dr-seuss-fans/index.html, accessed January 30, 2017; "Why Did Barnes and Noble Name Their E-reader 'Nook'?," *Quora*, April 4, 2015, https://www.quora.com/Why-did-Barnes-and-Noble-name-their-e-reader-Nook, accessed July 2, 2019. *voom, va va voom*: *OED*; "va va voom," *Wiktionary*. **Kagan**: Philip Swarts, "Supreme Court Justice Kagan uses Dr. Seuss in Case Argument," *Washington Times*, February 25, 2015; **Thacker**: Laurel Wamsley, "Quoting 'The Lorax,' Court Pulls Permit for Pipeline Crossing Appalachian Trail," NPR, December 14, 2018, https://www.npr.org/2018/12/14/676950106/quoting-the-lorax-court-pulls-permit-for-pipeline-crossing-appalachian-trail, accessed December 17, 2018. **Douthat**: Ross Douthat, "David Souter Killed the Filibuster," *NYT*, April 12, 2017. **Cruz**: Meagan Fitzpatrick, "Ted Cruz Anti-Obamacare Talk-a-thon Ends After 21 Hours," *CBC News*, September 25, 2013, https://www.cbc.ca/news/world/why-ted-cruz-read-green-eggs-and-ham-in-the-u-s-senate-1.1867499, accessed November 19, 2019. **Scholarly analysis of Seuss's terms**: Sarah Kaplan, "Scientists Have Figured Out What Makes Dr. Seuss So Silly," *WP*, December 2, 2015. *Grinch:* Philip Nel, *Dr. Seuss*, 25. **Sources of Geisel's creativity**: Judith Morgan and Neil Morgan, *Dr. Seuss & Mr. Geisel*, xix, 87, 272.

Dodgson's walk: Stuart Dodgson Collingwood, *The Life and Letters of Lewis Carroll*, Detroit: Gale, 1898, 1967, 171; David Denby, *Snark, It's Mean, It's Personal, and It's Ruining Our Conversation*, New York: Simon & Schuster, 2009.

Carroll: Morton N. Cohen, *Lewis Carroll: A Biography*, New York: Knopf, 1995.

snark: David Denby, *Snark*, 17–19; Martin Gardner, *The Annotated Snark: The Full Text of Lewis Carroll's Great Nonsense Epic, The Hunting of the Snark, and the Original Illustrations*, New York: Simon & Schuster, 1962, 17–18, 37. **Humpty Dumpty and Alice**: Martin Gardner, *The Annotated Alice: The Definitive Edition*, New York: Norton, 2000, 207–20. *chortle, galumph*: Ibid., 150; *OED*. *boojum*: Martin Gardner, *The Annotated Snark*, 53. **Carroll's coining methods**: Stuart Dodgson Collingwood, *The Life and Letters of Lewis Carroll*, 209–10, 274; Martin Gardner, *The Annotated Alice*, 148–54, 215–16; Robert Douglas Fairhurst, *The Story of Alice: Lewis Carroll and the Secret History of Wonderland*, Cambridge, MA: Belknap, 2015, 42–43, 147; Lederer, *The Miracle of Language*, 106–12. **"take care of the sounds"**: Gardner, *The Annotated Alice*, 150. *vorpal swords, Dungeons and Dragons*: "D&D Adventure System Wiki," https://ddadventuresystem.fandom.com/wiki/Vorpal_Sword, accessed February 6, 2018. *Team Vorpal Swords*: https://kurokonobasuke.fandom.com/wiki/Team_Vorpal_Swords, accessed February 6, 2018. *jabberwocky*: Martin Gardner, *The Annotated Alice*, 153. *uffish*: Martin Gardner, *The Annotated Snark*, 59. **Jabberwockian terms**: Ibid., 148–55. **Kipling, *Stalky & Co.***: Ibid., 149. **Eddington**: Ibid., 150–51; E. S. Eddington, *The Nature of the Physical World*, Whitefish, MT: Kessinger, 1927, 2010, 291. **Partridge**: Partridge, *Here, There and Everywhere*, 188.

goop, **Burgess**: *OED*; Mathews, *A Dictionary of Americanisms*, Vol. 1, 335; Sadie Stein, "Disgusting Lives," *The Paris Review* (Daily), March 11, 2014, https://www.theparisreview.org/blog/2014/03/11/disgusting-lives/, accessed July 4, 2019. **Goops excerpt**: Gelett Burgess, *Goops and How to Be Them: A Manual of Manners for Polite Infants Inculcating Many Juvenile Virtues Both by Precept and Example*, New York: Dover, 1900, 1968, 5, 3. **Geisel's mother**: E. Pease, *Theodor SEUSS Geisel*, 10–11. **Paltrow**: Alexandra Jacobs, "Meet the Goopies," *NYT*, June 14, 2017.

Wymps: Evelyn Sharp, "Why the Wymps Cried," *The Chap-book*, Vol. 7, 1897, 276–81; Evelyn Sharp, *Wymps: And Other Fairy Tales*, London: Lane, 1897. **Ade, "Wimp"**: George Ade, "The Two Unfettered Birds," in *Knocking the Neighbors*, Garden City, NY: Doubleday, Page, 1912, 218. *Arrowsmith*: Sinclair Lewis, *Arrowsmith*, New York: Harcourt Brace, 1925, 1945, 299. For whatever reason, Evelyn Sharp's books on *Wymps* are seldom given their due as the probable progenitor of "wimp," and "wimpy," even by the *OED*. Paul Dickson does in *Authorisms* (182), where Ade and Lewis's subsequent use of "wimp" and "wimpish" are also noted (although his excerpt from *Arrowsmith* is inaccurate). Others, such as *The Merriam-Webster New Book of Word Histories* (*M-W*, 504–5) and Robert Chapman's *New Dictionary of American Slang* (468) point to the Popeye character Wellington Wimpy as a source. During the 1930s radio comedian Bill Thompson portrayed an ineffectual character named Wallace "Wimp" Wimple, who later became a fixture on the popular *Fibber McGee and Molly* radio show. "Bill Thompson: King of Wimps," *WFMU's Beware of the Blog*, May 20, 2007, https://blog.wfmu.org/freeform/2007/05/bill_thompson_k.html, accessed July 4, 2019. Collectively, they all helped inspire our current use of *wimp*, but Sharp is the earliest inspiration of all.

"googles his way": George Ade, "The Joys of Single Blessedness," *The American Magazine*, June 1921, 11–13, 150, 13. **Kasner account**: *M-W*, 199–200; Edward Kasner and James Newman, *Mathematics and the Imagination*, New York: Simon & Schuster, 1940, 23. The charming origin story for "googol" involving Kasner and his young nephew is widely recounted with little acknowledgment of the popularity of "Barney Google" at the time. Steinmetz and Kipfer are a rare exception, noting in *The Life of Language* (167) that "being a child's invention, it [googol] may have been easily influenced by the name of the then very popular comic strip character Barney Google." See also Larry Bush, "The Etymology of 'Google' Is a Comedy of Errors," *Humor in America*, August 4, 2015, https://humorinamerica.wordpress.com/2015/08/04/the-etymology-of-google-is-a-comedy-of-errors/, accessed July 5, 2019. **Page and Brin**: David Koller reports that based on accounts by colleagues at Stanford who were present at the creation of their enterprise's name (in Wing B of Stanford's Gates Computer Science Building), including Sean Anderson, in September 1997 Page, Anderson, and others were brainstorming better names than "BackRub" (their working name) on a whiteboard. Anderson suggested "googolplex." Page countered with "googol." Anderson misspelled that word when he entered "google.com" into the computer before him. It was available. Page liked the misspelled version best and within hours they'd registered it. (Page himself doesn't mention Anderson when recounting how they got from "Googol" to "Google.") If this account is accurate, it would be yet another case of coinage by mistake. In any event, since "googol.com" had already been claimed, Page's stated preference for *Google* could be disingenuous. That may simply have been the name that was available. See David Koller, "Origin of the Name 'Google,'" January 2004, https://graphics.stanford.edu/~dk/google_name_origin.html, accessed June 17, 2011; Rachael Hanley, "From Googol to Google," *The Stanford Daily*, February 12, 2003. ***google-nose, the google***: Mathews, *A Dictionary of Americanisms*, Vol. 1, 716; Hardin E. Taliafero, *Fishers River (North Carolina) Scenes and Characters*, New York: Harper, 1859, 29; "Oddments," *Bulletin of the National History Survey*, Chicago Academy of Sciences, Issues 4–5, 1900, 47. **Nashville journalist**: *Nashville Union and American*, May 4, 1856, 2, https://www.newspapers.com/newspage/83322443/, accessed March 5, 2020. **Krazy Kat**: "'Google' in Krazy Kat (1912)," *The LINQUIST List*, August 6, 2003, http://listserv.linguistlist.org/piper-mail/ads-l/2003-August.txt, accessed February 17, 2020. **Louis Armstrong**: Louis Armstrong, *Satchmo: My Life in New Orleans*, New York: Prentice-Hall, 1954, 112. **Vickers**: V. C. Vickers, *The Google Book*, 1913, http://blogoscoped.com/googlebook/, accessed February 17, 2016; Richard Davies, "The Google Book: Worth Searching For," https://www.abebooks.com/books/features/google-book/index.shtml, accessed February 17, 2016. **1907 British magazine**: *Badminton Magazine*, September 1907, 289, cited in *OED*. **Page and Brin's digitization of *The Google Book***: Miguel Helft, "Ruling Spurs Effort to Form Digital Public Library," *NYT*, April 3, 2011.

Taser: Bruce Weber, "Jack Cover, 88, Physicist Who Invented the Taser Stun Gun, Dies," February 16, 2009; Victor Appleton, *Tom Swift and His Electric Rifle, or, Daring Adventures in Elephant Land*, New York: Grosset & Dunlap, 1911, 6, 8, 48–49, 64, 105.

I'm indebted to journalist Jamiles Lartey for calling my attention to the nature of this book in his article "Where Did the Word 'Taser' Come From? A Century-Old Racist Science Fiction Novel," *The Guardian*, November 30, 2015. **Tom Swift series**: "Tom Swift," Clute and Nicholls, *Encyclopedia of Science Fiction*, 1234. **Tom Swift Sr.**: "The Complete Tom Swift Sr. Home Page," https://www.tomswift.info/homepage/oldindex.html, accessed July 6, 2019. **Tom Swift Jr.**: "The Complete Tom Swift Jr. Home Page," https://www.tomswift.info/homepage/index.html, accessed July 6, 2019; Jeff Duntemann, "Tom Swift, Jr.: An Appreciation," http://www.duntemann.com/tomswift.htm, accessed April 5, 2016; Victor Appleton II, "Tom Swift and His Rocket Ship," https://www.tomswift.info/homepage/rocket2.html, accessed April 4, 2016.

"I have a harder job naming": Ibid. *Tom Swift and His Giant Robot*: Victor Appleton II, "Tom Swift and His Giant Robot," https://www.tomswift.info/homepage/robot.html, accessed April 4, 2016.

11. *NAMING THE FUTURE*

robot: Crystal, *The Story of English in 100 Words*, 199–202; "Josef Čapek—the Robot Inventor," *Weimar*, August 17, 2010, http://weimarart.blogspot.com/2010/08/josef-capek.html, accessed March 22, 2016; Karel Čapek, "Appendix: 'On the Word Robot,'" *Oxford Words Blog*, November 22, 2012, https://blog.oup.com/2012/11/words-were-thankful-for/, accessed January 11, 2016.

robotics: Isaac Asimov, "The Word I Invented," in Isaac Asimov, *Counting the Future*, Garden City, NY: Doubleday, 1983, 30–40, 33; Isaac Asimov, "Liar!," *Astounding Science Fiction*, May 1941, 43–55; "Runaround," *Astounding Science Fiction*, March 1942, 94–103.

test tube baby: Lee Server, *Encyclopedia of Pulp Fiction Writers*, New York: Facts on File/Checkmark, 2002, 104; Sam Fuller, *Test Tube Baby*, New York: Godwin, 1936. *genetic engineering*: OED; Prucher, *Brave New Words*, 77–78; Jack Williamson, *Dragon's Island*, New York: Simon & Schuster, 1951, 180. *body snatchers*: Jack Finney, *The Body Snatchers*, New York: Dell, 1955; "The Body Snatchers," in D'Ammassa, *Encyclopedia of Science Fiction*, 46; "Invasion of the Body Snatchers," *AMC filmsite*, https://www.filmsite.org/inva.html, accessed May 18, 1996. *pod, pod person*: Prucher, *Brave New Words*, 151; OED. *Stepford Wives*: Ira Levin, *The Stepford Wives*, New York: Random House, 1972; "Stepford," *UD*; "Literature / The Stepford Wives," *TV Tropes*, https://tvtropes.org/pmwiki/pmwiki.php/Literature/TheStepfordWives, accessed April 19, 2017. *Manchurian candidate*: Richard Condon, *The Manchurian Candidate*, New York: McGraw-Hill, 1959; *The Manchurian Candidate*, 1962, IMDb.

Clockwork Orange: Anthony Burgess, *A Clockwork Orange*: New York: Ballantine, 1962, 1965; Rees, *Cassel's Dictionary of Word and Phrase Origins*, 130; McArthur, *The Oxford Companion to the English Language*, 167.

dystopia, cacotopia: OED; Clute and Nicholls, *Encyclopedia of Science Fiction*, 360; Prucher, *Brave New Words*, 39–40. *Brave New World*: Ayto, *Twentieth Century Words*,

196; Aldous Huxley, *Brave New World Revisited*, New York: Harper, 1958, 4. *1984* **vocabulary, "doublethink"**: *OED*; George Orwell, *1984*, New York: Harcourt, Brace, 1949, 215; George Orwell, "From 'Nineteen Eighty-Four,'" in George Orwell, *The Orwell Reader: Fiction, Essays, and Reportage by George Orwell*, New York: Harcourt Brace, 1956, 396–419; James Wood, "A Fine Age, George Orwell's Revolutions," *NYer*, April 19, 2009, 54–63, 63; Lederer, *The Miracle of Language*, 139–40.

    Bokonism, karass, Cat's Cradle **vocabulary**: D'Ammassa, *Encyclopedia of Science Fiction*, 76–77; "Cat's Cradle Glossary," *GradeSave*, https://www.gradesaver.com/catscraret.e/study-guide/glossary-of-terms, accessed July 22, 2019. *grok*: *OED*. Based on a text search, the term *grok* is used 195 times in Robert Heinlein's *Stranger in a Strange Land* (New York: Putnam's, 1961). Wikipedia's "Grok" page covers the range of ways this word is used within Heinlein's novel, its countercultural uses, and the affinity of techies for the term. *grok* **among techies**: Chatfield, *Netymology*, 54–56; Brian Heater, "Hands-On with Apple's New Touch Bar MacBook Pro," *TechCrunch*, October 27, 2016, https://techcrunch.com/2016/10/27/macbook-pro-hands-on/, accessed November 4, 2016. **Maddow**: *The Rachel Maddow Show*, December 18, 2018, transcript, http://www.msnbc.com/transcripts/rachel-maddow-show/2018-12-18-0, accessed December 20, 2018.

    Space Cadet: Prucher, *Brave New Words*, 196; Clute and Nicholls, *Encyclopedia of Science Fiction*, 1233–34; "Tom Corbett, Space Cadet," *Solar Guard Academy*, http://www.solarguard.com/tchome.htmret, accessed July 23, 2019; IMDb.

    space, outer space: *OED*; "Where Does Outer Space Begin?," *worldatlas.com*, June 4, 2019, https://www.worldatlas.com/articles/where-does-outer-space-begin.html, accessed July 23, 2019. **Wells**: *OED*; H. G. Wells, *The First Men in the Moon*, London: Newnes, 1901, 45.

    satellite: *OED*; Steinmetz, *Semantic Antics*, 209; Jules Verne, *The Begum's Fortune*, Philadelphia: Lippincott, 1879, 179–80. *rocket*: H. C. Davis, *"To the Moon at 7 Miles a Second!,"* *Popular Science Monthly*, February 1927, 29. *countdown*: A. J. Hoberman, "When Fritz Lang Shot the Moon," *NYT*, June 27, 2019; "Fritz Lang—Woman in the Moon—1929. Launch," *YouTube*, https://www.youtube.com/watch?v=I8gu1p939a4, accessed July 24, 2019; **Margaret MacMillan**: Uri Friedman, "The Military Has Seen the Writing on the Wall," *ATL*, January 20, 2018, https://www.theatlantic.com/international/archive/2018/01/duckworth-trump-north-korea/551381/, accessed February 2, 2018. *blast off*: Dickson, *A Dictionary of the Space Age*, 2009, 26–28; James Schefter, *The Race: The Uncensored Story of How America Beat Russia to the Moon*, New York: Doubleday, 1999, 39–40.

    NASA task group, *Project Mercury*: Loyd S. Swenson, James M. Grimwood, Charles C. Alexander, *This New Ocean: A History of Project Mercury*, Washington, DC: National Aeronautics and Space Administration, 1966, 73, 131–32, 159–60. *astronaut*: Ibid., 160; Dickson, *A Dictionary of the Space Age*, 26–28; Allen O. Gamble, "The Selection of the Mercury Astronauts: Personal Recollections," unpublished, http://www.collectspace.com/review/kcstoever/gamble-essay6.pdf; James Schefter, *The Race*,

51; Scott Carpenter and Kris Stoever, *For Spacious Skies: The Uncommon Journey of a Mercury Astronaut*, New York: Harcourt, 2002, 160. **Grissom**: Ibid., 218. **Greg**: Percy Greg, *Across the Zodiac: The Story of a Wrecked Record*, Westport, CT: Hyperion, 1880, 1974, I:27, 32–33, 37, 72–73; II:18, 28, 226, 283, 286, 288; Michael Hellerman, "Across the Zodiac," *Kitbashed*, https://kitbashed.com/blog/across-the-zodiac, accessed November 4, 2016; "Astronautics," *NYT*, March 8, 1928; *Journal of the British Astronomical Association*, 1929, 331, cited by *OED* and Dickson, *A Dictionary of the Space Age*, 26–27.

   splashdown, go-no-go, and soft landing: Dickson, ibid., 207, 90, 184. **A-OK**: Steinmetz, *There's a Word for It*, 125–26; Dickson, *A Dictionary of the Space Age*, 14; Gene Kranz, *Failure Is Not an Option: Mission Control from Mercury to Apollo 13 and Beyond*, New York: Berkley, 2000, 2001, 54–55; "A-OK for Tomorrow's Missile Demands," Midvac Steels, 1952, in Jim Heimann, ed., *The Golden Age of Advertising— the 50s*, New York: Barnes & Noble, 2006, 57. **glitch**: *SPD*, 278–79; Ben Zimmer, "The Hidden History of 'Glitch,'" *Visual Thesaurus*, https://www.visualthesaurus.com/cm/wordroutes/the-hidden-history-of-glitch/, accessed April 16, 2018; Flesch, *Lite English*, 71–72; John Glenn, "Glitches in Time Save Trouble," in M. Scott Carpenter et al., *We Seven*, New York: Cardinal, 1963, 161.

   atomic bomb, Wells: *OED*; H. G. Wells, *The World Set Free*, New York: Dutton, 1914, 109; Angela Tung, "Atomic Bombs, Time Machines, and Lurve: Words from H. G. Wells," *wordnik*, September 21, 2012, https://blog.wordnik.com/atomic-bombs-time-machines-and-lurve-words-from-h-g-wells, accessed February 16, 2018; H. G. Wells, "The World Set Free," *Atomic Heritage Foundation*, https://www.atomicheritage.org/key-documents/hg-wells-world-set-free, accessed July 25, 2019.

   Asimov, techno-terms: *OED*; Isaac Asimov, "The Feeling of Power," in *If: Worlds of Science Fiction*, Buffalo, NY: Quinn, February 1958, https://themathlab.com/writings/short%20stories/feeling.htm, accessed June 16, 2011.

   cyberspace: "Burning Chrome," in William Gibson, *Burning Chrome*, New York: Harper, 1982, 2003, xvii, 179; William Gibson *Neuromancer*, New York: Penguin, 1984, 2016, 52; Prucher, *Brave New Words*, 31; Chatfield, *Netymology*, 40; Laura Sydell, "The Father of the Internet Sees His Invention Reflected Back Through a Black Mirror," *Morning Edition*, NPR, February 20 2018; "Q & A, William Gibson," *Newsweek*, February 23, 2003; William Gibson, interviewed by David Wallace-Wells, "The Art of Fiction No. 211," *Paris Review*, Summer 2011, https://www.gwern.net/docs/fiction/2011-gibson.html, accessed July 25, 2019; "Surface Tension," *High Profiles*, October 1, 2010, https://highprofiles.info/interview/william-gibson/, accessed July 25, 2019.

12. *LITERARY LINGO*

Catch-22: *M-W*, 95; Bernard, *Now All We Need Is a Title*, 59; "What's in a Name?," CBS News, March 3, 2008, https://www.cbsnews.com/news/whats-in-a-name-03-03-2008/, accessed May 13, 2008; Lynn Neary, "'Catch-22': A Paradox Turns 50 and Still Rings True," *Morning Edition*, NPR, October 13, 2011.

fug: Garson O'Toole, "Oh—You're the Man Who Can't Spell," *Quote Investigator*, March 12, 2019, https://quoteinvestigator.com/2019/03/12/fug/, accessed April 9, 2019; J. Michael Lennon, *Norman Mailer: A Double Life*, New York: Simon & Schuster, 2013, 94, 737, 793; Peter Mancuso, *Norman Mailer: His Life and Times*, New York: Simon & Schuster, 1985, 105–6; Denis Brian, *Tallulah, Darling*, New York: Macmillan, 1971, 1980, 8, 271; "Who the Fug Are You?," Lennon, *Norman Mailer*, 737. *factoid*: Norman Mailer, *Marilyn: A Biography by Norman Mailer*, New York: Grosset and Dunlap, 1973, 18, 63, 92, 106; Melvyn Bragg, "Norman Mailer Talks to Melvyn Bragg About the Bizarre Business of Writing a Hypothetical Life of Marilyn Monroe," in *Conversations with Norman Mailer*, ed. J. Michael Lennon, Jackson: University Press of Mississippi, 1988, 194; **in OED:** Jason Mosser, "Norman Mailer and the Oxford English Dictionary," *The Mailer Review, The Norman Mailer Society*, April 12, 2015, http://mailerreview.org/norman-mailer-and-the-oxford-english-dictionary, accessed November 10, 2016; "Factoid," *Grammarist*, April 2012, https://grammarist.com/usage/factoid/, accessed January 21, 2016; David Marsh, "A Factoid Is Not a Small Fact," *The Guardian*, January 17, 2014.

Alexander on Milton: John Crace, "John Milton—Our Greatest Word Maker," *The Guardian*, January 28, 2008; Andy McSmith, "A Literary Visionary: Milton and His Satanic Verses," *The Independent*, January 15, 2008. **Smith's favorite Miltonisms**: Smith, *Milton and His Modern Critics*, 64–65. **Lederer**: Lederer, *The Miracle of Language*, 82. **Dickson**: Dickson, *Authorisms*, 3–4; Alice Padwe, "Interview with Paul Dickson," *Washington Independent Review of Books*, June 3, 2014, http://www.washingtonindependentreviewofbooks.com/index.php/features/interview-with-paul-dickson, accessed June 18, 2014. **Smith on Milton's word-coining strategies**: Smith, *Milton and His Modern Critics*, 64. **Alexander on Milton's word-coining strategies**: John Crace, "John Milton—Our Greatest Word Maker." **Milton's blindness**: McSmith, "A Literary Visionary: Milton and His Satanic Verses." **Miltonisms**: *OED*; Crace, "John Milton—Our Greatest Word Maker"; Forsyth, *The Etymologicon*, 16–18. **More Alexander on Milton's word-coining strategies**: John Crace, "John Milton—Our Greatest Word Maker." *Quixotic*: Ilan Stavans, *Quixote: The Novel and the World*, New York: Norton, 2015, 81. See also "'Don Quixote' Speaks to the 'Quality of Being a Dreamer,'" Robert Siegel interview with Ilan Stavans, *All Things Considered*, NPR, September 8, 2015; "A Gargantuan Error: Quixotic Is Not the Only Word from a Book Character," Robert Siegel interview with Bruce Conforth, *All Things Considered*, NPR, September 8, 2015.

Pollyanna, Candide, Micawber: Keyes, *I Love It When You Talk Retro*, 227–28.

Dickens: Sørensen, *Charles Dickens*, 60–61; Ben Zimmer, "'Not to Put Too Fine a Point upon It': How Dickens Helped Shape the Lexicon," *Visual Thesaurus*, February 3, 2012, https://www.visualthesaurus.com/cm/wordroutes/not-to-put-too-fine-a-point-upon-it-how-dickens-helped-shape-the-lexicon/, accessed April 28, 2017. **Quinion**: Michael Quinion, "The Words of Dickens," *World Wide Words*, February 11, 2015. http://www.worldwidewords.org/articles/ar-dic1.htm, accessed June 29, 2015. *flummox*: *OED*; Sørensen, *Charles Dickens*, 25, 33, 134. *butterfingers*: *OED*; Quinion, "The Words of Dickens"; Sørensen, *Charles Dickens*, 33, 122; Gary Martin, "What's the

Origin of the Word 'Butterfingers'?," *The Phrase Finder*, 2012, https://www.phrases. org.uk/meanings/butterfingers.html, accessed February 8, 2018; Markham, *The English Housewife*, 64. *kibosh*: Anatoly Liberman, "Unable to Put the Kibosh on a Hard Word," *OUPblog*, May 19, 2010, https://blog.oup.com/2010/05/kibosh/, accessed August 8, 2018; Anatoly Liberman, "Three Recent Theories of 'Kibosh,'" *OUPblog*, August 14, 2013, https://blog.oup.com/2013/08/three-recent-theories-of-kibosh-word-origin-etymology/, accessed July 30, 2019. **Douglas-Fairhurst**: Robert Douglas-Fairhurst, *Becoming Dickens: The Invention of a Novelist*, Cambridge: Belknap/Harvard University Press, 2011, 336; **Oxford Companion**: Paul Schlike, ed., *The Oxford Companion to Charles Dickens*, Oxford: Oxford University Press, 2011, 554. **Dickensisms**: Michael Quinion, "The Words of Dickens." *common, dim*: Sørensen, *Charles Dickens*, 52, 126, 130. **theatrical terms**: Ibid., 49, 142. *makeup*: Fred E. Basten, *Max Factor's Hollywood*, Los Angeles: General, 1995, 2008, 41, 284. *door-mat*: *OED*; Sørensen, *Charles Dickens*, 55, 130. *the creeps*: Ibid., 128; Flesch, *Lite English*, 37. **Dickens's love of word-play**: Sørensen, *Charles Dickens*, 59. *Nellicide, spoffish, ponging, bacchanalially, prompterian, sea-sicky, touch-me-notness*: Sørensen, *Charles Dickens*, 49, 57, 59, 123, 164. *ravenless*: Ibid., 40. *metropolitaneously*: *OED*; Zimmer, "Not to Put Too Fine a Point upon It." **Dickens's word-creation strategies**: Sørensen, *Charles Dickens*, 25–61; Zimmer, "Not to Put Too Fine a Point upon It." *fraud*: Sørensen, *Charles Dickens*, 134. *logocracy*: *OED*; Nancy Aycock Metz, "Dickens, Irving, and the American 'Logocracy,'" *Dickens Studies Annual*, 47, 2016, 1–16.

Irving's new terms: *OED*; Babcock, *The Ordeal of American English*, 172–73. *boss*: *OED*; *M-W*, 59–60; van der Sijs, *Cookies, Coleslaw, and Stoops*, 182–83. *almighty dollar*: *OED*; William Safire, "Almighty Dollar," *NYT*, June 15, 2008; Washington Irving, "Creole Village," in *Full Text of Chronicles of Wolfert's Roost and Other Papers*, Edinburgh: Constable, 1855, 30, 36. **Words overheard by Irving**: *OED*; Wayne R. Kime, "Washington Irving and Frontier Speech," *American Speech* 42, no. 1, February 1967, 5–18. **"Lynch's Law"**: Washington Irving, "A Tour on the Prairies," in Washington Irving, *The Crayon Miscellany*, Philadelphia: Lippincott, 1870, 33–34; Thomas Walker Page, "The Real Judge Lynch," *ATL*, December 1901, 731–43. Other men named Lynch have been credited as the inspiration for "Lynch's Law," but none as credibly as Charles Lynch. See Christopher Waldrep, *The Many Faces of Judge Lynch: Extralegal Violence and Punishment in America*, New York: Palgrave/Macmillan, 2002, 2–28, 34, 36, 38–39, 44–46; Mac McLean, "Who Was Charles Lynch?," (Danville, VA) *Register & Bee*, August 1, 2005.

vet: *OED*; William Safire, "Vetter Vets 'Vet,'" *NYT*, March 28, 1993; Juliet Lapidos, "Vetting Vet," *Slate*, September 3, 2008; Rudyard Kipling, "The Army of a Dream," in Rudyard Kipling, *Traffics and Discoveries*, New York: Doubleday, 1904, 250. **Bertha Croker's novel**: *OED*; Bertha M. Croker, *Peggy of the Bartons*, London: Fenno, 1898, 138. *bite the bullet*: Rudyard Kipling, *The Light That Failed*, Chicago: Rand McNally, 1891, 1923, 179 ("Bite on the bullet, old man, and don't let them think you're afraid").

Pascal Tréguer cites some earlier references to soldiers biting bullets as they're being flogged in "The Authentic Origin of 'To Bite on the Bullet,'" *word histories*, July 24, 2017, https://wordhistories.net/2017/07/24/bite-the-bullet-origin/, accessed January 8, 2020. **hell for leather**: *OED* citing Kipling's *The Story of Gadsbys* (1889) "Here, Gaddy, take the note to Bingle and ride hell-for-leather," and an 1893 use by him as well. **gadgets**: *OED*; Kipling, *Traffics and Discoveries*, 54, 99, 165, 166, 175. Some sources, including the *OED* and Michael Quinion, note an 1886 book on nautical life in which the term *gadjet* had already appeared: *OED*; "Gadget," *World Wide Words*, May 12, 2007, http://www.worldwidewords.org/qa/qa-gad1.htm, accessed August 1, 2019; Flexner, *Listening to America*, 282, says this naval term dates to the 1850s. **traffic lights**: *OED*; Ayto, *Twentieth Century Words*, 181; Rudyard Kipling, "As Easy as A.B.C.," 1912, in Rudyard Kipling, *A Diversity of Creatures*, London: Macmillan, 1917, 1–42, 21, 41. **grinching**: *OED*; Angela Tung, "The Words of Rudyard Kipling," *wordnik*, December 27, 2012, https://blog.wordnik.com/the-words-of-rudyard-kipling, accessed December 8, 2015; Rudyard Kipling, "The Lament of the Border Cattle Thief," *Ballads and Barrack-Room Ballads*, New York: Macmillan, 1897, 54. **Svengali**: *OED*; Tung, "The Words of Rudyard Kipling"; George du Maurier, *Trilby*, London: Osgood, McIlvaine, 1894; Rudyard Kipling, "The Dog Hervey," 1914, in Rudyard Kipling, *A Diversity of Creatures*, 131–57, 145. **it, it girl**: *OED*; Angela Tung, "The Words of Rudyard Kipling"; Lindsay Baker, "Got It?," *The Guardian*, April 20, 2001; Rudyard Kipling, "Mrs. Bathhurst," in *Traffics and Discoveries*, 325; *It* (1927), IMDb. **penny-farthing**: *OED*; Tung, "The Words of Rudyard Kipling"; Rudyard Kipling, "Plain Tales from the Hills," 1888, in Rudyard Kipling, *Plain Tales from the Hills*, NY: Doubleday, Page, 1899, 1915, 91, 303. In addition to Kipling's use, the *OED* cites a 1652 reference to Jewish political figures as "pennyfarthing-Politicians," and a 1615 mention of "peny-farthing offences" worthy of forgiveness. **overseas**: *OED*; Tung, "The Words of Rudyard Kipling"; Rudyard Kipling, "Our Overseas Men," *The Times* (London), July 13, 1892, http://www.kiplingsociety.co.uk/rg_tideway_four.htm, accessed February 1, 2017. **slack-jawed, grass roots**: *OED*; Tung, "The Words of Rudyard Kipling"; Rudyard Kipling, *Kim*, Garden City, New York: Doubleday, 1901, 70, 338. **squiggly, squiggle, just-so stories**: Tung, "The Words of Rudyard Kipling"; Rudyard Kipling, "How the Rhinoceros Got His Skin," in Rudyard Kipling, *Just-So Stories*, Garden City, NY: Doubleday, Page, 1912, 34, 166. **old school tie**: *OED*; Tung, "The Words of Rudyard Kipling"; Rudyard Kipling, "The Tie," in *Limits and Renewals*, New York: Doubleday, Doran, 1932, 86. **white man's burden**: Rudyard Kipling, "The White Man's Burden," *The Times* (London), February 4, 1899, *New York Tribune*, February 5, 1899; Rudyard Kipling, *Rudyard Kipling: Complete Verse*, New York: Anchor, 1989, 321–23; Martin Nolan, "The Day Teddy Roosevelt, Admiral Dewey and 'Bayonet Rule' Converged in S.F.," *SFC*, May 11, 2003.

    banana republic: Malcolm D. McLean, "O. Henry in Honduras," *American Literary Realism, 1870–1910* 1, no. 3, Summer 1968, 39–46; O. Henry, *Cabbages and Kings*, New York: Burt, 1904, 132, 296; Barry Popik, "Banana Republic," *The Big Apple*,

July 6, 2009, https://www.barrypopik.com/index.php/new_york_city/entry/banana_republic, accessed February 2, 2017; T.W., "Where Did Banana Republics Get Their Name?," *The Economist*, November 21, 2013; Kat Eschner, "Where We Got the Term 'Banana Republic,'" *smithsonian.com*, January 18, 2017, https://www.smithsonianmag.com/smart-news/where-we-got-term-banana-republic-180961813/, accessed March 2, 2017; Pascal Tréguer, "The Appearance of 'Banana Republic' in the USA in 1901," *word histories*, https://wordhistories.net/2018/07/03/banana-republic-origin/, accessed January 8, 2020.

   neologeewhiz: Redfern, *Clichés and Coinages*, 238. **Joyce's neologisms**: Paul Anthony Jones, "17 Words Invented by James Joyce," *Huffington Post*, May 17, 2015, https://www.huffpost.com/entry/17-words-invented-by-james-joyce_b_6866424, accessed February 9, 2018; *Joyce Word Dictionary*, http://webcache.googleusercontent.com/search?q=cache:http://www.joycewords.com/about/, accessed August 5, 2019. **epiphany, epiphanised**: Steinmetz, *Semantic Antics*, 62–63; Herbert F. Tucker, "Epiphany and Browning: Character Made Manifest," *PMLA* 107, no. 5, October 1992, 1208–21; "James Joyce: Definition of Epiphany," http://theliterarylink.com/joyce.html, accessed May 8, 2018.

   Stein: Gertrude Stein, *Everybody's Autobiography*, New York: Random House, 1937, 298: Keyes, *The Quote Verifier*, 219–20; Ben Zimmer, "Why Gertrude Stein's 'No There There' Is Everywhere," *WSJ*, February 2, 2018.

   smoke and mirrors: SPD, 671–72; Jimmy Breslin, *How the Good Guys Finally Won*, New York: Viking, 1975; **Lowell Sun**: "Smoke and Mirrors," *The Phrase Finder*, https://www.phrases.org.uk/meanings/324700.html, accessed August 5, 2018. **Sen. John Johnston**: Pascal Tréguer, "Meaning and Origin of the Phrase 'Smoke and Mirrors,'" *word histories*, https://wordhistories.net/2017/04/12/smoke-and-mirrors/, accessed January 8, 2020.

   Gang Couldn't Shoot Straight: Jimmy Breslin, *The Gang That Couldn't Shoot Straight*, New York: Viking, 1969. Breslin discusses the ubiquity of this title in his memoir *I Want to Thank My Brain for Remembering Me*, New York: Little, Brown, 1996, 32, 132. **Venezuela allusion**: "How Venezuela's President Maintains His Grip on Power," interview with Jon Lee Anderson, *Weekend Edition Saturday*, NPR, December 23, 2017. **Chafee**: David Scharfenberg, "Lincoln Chafee's Unlikely Campaign," *BG*, May 8, 2015. **Gang Wouldn't Write Straight**: Marc Weingarten, ed., *The Gang That Wouldn't Shoot Straight: Wolfe, Thompson, Didion, Capote, and the New Journalism Revolution*, New York: Crown, 2006. **Krugman**: *NYT*, February 1, 2018.

   gamesmanship: Stephen Potter, *The Theory and Practice of Gamesmanship: Or, The Art of Winning Games Without Actually Cheating*, London: Hart-Davis, 1947; Ayto, *Twentieth Century Words*, 277, 287, 357. **brinkmanship**: Ibid., 329; SPD, 83–84; Barnhart and Metcalf, *America in So Many Words*, 253; "brinkmanship," *Online Etymology Dictionary*, https://www.etymonline.com/search?q=brinkmanship, accessed July 29, 2016; James Shepley, "How Dulles Avoided War," *Life*, January 16, 1956, 70.

whisperer: Neal Davies, "There's No Such Thing as a 'Horse Whisperer,'" *horse-talk.co.nz*, https://www.horsetalk.co.nz/2015/07/28/no-such-thing-horse-whisperer/, accessed February 19, 2020; Beth Slovic, "At the Church of Buck, Riders Commune with Their Horses," *Bozeman Daily Chronicle*, May 14, 2005; Mandalit del Barco, "'Vegetable Whisperer,' Chef Plants the Seeds of His Own Reinvention," *The Salt*, NPR, April 17, 2017; "One of Portland's Best New Breweries Opens Its First Taproom Monday with Picnic Blankets and a Half-Hidden Beer Garden," *The Oregonian*, May 18, 2018.

self-help: Samuel Smiles, *Self-Help: With Illustrations of Character and Conduct*, Boston: Ticknor and Fields, 1859, 1866, 1: *OED*; Asa Briggs, "Samuel Smiles: The Gospel of Self-Help," *History Today* 37, no. 5, May 5, 1987, https://www.historyto-day.com/archive/samuel-smiles-gospel-self-help, accessed April 20, 2016; "Samuel Smiles: On the Origin of Self-Help," *The Economist*, April 24, 2004, 86; Kate Williams, "Self Help Victorian Style," *BBC News Magazine*, July 2, 2009, http://news.bbc.co.uk/2/hi/uk_news/magazine/8130223.stm, accessed April 20, 2016. *pyschobabble*: *OED*. **Bushes**: David Jackson, "Bush Denounces 'Psychobabble' About His Father," *USA Today*, December 7, 2014; Taegan Goddard, "Bonus Quote of the Day," *Political Wire*, January 5, 2016, https://politicalwire.com/page/2/, accessed January 5, 2016.

R. D. Rosen: Richard Dean Rosen, "Psychobabble: The New Jargon of Candor," *New Times*, October 1975, 49; R. D. Rosen, *Psychobabble: Fast Talk and Quick Cure in the Era of Feeling*, New York: Atheneum, 1977; Richard Dean Rosen, "My Words," *Richard Dean Rosen*, http://rdrosen.com/my-words/, accessed August 6, 2019; "The Psychobabble Man," *Playboy*, June 1978, 23.

13. IVY-COVERED WORDS

bowling alone: Robert D. Putnam, *Bowling Alone: The Collapse and Revival of American Community*, New York: Simon & Schuster, 2000; Brian Lamb interview with Robert Putnam, *C-SPAN Booknotes*, December 24, 2000 https://www.c-span.org/video/?159499-1/bowling-alone, accessed August 6, 2019; Robert D. Putnam, "Bowling Alone," *Journal of Democracy* 6, no. 1, January 1995, 65–78. **New York Times essayist**: Cristobal Young, "You Don't Need More Free Time," *NYT*, January 8, 2016.

broken windows: James Q. Wilson and George L. Kelling, "Broken Windows," *ATL*, March 1982, 29–38, 31; Justin Peters, "Broken Windows: Policing Doesn't Work," *Slate*, December 3, 2014. **Kelling told Vedantam**: Shankar Vedantam, "How 'Broken Windows' Helped Shape Tensions Between Police and Communities," *All Things Considered*, NPR, November 16, 2016.

superpredators: John Dilulio, "The Coming of the Super-Predators," *The Weekly Standard*, November 27, 1995, 23–28. **Hillary Clinton's 1996 speech**: Keene State College, Keene, New Hampshire, https://www.youtube.com/watch?v=jouCrA7ePno, accessed August 7, 2019; Robert Mackey, Zaid Jilani, "Hillary Clinton Still Haunted by Discredited Rhetoric on 'Superpredators,'" *The Intercept*, February 25, 2016, https://

theintercept.com/2016/02/25/activists-want-hillary-clinton-apologize-hyping-myth-superpredators-1996/, accessed August 7, 2019. **Dilulio's epiphany**: Elizabeth Becker, "As Ex-theorist on Young 'Superpredators,' Bush Aide Has Regrets," *NYT*, February 9, 2001; Clyde Haberman, "When Youth Violence Spurred 'Superpredator' Fear," *NYT*, April 6, 2014; "The Superpredator Myth, 20 Years Later," *Equal Justice Initiative*, April 7, 2014, https://eji.org/news/superpredator-myth-20-years-later, accessed July 6, 2015.

pecking order: *OED*; Porter G. Perrin, "'Pecking Order' 1927–54," *American Speech* 30, no. 4, December 1955, 265–68; John Price, "A Remembrance of Thorleif Schjelderup-Ebbe," *Human Ethology Bulletin* 10, no. 1, March 1995, 1–6; Frans de Waal, *The Ape and the Sushi Master: Cultural Reflections by a Primatologist*, New York: Basic, 2001, 46–48. **Alverdes**: Friedrich Alverdes, *Social Life in the Animal World*, New York: Harcourt, 1927, cited in W. C. Alee, *Animal Aggregations: A Study in General Sociology*, Chicago: University of Chicago Press, 1931, 344–45; M. W. Schein, ed., *Social Hierarchy and Dominance*, Stroudsburg, PA: Dowden, Hutchinson and Ross, 1975. **Huxley**: Aldous Huxley *Point Counter Point*, Champaign, IL: Dalkey, 1928, 1996, 315; Mead: *SPD*, 533–34. **Alsops**: Porter G. Perrin, *American Speech*, 268.

Adichie: Chimamanda Ngozi Adichie, *Americanah*, New York: Anchor, 2014, 220. **McWhorter**: McWhorter, *Doing Your Own Thing*, 242. **Butler**: Judith Butler, *Frames of War: When Is Life Grievable?*, London: Verso, 2009; Judith Butler, *Gender Trouble: Feminism and the Subversion of Identity*, New York: Routledge, 1990, 1997.

intersectionality: *OED*; Kimberlé Williams Crenshaw, "Demarginalizing the Intersection of Race and Sex: A Black Feminist Critique of Antidiscrimination Doctrine, Feminist Theory and Antiracist Politics," *The University of Chicago Legal Forum*, no. 1, 1989, 139–67; **2015 article**: Patricia Hill Collins, "Intersectionality's Definitional Dilemmas," *Annual Review of Sociology* 41, no. 1, August 2015, 1–20; Kory Stamper, "A Brief, Convoluted History of the Word 'Intersectionality,'" The Cut, *New York*, https://www.thecut.com/2018/03/a-brief-convoluted-history-of-the-word-intersectionality.html, accessed June 12, 2020.

Telegraph: Ava Vidal, "'Intersectional Feminism': What the Hell Is It? (And Why You Should Care)," *The Telegraph*, January 15, 2014; **Crenshaw comment, "it's complicated"**: "Kimberlé Crenshaw on Intersectionality, More than Two Decades Later," *Columbia Law School*, https://www.law.columbia.edu/pt-br/news/2017/06/kimberle-crenshaw-intersectionality, accessed February 12, 2018.

natural selection: Charles Darwin, *On The Origins of Species by Means of Natural Selection*, Chicago: Britannica, 1859, 1952, 32. *survival of the fittest*: Herbert Spencer, *The Principles of Biology*, Vol. 2, New York: Appleton, 1864, 1898, 444; Charles Darwin, *The Variation of Animals and Plants Under Domestication*, London: John Murray, 1868, 1905, 7–8. **Darwinisms, Zimmer**: Ben Zimmer, "Darwin Words," *Visual Thesaurus*, February 11, 2009, https://www.visualthesaurus.com/worret.ists/15165, accessed April 28, 2017; Zimmer, "Happy Lincoln / Darwin Day," *Visual Thesaurus*, February 12, 2009, https://www.visualthesaurus.com/cm/wordroutes/happy-lincolndarwin-day/, accessed April 27, 2017; *OED*. **Darwin's Spanish loan words**: Ibid.; Hitchings, *The Secret Life of Words*, 256; Lynch, *The Lexicographer's Dilemma*, 145; *OED*.

knee jerk: Ann Scott, Mervyn J. Eadie, and Andrew Lees, *William Richard Gowers: Exploring the Victorian Brain*, Oxford: Oxford University Press, 2012, 101–2, 138, 146–48, 245. (The authors note speculation that it was another Doyle character, not Sherlock Holmes, who was modeled after William Gowers. Scott is Gowers's great-granddaughter.) Andrew J. Lees, "The Strange Case of Dr William Gowers and Mr Sherlock Holmes," *Brain* 138, no. 7, 2015, 2103–8; F. Clifford Rose, *History of British Neurology*, London: Imperial College, 2012, 131–37; William Richard Gowers, *A Manual of Diseases of the Nervous System*, London: Churchill, 1886–88, 1892. Although in 1885 Gowers had called this response *myotatic irritability*, by the time he published his opus he called it simply *the knee-jerk*, as it's been called ever since. On allegorical uses of *knee jerk*, see *SPD*, 375.

vegetative state: Bryan Jennett and Fred Plum, "Persistent Vegetative State After Brain Damage: A Syndrome in Search of a Name," *Lancet* 299, no. 7753, April 1, 1972, 734–37; Bryan Jennett, *The Vegetative State*, Cambridge: Cambridge University Press, 2002, 1–5; "A Brief History of the Vegetative State," *Minds and Brains*, April 28, 2014, https://philosophyandpsychology.wordpress.com/2014/04/28/a-brief-history-of-the-vegetative-state/, accessed May 8, 2017.

Dawkins, *meme*: Richard Dawkins, *The Selfish Gene*, Oxford: Oxford University Press, 1976, 203–15; Richard Dawkins, "The Selfish Meme," *Time*, April 19, 1999, 52–53; Chatfield, *Netymology*, 48–50; *OED*.

black hole: John Archibald Wheeler with Kenneth Ford, *Geons, Black Holes, and Quantum Foam: A Life in Physics*, New York: Norton, 2000, 296–97. **Wheeler obituary**: Dennis Overbye, "John A. Wheeler, Physicist Who Coined the Term 'Black Hole,' Is Dead at 96," *NYT*, April 14, 2008. In "Black Holes," *World Wide Words*, April 25, 2008, http://www.worldwidewords.org/topicalwords/tw-bla1.htm, accessed June 29, 2015, Michael Quinion reviews possible explanations for Wheeler's claim to have introduced (if not coined) *black hole* in 1967, even though it had appeared in print three years earlier, including the possibility that the same person had suggested this term both to Wheeler and to earlier parties. Quinion credits Fred Shapiro with digging up its use by Ann Ewing, *Science News Letter* 39, no. 1, January 18, 1964. The *OED* also includes this citation.

Merton quotes: Merton and Barber, *The Travels and Adventures of Serendipity*, xiv, xxi, 235. **Colleagues on Merton**: Gerald Holton, "Robert K. Merton," *Proceedings of the American Philosophical Society* 144, no. 4, December 2004, 506–17; Craig Calhoun, "Robert K. Merton Remembered," *Footnotes*, March 2003, https://www.asanet.org/sites/default/files/savvy/footnotes/mar03/indextwo.html, accessed April 26, 2016. **Merton's neologisms**: Piotr Sztompka, *Robert K. Merton: An Intellectual Profile*, New York: St. Martin's, 1986, 31–32; *OED*. *unanticipated consequences*: Robert K. Merton, "The Unanticipated Consequences of Purposive Action," *American Sociological Review* 1, no. 6, December 1936, 894–904; Robert K. Merton, *Social*

Theory and Social Structure, New York: Simon & Schuster, 1968, 117, 120; Frank de Zwart, "Unintended but Not Unanticipated Consequences," *Theory and Society* 44, no. 3, May 2015, 283–97. **self-fulfilling prophecy**: Robert Merton, "The Self-Fulfilling Prophecy," *Antioch Review* 8, no. 2, Summer 1948, 193–210, 195. **Matthew effect**: Robert K. Merton, "The Matthew Effect in Science," *Science* 159, no. 3810, January 5, 1968, 56–63. **Gladwell**: Malcolm Gladwell, *Outliers*, New York: Little, Brown, 2008, 15–34, 30.

focus group: "The Vocabularist: Where Did the Term Focus Group Come From?," *Magazine Monitor*, BBC News, April 2, 2015, https://www.bbc.com/news/blogs-magazine-monitor-32141190, accessed May 23, 2018; Robert K. Merton and Patricia L. Kendall, "The Focused Interview," *American Journal of Sociology* 51, no. 6, May 1946, 541–57.

Birdwhistell, kinesics: *OED*; Ray Birdwhistell, *Introduction to Kinesics: An Annotation System for Analysis of Body Motion and Gesture*, Washington, DC: Department of State, 1952, 3. **Birdwhistell's neologisms**: Alessandra Padula, "Kinesics," in *Encyclopedia of Communication Theory*, ed. Stephen W. Littlejohn and Karen A. Foss, Los Angeles: Sage, 2009, 581–83. **Birdwhistell on body language**: Thomas Barfield, *The Dictionary of Anthropology*, Hoboken, NJ: Wiley-Blackwell, 1998, 223–34. **online dictionary**: "kinesics," *Etymology Dictionary*, https://www.etymonline.com/word/kinesics, accessed August 12, 2019. **Times obituary**: Eric Pace, "Prof. Ray L. Birdwhistell, 76; Helped Decipher Body Language," *NYT*, October 25, 1994.

proxemics, personal space: Ani Kington, "Proxemics and Communication Styles," May 6, 2013, *InterExchange*, https://www.interexchange.org/articles/career-training-usa/2013/05/06/proxemics-and-communication-styles/, accessed April 6, 2019; Robert Sommer, *Personal Space: The Behavioral Basis of Design*, Englewood Cliffs, NJ: Prentice-Hall, 1969. **Biden**: *NYT*, April 3, 2019.

Grafenberg, G-Spot: Elizabeth Hess, "Sexual Speculation: The Story of G," *WP*, September 19, 1982; Emily Dugan, "Mystery of the G Spot Explored," *The Independent*, February 21, 2008; Goldy Levy, "1957: The Doctor Who Discovered the G-spot, if There Is One, dies," *Haaretz*, October 28, 2016; Ernest Grafenberg, "The Role of the Urethra in Female Orgasm," *The International Journal of Sexology* 3, no. 3, February 1950, 145–48; Frank Addiego, Edwin G. Belzer Jr., Jill Comolli, William Moger, John D. Perry, and Beverly Whipple, "Female Ejaculation: A Case Study," *The Journal of Sex Research* 17, no. 1, 1981, 13–21; Alice Kahn Ladas, Beverly Whipple, and John D. Perry, *The G-Spot and Other Discoveries About Human Sexuality*, New York: Holt, Rinehart & Winston, 1982. **music critic**: *Independent*, January 5, 1991, cited in *OED*.

dephlogisticated air, oxygen: Hitchings, *The Language Wars*, 101; American Chemical Society, "Joseph Priestley and the Discovery of Oxygen," https://www.acs.org/content/acs/en/education/whatischemistry/landmarks/josephpriestleyoxygen.html, accessed August 13, 2019.

Einstein, invariance, relativity: Arthur I. Miller, *Albert Einstein's Special Theory of Relativity*, Reading, MA: Addison-Wesley, 1981, xiii, 1–2, 4, 88–89, 232, 234; Brandon

R. Brown, *Planck: Driven by Vision, Broken by War*, New York: Oxford University Press, 2015, 6; Irving Klotz, "Postmodernist Rhetoric Does Not Change Fundamental Scientific Facts," *The Scientist* 10, no. 15, July 1996, 9; Craig Rusbult, "Einstein's Theory of Relativity Should Be Called a Theory of Invariance Because It Is Based on Constancy, Not Relativity," 2007, https://www.asa3.org/ASA/education/views/invariance.htm, accessed August 2, 2016; email to author from Daniel Kennefick, coauthor of *An Einstein Encyclopedia* (Princeton, NJ: Princeton University Press, 2015), May 3, 2018.

peak experience, hierarchy of needs, self-actualization: Edward Hoffman, *The Right to Be Human: A Biography of Abraham Maslow*, Los Angeles: Tarcher, 1988, 339, 340–41; Erin Sullivan, "Self-Actualization," *Encyclopedia Britannica*, https://www.britannica.com/science/self-actualization, accessed August 13, 2019; Joaquín Selva, "What Is Self-Actualization? A Psychologist's Definition," *PositivePsychology*, May 5, 2017, https://positivepsychology.com/self-actualization/, accessed August 13, 2019. **gun-owners' hierarchy of needs**: Amy Walter, "It's Not All About the NRA," *The Cook Political Report*, February 22, 2018, https://cookpolitical.com/analysis/national/national-politics/its-not-all-about-nra, accessed February 24, 2018. **Maslow's tongue-twisters**: Edward Hoffman, *The Right to Be Human*, 337, 339, 341. **postmortem life**: Ibid., 325. **holistic**: Abraham Maslow, "A Symbol for Holistic Thinking," *Persona* 1, no. 1, March 1947, 24–25; J. C. Smuts, *Holism and Evolution*, New York: Macmillan, 1926, 98, ix.

14. COINED WITH INTENT

Browne: Hugh Aldersey-Williams, *In Search of Sir Thomas Browne: The Life and Afterlife of the Seventeenth Century's Most Inquiring Mind*, New York: Norton, 2015; Denny Hilton, "Sir Thomas Browne and the Oxford English Dictionary," *Oxford Dictionaries*, August 8, 2012, http://blog.oxforddictionaries.com/2012/08/sir-thomas-browne/, accessed August 4, 2015. **Browne's neologisms**: Ibid.; *OED*; Hugh Aldersey-Williams, *In Search of Sir Thomas Browne*, xix, 10–14. **electricity**: Ibid., 150. **botanologer, botanist**: Ibid., 138. **Johnson on Browne**: Ibid., 10. **Browne's admirers**: Ibid., 14–22. **Browne's admired neologisms**: Hilton, "Sir Thomas Browne and the Oxford English Dictionary"; Hugh Aldersey-Williams, *In Search of Sir Thomas Browne*, 10–14, 27, 151, 181. **Aldersey-Williams**: Ibid., 11. **Hilton told Aldersey-Williams**: Ibid., 13.

Thomas Huxley: Russell Grigg, "Darwin's Bulldog—Thomas H. Huxley," *Creation* 31, no. 3, June 2008, 39–41; Ann Scott et al., *William Richard Gowers*, 71.

agnostic: *OED*; *M-W*, 5–6; Mead, *Word-Coinage*, 67; Bill Young, "The Origin of the Word *Agnostic*," *The Secular Web*, https://infidels.org/library/modern/reason/agnosticism/agnostic.html, accessed November 17, 2015; "More on Huxley and the Definition of Agnosticism," *The Secular Web*, https://infidels.org/library/modern/mathew/sn-huxley.html, accessed November 17, 2015; Thomas H. Huxley, "Agnosticism," in *Christianity and Agnosticism*, New York: Humboldt, 1889, 20–21, https://archive.org/details/agnosticism00variuoft/page/n3, accessed November 19,

2015. **Bertrand Russell**: Bertrand Russell, *The Autobiography of Bertrand Russell, 1914–1944*, Boston: Atlantic Monthly/Little, Brown, 1951, 1968, 30.

    Douglas, Wilde: Montgomery H. Hyde, *The Trials of Oscar Wilde*, New York: Dover, 1962, 1973, 106–17, 121–12, 129, 201–2, 204; Keyes, *The Wit and Wisdom of Oscar Wilde*, 1, 157–58. **British homosexuality**: Ibid., 12–13, 18; Gary Schmidgall, *The Stranger Wilde*, New York: Dutton, 1994, 172.

    euphemisms for homosexuality: Flexner, *Listening to America*, 283–84; Keyes, *The Wit and Wisdom of Oscar Wilde*, 12–13, 18; Keyes, *Euphemania*, 232–33; R. W. Holder, *How Not to Say What You Mean: A Dictionary of Euphemisms*, Oxford: Oxford University Press, 1987, 2007, 269, 285, 294; Ann Bertram, *NTC's Dictionary of Euphemisms*, Chicago: NTC, 1998, 1999, 59, 163, 271, 281; Ayto, *Wobbly Bits and Other Euphemisms*, 104–10; Pei, *Words in Sheep's Clothing*, 213.

    homosexuals: GVGK Tang, "150 Years Ago, the Word 'Homosexual Was Coined in a Secret Correspondence," *medium,* May 6, 2018, https://medium.com/@gvgk-tang/150-years-ago-the-word-homosexual-was-coined-in-a-secret-correspondence-1803ff9a79bc, accessed September 23, 2020; Manfred Herzer, "Kertbeny and the Nameless Love," *Journal of Homosexuality* 12, no. 1, Fall 1985, 1–26; Rictor Norton, "The Term Homosexual," *A Critique of Social Constructionism and Postmodern Queer Theory*, http://rictornorton.co.uk/social14.htm, accessed August 6, 2016; Dan Heching, "The Word 'Homosexuality' Is Born," *Out*, May 6, 2016, https://www.out.com/today-gay-history/2016/5/06/birth-term-homosexuality, accessed February 13, 2018. *heterosexual*: Ibid.

    Symonds: Manfred Herzer, "Kertbeny and the Nameless Love"; Phyllis Grosskurth, *Havelock Ellis: A Biography*, New York: Penguin/Putnam, 1980, 174–75.

    Ellis on *homosexual*: Lawrence Paros, *The Erotic Tongue: A Sexual Lexicon*, New York: Owl/Holt, 1984, 152; Grosskurth, *Havelock Ellis*, 185. **Havelock Ellis, *Sexual Inversion***: Ibid., 179, 184–90. *eonism, transvestism*: Havelock Ellis, *Studies in the Psychology of Sex, Vol. 7: Eonism and Other Supplementary Studies*, Philadelphia: Davis, 1928, v–vi, 1–4, cited in Phyllis Grosskurth, *Havelock Ellis*, 359, 379; Magnus Hirschfeld, *Die Transvestiten*, cited in Phyllis Grosskurth, *Havelock Ellis*, 379; Havelock Ellis, *Eonism*, v; Vern L. Bullough and Bonnie Bullough, *Cross Dressing, Sex, and Gender*, Philadelphia: University of Pennsylvania Press, 1993, vii. **Ellis's neologisms**: Phyllis Grosskurth, *Havelock Ellis*, 221, 233–34, 291–92, 390; Fritz Wittels, *Sigmund Freud: His Personality, His Teaching and His School*, New York: Routledge, 2013, 112. *narcissism*: Ibid., 200, 291, 362, 391; *M-W*, 315; S. H. Konrath, "Narcissism," *Deep Blue*, 2007, 1–4, https://deepblue.lib.umich.edu/bitstream/hanret.e/2027.42/57606/skonrath_2.pdf?sequence=2, accessed March 13, 2018. **Coleridge**: *OED*; Angela Tung, "The Rime of a Romantic Poet: 10 Words Coined by Samuel Taylor Coleridge." *wordnik*, October 21, 2015, https://blog.wordnik.com/the-rime-of-a-romantic-poet-10-words-coined-by-samuel-taylor-coleridge, accessed August 26, 2019; Jeffrey Aronson, "When I Use a Word . . . Narcissism," *thebmjopinion*, August 12, 2016, https://blogs.bmj.com/bmj/2016/08/12/jeffrey-aronson-when-i-use-a-word-narcissism/, accessed August 26, 2019.

Sanger: Jean H. Baker, *Margaret Sanger: A Life of Passion*, New York: Hill and Wang, 2011, 89, 91–93. **Sanger and Ellis**: Ibid., 61, 92–93; Phyllis Grosskurth, *Havelock Ellis*, 242–87, 292, 325–26, 371–75, 432; Margaret Sanger, *An Autobiography*, New York: Dover, 1938, 2004, 94, 133–41, 277–78. Margaret H. Sanger, *Family Limitation*, rev. 6th ed., 1917, https://archive.lib.msu.edu/DMC/AmRad/familylimitations.pdf; Jean H. Baker, *Margaret Sanger*, 85–88; "Sanger's Boardwalk Empire Cameo," *Margaret Sanger Papers Project*, https://sangerpapers.wordpress.com/2010/09/24/sangers-boardwalk-empire-cameo/, accessed August 6, 2016. *climax*: *OED*; Margaret H. Sanger, *Family Limitation*, 10. *coitus interrupts, douche, condoms*: Ibid., 6–7, 9–10. **Sanger, "At that time"**: Margaret Sanger, "Early Years of Margaret Sanger's Work in the Birth Control Movement," 1930, Margaret Sanger Papers, Library of Congress, 128:0346-034. **Sanger's apartment meeting**: Margaret Sanger, "Early Years of Margaret Sanger's Work in the Birth Control Movement," Margaret Sanger Papers, Library of Congress (microfilm), August 1952, 28: 349; Margaret Sanger, *My Fight for Birth Control*, Oxford: Pergamon, 1931, 1969, 83–84; Margaret Sanger, *An Autobiography*, 107–8; Rudolph Brasch, *How Did Sex Begin? Sense and Nonsense of Sexual Customs and Traditions*, Sydney, Australia: Angus & Robertson, 1974, 100; "Birth Control," in Vern L. Bullough, ed., *Encyclopedia of Birth Control*, Santa Barbara, CA: ABC-CLIO, 2001, 31. **Sanger's return from abroad**: Margaret Sanger, *An Autobiography*, 180. **Sanger told writer**: Miriam Reed, ed., *Margaret Sanger: Her Life in Her Words*, Fort Lee, NJ: Barricade, xiii.

genocide: "Coining a Word and Championing a Cause: The Story of Raphael Lemkin," *Holocaust Encyclopedia*, https://encyclopedia.ushmm.org/content/en/article/coining-a-word-and-championing-a-cause-the-story-of-raphael-lemkin, accessed August 16, 2019; "Raphael Lemkin Defines Genocide," *Genocide Watch*, March 14, 2013, http://genocidewatch.net/2013/03/14/raphael-lemkin-defines-genocide-2/, accessed August 18, 2019; Douglas Irvin-Erickson, *Raphaël Lemkin and the Concept of Genocide*, Philadelphia: University of Pennsylvania Press, 2016; "Chapter IX: 'Genocide,'" from Raphael Lemkin, *Axis Rule in Occupied Europe: Laws of Occupation—Analysis of Government—Proposals for Redress*, Washington, DC: Carnegie Endowment for International Peace, 1944, 79–95, http://www.preventgenocide.org/lemkin/AxisRule1944-1.htm, accessed February 4, 2020; (London) *Sunday Times*, October 21, 1945, cited in *OED*.

cybernetics: Norbert Wiener, *I Am a Mathematician*, Garden City, NY: Doubleday, 1956, 321–2; Norbert Wiener, *Cybernetics: Or Control and Communication in the Animal and the Machine,* New York: MIT/Wiley, 1948, 19; Flo Conway and Jim Siegelman, *Dark Hero of the Information Age: In Search of Norbert Wiener The Father of Cybernetics*, New York: Basic, 2005, 174–75; Chatfield, *Netymology*, 39–40; Steinmetz, *There's a Word for It*, 85. **Shannon**: In "Defining 'Cybernetics,'" The American Society for Cybernetics cites the sentence from Claude Shannon's letter to Norbert Wiener as "widely quoted, attributed to Claude Shannon," http://www.asccybernetics.org/foundations/definitions.htm, accessed August 22, 2019. Since the relationship of Shannon and Wiener was edgy, this popular account, whose original source I can't locate, at best must be considered unconfirmed. **"a background in cyber"**: Morgan Chalfant, "Five Key Players for Trump on Cybersecurity," *The Hill*, May 6, 2017. **feed-back**: Norbert Wiener, *Cybernetics*, 13; Flo Conway and Jim Siegelman, *Dark Hero of the Information Age*, 178–79, 373.

locavore: Olivia Wu, "The Challenge: Eat Locally for a Month (You Can Start Practicing Now)," *SFC*, June 1, 2005; Larry West, "What Is the Origin of the Term 'Locavore?,'" *ThoughtCo*, https://www.thoughtco.com/the-origin-of-the-term-locavore-1204000, accessed August 16, 2019. Jessica Prentice, "The Birth of Locavore," *OUPblog*, November 20, 2007, https://blog.oup.com/2007/11/prentice/, accessed July 2, 2016; "Oxford Word of the Year: Locavore," *OUPblog*, November 12, 2007, https://blog.oup.com/2007/11/locavore/, accessed March 20, 2010.

Pei: Pei, *The Story of Language*, 159.

bromide: Gelett Burgess, *Are You a Bromide?*, New York: Huebsch, 1907 (based on a magazine article published a year earlier); Paul Dickson, foreword to Burgess, *Burgess Unabridged*, vii–xii, x. **blurb**: "It's a 'Blurb' Now to Puff a New Book: Gelett Burgess Coins Odd Word for Booksellers' Annual Dinner," *NYT*, May 16, 1907; Burgess, *Burgess Unabridged*, xiv, 7; *M-W*, 54–55; Crystal, *The Story of English in 100 Words*, 213–15; Stan Carey, "Gelett Burgess and the Blurb," *Sentence First*, https://stancarey.wordpress.com/2009/04/14/gelett-burgess-and-the-blurb/, accessed February 10, 2018; Colin Dwyer, "Forget the Book, Have You Read This Irresistible Story on Blurbs?," NPR, September 27, 2015, https://www.npr.org/2015/09/27/429723002/forget-the-book-have-you-read-this-irresistible-story-on-blurbs, accessed February 10, 2018; Pascal Tréguer, "The Noun 'Blurb' Was Coined by Gelett Burgess in 1907," *word histories*, January 17, 2018, https://wordhistories.net/2018/01/17/blurb-gelett-burgess/, accessed August 19, 2019. **Burgess's neologisms**: Burgess, *Burgess Unabridged*, 67, 88–89, 112.

widget: George S. Kaufman and Marc Connelly, *Beggar on Horseback: A Play in Two Parts*, New York: Liveright, 1924, 94–99, 104–11, 132–33; "Widgets," *NYer*, January 1, 1938, 13–14; Handy (Jam) Organization, "Round and Round (Widgets)," 1939, https://archive.org/details/Roundand1939, accessed August 19, 2019; **Surowiecki**: James Surowiecki, "The Goldilocks Effect," *NYer*, May 27, 2002, 50.

Minkova and Stockwell: Minkova and Stockwell, *English Words*, 12–13, 21.

Kodak: Ibid., 12; Carl W. Ackerman, *George Eastman: Founder of Kodak and the Photography Business*, Hopkins, MN: Beard, 1930, 2000, 75–76. Eastman's claim that *Kodak* was an arbitrary coinage is more credible than the same, more dubious claim made by Augustin Thompson about *Moxie*. After considering a wide range of possible etymologies for *Kodak*, biographer Elizabeth Brayer concluded that Eastman should be taken at his word: that this brand name was a pure invention whose value lay in its terseness, uniqueness, and ease of pronunciation. Elizabeth Brayer, *George Eastman: A Biography*, Baltimore: Johns Hopkins University Press, 1996, 63–64, 548–49.

Heroin: *OED*; Forsyth, *Etymologicon*, 107–8; Laura Secorun Palet, "The Deadly Drug that Used to Be a Popular Medicine," OZY, https://www.ozy.com/flashback/the-dearet.y-drug-that-used-to-be-a-popular-medicine/39174, accessed August 20, 2019;

Mark Borigini, "When Heroin Was Available to Housewives and Aspirin Was Bad for the Heart," *Psychology Today*, January 12, 2012, https://www.psychologytoday.com/us/blog/overcoming-pain/201201/when-heroin-was-available-housewives-and-aspirin-was-bad-the-heart, accessed August 20, 2019.

Escalator, escalate, escalation: *OED*; Crystal, *The Story of English in 100 Words*, 197–99; Steinmetz, *There's a Word for It*, 11. Herman Kahn, *On Escalation: Metaphors and Scenarios*, New York: Praeger, 1986.

zipper: *OED*; Robert O. Friedel, *Zipper: An Exploration in Novelty*, New York: Norton, 1994, 1996, 148–49; Henry Petroski, *The Evolution of Useful Things: How Everyday Artifacts—From Forks and Pins to Paper Clips and Zippers—Came to Be as They Are*, New York: Vintage, 1992, 1994, 110–11.

cellophane: David A. Hounshell and John Kenly Smith Jr., *Science and Corporate Strategy: Du Pont R&D, 1902–1980*, Cambridge: Cambridge University Press, 1988, 170, 179, 647; "The Name Nylon and Some of Its Adventures," from notes by Charles R. Rutledge, Textile Fibers Department, June 20, 1966, *Dupont Background*, January 1988. **nylon**: Ibid., 268–69; Susannah Handley, *Nylon: The Manmade Fashion Revolution*, London: Bloomsbury, 1999, 36–37.

transistor: Jon Gertner, *The Idea Factory: Bell Labs and the Great Age of American Innovation*, New York: Penguin, 2012, 98; Michael Riordan and Lillian Hoddeson, *Crystal Fire: The Birth of the Information Age*, New York: Norton, 1997, 159. A different origin story credits Bell engineer John Pierce, later a science fiction writer, with conjuring this name. "Naming the Transistor," PBS (Public Broadcasting Service), http://www.pbs.org/transistor/album1/pierce/naming.html, accessed August 20, 2019. Pierce himself propagates this alternative history in J. R. Pierce, "The Naming of the Transistor," *Proceedings of the IEEE* 86, no. 1, January 1998, *IEEE Xplore*, https://ieeexplore.ieee.org/document/658756, accessed August 20, 2019. However, a blog post recounting the contest version includes an actual reproduction of the naming ballot itself, including the instruction "(to be returned to Miss G. R. Callender, in 1A-323 at Murray Hill)," in which the winning name—*Transistor*—competed with *Semiconductor Triode, Surface States Triode, Crystal Triode, Solid Triode*, and *Ictatron* for naming rights. "How the Transistor Got Its Name," *adafruit.com*, September 5, 2011, https://blog.adafruit.com/2011/09/05/how-the-transistor-got-its-name/, accessed August 20, 2019. The original memo and ballot used for voting on names is linked at "History of the Transistor (the 'Crystal Triode')," *The Porticus Center*, https://www.beatriceco.com/bti/porticus/bell/belllabs_transistor.html, accessed August 20, 2019. As noted in the text, Pierce may have been the source of *transistor* on the contest ballot.

scofflaw: "Delcevare King, Banker, 89, Dead," *NYT*, March 22, 1964; Metcalf, *Predicting New Words*, 44–51; Mencken, *AL*, 174–75; **Barry Popik**: "Scofflaw," *ADS-L Digest*, December 7, 1997, http://www.americandialect.org/americandialectarchives/decxx97105.html, accessed May 22, 2018; Barry Popik, "Scofflaw," *The Big Apple*, December 18, 2004, https://www.barrypopik.com/index.php/new_york_city/entry/scofflaw, accessed August 15, 2019.

Spam: Darrell Ehrlick, *It Happened in Minnesota*, Lanham, MD: Rowman & Littlefield, 2008, 100–101; Forsyth, *Etymologicon*, 105; Judith Stone, "More Than You Wanted to Know About Spam," *NYT Magazine*, July 3, 1994, 243, 366–68; "SPAM: The Wonder Food," Hormel Foods, https://www.hormelfoods.com/newsroom/company-news/spam-the-wonder-food/, accessed August 15, 2019; Gene Gable, "Heavy Metal Madness: Spam vs. Spam," *Creative Pro Week*, August 22, 2005 https://creativepro.com/heavy-metal-madness-spam-vs-spam/, accessed August 15, 2019; "Kenneth Daigneau," *Powers Behind Grand Rapids*, https://powersbehindgr.wordpress.com/powers-theatre/stock-theatre/broadway-players/kenneth-daigneau/, accessed August 15, 2019. *Spam* **as slang**: Dickson, *War Slang*, 216, 328; Alan Green, "Milestone for a Much-Mocked Meat," *Philadelphia Inquirer*, March 29, 1987. *Spam* **as 'Net name**: Tom Zeller, "Spamology," *NYT*, June 1, 2003; Chatfield, *Netymology*, 145–47; Finn Brinton, *Spam: A Shadow History of the Internet*, Cambridge, MA: MIT Press, 2003, xiv, xxii, 12–14, 25; Brad Templeton, "Origin of the Term 'Spam' to Mean Net Abuse," *templeton.com*, 2003, https://www.templetons.com/brad/spamterm.html, accessed August 15, 2019; Darren Waters, "Spam Blights E-mail 15 Years On," BBC News, http://news.bbc.co.uk/2/hi/technology/7322615.stm, accessed August 15, 2019; Andrea Seabrook, "At 30, Spam Going Nowhere Soon," *All Things Considered*, NPR, May 3, 2008.

millennials, **etc.**: Neil Howe and William Strauss, *Generations:: The History of America's Future 1584 to 2069*, New York: Morrow, 1991, 335–43. **2005 Internet contest**: Bruce Horovitz, "After Gen X, Millennials, What Should Next Generation Be?," *USA Today*, May 4, 2012; Neil Howe, "Introducing the Homeland Generation," *forbes.com*, October 27, 2014, https://www.forbes.com/sites/neilhowe/2014/10/27/introducing-the-homeland-generation-part-1-of-2/#5cb1bc92bd67, accessed August 16, 2019. See also Jeremy W. Peters, "They Predicted 'The Crisis of 2020' . . . in 1991. So How Does This End?" *NYT*, May 28, 2020.

15. NONSTARTERS

ecdysiast: Mencken, *The American Language, Supplement I*, 585–87, Mencken, *The American Language, Supplement II*, 694; Rachel Shteir, *Striptease:: The Untold History of the Girlie Show*, New York: Oxford University Press, 2004, 216; Rachel Shteir, *Gypsy: The Art of the Tease*, New Haven, CT: Yale University Press, 2009, 104–5. The reporter who interviewed Gypsy Rose Lee, H. Allen Smith, later became a prominent humorist. In his 1941 book *Low Man on a Totem Pole* (Lake Oswego, OR: eNet Press, 1941, 2015, 82–84), Smith described his encounter with Lee the previous year. *ecdysiast* **in musical**: Arthur Laurents, Jule Styne, Stephen Sondheim, and Gypsy Rose Lee, *Gypsy: Gypsy, a Musical: Suggested by the Memoirs of Gypsy Rose Lee*, New York: Theatre Communications, 1959, 1994, 97.

Sniglets: Rich Hall & Friends, *Sniglets (Snig'Lit): Any Word That Doesn't Appear in the Dictionary, but Should*, New York: Collier/Macmillan, 1984, 36, 43, 55, 74; Metcalf, *Predicting New Words*, 22–27.

Academy: Mead, *Word-Coinage*, 211; "Our Literary Competitions: Result of No. 14," *The Academy* 56, no. 1393, January 14, 1899, 73–74; *The Academy* 56, no. 1395, January 28, 1899, 116–17. *Forum*: *AL*, 175. **NPR contest**: "NPR Announces 'Word Fugitive' Winner," *All Things Considered*, NPR, March 17, 2006.

Wallraff, "recreational coining": Wallraff, *Word Fugitives*, 8–10, 12, 16–17, 79, 121, 137, 140, 146, 177, 186, 190; Joshua J. Friedman, "Sniglets and Slithy Toves"; Barbara Wallraff, "Shouldn't There Be a Word . . . ?," *American Scholar* 75, no. 2, Spring 2006, 76–87, https://theamericanscholar.org/shouldnt-there-be-a-word/ #.XuoQ9ZNKhao, accessed June 11, 2016. **Wallraff quotations**: Ibid.; Joshua J. Friedman, "Sniglets and Slithy Toves." **McFedries, "stunt words"**: McFedries, *Word Spy*, ix, 242–43, 288.

snowmageddon: Jeff Clark, "Snowmageddon Twitter Analysis," *Neoformix*, January 30, 2009, https://www.neoformix.com/2009/Snowmageddon.html, accessed August 10, 2016; Andrew Freedman, "'Snowmageddon' Name Traced Back to CWG Reader," *Capital Weather Gang*, washingtonpost.com, February 19, 2010, http://voices.washington-post.com/capitalweathergang/2010/02/weve_been_challenged_-_to_a_sn.html, accessed August 10, 2016. *Frankenstorm, Superstorm Sandy*: Doyle Rice, "What's in a Name? Frankenstorm vs. Sandy," *USA Today*, October 26, 2012.

toe-tapper: "toe-tapper," *UD*; *wide stance*: "wide stance," *UD*; Rebecca Boone, "Craig's 'Wide Stance' Enters Lexicon," *The Oklahoman*, October 10, 2007.

Hobsonize: Richard W. Turk, introduction to *The Sinking of the "Merrimac,"* by Richmond Pearson Hobson, Annapolis, MD: Naval Institute, 1899, 1987, xiii–xix, xxiv; Mead, *Word-Coinage*, 64–65; *Baltimore American* cited in Mathews, *A Dictionary of Americanisms*, Vol. 1, 812. **Fletcherism**: Ibid., 627; Forsyth, *Horologicon*, 104–6. **Grahamism, Grahamites**: Mathews, *A Dictionary of Americanisms*, Vol. 1, 727.

Romeike, Romeikitis: Mead, *Word-Coinage*, 111–12.

internestic: Nancy Gibbs, "The Many Lives of Madeleine Albright," *Time*, February 17, 1997, 52. *chaordic*: Harriet Rubin, "C.E.O. Libraries Reveal Keys to Success," *NYT*, July 21, 2007. *dontopedalogy*: Redfern, *Clichés and Coinages*, 232; Karan Thapar, "Dontopedalogy: The Science Prince Philip Taught the World," *Hindustan Times*, May 15, 2018.

Shakespeare's nonstarters: Patricia T. O'Conner and Stewart Kellerman, "Neologisms: Winners and Losers," *Grammarphobia*, August 28, 2011, https://www. grammarphobia.com/blog/2011/08/neologisms.html, accessed April 23, 2018; Anu Garg, "fustilarian," "rampallion," *A.Word.A.Day*, wordsmith.org, https://wordsmith. org/words/fustilarian.html and https://wordsmith.org/words/rampallion.html, respectively, accessed May 17, 2018; "fustilarian," *Henry IV*, Pt. 2, II.i.62, cited in *OED*. See http://shakespeare.mit.edu/2henryiv/full.html, accessed August 30, 2019.

Thackeray, Cooper, Tolkien, Trollope, Greene, Browne, and Milton's nonstarters: O'Conner and Kellerman, "Neologisms: Winners and Losers"; "Definition of Americaness," *Merriam-Webster*, https://www.merriam-webster.com/dictionary/

Americaness, accessed June 26, 2015; Smith, *The English Language*, 46; Hitchings, "'Authorisms' by Paul Dickson"; Dickson, *Authorisms*, 20, 66; *OED*.

Dahl told daughter: Ariel Levy, "Poetry of Systems," *NYer*, December 18 and 25, 2017, 60–68, 60. **Dahlisms**: Susan Rennie, ed., *Oxford Roald Dahl Dictionary*, Oxford: Oxford University Press, 2016. "Oxford English Dictionary Updates with 6 Dahl Words," *Morning Edition*, NPR, September 14, 2016; Kimberley Reynolds, "From Muggle to Whizpopper: Invented Words in Children's Literature," *OxfordDictionaries.com*, November 26, 2014, http://blog.oxforddictionaries.com/2014/11/children-literature-dahl, accessed January 22, 2016; Robert Hughes, "The Language of Roald Dahl," *OxfordDictionaries.com*, September 2011, http://blog.oxforddictionaries.com/2011/9/the-language-of-roald-dahl, accessed January 22, 2016.

Gibson: Maria Popova, "William Gibson on Cultivating a 'Personal Microculture,'" *brainpickings*, February 24, 2012, https://www.brainpickings.org/2012/02/24/william-gibson-personal-micro-culture/, accessed May 9, 2018.

David Lewis: "Road Rage," *art.spoke.soul.*, April 17, 2012, https://artspoke-soul.wordpress.com/2012/04/17/190/, accessed December 13, 2012. **internot**: Paul McFedries, "Internot," *Word Spy*, February 7, 1998, http://www.logophilialimited.com/index.php?word=internot, accessed May 14, 2008. **Paul Lewis**: "Parlancer: When Language Needs Inventing, Paul Lewis Is the Man to Do It," *Boston College Magazine*, Spring 1996, 14. In *Predicting New Words*, Allan Metcalf reviews at length the Paul Lewis's many nonstarters (16–22). **Rosen**: R. D. Rosen, "My Words," *Richard Dean Rosen* website, http://rdrosen.com/my-words/, accessed August 6, 2019.

BBC committee: Jürg R. Schwyter, *Dictating to the Mob: The History of the BBC Advisory Committee on Spoken English*, Oxford: Oxford University Press, 2016, ix–x, 27–28, 80, 86, 113–14, 129–44, 157–60. **online discussion, *roundabout-gyratory circus***: Nick Kapur (@nick_kapur), Twitter post, June 26–28, 2017, https://twitter.com/nick_kapur/status/879443654598955008?lang=en, accessed April 20, 2018.

Pitman's neologisms, Bryson's comment: Bryson, *The Mother Tongue*, 129; "Isaac Pitman," *Encyclopedia Britannica*, January 8, 2019, https://www.britannica.com/print/article/462091, accessed September 3, 2019; Thomas Allen Reed, *Biography of Isaac Pitman* (*Inventor of Phonography*), London: Griffith, 1890. **shorthand**: *OED*.

Talbot: Larry J. Schaaf, *The Photographic Art of William Henry Fox Talbot*, Princeton, NJ: Princeton University Press, 2000, 17–21, 235–36, has an extensive consideration of the different names given to Talbot's process. In endnotes, Schaaf notes John Herschel's longtime interest in terminology, and his preference for "words and signs used in our reasonings that are full and true representatives of the things signified" (235). Schaaf acknowledges that at least one other colleague advised Talbot that *photography* improved on *sciagraphy* and *photogenic drawing*, but says Herschel lobbied most forcefully for this neologism. See also *William Henry Fox Talbot: Photographs from the J. Paul Getty Museum*, Los Angeles: Getty, 2002, 112–13 (which includes a reproduction of the cover of the 1846 pamphlet titled *Specimens of the Talbotype or Sun Pictures* on p. 144), and Roger Watson and Helen Rappaport, *Capturing the Light: The Birth of*

Photography, a True Story of Genius and Rivalry, New York: St. Martin's, 2013, 134, 137, 184–87.

Sphairistikè, lawn tennis: "Anyone for Sphairistikè?," *BBC Wales History*, April 18, 2012, https://www.bbc.co.uk/blogs/wales/entries/d4437526-3b92-32f4-89a6-bd3c29f296f0, accessed February 8, 2016; Chris Pearce, "Origins of the Wimbledon Tennis Tournament," June 29, 2015, https://chrispearce52.wordpress.com/2015/06/29/origins-of-the-wimbledon-tennis-tournament/, accessed February 8, 2016; Bodleian Library, ed., *The Original Rules of Tennis*, Carlton Victoria, Australia: Miegunyah, 2010, 13–18.

electric speech, speaking telegraph, harmonic telegraph, telephone: Daniel A. Wren, *Management Innovators: The People and Ideas that Have Shaped Modern Business*, New York: Oxford University Press, 1998, 98; Tom Standage, *The Victorian Internet: The Remarkable Story of the Telegraph and the Nineteenth Century's On-line Pioneers*, New York: Walker, 1998, 195–98; American Heritage editors, *Word Histories and Mysteries*, 280–81; John Brooks, *Telephone: The First Hundred Years*, New York: Harper, 1976, 35; Edwin S. Grosvenor and Morgan Wesson, *Alexander Graham Bell: The Life and Times of the Man Who Invented the Telephone*, New York: Abrams, 1997, 44–53; James Meyers, *Eggplants, Elevators, Etc.: An Uncommon History of Common Things*, New York: Hart 1978, 268; *OED*.

eonite, Saran Wrap: Doug Henze, "Dow's Plastic Wrap Celebrates 40th Birthday," *Ludington* (MI) *Daily News*, March 5, 1994; Mary Bellis, "Inventors: Saran Wrap," theinventors.org, http://theinventors.org/library/inventors/blsaranwrap.htm, accessed March 31, 2006; "What Is the Origin of the Brand Names Saran Wrap and Oral B?," *FunTrivia*, December 5, 2001, https://www.funtrivia.com/askft/Question14824.html, accessed February 8, 2016.

Buckminster Fuller: John McHale, *R. Buckminster Fuller*, New York: Braziller, 1962; Sidney Rosen, *Wizard of the Dome: R. Buckminster Fuller, Designer for the Future*, Boston: Little, Brown, 1969; Robert Marks and R. Buckminster Fuller, *The Dymaxion World of Buckminster Fuller*, New York: Anchor/Doubleday, 1973; Lloyd Steven Sieden, *Buckminster Fuller's Universe*, New York: Plenum, 1989; Loretta Lorance, *Becoming Bucky Fuller*, Boston: MIT Press, 2009; Jonathon Keats, *You Belong to the Universe: Buckminster Fuller and the Future*, New York: Oxford University Press, 2016. **4D, dymaxion**: Sidney Rosen, *Wizard of the Dome*, 59–66; Robert Marks and Fuller, *The Dymaxion World of Buckminster Fuller*, 3–4, 9, 18–21, 58; Lloyd Steven Sieden, *Buckminster Fuller's Universe*, 119, 125–32, 256; Loretta Lorance, *Becoming Bucky Fuller*, 83–84, 118, 127, 133, 160–62, 164, 265 261; Keats, *You Belong to the Universe*, 39; Sarah Fallon, "Hey Silicon Valley—Buckminster Fuller Has a Lot to Teach You," *Wired*, March 29, 2016, https://www.wired.com/2016/03/buckminster-fuller-brilliant-crank-lot-teach-silicon-valley/, accessed April 25, 2016. Some, including Fuller, believe Waldo Warren introduced the word *radio* to common parlance as a noun (Keats, *You Belong to the Universe*, 59). **Fuller's neologisms**: Sidney Rosen, *Wizard of the Dome*, 143; Robert Marks and R. Buckminster Fuller, *The Dymaxion World of Buckminster*

Fuller, 2–5, 57, 59; Sieden, *Buckminster Fuller's Universe*, 102–4, 269, 317, 377–79, 388; Elizabeth Kolbert, "Dymaxion Man," *NYer*, June 9 and 16, 2008, 64–69, 66–67. **synergy, synergetics**: *OED*; Dave Wilton, "Synergy," *Wordorigins.org*, January 16, 2014, http://www.wordorigins.org/index.php/site/comments/synergy/, accessed February 8, 2016; R. Buckminster Fuller, *Synergetics: Explorations in the Geometry of Thinking*, New York: Macmillan, 1975. **spaceship earth**: Lloyd Steven Sieden, *Buckminster Fuller's Universe*, 127, 256, 269. According to the descriptive copy for Fuller's *Operating Manual for Spaceship Earth* (Carbondale, IL: Southern Illinois, 1969), the economist Barbara Ward had already used this phrase as a book title before Fuller's own book was published in 1969 but acknowledged him as its source. https://www.amazon.com/Operating-Manual-Spaceship-Buckminster-Fuller/dp/089190235X, accessed September 5, 2019. **geodesic**: John McHale, *R. Buckminster Fuller*, 44; Sidney Rosen, *Wizard of the Dome*, 120–22, 126; Lloyd Steven Sieden, *Buckminster Fuller's Universe*, 305–7, 313, 315–17. **syntropy**: Gene Keyes email to author, August 15, 2007; Antonella Vannini, "Entropy and Syntropy. From Mechanical to Life Science," *NeuroQuantology* 3, no. 2, September 2007; Linda Rae Reneau, "Syntropy—The Rest of Reality," *Life Energy Powers*, https://www.lifeenergypowers.com/entropy-and-syntropy.html, accessed September 5, 2019.

16. VAN WINKLE WORDS

Walpole letter to Mann: Merton and Barber, *The Travels and Adventures of Serendipity*, 9, 30, 285; W. S. Lewis, Warren Hunting Smith, and George L. Lam, *Horace Walpole's Correspondence with Sir Horace Mann*, New Haven, CT: Yale University Press, 1960, 407. **Walpole's neologisms**: *OED*; Merton and Barber, *The Travels and Adventures of Serendipity*, 8–9, 30–32; Lynch, *The Lexicographer's Dilemma*, 254; Hitchings, *The Secret Life of Words*, 210, 216. Walpole used *airgonaut* repeatedly in his letters, as well as *airgonation*. *Muckubus* appears only once. See *The Letters of Horace Walpole: Earl of Orford*, Vol. II, Philadelphia: Lea and Blanford, 1842, 320–21; Paget Toynbee, ed., *The Letters of Horace Walpole: Fourth Earl of Orford*, London: Oxford University Press, 1891, 199, 225, 241, 264, 278, 300. The *OED* cites *betweenity* being used in a 1760 letter by Walpole, then elsewhere from the 1820s. **Circuitous path of *serendipity***: Merton and Barber, *The Travels and Adventures of Serendipity*, 30, 75, 132–33. **American magazine columnist**: "The Spectator," *The Outlook*, July 18, 1903, cited in ibid., 75, 132. **"curious,"** etc.: Merton and Barber, *The Travels and Adventures of Serendipity*, 90, 92. **Meynell**: Ibid., 63–4, 73–74, 128–29. **Crothers, Cannon**: Ibid., 133–34, 137, 228–29, 292; Samuel McChord Crothers, "Humanly Speaking," in Samuel McChord Crothers, *Humanly Speaking*, Boston: Houghton Mifflin, 1912, xiii. **Cannon, *fight or flight*, homeostasis**: David Goldstein, "Walter Cannon: Homeostasis, the Fight-or-Flight Response, the Sympathoadrenal System, and the Wisdom of the Body," *brainimmune*, May 16, 2009, http://www.brainimmune.com/walter-cannon-homeostasis-the-fight-or-flight-response-the-sympathoadrenal-system-and-the-wisdom-of-the-body/, accessed February 21, 2020. **Van Loon, Dine**: Merton and Barber, *The Travels and Adventures of*

Serendipity, 69. **Joyce, *serendipitist***: Ibid., 260. ***Free Press* columnist**: James S. Pooley, ibid., 79–80, 147, 169; **book reviewer (*World Telegram and Sun*)**: Ibid., 286. **lists of favorite words**: Ibid., 288. **foreign translations**: Ibid., 143–44, 250. **variations in English**: Ibid., 102. **Merton on discovering *serendipity*, quoted**: Ibid., 233–35, 238, 289. **Merton on revived words**: Ibid., 22, 67. **Steinmetz**: Steinmetz, *There's a Word for That*, 237; **Barnhart and Metcalf**: Barnhart and Metcalf, *America in So Many Words*, ix.

   cheesiness: OED; Sørensen, *Charles Dickens*, 123. ***aspirational, optics***: Ibid., 45–46, 115. ***dunno, monetize***: *OED* records "dunno" being used in the modern sense as early as 1759, "monetize" in 1867.

   O.M.G.: *OED*; Lord Fisher, *Memories*, London: Hodder and Stoughton, 1919, 77–78; David Sharlatmadan, "11 Words That Are Much Older than You Think," *theguardian.com*, July 1, 2014, https://www.theguardian.com/commentisfree/2014/jul/01/words-much-older-than-you-think-language, accessed January 16, 2016; Rebecca Hiscott, "LOL, WTF? The Origin Stories of Your Favorite Internet Acronyms," *HuffPost*, July 17, 2014, https://www.huffpost.com/entry/internet-acronyms_n_5585425, accessed December 29, 2017; Ben Zimmer, "OMG! It Started in 1917 with a Letter to Churchill," *WSJ*, September 8, 2017, https://www.wsj.com/articles/omg-it-started-in-1917-with-a-letter-to-churchill-1504882081, accessed September 11, 2019.

   vegan: *OED*; "George D Rodger's Interview with Donald Watson (December 2002, Unabridged)," *veganplace*, November 1, 2014, https://veganplace.blog/2014/11/01/george-d-rodgers-interview-with-donald-watson-december-2002-unabridged/, accessed September 11, 2019; "Wanted: A Name," in *The Vegan News*, no. 1, November 1944, http://www.ukveggie.com/vegan_news/, accessed September 24, 2016; "History," *Vegan Society*, https://www.vegansociety.com/about-us/history, accessed September 11, 2019; "Ripened by Human Determination: 70 Years of the Vegan Society," *The Vegan Society,* 2016, https://www.vegansociety.com/sites/default/files/uploads/Ripened%20by%20human%20determination.pdf , accessed September 15, 2020; Rico Nascence, "What Is the Origin of the Word Vegan?," *Quora*, May 18, 2018, https://www.quora.com/What-is-the-origin-of-the-word-vegan, accessed September 11, 2019; Kent Roll, "Who Coined the Term Vegan?," *Quora*, July 17, 2019, https://www.quora.com/Who-coined-the-term-vegan/answer/Kent-Roll, accessed September 11, 2019; Lee Hall, "In Memory and Celebration: Donald and Dorothy," *veganplace.blog*, May 26, 2014, https://veganplace.blog/2014/05/26/remembering-donald-and-dorothy/, accessed September 11, 2019.

   free-range: David Kamp, *The United States of Arugula*, New York: Crown, 2009, 272-73; Gael Greene, "Gettin' Fresh: Larry Forgione and the Homegrown Revolt Against the Tyranny of French Cuisine," *New York*, March 28, 2003, http://nymag.com/nymetro/news/anniversary/35th/n_8573/, accessed June 14, 2011. **Earlier uses of *free-range***: *OED*.

   Ms.: Steinmetz, *There's a Word for It*, 75; Barnhart and Metcalf, *America in So Many Words*, 249; Metcalf, *From Skedaddle to Selfie*, 142–43; *Springfield (MA) Sunday Republican*, November 10, 1901, cited in *OED*.

slacker: *OED*; Metcalf, *From Skedaddle to Selfie*, 166; John Corbin, "A Harvard Man at Oxford," *Harper's Weekly*, February 26, 1898, https://archive.org/stream/ aag4066.1898.001.umich.edu/aag4066.1898.001.umich.edu_djvu.txt,   accessed September 10, 2019.

fiscal cliff: Tom Geogheghan, "Who, What, Why: Who First Called It a 'Fiscal Cliff'?," *BBC News Magazine*, November 14, 2012, https://www.bbc.com/news/ magazine-20318326, accessed November 6, 2019; Margalit Fox, "Water H. Stern, 88, Dies; Coined Term 'Fiscal Cliff,'" *NYT*, November 8, 2013; "The Origin of the Term: Fiscal Cliff," interview with Ben Zimmer, *Morning Edition*, NPR, November 20, 2012; Stephen L. Carter, "The Surprisingly Long History of the Fiscal Cliff," *bloomberg. com*, November 29, 2012, https://www.bloomberg.com/opinion/articles/2012-11-29/ the-long-history-of-the-fiscal-cliff, accessed January 8, 2013. ***credit crunch***: Matthew Parris, "Now That We've Come to the Crunch . . . Who Coined the Fateful Phrase that Has Exploded into Our Daily Lives?," *The Times* (London), October 25, 2008. ***launder***: Greenman, *Words in Action*, 13.

bomb cyclone: Alan Blinder, Patiricia Mazzei, and Jess Bidgood, "'Bomb Cyclone': Snow and Bitter Cold Blast the Northeast," *NYT*, January 4, 2018; Rachel Feltman, "What the Heck Is a Bomb Cyclone?," *Popular Science*, January 3, 2018, https://www.popsci.com/bomb-cyclone/, accessed January 12, 2018; Dan Boyce, "Rare Blizzard Meteorologists Are Calling 'Bomb Cyclone' Hits Central U.S.," *All Things Considered*, NPR, March 13, 2019; Alexander C. Kaufman, "This Is the Man to Blame tor the Term 'Bomb Cyclone'" *HuffPost*, January 3, 2018, updated January 5, 2018, https:// www.huffpost.com/entry/bomb-cyclonedefinition_n_5a4d5beae4b06d1621bcfd56, accessed April 8, 2019; Frederick Sanders and John R. Gyakum, "Synoptic-Dynamic Climatology of the 'Bomb,'" *Monthly Weather Review* 108, no. 10, October 1980, 1589–1606. Apparently military ordnance lends itself to descriptions of severe weather. Before it was applied to whiteout snowstorms in the 1870s, *blizzard* had referred to a sharp volley, as from a gun.

greenhouse effect: J. H. Poynting, "On Prof. Lowell's method for evaluating the surface-temperatures of the planets; with an attempt to represent the effect of day and night on the temperature of the earth," *The London, Edinburgh, and Dublin Philosophical Magazine and Journal of Science* 14, no. 84, 1907, 749–60, 749; Steve Easterbrook, "Who First Coined the Term 'Greenhouse Effect'?," *Serendipity*, August 18, 2015, https://www.easterbrook.ca/steve/2015/08/who-first-coined-the-term-greenhouse-effect/, accessed September 12, 2019. **Bell**: Edwin S. Grosvenor and Morgan Wesson, *Alexander Graham Bell*, 274, 292, citing a February 1, 1917, speech, reprinted in *National Geographic*, February 1917, 131–46; Nina Strochlic, "100 Years Ago, Alexander Graham Bell Predicted Life in 2017," https://www.nationalgeographic.com/magazine/2017/06/explore-alexander-graham-bell-progress/, accessed September 12, 2019. **Kaplan**: "Florida and Ice Caps," editorial, *Palm Beach Post*, May 31, 1957.

global warming: Wallace S. Broecker, "Climatic Change: Are We on the Brink of a Pronounced Global Warming?," *Science* 189, no. 4201, August 8, 1975, 460–63.

Broecker told a reporter: Abby Gruen, "N.J. Scientist Who Coined 'Global Warming' Term Tries to Avoid the Limelight 35 Years Later," (Newark) *Star-Ledger*, August 8, 2010; *SPD*, 279–80; *Hammond Times*, November 6, 1957. **Russell and Landsberg**: Clifford Russell and Hans Landsberg, "International Environmental Problems—a Taxonomy," *Science* 172, no. 3990, June 25, 1971, 1307–14; *San Antonio Express*, April 28, 1952.

Luntz: Memo to White House: Oliver Burkeman, "Memo Exposes Bush's Green Strategy," *The Guardian*, March 3, 2003; Frank Luntz, "Straight Talk," Luntz Research Corporation, 2002, 142, http://www.exponentialimprovement.com/cms/uploads/a-cleaner-safer-healthier.pdf, accessed September 12, 2019; "Global Warming vs Climate Change," *Skeptical Science*, https://skepticalscience.com/climate-change-global-warming.htm, accessed January 1, 2018; Dan Zak, "How Should We Talk About What's Happening to Our Planet?," *WP*, August 27, 2019. **Hammond Times**: Editorial, November 6, 1957. According to this editorial, "if continued unchecked emissions of pollutants could result in a large scale global warming, with radical climate changes."

recency illusion: Arnold Zwicky, "Just Between Dr. Language and I," *Language Log*, August 7, 2005, http://itre.cis.upenn.edu/~myl/languagelog/archives/002386.html, accessed April 29, 2016; "The Word: Recency Illusion," *The Word, New Scientist* 196, no. 2630, November 17, 2007, 60; Sharlatmadan, "11 Words." See also Kory Stamper, "Slang for the Ages," *NYT*, October 3, 2014.

munchkin: James Lowder, *The Munchkin Book: The Official Companion*, Dallas: Smart Pop, 2016; "What's a Munchkin?," *Steve Jackson Games*, January 2, 2006, http://forums.sjgames.com/showthread.php?t=11529, accessed November 1, 2016; Mike Holmes, "Odd Note About the Term Munchkin," http://www.indierpgs.com/archive/index.php?topic=2590.0;wap2, accessed November 1, 2016. *moxie*: Vinnie Mancuso, "Aubrey Plaza, 'Legion' Mental Case, Has What the Kids These Days Call 'Moxie,'" *Observer*, February 2, 2017.

Dalzell: Dalzell, *Flappers 2 Rappers*, xii, 57–60, 154–56, 158–59. **1960s terms**: Ibid., 131–33. *vibe*: Elbert Hubbard, *Courtesy as an Asset*, East Aurora, NY: Roycrofters, 1911, 3.

hobbit, **Tolkien**: "A Definition of 'Hobbit' for the OED," *OUPblog*, January 4, 2013, https://blog.oup.com/2013/01/oed-hobbit-definition-word-origin-etymology/, accessed September 13, 2019; Ewen Callaway, "Did Humans Drive 'Hobbit' Species to Extinction?," *nature.com*, March 30, 2016, https://www.nature.com/articles/nature.2016.19651, accessed September 13, 2019; **Tolkien to Burchfield**: J.R.R. Tolkien, *The Letters of J.R.R. Tolkien*, New York: Houghton Mifflin Harcourt, 2014, 404–5.

muggle: "Muggle," *Language Realm*, undated, http://www.languagerealm.com/hplang/muggle.php, accessed January 22, 2016; Dickson, *Authorisms*, 117–18; Crystal, *The Story of English in 100 Words*, 248–50. *wordnik*: Angela Tung, "Attention all Muggles and Squibs!," *wordnik*, July 15, 2011, https://blog.wordnik.com/attention-all-muggles-and-squibs, accessed December 8, 2015. *mug*: *OED*; Mathews, *Dictionary of Americanisms*, Vol. 2, 1098; Lighter, *Random House Dictionary of American Slang*, Vol. 2, 613–15.

grit: Angela Duckworth, *Grit: The Power of Passion and Perseverance*, New York: Scribner, 2016; **Duckworth credited with coining grit**: Tovia Smith, "Does Teaching Kids to Get 'Gritty' Help Them Get Ahead?," *Morning Edition*, NPR, March 17, 2014; "Got Grit? Angela Lee Duckworth on Educational Perseverance," Early Math Collaborative, Erikson Institute, October 31, 2014, https://earlymath.erikson.edu/got-grit/, accessed April 4, 2019; "Leading & Learning—My First Blog Post," *soldisays*, August 2018, https://soldidays.wordpress.com. **grit etymology**: *OED*; Mathews *Dictionary of Americanisms*, Vol. 1, 746. **Grit**: *Rural American Know-How*, https://www.grit.com/, accessed June 21, 2019; Michael Cieply, "A Publicist's Sly Push for the Novel 'True Grit,'" *NYT*, December 24, 2010.

groupthink: Irving L. Janis, *Victims of Groupthink: A Psychological Study of Foreign-Policy Decisions and Fiascoes*, Boston: Houghton Mifflin, 1972; Irving L. Janis, "Groupthink," *Yale Alumni Magazine* 36, no. 4, January 1973; Kathrin Lassila, "A Brief History of Groupthink," *Yale Alumni Magazine* 71, no. 3, January–February 2008; **Janis obituary**: *NYT*, November 18, 1990; Irving L. Janis, "Groupthink," *Psychology Today* 5, no. 6, November 1971, 43–46, 74–76. **Whyte**: William H. Whyte Jr., "Groupthink," *Fortune*, March 1952, 114–17, 142, 146.

perfect storm: "Annotation Tuesday! Sebastian Junger and the Perfect Storm," *Nieman*, August 19, 2013, https://niemanstoryboard.org/stories/annotation-tuesday-sebastian-junger-and-the-perfect-storm/, accessed April 24, 2017; "Meteorologists Say 'Perfect Storm' Not So Perfect," *Science Daily*, June 29, 2000, https://www.sciencedaily.com/releases/2000/06/000628101549.htm, accessed April 25, 2017. **Earlier uses of perfect storm**: *OED*; Dickson, *Authorisms*, 164–65; Patricia T. O'Conner and Stewart Kellerman, "The Imperfect Storm," *Grammarphobia*, May 3, 2008, https://www.grammarphobia.com/blog/2008/05/the-imperfect-storm.html, accessed December 26, 2017; **1936 news account**: *Port Arthur (TX) News*, March 20, 1936, cited in *OED*.

2007 list of overused catchphrases: Andrew Stern, "'Perfect Storm' of Clichés Make Bad English List," *Reuters*, December 31, 2007, https://www.reuters.com/article/us-words-list/perfect-storm-of-cliches-make-bad-english-list-idUSN2846970520071231?sp=true, accessed September 14, 2019.

tipping point: Morton Grodzins, "Metropolitan Segregation," *Scientific American* 197, no. 4, October 1957, 34; Thomas C. Schelling, "Dynamic Models of Segregation," *Journal of Mathematical Sociology* 1, no. 2, July 1971, 143–86; William Safire, *NYT Magazine*, July 27, 2003, 15; Gavin McNett, "Idea Epidemics," *Salon*, March 17, 2000. Matt Elzweig, "Gladwell Hunting," *New York Press*, April 2–8, 2008, covers thoroughly Gladwell's barely acknowledged debt to Thomas Schelling, and entirely unacknowledged debt to Morton Grodzins. This well-reported article includes an interview with Schelling, who said he felt aggrieved about having his work borrowed by Gladwell with but a single citation buried in notes at the end acknowledging this fact. As Schelling told Elzweig, "people don't read endnotes." (And yes, I'm aware of the irony of including Schelling's observation in the endnotes of my book.) **Early twentieth century reference to "tipping point"**: *Oakland Tribune*, June 30, 1910.

emotional intelligence: Peter Salovey and John D. Mayer, "Emotional Intelligence," *Imagination Cognition and Personality* 9, no. 3, 1989–90, 185–211; Annie Murphy Paul, "Promotional Intelligence," *Salon*, June 28, 1999, details how unhappy Salovey and Mayer were about the way they thought Daniel Goleman misinterpreted their work on emotional intelligence; Wayne Leon Payne, "A Study of Emotion: Developing Emotional Intelligence; Self-Integration; Relating to Fear, Pain and Desire (Theory, Structure of Reality, Problem-Solving, Contraction / Expansion, Tuning in / Coming Out / Letting Go)," PhD dissertation, The Union for Experimenting Colleges and Universities, 1985, in Steve Hein, "Wayne Payne's 1985 Doctoral Dissertation on Emotions and Emotional Intelligence," *EQI.org*, July 2011, updated 2015, https://eqi.org/payne.htm, accessed September 14, 2019.

baby boomers: Landon Y. Jones, *Great Expectations: America and the Baby Boom Generation*, New York: Coward, McCann & Geoghegan, 1980; Landon Y. Jones, "How 'Baby Boomers' Took Over the World," *WP*, November 6, 2015; "Baby Boomer," *The Phrase Finder*, undated, https://www.phrases.org.uk/meanings/baby-boomer.html, accessed September 16, 2019; *Coshocton (OH) Tribune*, August 7, 1920; *Life*, December 1, 1941, 73–74; *Time*, December 8, 1941, 38.

Gen X: Douglas Coupland, *Generation X: Tales for an Accelerated Culture*, New York: St. Martin's, 1991. **Coupland's comment**: Vann Wesson, *Generation X Field Guide & Lexicon*, Birmingham, UK: Orion, 1996, excerpted in https://people.uva-wise.edu/pww8y/Supplement/-ConceptsSup/PopulationSup/GenX.html, accessed April 26, 2016. **Coupland's changing origin story for *Generation X* title**: Doody, "X-Plained: The Production and Reception History of Douglas Coupland's *Generation X*," *Papers of the Bibliographical Society of Canada* 49, no. 1, 2011, 5–34, 25–27 https://doi.org/10.33137/pbsc.v49i1.21940, accessed September 17, 2019; Douglas Coupland, "Generation X'd," *Details*, June 1995, reprinted in http://coupland.tripod.com/details1.html, accessed September 16, 2019. **Deverson and Hamblett**: Jane Deverson and Charles Hamblett, *Generation X*, London: Tandem, 1964; Alan Dein, "The Original Generation X," *BBC News Magazine*, March 1, 2014, https://www.bbc.com/news/magazine-26339959, accessed April 26, 2016. **Capa**: Richard Whelan, *Robert Capa: A Biography*, Lincoln: University of Nebraska Press, 1994, 279, 287, 315; John M. Ulrich, "Introduction: Generation X, A (Sub)Cultural Genealogy," in *GenXegesis: Essays on Alternative Youth (Sub)Culture*, ed. John McAllister Ulrich and Andrea L. Harris, Madison: University of Wisconsin Press, 2003, 5.

17. DISPUTATION

gonzo: William McKeen, *Hunter S. Thompson*, Boston: Twayne/Hall, 1991, 11, 35; E. Jean Carroll, *Hunter: The Strange and Savage Life of Hunter S. Thompson*, New York: Dutton, 1993, 124; Douglas Brinkley, "Editor's Note," in Hunter S. Thompson, *The Proud Highway: Saga of a Desperate Southern Gentleman, 1955–1967*, ed. Douglas Brinkley, New York: Villard, 1997, xxvii; Kevin T. McEneaney, *Hunter S. Thompson: Fear,*

Loathing, and the Birth of Gonzo, Lanham, MD: Rowman & Littlefield, 2016, 67–69. **Thompson's definition of *gonzo***: Douglas Brinkley, ed., Hunter S. Thompson, *Fear and Loathing in America: The Brutal Odyssey of an Outlaw Journalist, 1968–76*, New York: Simon & Schuster, 2000, 450. In his foreword to this second volume of Hunter Thompson's letters, David Halberstam paid tribute to Thompson as "a man of Gonzo," who had "a great resonance with the non-Gonzoists among us" (xi). In an editor's note to this 2000 book, historian Douglas Brinkley noted that Thompson was credited with coining "gonzo" by at least two dictionaries (Webster's and Random House). Two decades later, all I can find in any dictionary of any vintage is reference to Thompson being a first or early user of this term. This was true in Thompson's own copy of the *Random House Dictionary*. See http://www.openculture.com/2019/05/gonzo-defined-by-hunter-s-thompsons-personal-copy-of-the-random-house-dictionary.html, accessed February 22, 2020.

Cardoso obituary: *SFC*, March 5, 2006. **flap copy**: Dickson, *Authorisms*, 60–61; Dalzell and Victor, *The New Partridge Dictionary of Slang and Unconventional English*, 1018. **Hirst on etymology of gonzo**: Martin Hirst, "What Is Gonzo? The Etymology of an Urban Legend," *UQ Eprint edition*, January 19, 2004, 2–16, 5. **Hirst concluded**: Ibid., 5–7. **Giuliano**: "The Origin of Gonzo," *ANBA*, February 24, 2005, http://anaba.blogspot.com/2005/02/origin-of-gonzo.html, accessed November 9, 2015; Charles Giuliano, "British Rocker Alvin Lee Dead at 68: Inspired Birth of Gonzo Journalism," *Berkshire Fine Arts*, March 7, 2013, https://www.berkshirefinearts.com/03-07-2013_british-rocker-alvin-lee-dead-at-68.htm, accessed November 9, 2015; Charles Giuliano, "The Maltese Sangweech and Other Heroes," *Berkshire Fine Arts*, June 4, 2014, https://www.berkshirefinearts.com/06-04-2014_dr-gonzo-william-j-cardoso.htm, accessed November 9, 2015. **Baker**: Billy Baker, "It's Totally Gonzo," *BG*, https://groups.google.com/forum/#!topic/alt.folklore.urban/sDMvOrnXgqU, November 21, 2010. **Brinkley**: In Kevin T. McEneaney, *Hunter S. Thompson*, 68. **Baker**: Baker, "It's Totally Gonzo."

fifteen minutes of fame: Garson O'Toole, "In the Future Everyone Will Be Famous for 15 Minutes"; **Warhol's fellow artists, photographer**: Blake Gopnik, "In the Future, Everyone Will be World-Famous for 15 Minutes," *Warholiana*, updated February 6, 2019, https://warholiana.com/post/81689862604/in-the-future-everyone-will-be-world-famous-for, accessed September 19, 2019.

mojo: Evan Morris, "Mojo," *The Word Detective*, January 16, 2009, http://www.word-detective.com/2009/01/mojo/, accessed September 19, 2019; "etymology of the word 'mojo,'" *alt.folksore.urban*, August 6, 1999, https://groups.google.com/forum/#!topic/alt.folklore.urban/sDMvOrnXgqU, accessed September 19, 2019; Terry Victor, "Finding Mojo," *#Grammar's Blog of Wordliness*, February 25, 2017, https://terryvictor-couk.wordpress.com/2017/02/25/finding-mojo/amp/, accessed June 6, 2020; "The Origin of Mojo," *Mojoland*, http://mojoland.net/origin/, accessed May 23, 2017; Ben Zimmer, "How 'Mojo' Got Its Magic Working," *WSJ*, October 4, 2018; "My Daddy's Got the Mojo, But I Got the Say So," by Butterbeans and Susie, https://www.youtube.com/watch?v=CwzOLW3BwJs, accessed November 6, 2019.

Stamper: Stamper, *Word by Word*, 197–98.

bad hair day: Jane Pauley, *TV Guide*, May 7, 1994, 39; Belinda Luscombe, "10 Questions with Jane Pauley," *Time*, January 20, 2014. **Swartz, OED citing *Santa Rosa Press Democrat*, July 24, 1988:** Valerie Hillow, "Not Just Another Bad Hair Day," *The Ohio Journalist*, June 6, 2002, text posted by Allan Metcalf on *The LINGUIST List*, June 17, 2002, http://listserv.linguistlist.org/pipermail/ads-l/2002-June/023004.html, accessed March 9, 2017. **Brooklyn judge**: *Almanac of the Federal Judiciary* (Aspen), Vol. 1–2, 1988, 90, https://books.google.com/books?ppis=_c&id=DNNFAQAAIAAJ&dq=Korman+%22bad+hair+day%22+aspen+1988&focus=searchwithinvolume&q=%22bad+hair+day%22+, accessed March 26, 2019. Since this comment was published in a 1988 book, it presumably antedated Swartz's usage in July of that year, suggesting *bad hair day* was in common use at that time. **Simmons**: Brent Simmons, "Origin of Good (and Bad) Hair Day," *inessential*, February 9, 2016, https://inessential.com/2016/02/09/origin_of_good_and_bad_hair_day, accessed March 10, 2017. Pascal Tréguer found two references to "bad hair day" in a barbershop ad that appeared in the *State Journal* of Lansing, Michigan, on February 14, 1970 (one suggesting that men experiencing such a day might benefit from a trip to their shop): Pascal Tréguer, " 'Bad Hair Day' (When Everything Seems to Go Badly)," *word histories*, https://wordhistories.net/2017/08/04/bad-hair-day-origin/, accessed January 8, 2020.

Kingsley, Papworth: Fiona Hicks, "The Man Who Saved Audrey's Hair," *The Lady*, October 3, 2013, https://lady.co.uk/man-who-saved-audreys-hair, accessed March 26, 2019; "Champagne Shampoo? Not Without Philip Kingsley's Approval," *Spears Wealth Management Awards Feed*, July 14, 2015, http://wma.spearswms.com/2015/07/14/champagne-shampoo-not-without-philip-kingsleys-approval/, accessed March 9, 2017; "Philip Kingsley, Celebrity Trichologist—Obituary," *The Telegraph*, September 16, 2016; "U.K. Trichologist First Coined 'Bad Hair Day,'" *Montreal Gazette*, September 30, 2016.

hot dog: Bruce Kraig and Patty Carroll, *Man Bites Dog: Hot Dog Culture in America*, Lanham, MD: Alta Mira/Rowman & Littlefield, 2012, 44, 47–49, 51–52, reviews this presumed etymology at length, then thoroughly debunks it. In *Origin of the Term "Hot Dog,"* George Leonard Cohen, David Shulman, and Barry A. Popik (Rolla, MO: Gerald Cohen, 2004) had already done so in impressive detail. **Mencken, Bryson, National Hot Dog and Sausage Council**: *AL*, 186; Bill Bryson, *Made in America*, 198–99. Although this book was published in 1994, Bryson continued to recount the apocryphal Tad Dorgan etymology in his 2013 book *One Summer* (New York: Doubleday, 2013, 119), long after it had been thoroughly discredited. At one time, the National Hot Dog and Sausage Council also endorsed this origin story (see "Etymology of Hot Dog," *Snopes.com*, July 23, 2007, https://www.snopes.com/fact-check/hot-dog/, accessed May 5, 2011), but the Council subsequently added more credible etymologies to their website, https://www.hot-dog.org/culture/hot-dog-history, accessed September 20, 2019. A solid recounting of *hot dog*'s etymology (as of mid-2011) can be found at "Ben Zimmer, 'Hot Dog': The Untold Story," *Visual Thesaurus*, May 13, 2011, https://www.visualthesaurus.com/cm/

wordroutes/hot-dog-the-untold-story/, accessed December 26, 2016. Barry Popik's dogged research on this topic is reported by Sara David, "Food Historian Explains His Quest to Define the Hot Dog as a Sandwich," *First We Feast*, November 17, 2016, https:// firstwefeast.com/features/2016/11/hot-dog-sandwich-debate-food-historian, accessed December 26, 2016. Popik updates findings about *hot dog's* etymology on his *Big Apple* website, Barry Popik, "Hot Dog," *Big Apple*, July 25, 2004, https://www.barrypopik. com/index.php/new_york_city/entry/hot_dog_polo_grounds_myth_original_mono-graph/, accessed September 20, 2019. **Dorgan cartoons**: Ibid.; Cohen et al., *Origin of the Term "Hot Dog,"* 3, 103–4, 141–45, 150, 157–59, 161, 163–67, 171–72, 174, 179, 198, 225, 252, 255–57, 259, 264, 270–74, 277, 282–83. On pages 130–32, this book reproduces two Dorgan cartoons from December 12 and 13, 1906, in which the term *hot dog* does appear. **1895 *Judge* cartoon**: Ibid., 118; **campus hot dog humor, Yale**: Ibid., 20–21.

Tennessee newspapers: *The Nashville Tennessean*, November 14, 1886, and the *Nashville Daily American*, February 9, 1891, located by Fred Shapiro, cited by Allan Metcalf, "Hot Dog," *Lingua Franca, The Chronicle of Higher Education*, May 17, 2013, https://www.chronicle.com/blogs/linguafranca/2013/05/17/hot-dog/, accessed September 19, 2019, and Metcalf, *From Skedaddle to Selfie*, 33–36, where 1892 press accounts are also noted. Barry Popik, "Hot Dog," *The Big Apple*, includes all of these references, and the Asbury Park ordinance as well. To stay abreast of *hot dog* sightings, check *The Big Apple* first. See also Pascal Tréguer, "History of the Word 'Hot Dog,'" *word histories*, https://wordhistories.net/2017/03/27/hot-dog/, accessed January 8, 2020. **Coney Island**: *AL*, 186.

affluenza: Marja Mills, "Who Coins New Words? Tracing One Back to the Big Bang," *Chicago Tribune*, April 10, 2001; Christine Hauser, "'Affluenza' Sets Off a Linguistic Contest," *NYT*, December 13, 2013; Nancy Friedman, "Word of the Week: Affluenza," *Fritinancy*, December 16, 2013, https://nancyfriedman.typepad.com/ away_with_words/2013/12/word-of-the-week-affluenza.html, accessed September 23, 2019; Sarah Kershaw, "Affluenza: A Plague on Both Their Houses, Their Cars, and Their Yacht," *The Guardian*, January 4, 2016. **G. Dick Miller**: John Luciew, "Psychologist Behind Rich Kid's 'Affluenza' Defense Regrets Term as Teen's No-Jail DUI Homicide Sentence Touches a Nerve," *PennLive*, (Harrisburg, PA) *Patriot-News*, December 12, 2013, https://www.pennlive.com/midstate/2013/12/psychologist_behind_rich_kids. html, accessed September 23, 2019; "What Is the Affluenza Defense?," *HG.org*, https:// www.hg.org/legal-articles/what-is-the-affluenza-defense31843, accessed July 6, 2015. **O'Neill**: Bill Hoffman, "Therapist Who Coined Term 'Affluenza' Doesn't Excuse DUI Teen," *Newsmax*, December 16, 2013. **Comstock**: Gregory S. McNeal, "Is Affluenza Real? Ask Senator Elizabeth Warren and Other Experts," *forbes.com*, December 13, 2013, https://www.forbes.com/sites/gregorymcneal/2013/12/13/is-affluenza-real-ask-senator-elizabeth-warren-and-other-experts/#174c04913b60, accessed July 6, 2015. **Levy**: Mills, "Who Coins New Words?"; **de Graaf**: Ibid.; Christine Hauser, "'Affluenza Sets Off a Linguistic Contest"; Kershaw, "Affluenza"; John de Graaf, "Co-Author of *Affluenza*: 'I'm Appalled by the Ethan Couch Decision,'" *Time.com*, December 14,

2013, http://ideas.time.com/2013/12/14/co-author-of-affluenza-im-appalled-by-the-ethan-couch-decision/, accessed December 14, 2013. **Whitman**: Kershaw, "Affluenza"; Mills, "Who Coins New Words?" **Marja Mills**: Ibid. **Levy**: Ibid. **Garson O'Toole, 1908 London newspaper column**: Nancy Friedman, "Word of the Week: Affluenza"; Sarah Kershaw, "Affluenza." **Sheidlower**: Marja Mills, "Who Coins New Words?"

postmodern, **Ihab Hassan obituary**: Meg Jones, "Hassan Coined Term Postmodernism for Change in '60s Literature," *Milwaukee Journal Sentinel*, September 14, 2015; Ihab Hassan, *The Postmodern Turn: Essays in Postmodern Theory and Culture*, Columbus: Ohio State University Press, 1987, 85, includes a good if partial review of the many appearances of *postmodern* before his use of that term; **John Watkins Chapman**: "Postmodernism," *New World Encyclopedia*, https://www.newworldency-clopedia.org/entry/Postmodernism, accessed September 23, 2019; "Postmodernism," *Social Research Glossary*, https://www.qualityresearchinternational.com/socialre-search/postmodernism.htm, accessed September 23, 2019. **Higgins**: Dick Higgins, *A Dialectic of Centuries* (Bloomington: Indiana University Press, 1978, 7. **Alternative attributions of** *postmodern* **coinage**: Vijaya Tamiya, "Postmodernism: A Theoretical Perspective," *Slideshare*, March 7, 2015, https://www.slideshare.net/wretchedguy/postmodernism-45546726, accessed September 23, 2019.

1913 article: J. M. Thompson, "Post-Modernism," *The Hibbert Journal* 12, no. 4, July 1913, 733–35. (This century-old article prompted a lively response in which the term "post-modernism" was bandied about freely.) **de Onis**: Perry Anderson, *The Origins of Postmodernism*, London: Verso, 1998, 3–4, 102. **Toynbee**: Arnold J. Toynbee, *A Study of History*, New York: Oxford University Press, 1947, 323. **Jencks**: Charles Jencks, "The Rise of Post-Modern Architecture," *The Language of Post-Modern Architecture*, New York: Rizzoli, 1977; Elie Haddad, "Charles Jencks and the Historiography of Post-Modernism," *The Journal of Architecture* 14, no. 4, 2009, 493–510; Witold Rybczysnki, "Was Postmodern Architecture Any Good?," *Slate*, November 17, 2011. **Hudnut**: Jill Pearlman, *Inventing American Modernism: Joseph Hudnut, Walter Gropius, and the Bauhaus Legacy at Harvard*, Charlottesville: University of Virginia Press, 2007. **Mills**: Ann Nilsen and Julia Brannen, "Contextualizing Lives:: The History-Biography Dynamic Revisited," in John Scott and Ann Nilsen, *C. Wright Mills and the Sociological Imagination: Contemporary Perspectives*, Cheltenham, UK: Edward Elgar, 2013, 90. **Lyotard**: Helen Pluckrose "How French Intellectuals Ruined the West: Postmodernism and Its Impact Explained," *Areo*, https://areomagazine.com/2017/03/27/how-french-intellectuals-ruined-the-west-postmodernism-and-its-impact-explained/. To the best of my knowledge, none of these alleged coiners of *postmodern* themselves took credit for its coinage.

booty call: Jinelle Shengulette, "Laughter Is Still No. 1 for Bill Bellamy," *Rochester Democrat and Chronicle*, February 20, 2014; Elon Green, "The Lost History of the 'Booty Call,'" *Esquire.com*, June 23, 2016, https://www.esquire.com/lifestyle/sex/a46054/the-lost-history-of-the-booty-call/, accessed December 15, 2016. **Takashi Bufford, Anthony Darlington, Jesse Weaver**: Ibid. **Elon Green's** *Esquire* **piece**: Ibid.

Online discussion of *booty call* etymology: "Talk: Booty Call," *Wikipedia*, https://en.wikipedia.org/wiki/Talk:Booty_call, accessed December 15, 2016. **Waller**: "Come and Get It," Fats Waller and Ed Kirkeby, 1941.

Chast: Roz Chast, *Theories of Everything: Selected, Collected, and Health-Inspected Cartoons, 1978–2006*, New York: Bloomsbury, 45. **Kahn, Greene**: "Yuppie," *Spy*, October 1988, 133. **Kahn columns**: *East Bay Express*, June 10, 1983, July 26, 1985, discussed in *Spy*; Alice Kahn, *My Life as a Gal*, New York: Dell, 1987, 43–45. **Greene column**: *Chicago Tribune*, March 23, 1983: "Yuppie," *Spy*. **Kahn responded**: Ibid.; Kahn, *My Life as a Gal*. **Rottenberg**: Dan Rottenberg, "About That Urban Renaissance . . . There'll Be a Slight Delay: Yuppies Flood the Lakefront, but It Takes Families to Save a City," *Chicago*, May 1980, 154–57, 192, 194, 198, 155; Luke Seeman, "The Yuppie Turns 35," *Chicago*, June 3, 2015, https://www.chicagomag.com/city-life/June-2015/Yuppie-Dan-Rottenberg/, accessed February 11, 2016. ***Newsweek*, "The Year of the Yuppie"**: cover story, *Newsweek*, December 31, 1984.

WASP: E. Digby Baltzell, *The Protestant Establishment: Aristocracy & Caste in America*, New Haven, CT: Yale University Press, 1964, 9; Eric Pace, "E. Digby Baltzell Dies at 80; Studied WASP's," *NYT*, August 20, 1996. **Hacker**: Andrew Hacker, "Liberal Democracy and Social Control," *American Political Science Review* 51, no. 4, 1957, 1009–26, 1011. **Shapiro**: "The First WASP?," Fred Shapiro letter to *New York Times*, March 14, 2012. **Kennedy**: *New York Amsterdam News*, April 17, 1948, cited in ibid. **Fairlie**: Henry Fairlie, "Political Commentary," *The Spectator*, September 23, 1955, 5–7. **Fairlie felt knighted**: Henry Fairlie, "The Language of Politics," *ATL*, January 1975, 25–33, 25. **"Establishment good looks"**: Marc Weingarten, *The Gang That Wouldn't Write Straight*, 217. **Taylor, Pearson, Golding/Ford**: Henry Fairlie, "Evolution of a Term," *NYer*, October 17, 1968, 173–74, 176, 178, 180, 182, 184–88, 191–94, 197–200, 203–6, 184–86. **Taylor**: A. J. P. Taylor, "Books in General," *The New Statesman and Nation*, August 29, 1953, 236–37, excerpted in Philip Maughan, "The Origins of 'the Establishment': An Etymological Intrigue," *New Statesman*, February 7, 2013. **book on 1920s**: Douglas Golding, *The Nineteen Twenties: A General Survey and Some Personal Memories*, London: Nicholson and Watson, 1945, cited by Fairlie, "Evolution of a Term," 186. **Pearson**: Hesketh Pearson, *Labby (The Life and Character of Henry Labouchère)*, London: Hamish Hamilton, 1936, 247–49. **Emerson**: "The Conservative," https://archive.vcu.edu/english/engweb/transcendentalism/authors/emerson/essays/conservative.html, accessed April 4, 2019. **Fairlie's concession**: Fairlie, "Evolution of a Term," 187.

almighty dollar: **Bulwer-Lytton**: "Our Story," *The Bulwer-Lytton Fiction Contest*, https://www.bulwer-lytton.com/about, accessed September 25, 2019; San Jose State University professor Scott Rice interviewed about Bulwer-Lytton Fiction Contest, *Weekend Edition Sunday*, NPR, July 1, 2007. **Irving**: See notes for Chapter 12. **Jonson "almighty gold"**: "Almighty Dollar," *Historically Speaking*, January 13, 2015, https://idiomation.wordpress.com/tag/edward-bulwer-lytton/, accessed September 25, 2019; Ian Donaldson, *Ben Jonson: A Life*, London: Oxford University Press, 2002, 146.

iron curtain: *OED*; *SPD*, 354–55; Keyes, *The Quote Verifier*, 100–101, 300; Martin Tolchin, "About: New Words," *NYT Magazine*, September 8, 1957 reprinted in Babcock, *The Ordeal of American English*, 129–30; George Crile, *A Mechanistic View of War and Peace*, New York: Macmillan, 1915, 69.

brunch: *OED*; Pascal Tréguer, "History of the Portmanteau Word 'Brunch,'" *word histories*, December 2, 2016, https://wordhistories.net/2016/12/21/brunch/, accessed January 8, 2020.

The Goon Show, **Spike Milligan**: Michael Quinion, "Goon," *World Wide Words*, December 5, 2015, http://www.worldwidewords.org/qa/qa-goo4.htm, accessed February 28, 2018.

Goon: See notes for Chapter 8.

fashionista: See notes for Chapter 4; *OED*; **Popik, O'Toole, Shapiro, Yagoda**: Barry Popik, "Fashionista," *Big Apple*, April 20, 2013, https://www.barrypopik.com/index.php/new_york_city/entry/fashionista, accessed October 14, 2015; Yagoda, Conway-Jones in Ben Yagoda, "Local Boy Makes Word?," in Chapter 4 notes.

18. WORD WARS

The origins of American English are considered at length in Mencken, *The American Language*; Read, *Milestones in the History of English in America*; Flexner, *I Hear America Talking* and *Listening to America*; de Vere, *Americanisms*; Pyles, *Words and Ways of American English*; Dohan, *Our Own Words*; Dillard, *All-American English* and *American Talk*; Babcock, *The Ordeal of American English*; Bryson, *Made in America*; and McQuain, *Never Enough Words*.

Jefferson to Adams on "neology": Letter from Thomas Jefferson to John Adams, August 15, 1820, *The Writings of Thomas Jefferson*, Vol. 14, Washington, DC: Thomas Jefferson Memorial Association, 1904, 269–76, 272. **Jefferson to Waldo about "neologize"**: Letter from Thomas Jefferson to John Waldo, June 27, 1813, *The Writings of Thomas Jefferson*, Vol. 13, Washington, DC: Thomas Jefferson Memorial Association, 1903, 338–47, 346.

Miscellaneous Americanisms: *AL*, 114–15; Pyles, *Words and Ways of American English*, 6–7; Babcock, *The Ordeal of American English*, 172–73; Dohan, *Our Own Words*, 83–89, 97; Flexner, *I Hear America Talking*, 7–9; Bryson, *Made in America*, 20; McArthur, *The Oxford Companion to the English Language*, 39–40. **the help, sleigh**: M-W, 60; Mead, *Word-Coinage*, 127, 129–30; Dohan, *Our Own Words*, 106; Flexner, *I Hear America Talking*, 8; Tracy Chevalier, *The Last Runaway*, New York: Harper, 2013, 185.

British reviewer of *Notes on the State of Virginia*: *The European Magazine and London Review*, August, 1787, 114; Read, *Milestones in the History of English in America*, 50; Pyles, *Words and Ways of American English*, 17–18. A good summary of this contretemps, including a facsimile excerpt of *The European Magazine* review, can be found in "How Thomas Jefferson Was Berated for Coining 'Belittle,'" Pascal Tréguer, *word histories*, March 25, 2018, https://wordhistories.net/2018/03/25/belittle-thomas-jefferson/, accessed October 7, 2019. ***Anglophobia***: In 1793 Jefferson wrote to James Madison, "The Anglophobia has seized violently on three members of our council," *The Writings of Thomas Jefferson*, Vol. 9, Washington, DC: Thomas Jefferson Memorial Association, 87–89; *OED*. **Jefferson to Waldo**: *The Writings of Thomas Jefferson*, Vol. 13, 338-47. **Jefferson as neologizer**: "Thomas Jefferson," OED; Dickson, *Words from the White House*, 10; O'Conner and Kellerman, *Origins of the Specious*, 51. ***stump-orators***: Jefferson letter to Adams, June 27, 1813, in *The Writings of Thomas Jefferson*, Vol. 13, 281.

Adams's letter to Rush: "From John Adams to Benjamin Rush, 10 February 1812," *Founders Online*, National Archives, https://founders.archives.gov/documents/Adams/99-02-02-5753, accessed October 1, 2019.

Johnson on Americans: James Boswell, *Life of Johnson*, London: Oxford University Press, 1953, 590, 946. According to Boswell, Dr. Johnson was prone to grow apoplectic on the topic of Americans, whom he considered "Rascals—Robbers—Pirates." Ibid., 946.

British tourists: Allen Walker Read, "British Recognition of American Speech, in the Eighteenth Century" in Read, *Milestones in the History of English in America*, 37–54. **Moore's report**: *AL*, 3; Hitchings, *The Secret Life of Words*, 248; Richard W. Bailey, "American English Abroad," in Algeo, *The Cambridge History of the English Language*, Vol. 6, 455–96, 476. ***bluff***: Pyles, *Words and Ways of American English*, 6; Dohan, *Our Own Words*, 95; Flexner, *I Hear America Talking*, 8. ***foothill, eel grass, skunk***: *AL*, 104, 114–15.

"Motley gibberish": Martin, *Dictionary Wars*, 20; **British Critic**: *British Critic* 35, February 1810, Article 11, 181–82. **American recoinage of British terms**: *AL*, 24; Dohan, *Our Own Words*, 6, 84–87; McQuain, *Never Enough Words*, 7–8; O'Conner and Kellerman, *Origins of the Specious*, 9–10, 14, 170. **Hamilton**: Thomas Hamilton, *Men and Manners in America*, Vol. 1, Edinburgh: Blackwood, 1833, 233.

barbarisms, barborous, barbarizing, OED; *M-W*, 37; George Puttenham, *The Arte of English Poesie*, 336; Pei, *The Story of Language*, 204; Liberman, *Word Origins*, 9; Elisabeth Showalter Muhlenfeld, "Analyzing Becky Sharp's Trash," *Gifts of Speech*, April 11, 2008, http://gos.sbc.edu/m/muhlenfeld3.html#_edn39, accessed October 3, 2019; Hitchings, *Defining the World*, 146. **Johnson, "barbarous"**: Greenman, *Words in Action*, 11; Martin, *The Dictionary Wars*, 4; Hitchings, *Defining the World*, 146; Hitchings, *The Secret Life of Words*, 206. **Words disdained by Johnson**: Hitchings, *Defining the World*, 146; Mugglestone, *Lost for Words*, 144. **Hamilton**: Hamilton, *Men and Manners in America*, 234.

Webster: **"New circumstances"**: Lepore, *A Is for American*, 6. **"As an independent nation,"**: Martin, *The Dictionary Wars*, 21. **Declaration of Linguistic Independence**: Babcock, *The Ordeal of American English*, 45–46; Rosemarie Ostler, *Founding Grammars: How Early America's War over Words Shaped Today's Language*, New York: St. Martin's, 2015, 12. **"New words will be formed"**: Joshua Kendall, *The Forgotten Founding Father: Noah Webster's Obsession and the Creation of an American Culture*, New York: Putnam's, 2010, 284.

Introduction to dictionary: David Micklethwait, *Noah Webster and the American Dictionary*, Jefferson, NC: McFarland, 2000, 174. **Webster's attitude**: Hitchings,

The Secret Life of Words, 250–51; Hitchings, *The Language Wars*, 110–12; Lynch, *The Lexicographer's Dilemma*, 122–24; O'Conner and Kellerman, *Origins of the Specious*, 13; Jill Lepore, "Noah's Mark," *NYer*, November 6, 2006, 78–82, 85–87; 81.

Webster's inclusions: Crystal, *The Story of English in 100 Words*, 181; Jill Lepore, "Noah's Mark," 81. **Hall-Webster exchange**: Capt. Basil Hall, "A Naval Officer Sees All Sections, 1827–8," in *American Social History as Recorded by British Travelers*, ed. Allan Nevins, New York: Holt, 1923, 139–58, 157.

Language tourism: *AL*, 23–28; Frances Trollope, Martin, *Dictionary Wars*, 9–10. **American speech**: *AL*, 300–311. **Dickens**: Charles Dickens, *American Notes*, Greenwich, CT: Fawcett, 1842, 1961, 195. **Dickens's visits to U.S.**: Sørensen, *Charles Dickens*, 47–48; *AL*, 26–27.

Witherspoon, *Americanisms*: Ibid., 4–7; Pyles, *Words and Ways of American English*, 5; Flexner, *I Hear America Talking*, 9; Dohan, *Our Own Words*, 6, 167; McQuain, *Never Enough Words*, 7–8; *The Works of the Rev. John Witherspoon, D.D. L.L.D. Late President of the College, at Princeton New-Jersey*, Philadelphia: Woodward, 1801, 181–82, 186, 191–92, 460. See also Gilbert Milligan Tucker, *American English: A Paper Read Before the Albany Institute, June 6, 1882, with Revision and Additions*, Albany, NY: Weed, Parsons, 1883, 358. In a paper on the origins of the word *campus*, etymologist Albert Matthews speculated that Witherspoon may have introduced this Latin-based Americanism, which was first used at Princeton early in his 1768–94 tenure as its president. See Albert Matthews, "Campus," *Transactions*, Vol. 3, 1895–1897, Colonial Society of Massachusetts, March Meeting, 1897, 431–36, 431.

Franklin to Webster: *AL*, 7. **Dennie**: Joshua Kendall, *The Forgotten Founding Father*, 234; Jill Lepore quoted Dennie as calling verbal barbarisms "anxious weeds," not "noxious weeds," perhaps due to auto-correct: Jill Lepore, "Noah's Mark," 79.

"O'Grabble" letter to *Gazette*: Harlow Giles Unger, *Noah Webster: The Life and Times of an American Patriot*, New York: Wiley, 1998, 249. **Dutton**: Martin, *The Dictionary Wars*, 44.

John Pickering's glossary: *AL*, 35; Pyles, *Words and Ways of American English*, 19; Lepore, *A Is for American*, 70–73; Hitchings, *The Language Wars*, 108; John Pickering, "An Essay on the Present State of the English Language in the United States," excerpted from *A Vocabulary, or Collection of Words and Phrases Which Have Been Supposed to Be Peculiar to the United States of America*, Boston: Cummings and Hilliard, 1816, in Babcock, *The Ordeal of American English*, 28–30, 30. **Edinburgh Review critic**: Read, *Milestones in the History of English in America*, 61. **Coleridge**: *OED*; *AL*, 28; Thomas Allsop, ed., *Letters, Conversations and Recollections of S. T. Coleridge*, London: Farrah, 1864, 139. **Ruskin**: *OED*; John Ruskin, "Letter the 42nd," August 1, 1873, in *Fors Clavigera, Letters to the Workmen and Labourers of Great Britain*, Vol. 4, Kent, UK: George Allen, 1874, 118. **Fowlers**: Henry and Frank Fowler, *The King's English*, Whitefish, MT: Kessinger, 1906, 2009, 23. **Whibley**: *AL*, 31; Charles Whibley, "The American Language," *The Bookman* 27, January 1908, reprinted with response by H. W. Boynton, H.L. Mencken "The American Language," 63–71, 65, 70. **Murphy**: Murphy,

The Prodigal Tongue, 2–3, 10. **Prince Charles**: Mike Handley, "I Say, What Did He Say?," *WP*, April 2, 1995; **O'Conner and Kellerman**: O'Conner and Kellerman, *Origins of the Specious*, 4. **Wilson, Nashe**: Greenman, *Words in Action*, 29. **Bryant's list**: Brander Matthews, "The Art of Making New Words," 60. **Defoe**: Redfern, *Clichés and Coinages*, 191; Lynch, *The Lexicographer's Dilemma*, 58–60. **Swift**: Greenman, *Words in Action*, 11; *AL*, 169; Hitchings, *The Language Wars*, 54–56; Lynch, *The Lexicographer's Dilemma*, 62–65; Jonathan Swift to The *Tatler No. 230*, September 27–28, 1710, in *The Works of the Rev. Jonathan Swift*, Vol. 5, https://en.wikisource.org/wiki/The_Works_of_the_Rev._Jonathan_Swift/Volume_5/Tatler_Number_230, accessed October 9, 2019; Jonathan Swift, *A Proposal for Correcting, Improving and Ascertaining the English Tongue*, ed. Jack Lynch, (paragraphs 6, 8), 1712, http://jacklynch.net/Texts/proposal.html, accessed October 9, 2019; "Jonathan Swift's *A Proposal for the English Tongue*," *British Library*, https://www.bl.uk/collection-items/jonathan-swifts-a-proposal-for-the-english-tongue, accessed October 7, 2019.

   Samuel Johnson's changing attitudes: Jack Lynch, "Dr. Johnson's Revolution," *NYT*, July 2, 2005; Jack Lynch, ed., *Samuel Johnson's Dictionary: Selections from the 1755 Work That Defined the English Language*, New York: Walker, 2002, 41; Hitchings, *The Language Wars*, 92; Greenman, *Words in Action*, 11. **Words Johnson railed against**: *AL*, 126; Mugglestone, *Lost for Words*, 144.

   Priestley: Hitchings, *The Language Wars*, 102. **Evelyn**: Lynch, *The Lexicographer's Dilemma*, 73; Hitchings, *The Secret Life of Words*, 185.

   The Oxford English Dictionary: Mugglestone, *Lost for Words*. **excluded words**: Ibid., 94-5, 113, 134, 142. **exclusion of scientific and technical terms**: Ibid., 27-8, 110-21, 126. *appendicitis, electronic*: Ibid., 140, 211. **Coleridge, *linguipotence*, Swinburne, *harvestry***: Ibid., 101, 179. **"linguistic apartheid"**: Ibid., 121. *scientist*: Ibid., 116.

   Whewell, Faraday, Kelvin: Sydney Ross, "Scientist: The Story of a Word," 72–73.

   Lynch: Lynch, *The Lexicographer's Dilemma*, 271. **Hitchings**: Hitchings, *The Language Wars*, 170, 166. **Merton**: Merton and Barber, *The Travels and Adventures of Serendipity*, 11.

   class-based attitudes in birth of *OED*: Mugglestone, *Lost for Words*, 162-6, 175, 207, 220. **"The English of educated people"**: 207: *Anglicity*: 74, 83. **racial bias**: Martin, *The Dictionary Wars*, 44; Pei, *The Story of Language*, 194; Mugglestone, *Lost for Words*, 163-6. **"A man of honourable character"**: Ibid., 163. **"Cuffee" letter to *Gazette***: Unger, *Noah Webster*, 249; Lepore, *A Is for American*, 6.

   preserved Britishisms: Pyles, *Words and Ways of American English*, 21–27; McQuain, *Never Enough Words*, xvii; O'Conner and Kellerman, *Origins of the Specious*, 9, 14; Murphy, *The Prodigal Tongue*, 103–5. **Daily News writer on *scientist***: Sydney Ross, "Scientist: The Story of a Word," 79. **BBC list**: Murphy, *The Prodigal Tongue*, 126.

   stiff upper lip: *OED*; "A Stiff Upper Lip," *Grammarphobia*, October 5, 2016, https://www.grammarphobia.com/blog/2016/10/stiff-upper-lip.html, accessed September 25, 2020; Pascal Tréguer, "An American Phrase for a British Trait: 'A Stiff Upper Lip,'" *word histories*, May 6, 2018, https://wordhistories.net/2018/05/06/stiff-upper-lip/, accessed December 13, 2019.

Archer: Mead, *Word-Coinage*, 16–17; Archer, *America To-Day*, 219, 238, 247–53. **Woolf**: Virginia Woolf, "American Fiction," *The Saturday Review of Literature*, August 1, 1925, in Virginia Woolf, *The Moment and Other Essays by Virginia Woolf*, ed. Leonard Woolf, Boston: Harvest/Houghton Mifflin, 1947, 1974, 113–27, 126–27. **Cooke**: Hepzibah Anderson, "How Americanisms Are Killing the English Language," *BBC*, September 6, 2017 (reviewing Matthew Engels's *That's the Way It Crumbles: The American Conquest of English*, London: Profile, 2017), http://www.bbc.com/culture/story/20170904-how-americanisms-are-killing-the-english-language, accessed January 6, 2020.

Hitchings: Hitchings, *The Secret Life of Words*, 252. **Fairlie**: Henry Fairlie, "Evolution of a Term," 192, 206.

19. COINER'S REMORSE

Greenspan to Gross: *Fresh Air*, NPR, November 18, 2007; *SPD*, 355–56. "Remarks by Chairman Alan Greenspan at the Annual Dinner and Francis Boyer Lecture of the American Enterprise Institute for Public Policy Research, Washington, D.C., December 5, 1996," https://www.federalreserve.gov/boarddocs/speeches/1996/19961205.htm, accessed October 16, 2019.

Hoyle comment: John Horgan, "Fred Hoyle: The Return of the Maverick," *Scientific American* 272, no. 3, March 1995, 46–48.

nuclear option: William Safire, "Nuclear Options," *NYT*, March 20, 2005; Dan Merica, "The Man Who Coined the Term 'Nuclear Option' Regrets Ever Pursuing It," *politicalticker*, CNN, November 21, 2013, http://politicalticker.blogs.cnn.com/2013/11/21/the-man-who-coined-the-term-nuclear-option-regrets-ever-perusing-it/, accessed December 16, 2016.

Gov. Moonbeam: F. Richard Ciccone, *Royko: A Life in Print*, New York: Public Affairs, 2001, 297; William Safire, "Moon Bats & Wing Nuts," *NYT*, September 3, 2006; Jesse McKinley, "How Jerry Brown Became 'Governor Moonbeam,'" *NYT*, March 6, 2010; Mark Christman, "Royko's Love/Hate Relationship with 'Gov. Moonbeam,'" *nbcchicago.com*, March 7, 2010, https://www.nbcchicago.com/news/politics/Mike-Royko-Governor-Moonbeam-California-who-gave-brown-nickname-86756107.html, accessed December 3, 2015. **Royko-Brown conversation, Royko's 1991 column**: Mike Royko, "Lunar Label Eclipses Brown," *Dayton Daily News*, September 8, 1991.

Luntz's change of heart: Anthony Adragna, "Luntz: 'I Was Wrong' on Climate Change," *Politico*, August 21, 2019; Kate Yoder, "Frank Luntz, the GOP's Message Master, Calls for Climate Action," *grist*, July 25, 2019, https://grist.org/article/the-gops-most-famous-messaging-strategist-calls-for-climate-action/, accessed September 12, 2019; Dan Zak, "How Should We Talk About What's Happening to Our Planet?"

truthful hyperbole: Donald Trump with Tony Schwartz, *The Art of the Deal*, New York: Random House, 1987, 58. **Schwartz to Mayer**: Jane Mayer, "Trump's Boswell Speaks," *NYer*, July 25, 2016, 20–26, 21, 23.

fake news: Craig Silverman, "I Helped Popularize the Term 'Fake News' and Now I Cringe Every Time I Hear It," *BuzzFeed News*, December 31, 2014, https://www.buzzfeednews.com/article/craigsilverman/i-helped-popularize-the-term-fake-news-and-now-i-cringe, accessed May 19, 2020.

deep state: "Anatomy of the Deep State," *billmoyers.com*, February 21, 2014, https://billmoyers.com/2014/02/21/anatomy-of-the-deep-state/, accessed November 7, 2019. After Lofgren's book on this subject was published, several more appeared that were either titled *The Deep State* or had *Deep State* in their title. **le Carré**: John le Carré, *A Delicate Truth*, New York: Viking, 2013, 252. Joseph Bernstein, "The Guy Who Wrote the Book on the Deep State Wishes Trumpworld Would Shut Up About the Deep State," *BuzzFeed News*, April 5, 2018, https://www.buzzfeednews.com/article/joseph-bernstein/deep-state-mike-lofgren, accessed November 6, 2019; Greg Myre, "The Man Who Popularized the 'Deep State' Doesn't Like the Way It's Used," *All Things Considered*, NPR, November 6, 2019. (footnote) **invisible** government: *SPD*, 352–53.

profit center: Peter Drucker, *Managing in the Next Society*, New York: Talley/St. Martin's, 2002, 49, 84.

Arab Spring: Marc Lynch, "Obama's 'Arab Spring,'" *Foreign Policy*, January 6, 2011, https://foreignpolicy.com/2011/01/06/obamas-arab-spring/, accessed October 16, 2019; Marc Lynch, *The Arab Uprising: The Unfinished Revolutions of the New Middle East*, New York: Public Affairs, 2012, 9; Habib Toumi, "Who Coined 'Arab Spring'?," *gulfnews.com*, December 17, 2011, https://gulfnews.com/world/gulf/who-coined-arab-spring-1.952310, accessed January 3, 2013; *OED*. **Lynch told an interviewer**: Joyce Hackel, "Syria Crisis Spilling Over into Regional Conflict," *The World*, PRI, April 11, 2013; see also Spencer Blair, "After the Arab Spring," *World Outlook*, November 4, 2013, https://sites.dartmouth.edu/worldoutlook/category/arab-spring/, accessed December 17, 2016.

Gyakum told *HuffPost*: Alexander C. Kaufman, "This Is the Man to Blame for the Term 'Bomb Cyclone.'"

"Manic Pixie Dream Girl": Nathan Rabin, "The Bataan Death March of Whimsy Case File #1: *Elizabethtown*," *A.V.Club*, January 25, 2007, https://film.avclub.com/the-bataan-death-march-of-whimsy-case-file-1-elizabet-1798210595, accessed May 25, 2015; Gretchen Brown, "How to Avoid Becoming Your Partner's 'Manic Pixie Dream,'" *Rewire*, January 28, 2020, https://www.rewire.org/love/manic-pixie-dream/, accessed February 7, 2020; Nathan Rabin, "I'm Sorry for Coining the Phrase 'Manic Pixie Dream Girl,'" *Salon*, July 25, 2014.

world music: Robin Denselow, "We Created World Music," *The Guardian*, June 29, 2004; David Byrne, "Crossing Music's Borders in Search of Identity; 'I Hate World Music,'" *NYT*, October 3, 1999; **Boyd**: "Happy 30th Birthday, 'World Music,'" *The World*, PRI, February 3, 2017.

Asperger's syndrome: David Simpson, "Asperger's Syndrome and Autism: Distinct Syndromes with Different Personalities," in *The Many Faces of Asperger's Syndrome*, ed. Maria Rhode and Trudy Kauber, London: Kamac, 2004, 25–38, 32; Adam Feinstein, *A History of Autism*, Malden, MA: Wiley-Blackwell, 2010, 3–9, 79, 203–4. **Lorna Wing comment, interview with Feinstein**: Ibid., 204. (footnote) **Asperger's Nazi collaboration**: Edith Sheffer, "The Nazi History Behind 'Asperger,'" *NYT*, March 31, 2018. *Aspies*: Liane Holliday Willey, *Pretending to Be Normal: Living with Asperger's Syndrome*, London: Jessica Kingsley, 1999, 35, 71, 104. **Willey's regret**: Liane Holliday Willey, ed., *Asperger Syndrome in Adolescence: Living with the Ups and Downs and Things in Between*, London: Jessica Kingsley, 2003, 12.

Maverick: Richard B. Henderson, *Maury Maverick*, 305.

network neutrality: Tim Wu, "Network Neutrality, Broadband Discrimination," *Journal of Telecommunications and High Technology Law* 2, no. 1, 2003, 141–79. **Wu's exchange with Sydell**: Laura Sydell, "FCC Proposal Would Regulate Internet Like a Public Utility," *All Things Considered*, NPR, February 4, 2015.

grey goo, nanotechnology: Eric Drexler, *Engines of Creation: The Coming Era of Nanotechnology*, New York: Anchor, 1986, 172–73, 275; Jim Giles, "Nanotech Takes Small Step Towards Burying 'Grey Goo,'" *Nature* 429, no. 6992, June 10, 2004, 591; "Drexler, K. Eric," in *Encyclopedia of Nanoscience and Technology*, Vol. 1, ed. David H. Guston, Los Angeles: Sage, 2010, 168–69; **Norio Taniguchi**: N. Taniguchi, "On the Basic Concept of 'Nano Technology,'" *Proceedings of the International Conference on Production Engineering*, Tokyo, Part II (Tokyo: Japan Society of Precision Engineering, 1974). This is the first known use of *nano technology*.

Lederman: Leon Lederman with Dick Teresi, *The God Particle*, New York: Dell, 1993, 2006, xi, 22; Kelly Dickerson, "Here's What Scientists Really Wanted to Call the World's Most Famous Particle," *Business Insider*, May 20, 2015, https://www.businessinsider.com/why-the-higgs-is-called-the-god-particle-2015-5, accessed October 18, 2019. **Christian woman**: Leon M. Lederman and Christopher T. Hill, *Beyond the God Particle*, Amherst, NY: Prometheus, 2013, 32–33. **Soloney**: Tony Adams, "Higgs Boson Discovery Could Usher in 'New, Wonderful Technologies,' Says Physicist," *CSMonitor.com*, https://www.csmonitor.com/Science/2012/0705/Higgs-boson-discovery-could-usher-in-new-wonderful-technologies-says-physicist, accessed May 25, 2015.

Dawkins: Richard Dawkins, *The Selfish Gene*, Oxford: Oxford University Press, 1976, 2006, vii–viii. See also Sophie Elmhirst, "Is Richard Dawkins Destroying His Reputation?," *The Guardian*, June 9, 2015. **Dawkins on *meme***: Richard Dawkins, "The Selfish Meme," *Time*; Olivia Solon, "Richard Dawkins on the Internet's Hijacking of the Word 'Meme,'" *Wired*, June 20, 2013, https://www.wired.co.uk/article/richard-dawkins-memes, accessed September 18, 2019.

Mailer, *factoid, fug,* panel discussion: Bob Fulford, "Mailer, McLuhan and Muggeridge on Obscenity," in J. Michael Lennon *Conversations with Norman Mailer*, 116–38, 117. **Mailer greets new acquaintances**: J. Michael Lennon, *Norman Mailer*, 737.

Jong: Alexandra Alter, "Erica Jong's 'Fear of Dying' Defies the Sunset of Sex," *NYT*, September 7, 2015.

Whipple: Tom Geoghegan, "Err on a G-spot," *BBC News Magazine*, January 6, 2010; Wendy Zukerman, "If You're Still Hunting for the Elusive Area You Might Be Wasting Your Time . . . ," *The Sun*, September 18, 2016.

Crenshaw: Kory Stamper, "A Brief, Convoluted History of the Word 'Intersectionality.'"

sexual harassment: Lin Farley, "I Coined the Term 'Sexual Harassment.' Corporations Stole It," *NYT*, October 18, 2017.

Gibson comments: *Dayton Daily News*, November 1, 1999; George Gibson interview, Deborah Solomon, "Back from the Future," *NYT Magazine*, August 9, 2007, MM13.

20. YOU TOO CAN COIN A WORD

Churchill's memo, speech: Langworth, *Churchill by Himself*, 53, 61. **McFedries on short words**: McFedries, *Word Spy*, 17–18. **McFedries, McKean on pronunciation**: Ibid., 17; McKean, *Totally Weird and Wonderful Words*, 255–61; Erin McKean, "The Way We Live Now; On Language: Neologist," *NYT Magazine*, August 25, 2002.

Thun on playfulness: Thun, *Reduplicative Words in English*, 303.

pooh-bah: *OED*; Flesch, *Lite English*, 149–50.

YAP: C. E. Crimmins, *Y.A.P.: The Official Young Aspiring Professional's Fast Track Handbook*, Philadelphia: Running Press, 1983. *bleep*: *OED*; William Safire, "On Language: Bull Market in Words," *NYT Magazine*, November 14, 1982, 24, 26.

cha ching: 1992 ads for Rally's hamburgers featuring actor Seth Green, https://www.youtube.com/watch?v=KdjVZr1P7FU, accessed June 22, 2019; Stacy Ritzen, "Seth Green on Being the 'Cha Ching Guy' in Those Rally's Fast Food Commercials," *UPROXX*, September 4, 2014, https://uproxx.com/tv/seth-green-on-being-the-cha-ching-guy-in-those-rallys-fast-food-commercials/, accessed March 24, 2017.

Jones on *baby boomers*: Landon Y. Jones, "How 'Baby Boomers' Took Over the World." **translations of *baby boomers***: Ibid.

Glickman: Marty Glickman, *The Fastest Kid on the Block: The Marty Glickman Story*, Syracuse, NY: Syracuse University Press, 1996, 73–74; Stephen A. Riess, *Sports in America from Colonial Times to the Twenty-First Century*, New York: Routledge, 2015, 394; Marc Bona, "Marty Glickman, Pioneering Athlete Turned Broadcaster, Remembered in Well-Done Documentary, *cleveland.com*, August 16, 2013, https://www.cleveland.com/tv/2013/08/marty_glickman_remembered_in_w.html, accessed October 24, 2019.

air ball, slam dunk: "Mr. Lakers," *Newsweek*, August 18, 2002, 13; Ben Zimmer, "Of Pinpricks and Slam-Dunks: The Rhetoric of the Syrian Conflict," *Visual Thesaurus*, September 13, 2013, https://www.visualthesaurus.com/cm/wordroutes/of-pinpricks-and-slam-dunks-the-rhetoric-of-the-syrian-conflict/, accessed March 16, 2018.

gung ho: Jess Kung, "The Long, Strange Journey of 'Gung-Ho,'" *Code Switch: Word Watch*, NPR, October 18, 2019, https://www.npr.org/sections/codeswitch/2019/10/18/406693323/the-long-strange-journey-of-gung-ho, accessed October 18, 2019; R. W. Gaines, "Gung Ho! According to Evans F. Carlson," *Gunny G's Globe and Anchor*, www.angelfire.com/ca/dickg/gungho.html, accessed January 12, 2008; Dickson, *War Slang*, 170–71, 243–44; Pascal Tréguer, "'Gung-Ho,' and the American Admiration for Communist China," *word histories*, May 5, 2018, https://wordhistories.net/2018/05/05/gung-ho-origin/, accessed December 13, 2019.

buzzword: *OED*; F. M. Hallgren and H. Weiss, "'Buzz Words' at the 'B School,'" *American Speech* 21, no. 4, December 1946, 263; Geoff Nunberg, "From TED Talks to Taco Bell, Abuzz with Silicon Valley-Style 'Disruption.'" In *SPD*, 92–93, William Safire references Robert Kirk Mueller's 1974 book *Buzzwords*, in which Harvard professor Ralph Hower is cited as an introducer (if not coiner) of this term.

BlackBerry: Jacquie McNish and Sean Silcoff, *Losing the Signal: The Untold Story Behind the Extraordinary Rise and Spectacular Fall of BlackBerry*, New York: Flatiron, 2015, 63–64; "The Epic Rise and Fall of BlackBerry," *Here & Now,* NPR, May 28, 2015; Frankel, *Wordcraft*, 68–74.

Brexit: Steven Poole, "From Woke to Gammon." ***bork***: "Bork," *UD*; Richard Speed, "Borked Capsule Makes a Successful Return to Earth," *The Register*, December 23, 2019. **Gardner, *bomb***: Martin Gardner, *The Annotated Snark*, 24. **First edition of *OED* on *b***: McKnight, *English Words and Their Background*, 164–65. "***Bubble up with***": Ellen McCarthy, "In 2020 Back-to-School Shopping Means Frantically Looking for Other Families to 'Bubble Up' With," *WP*, August 9, 2020.

Burgess on *g*: Burgess, *Burgess Unabridged*, xvii. ***G-men***: "A Byte Out of History: 'Machine Gun' Kelly and the Legend of G-Men," *Federal Bureau of Investigation Archives*, September 26, 2003, https://archives.fbi.gov/archives/news/stories/2003/september/kelly092603, accessed April 18, 1017. ***G-spot***: See notes to Chapter 13.

Metcalf on "power of *k*": Metcalf, *OK*, 9, 71. **Eastman**: Elizabeth Brayer, *George Eastman*, 63; Carl W. Ackerman, *George Eastman*, 76. **Krazy Kat**: George Herrimann, *Krazy & Ignatz, 1922–1924*, Seattle: Fantagraphics, 2012, 250; Bill Watterson, "A Few Thoughts on Krazy Kat," in *Krazy Kat & the Art of George Herriman*, ed. Craig Yoe, New York: Abrams, 2011, 9–10, 10. **Pound**: Louise Pound, "The Kraze for K," in Pound, *Selected Writings of Louise Pound*, 321–23. **Catskill comedians**: Roy Blount, Jr., foreword to *The F Word*, 2nd ed., ed. Jesse Sheidlower, New York: Random House, 1995, 1999, xvii. ***canoe***: Robert Chapman, *New Dictionary of American Slang*, 61.

Blount: Jesse Sheidlower, *The F Word*, xvi. **Robbins's fondness for *z***: Tom Robbins, "The Spirit of the Letter," *Esquire*, June 1996, 68–69. **Burgess**: Burgess, *Burgess Unabridged*, xxvi, 39, 119–20. **Geisel's words with *z***: amberella, "Words Made Up by Dr. Seuss," *wordnik*, https://www.wordnik.com/lists/words-made-up-by-dr-seuss, accessed September 23, 2014.

pop culturists: Maureen Tkacik, "'Z' Zips into the Zeitgeist, Subbing for 'S' in Hot Slang," *WSJ*, December 30, 2002. **Zinzin**: https://www.zinzin.com/, accessed

June 22, 2019. *sizzle*: *Parade*, November 12, 2006, 8; Elmer Wheeler, *Tested Sentences That Sell*, New York: Prentice-Hall, 1938, 3; *OED*. **Zoom, Zoomers, Zbellion**: Nick Turse, "Pentagon War Game Includes Scenario for Military Response to Domestic Gen Z Rebellion," *The Intercept*, June 5, 2020 https://theintercept.com/2020/06/05/pentagon-war-game-gen-z/ accessed June 10, 2020.

Zimmer: Ben Zimmer, "Spreading the Word"; Metcalf, *Predicting New Words*, 152.

neologisms unspectacular, unobtrusive: Ibid., 152, 155–57, 167, 171, 173, 177–84; Wallraff, *Word Fugitives*, 184; Hitchings, *The Language Wars*, 280; Sørensen, *Charles Dickens*, 25, 123, 127.

Lignos and Pritchard on "naturalness": "Why Did *Frenemy* Stick?," *Time*, July 6, 2015; Constantine Lignos and Hilary Pritchard, "Quantifying Cronuts: Predicting the Quality of Blends," July 6, 2015, https://lignos.org/blends/, accessed March 15, 2016. **Zimmer comment**: Ben Zimmer, "Spreading the Word." *comrade*: Amor Towles, *A Gentleman in Moscow*, New York: Viking, 2016, 181. *hookup*: Kathleen A. Bogle, *Hooking Up: Sex, Dating, and Relationships on Campus*, New York: New York University, 2008. Bogle's work is reviewed in Tara Parker-Pope, "The Myth of Rampant Teenage Promiscuity," *NYT*, January 27, 2009, and in Brenda Wilson's interview with her, "Sex Without Intimacy: No Dating, No Relationships," *Morning Edition*, NPR, June 29, 2009.

uptalk: James Gorman, "Like, Uptalk?" *NYT Magazine*, August 15, 1993, 14; Metcalf, *Predicting New Words*, 161; Ben Zimmer, "'Uptalk' in the *OED*," *Language Log*, September 12, 2016, https://languagelog.ldc.upenn.edu/nll/?p=28086, accessed October 26, 2019. *Type A*: Meyer Friedman and Ray H. Rosenman, *Type A Behavior and Your Heart*, New York: Knopf, 1974. It should be noted that Allan Metcalf believes gap filling is overrated as a quality of successful neologisms (*Predicting New Words*, 63–67).

Hoyle, C-field, etc.: Fred Hoyle, *Home Is Where the Wind Blows*, 401, 404–7, 420; Mitton, *Conflict in the Cosmos*, 125. **Hoyle's rueful comment**: Ibid., 209.

Murray, echoic: Murray, "Ninth Annual Address of the President to the Philological Society," 117–76; Considine, *Adventuring in Dictionaries*, 236; *OED*.

names for children's in-laws: Bob Levey, "O.K., Out There, Clean Up That In-Law Language," *WP*, August 30, 1982; Wallraff, *Word Fugitives*, 169–70, 185; Rosten, *The New Joys of Yiddish*, 228–29; email from the author's svakha Halyna Mironets, December 19, 2019.

(footnote) **abbreviations, *LGBTQPAN, LGBTQIAPK*:** Miriam Kramer, "LGBTQ+ Individuals Face Harassment in Astronomy, Planetary Science," *Axios*, December 17, 2019, https://www.axios.com/harassment-sexual-sciences-lgbt-women-of-color-db9913c3-9690-4e74-8ec8-bc5adfea7539.html, accessed December 24, 2019; *LGBTQIAPK*: "Your Guide to LGBTQIAPK Addiction Treatment," *American Addiction Centers*, December 10, 2019, https://americanaddictioncenters.org/lgbtqiapk-addiction, accessed December 24, 2019.

guy: See notes for Chapter 7. **Leacock**: Stephen Leacock, *How to Write*, London: Bodley Head, 1944, 110–11; **Flesch**: Flesch, *Lite English*, 80–81.

Acknowledgments

NO AUTHOR WORKS in a vacuum, least of all this one. That is why I'm so grateful for the help I've received while writing this book. As with so many of my books, my brother Gene carefully read the manuscript and gave me the kinds of helpful response I've come to expect from him. The same thing is true of my friend and sometime editor Bill Phillips, whose decades of support and sound counsel mean so much to me. Other readers whose responses improved my manuscript are Jay Smith, Lanny Jones, and Rosalie Maggio.

Help with specific chapters came from Halyna Mironets, Lottesophia Gordon, Nicky Keyes, Bob Fogarty, Jessica Zagory, Steve Conn, John Dickinson, Raul Ramos, Priscilla Long, Dan Rottenberg, Jeff Evans, Robert Priest, Daniel Kennefick, and Alice Calaprice.

Librarians whose assistance was invaluable include Sandy Coulter and Scott Sanders of the Olive Kettering Library at Antioch College, Karl Colón and Connie Collett of Ohio's Greene County Public Library, as well as librarians at the Multnomah County Library and Concordia University Library of Portland, Oregon.

Tech and spiritual support has come from members of my extended family: Gene, Steve, Nicky, David, Scott, Rachel, and Anya, as well as friends such as Gay Courter, Kathy Rippey, Dan Friedman, and Gary Klein.

I'm grateful to Robert Wilson, who accepted and shepherded my original article on coined words that appeared in *The American Scholar*, then hired me to write a column about language for them. This book was enriched by the thoughtful editing of Timothy Bent (to say nothing of his patience with the inordinate amount of time it took me to complete it). Thanks too to his assistant, Zara Cannon-Mohammed, for pitching in when needed, corralling illustrations especially. The meticulous, well-informed oversight of production editor Joellyn Ausanka and copy editor Mary Anne Shahidi made this a far better book than it would have been without their keen editorial eyes.

My agent, Colleen Mohyde, has been this book's cheerleader from the moment years ago when I first said to her, "How about a book on coined words?" In the years since Colleen has been supportive far beyond the call of duty during the many twists and turns it took to actually write that book.

Most importantly, my wife, Muriel, has given me her usual stellar help critiquing my work, editing, proofreading, and formatting the manuscript, then creating an album of illustrations, along with other forms of support too numerous to mention.

Illustration Credits

Goops cover, Gelett Burgess, author and illustrator, *Goops and How to Be Them: A Manual of Manners for Polite Infants,* Philadelphia: Stokes, 1900. *Wymps* cover, Evelyn Sharp, author; Mabel Dearmer, illustrator, *Wymps and Other Fairy Tales,* New York: Lane, 1897.   119

Three "Robots": unknown production of Karel Čapek's 1921 play *R.U.R.*   124

Trilby and Svengali, 1931 / WARNER BROS / Ronald Grant Archive / Alamy Stock Photo   138

Blackboard Jungle still, 1955 / Entertainment Pictures / Alamy Stock Photo   143

"Knee-jerk" drawings / by William Richard Gowers, *Manual of Diseases of the Nervous System*, London: J & A Churchill, 1888.   152

Antioch Review page / Copyright © 1948 by the Antioch Review, Inc. First appeared in the *Antioch Review* 8, no. 2 (Spring 1948). By pernission of the *Antioch Review.*   155

General Jan Smuts / ca. 1920, Bain News Service, Library of Congress   159

"Blurb" / 1907 jacket of *Are You a Bromide?* by Gelett Burgess, New York: Huebsch, 1906.   171

"Splooch" / Gelett Burgess, author; Herb Roth, illustrator, *Burgess Unabridged: A New Dictionary of Words You Have Always Needed,* New York: Frederick A. Stokes, 1914.   172

Bottle of Heroin, early twentieth century / uploaded by Mpv_51, *English Wikipedia*, October 23, 2005   174

Striporama poster, 1953 / Everett Collection, Inc. / Alamy Stock Photo   180

Painting of Lieutenant Richmond P. Hobson, ca. 1898 / Naval History and Heritage Command   184

Walter Clopton Wingfield, *Illustrated Sporting and Dramatic New* 15, June 1881. Lawn tennis rule book, February 1874, author unknown.   189

Dymaxion House / Henry Ford Museum, Dearborn, Michigan, 2014; author's photo.   190

Horace Walpole / 1754 engraving by G. E. Madeley. From catalog sale of Walpole's Strawberry Hill Collection, 1842   193

First issue of *The Vegan News* / ©The Vegan Society, by permission.   196

Earliest known mug shot: Belgium, 1843, photographer unknown   201

Roz Chast cartoon / in Roz Chast, *Theories of Everything,* New York: Bloomsbury, 2006. By permission of Roz Chast.   215

Muskrats / print by John James Audubon, 1849, University of Michigan Library Digital Collection   220

Kirsten Dunst, in *Elizabethtown* / PictureLux / The Hollywood
　　Archive / Alamy Stock Photo 237
Pooh Bah cigarette card / Lebrecht Music & Arts / Alamy Stock Photo 246
"Huzzlecoo" / Gelett Burgess, author; Herb Roth, illustrator, *Burgess
　　Unabridged: A New Dictionary of Words You Have Always Needed,*
　　New York: Frederick A. Stokes, 1914. 252

Index

Note: Page numbers in italics indicate pages with illustrations.